THE COMPLETE
WINE & FOOD
COOKBOOK

THE COMPLETE WINE & FOOD COOKBOOK

HAROLD C. TORBERT

NASH PUBLISHING

Los Angeles

Illustrations by Laurie Jordan

Library of Congress Catalog Card Number: 71-127490
Standard Book Number: 8402-1154-6

Published simultaneously in the United States and Canada
by NASH PUBLISHING, 9255 Sunset Boulevard
Los Angeles, California 90069.

Printed in the United States of America

Current printing (last digit):
10 9 8 7 6 5 4 3 2 1

FOR FRANCES

Who patiently tasted, sipped and criticized her way through all of the recipes and then urged, persuaded, and nagged me until I revised each chapter to her liking. I am grateful.

CONTENTS

THE COMPLETE
WINE & FOOD
COOKBOOK

WHY A BOOK ON FOOD AND WINE ?

Good food and drink are a delight.

They matter to us as much as to any people in the world. No country spends more on its table than ours. Yet both at home and in most of our restaurants we eat and drink less well than many families in continental Europe with incomes far below ours. And they manage to accompany every dinner with a pleasant glass of wine. We cannot excuse ourselves with the thought that the cost of living is higher here. Costs are as high in Paris as in New York, and the same is true of every other large city.

People in Europe care a lot about good meals. Happily, younger generations and some older ones in this country are beginning to share this attitude. Americans are re-learning what others have always known, that ice water is a barbarous drink and that good food calls for good wine; good, wholesome wine, not necessarily rare or expensive wine.

My aim in this book is threefold:

To show you how you can eat and drink better than you ever have without disrupting your pocketbook.

To help you rear your children knowing and liking a wide variety of dishes chosen from the cultures of many countries.

To show you how to order and serve wine without spending too much money, but with pleasure and confidence.

The book gives you suggestions about wine so that you can start using it with enjoyment. If you already know about wine the recommendations on that subject will still be useful. The recipes are for dishes which range from simple and inexpensive to those elegant enough to grace the tables of France's greatest restaurants. Some of them, in fact, are for dishes which *do* appear on the tables of France's three-star eating places.

In a few months, I shall publish a book which will tell you what you need to know about wines, in simple language, and without the technical details found in some books on the subject or the extravagance and snobbery of some of the others. Many books tell more about wine than most of us need to know; booklets and cards found in stores tell far too little. I am also struck with the near unanimity with which they give false information: "Red wines with red meat; white wines with fish or chicken; rosé wines with everything." Chicken is a rather strongly flavored meat. For all but a few recipes using cream and delicate seasonings you are likely to prefer a good, light red wine with chicken. On the other hand, pork nearly always benefits from a white wine, and a rather sweet one at that, more than from a red. It is deplorable to use rosé wine as a universal accompaniment with every sort of food. Rosés are light, unimportant wines which may be preferable to water at picnics or beach suppers on summer days, or for ladies' luncheons where the ladies know nothing of wine. In the opinion of most real wine experts, they are fit for little else, as one usually learns quickly from one's own palate.

Red Wine with Chicken

Many American restaurants mishandle wine. You may have had the chilling experience (no pun intended) of receiving a red wine straight from a refrigerator. I have seen too many waiters handle a bottle of old red wine so carelessly that the sediment was mixed thoroughly with the wine. Further, the outrageous markups that too many restaurant owners put on their wines and the too-limited assortment on their wine cards do nothing to encourage the use of wine.

This book will try to offer you menus and recipes which will, with suitable wines, make each meal a pleasure. Good cooking and pleasurable dining need wine as much as they need other essential seasonings. But neither the wines nor the dishes need be rare or costly.

Gastronomy is an art to enjoy in youth and in age, alone and in company, in health and, most of the time, in sickness. The dollar costs are less than most persons realize. Gastronomy is an art which never grows old. It caresses our youth, lends joy to our middle years, and enhances our age when the weight of years may force us to forego other pleasures.

No book gives a complete knowledge of wine. You learn about wine from drinking it. The cultivated Frenchman learns his wines at his father's elbow, as we all learn our morals at our mother's knee. But up to the present, most Americans have not had fathers knowledgeable in wine. Our Bourbon and Scotch culture and the national disaster of Prohibition are largely to blame.

This book is written with prejudices. It makes no attempt whatever to be fair. However, the prejudices are concerned with but one thing: that we all have as pleasant a time as possible while nourishing ourselves. Here are some of my prejudices.

First, I am convinced that the fine wines of France and of a very small area in southwestern Germany, embracing short sections of the Rhine and Mosel rivers and their tributaries, set the standards by which *all* the other wines of the world must be judged.

Second, I believe that the cooking of France, by which I really mean the butter-cream-and-mild herb cuisine of the Ile de France and the northern provinces, sets the standard for all other cooking. The olive oil-tomato-and-garlic cookery of southern France and Italy are second, that of Spain a distant third, with German sugar-lard-and-vinegar cooking far down the list, and the public cooking of Great Britain at the bottom.

Nevertheless, good cooking is where you find it. In this book you will find recipes from Great Britain, Mexico, Spain, Greece, from both New England and the South in our own country.

Third, I have a prejudice against sugar with meat, from whatever country's cuisine it springs. I dislike the three-star French restaurant's duck with orange as much as I do the British mint jelly with lamb or Germany's and our own country's applesauce with roast pork or roast goose. I think countless good hams have been ruined by smearing them with brown sugar or serving them with a raisin sauce.

Fourth, I believe that with the possible exception of warm apple pie, *warm* is a temperature to be avoided in serving food. Hot dishes deserve to reach the dinner *hot*,

3

and cold ones should arrive at the table truly *cold*. To do less shows lack of consideration for your guests and for yourself.

Finally, I agree wholeheartedly with Brillat-Savarin's assertion that men who stuff themselves or grow tipsy know neither how to eat nor how to drink.

I am not concerned in this book with elaborate dinners of many courses and expensive wines. Life would be barren without its feasts, and feasts would lack much of their enjoyment without fine wines to go with them. But most of the time we live simply, eating plain three-course dinners. And this is what we ought to do. Our palates would become jaded if every meal were an elaborate multi-coursed one accompanied by the choicest wines!

I have friends who always drink the finest vintages of Burgundy and Bordeaux, the Rhine and the Mosel. Others drink only fine wines, but serve them only with special meals. I find both practices wrong.

In every language, the word signifying a good meal, feast, fete, fiesta, fest, is synonymous with a holiday, a celebration, an occasion for joy. This is as it should be; rejoicing and good eating and drinking belong together. But our palates, our digestions, and in most cases, our purses, forbid us to feast every day.

Every country in the world where the climate supports the wine grape *vitis vinifera* makes wine. Most of this wine is an agreeable, wholesome beverage, much more pleasurable and healthy for washing down ordinary, every-day food than water. For millions of our fellow human beings wine is as much a necessity as the bread it is eaten with, equally as good, and with as little pretense to elegance. It was such wine that was involved in the miracle at Cana, and at the Last Supper, a humble meal eaten by humble men.

We are concerned with good daily fare and with occasional feasts; with good simple wines, red and white, and with some of the most precious liquids ever offered men by their fellow men. In choosing recipes for the book I have been guided by three considerations: each recipe is for a dish I have cooked and my family has liked; the items called for are available in middle-sized cities or by mail order; the recipes are of a scope and complexity within the reach of a competent American, whether a woman who keeps house or a man who cooks occasionally for his own pleasure or for that of his family and his friends.

My acquaintance with wine began as a Stanford student purchasing bootleg "Dago red" in the hills back of Palo Alto and Menlo at a dollar a gallon, bring your own jug. I worked my way through the university, and many a week's lunches consisted of a loaf of San Francisco's incomparable sourdough bread and a jug of not-to-be-despised wine.

Later I was an assistant resident in medicine at the Stanford University Hospitals. Because it was the time of the Depression, all University officers whose salaries were $3000 yearly or less suffered a five percent pay cut. Each month, after I cashed my check for $23.75, my first and most pleasurable purchase was two bottles of wine, one for drinking and the other for laying down. Thus was my cellar born. During subsequent years, I have at times spent on the cellar sums which startled my wife, who has herself become perceptive about the fine points of a good vintage.

We regret not one penny of our expenditures. My only concern is that the cellar shall continue to furnish us a bottle of *ordinaire,* or a little better, every day, with a good bottle often enough to add interest, and an occasional great one for special events. I know of no way in which I could have better invested whatever the cellar has cost. I am sure our wines have not cost more than we could afford. I will go further. I could not have afforded not to have my cellar.

I am, I think, no wine snob. If you gain the impression that I think *some* French wines are better than most California wines and that the very best of the French and German vintages exceed anything California has yet produced, it is because more than thirty years of critical wine tasting have convinced me that these things are so. Nevertheless, with the exception of France and Germany, it is clear that the vintners of California have succeeded in producing finer vintages than any other wine-growing region in the world. This was clearly demonstrated at a tasting of the International Wine and Food Society in London in the autumn of 1969.

red burgundy

There is no mystique to drinking wine. But many billions of gallons of fermented grape juice have gone down countless human throats, and out of this experience one can draw some conclusions and make some suggestions.

Most wine, even very modest wine, is beautiful. Since it is beautiful it is good to look at. Thus the glass from which you drink should be clear and colorless.

Part of wine's delight is its bouquet, its perfume. Therefore it is better that your glass be of a shape that will concentrate the aroma at your nose.

Even if you have not yet tasted wine, a moment's reflection will tell you that it is better to drink a thin wine before a full-bodied one, a simple wine before one that is complex, a youthful wine before an old.

However, these are only suggestions passed from one generation of wine drinkers to the next. They are not even conventions, really. Many persons like only white wines and drink their favorite with all sorts of food. This is in no way wrong. But if you are a beginner you will do well to follow the simple suggestions I outline, simple because the majority of those who drink wine have found that in this way their pleasure is enhanced.

I suggest you will get the most out of the book if you will observe three points, the first two of which may at first seem to contradict each other. The first time you use one of these recipes follow it accurately. The result will be an attractive dish. Second, after using the recipe once, vary it to suit yourself. In this way you will become a creative and original cook, the only kind worth trying to be. Finally, may I urge you to study the first four chapters of the cooking section with the greatest attention. They furnish the bases for all good cooking.

If you can make good doughs, sauces and stocks and can use with love and skill the short list of herbs and spices, the rest is merely detail which comes with practice. And I am sure that you will agree that the continual repetition of the directions for making a white sauce, for example, is a needless clutter of subsequent recipes. Incidentally, making fine sauces is not the mystery involving esoteric knowledge and days of labor that tradition would have you believe. Modern products and methods have shortened many formerly tedious procedures.

My qualifications for writing this book?

My mother determined that her sons were not going to grow up as helpless around the house as their father. Very early she set my brother and me to learning all the tasks of running a house. From the beginning I liked cooking and I have continued to cook for more than five decades. I have eaten and cooked my way from northern Idaho to Mexico, from San Diego to New York, from New Orleans to Boston. My wife and I have lived in France and

Italy and traveled in other countries of western Europe. In a Paris apartment, we had first a Parisienne and then a Bretonne as cooks. Flattered to have the man of the house show interest in their activities, these ladies taught me a great deal.

We have dined in three-star restaurants in Paris and the provinces, in city bistros and in country inns. Everywhere I have talked with chefs, maitres d'hotel, patrons and patronesses, and whenever the opportunity offered, with ordinary housewives, both in Paris and the country. I read cookbooks the way some people read detective stories. We do not hesitate to try new recipes on dinner guests because I know I can define the taste of a dish from reading its recipe. And I can usually, but not always, closely duplicate any dish I have tasted.

One final wish from me to you:

I hope you have as much fun using this book as I did writing it.

THE PHYSIOLOGY OF TASTE

1

Eating and drinking are sensuous experiences; that is, known through our senses. In being sensuous experiences, they differ in no way from other activities of necessity and pleasure that human beings engage in. And despite any statements to the contrary by our Puritan forebears, it is nonsense to think of some of our senses as noble and others as base: to erect a hierarchy of the senses.

Listening to music at whatever level we like is an elevating way to pass the time. It is also sensuous. If we were deprived of the sense of hearing, music would be a closed book to us. But listening to music involves far more sensuous activity than merely hearing. How close attention can you pay to the performance if your seat is uncomfortable? How many times have you been put to sleep by the bad air in an auditorium? How frequently has your attention wandered because you were too hot or too cold?

There is no more elevating experience than looking at beautiful scenery or masterpieces of art. But few of us are ardent enough lovers of beauty to expose ourselves to too much cold or heat while we view it. Poorly lighted and ventilated exhibition rooms will keep people away from museums showing masterpieces.

No hierarchy of the senses exists. Whatever you think about man's ultimate nature or his destiny, all that we experience reaches us through our senses.

Wise men cultivate and refine *all* of their senses, not just some of them. The senses involved in the enjoyment of food and drink are as worthy of cultivation as those used in enjoying music or philosophy. Cultivation of these senses can refine and sharpen one's delight in the things of the table and, like art and music, make more vivid and enjoyable the hours and days which are all we will ever have of life here and now.

Most persons think that enjoyment of food and drink arises from *taste*. This is so only to a most limited extent. The nerve receptors in the taste buds distributed over our tongues and the upper parts of our throats act as transducers, sending electrical impulses to the taste centers in the brain, where the various kinds of electrical impulses are sorted out into the different tastes. Our taste buds are capable of differentiating only five perceptions: sweet, bitter, sour, acrid, and salt.

All other components of the complex sensation we commonly call taste are really odors, perceived by the receptors in the roof of our noses. Coffee, for example, registers merely as bitter to our taste buds. The marvelous flavor of a good, fresh cup of coffee is due to its *aroma,* perceived by our sense of smell. This is why the best of food or drink has little flavor when we have severe head colds: the volatile particles of the food or drink cannot come into contact with the nerve endings in the olefactory area, so the detection of aroma is faulty or absent.

Taste and aroma, then, are the primary sense stimuli through which we are pleased or displeased by what we eat or drink; but the total experience of taste is even more complex. The linings of the mouth, palate and pharynx are richly supplied with nerves which convey the sensations of touch, and by others which feed our brains information about the degree of heat or cold. Most of us find that the combined information that a particular morsel is rather cold and greasy gives us a feeling of unpleasantness. Coffee not really hot loses much of its attractiveness. The tingling sensation of the bubbles of carbon dioxide combined with a pleasant sensation of coldness is what makes champagne, a cola drink, or beer attractive to those who like them.

Numerous other varieties of sense experience are also involved in pleasurable dining. We cannot fully enjoy food if the place where we are dining is too hot or too cold. An uncomfortable chair distracts from the pleasure of a meal as much as it does from the enjoyment of a concert.

Our aesthetic sensibilities are also involved. Appropriate furnishings for the table are important. This is no plea for expensive linens, china, or silver; proper appreciation of gastronomy does not depend on the depth of one's purse. Table linen does not have to be elegant, but it should be appropriate and, above all, it should be fresh. Paper napkins, even big ones, are inappropriate. A few fresh flowers, a bowl of fruit or other products of farm or garden, candles, or a small piece of sculpture in the center of the table stimulate the aesthetic sense, adding charm to a good meal and mitigating one less than good.

It is important to come to the table in a state of repose. If marital conflicts must be aired, financial problems discussed, children disciplined, or bad news conveyed, wait, in the name of happiness, until after dinner. This need to be relaxed is the raison d'être of the cocktail hour. Guests do not all arrive at the same moment. No wife can predict the exact moment of a husband's arrival home. What better way to allow guests to come to know each other and to soothe nerves jangled by traffic or the cares of the day than to spend a little while relaxing over a sensible drink.

Alcohol is often thought of as a stimulant. What makes the premeal drink, the apéritif, useful is that the action is precisely the opposite of stimulation. It is a central nervous system sedative. Further, by happy chance, the parts of the central nervous system first affected by alcohol are the higher centers, those most susceptible of irritation by the trials of life. A glass of sherry, a Manzanilla or Fino by preference, a glass of vermouth, or one of the bitter apértifs, or *one* Martini or Scotch allows guests time to become accustomed to one another, for the host's nerves to be calmed, and for the hostess to put the finishing touches to the dinner. Used in this way the premeal drink can do no harm and helps prepare every one in the party for the pleasures to come.

COMPOSING A MEAL: A FINE ART

Just as a beautiful painting is a blend of line, color and design, a good meal is a skillful blend of color, texture and flavor. And the proper finishing touch to any gastronomic masterpiece is the proper meeting of the foods and wine. You may be an excellent cook, but to be a true connoisseur, you have to learn this art of matching food and drink. Acquiring skill in this art means greater joy and satisfaction for yourself and your family.

Attention to the color of different dishes can add to a meal's attractiveness. In France, a generation ago, there was a fad for monochromatic effects, such as an all-red dinner. The vegetables were all colored with beet juice; in an all-green dinner the only cheese admitted was Roquefort. But a monochromatic dinner soon becomes as monotonous to the palate as to the eye and the absurd idea was soon abandoned.

Let us look at some simple three-course family dinners. If your main course is chicken in a rich white sauce, or creamed tuna, you will not want a heavy cream soup for your first course. A fresh, crisp green salad with a mild vinaigrette will afford a contrasting color, crisp crunchiness in contrast to the rich softness of the main dish, and a fresh, light flavor which will make the richness of the creamed main dish all the more delicious by contrast. A good apple pie with buttery, cinnamon flavored juice oozing from its rich crust is a fine dessert, but both its richness and its color suggest that it not follow a pot roast, savory with herbs and full of fat. A dish of raspberries or a crisp, cool apple will provide a better termination. An entrée of macaroni and cheese or *Fettucine Alfredo,* bland and soft, and largely starchy, could be properly introduced by thin slices of dark red prosciutto with artichoke hearts.

A Frenchman whose name I have forgotten but whose Cartesian logic I admire, has described a simple menu classification. He lists dinners as follows: (1) the everyday family dinner, (2) dinners for intimate friends

13

(the author suggests that this classification may properly include parents), more festive dinners, served with greater care than other meals. In this category are dinners celebrating anniversaries and holidays such as Christmas and Easter. (3) More formal and sometimes larger dinners, the ones the housewife considers as "owed" are ones for which she gets out her best linens and most elegant china. (4) Dinners of ceremony: these require every refinement of table service.

In this book we will deal chiefly with the first three categories, although the menus of dinners of the fourth type will be cited to illustrate a point. An example of this fourth category is one of the dinners given by the Sisters of Charity in the cellars of the Hôtel Dieu at Beaune, in the heart of Burgundy, at the time of the annual auction of the wines of the Hospices de Beaune. Let us see how such a dinner worked out from the standpoint of variety of flavors and textures, the harmonious combination of dishes and the skillful choice of wines.

The dinner menu:

Le Consommé de Canard Cyrano
La Tourte de Volaille Truffée
Beaune-Clos de Mouches Blanc 1964

La Truite Braisée au Vin de Meursault
Meursault-Genevrières, Cuvée Philippe le Bon 1963

Le Cuissot de Marcassin Grand Veneur
Charmes-Chambertin 1961

La Caille Poêlèe à la Berchoux
Beaune, Cuvée Guigone de Salins 1961

Les Fromages

La Dame Glacée de la Cour de Bourgogne
Champagne Perrier-Jouët Brut 1961

Le Café
Le Vieux Marc et la Prunelle de Bourgogne

The first course was a consommé. That it was made of duck gave it an unusual flavor but it was what a consommé should be, a clear soup providing little nourishment. The truffled tart of fowl complemented the flavor of the consommé nicely, and its crisp crust gave a texture contrast. The white Beaune wine was young and fresh and not too subtle, so that its flavor did not compete with that of the tart.

The trout braised in Meursault wine was a lighter color than the *Tourte* and was soft. The Meursault-Genevrières was crisp and dry and was similar to, although of better quality, than that in which the fish was cooked.

A leg of young wild boar, prepared hunter's style, provided the greatest possible contrast, both in flavor and in texture, to the previous course. The meat was chewy, the fish fell apart. The spicy purée of vegetables added flavor and color. The red Charmes-Chambertin had great body and a bold perfume. It was fuller, with more complexity than the preceding wines. (The wines got older and more flavorful as the meal progressed; this is precisely the order in which several wines should be served.)

This dinner was unusual in that two game courses were offered. I suppose that here we are to regard the joint of boar as the roast and the skillet-cooked quail as the game. The wine accompanying the quail, a Beaune red from one of the finest grown and owned by the Hôtel Dieu, was still fuller and more complex than the red wine served with the boar. It was good with the quail and superb with the following cheeses, all of which were precisely ripe, neither hard nor too strong.

The dessert was a very light ice. The pretty conceit of molding it into the figure of a lady of the medieval Burgundian court added a note of festivity. The ice was cold and refreshing to palates by now a little jaded and to stomachs a whisper too full. Champagne contributed to the gaiety of the occasion, with its frothiness in the glass and its tingle on the tongue. This excellent vintage champagne made a fitting end to the wine list. The change back to a white from a red wine, and to a sparkling one from a still again afforded contrasts of taste, texture and color.

Coffee Finale

Good, strong, hot, black-roast coffee is, so far as I am concerned, the proper finale to any good dinner. I do not usually accompany it with brandy. But we were the guests of the growers, wine merchants, and the Sisters who depend on the auction for funds to operate their 500-year-old, yet modern hospital, we loyally sipped a glass of the marc—and thereby began a love affair which still continues.

It is evident how the choices throughout the meal afforded constant contrasts which added to the guests' enjoyment. One readily sees that care in choosing contrasting yet harmonious items is perhaps even more important in simple meals. We shall concentrate on foods and wines for one's own family and for the small, intimate parties which we enjoy with our friends and, if we are fortunate, with our relatives.

Although I maintain that classical French cooking is the standard by which all others has to be measured, the menus and recipes which follow include dishes from many lands. French pastry makers rarely surpass a good American apple or pecan pie. A New England clam chowder is among the world's best soups. Mexican cooking has much to recommend it, although I dislike the greasy, too-spicy dishes of the border, more Texan than Mexican.

A colleague, a man who cares enough about intellectual matters to have earned a Ph.D. in addition to his medical degree, observed with some scorn that the reason the French invented so many sauces was that their meats needed disguising. In the past the accusation was not wholly libellous, although the Charollais cattle, unhappily not yet supplying all of France's beef, produce meat to rival that from the finest Herefords or Aberdeen Angus of our land. Furthermore, the best French sauces are superb. But the man is a fool who sits down to a multicourse feast and drinks the finest wine every night of his life. How is he going to mark the occasion of his joys and triumphs?

Here are some examples of simple three-course dinners and modest wines to match. With such dinners one wine is always sufficient, drunk usually with the main course but also with the cheese when you are having it. Wine is not good with salad dressings containing vinegar, and most dry wines add nothing to desserts.

*Menus Include Dishes
From Many Lands*

I

*Romaine and Iceberg Lettuce Vinaigrette
Broiled Lamb Chops with Tarragon
New Peas, French Style*

Camembert and Liederkranz Cheeses
French Bread

Beaujolais*
Coffee

II

*Crudities (Raw Cauliflower, Celery, Cucumber,
Radishes, and Black and Green Olives) with
Flavored Mayonnaise*

Ground Chuck Steak, Broiled
Potatoes Anna

Deep French Apple Pie

Beaujolais
Coffee

* When in these menus I use the term *Beaujolais* without a modifying adjective I mean a modest French wine sold in its native land in a *pichet* or carafe and in this country at around a dollar a bottle.

III

Oysters on the Half Shell
Boiled Beef with Mustard and Horseradish
Brussels Sprouts with Butter

Fresh Raspberries with Cream

Beaujolais
Coffee

IV

Grated Raw Carrots

Dover Sole Meunière with Steamed Rice

Fresh Strawberries
Erbacher Marcobrunn Spatlëse 1959
Coffee

V

String Bean and Onion Salad

Boiled Smoked Tongue
Yellow Crooknecked Squash

Coffee Ice Cream

Torres Vino Tinto (Spanish)
Coffee

VI

Hearts of Celery Vinaigrette

Fillet of Beef, Braised with Tarragon
and Butter over Noodles

Fresh Pineapple with Kirsch

Vino Tinto
Coffee

VII

Eggs in Aspic, Garnished with
Sliced Tomatoes and Olives

Onion Soup with French Bread and Parmesan Cheese

Coffee

VIII

Green Salad with Chives

Deviled Crab with Steamed Rice

Ambrosia
Beaujolais
Coffee

IX

Little Neck Clams Farci

Chicken à l'Indienne
Steamed Rice

Green Salad Vinaigrette

Bisquit Tortoni

Vino Tinto
Coffee

X

Sliced Cucumbers with Dill-Flavored Mayonnaise

Southern Hash

Apricot Mousse

Charmes-Chambertin 1959
Coffee

XI

Celery Rémoulade

Poached Salmon with Hollandaise Sauce
Green Beans with Little Onions

Honeydew Melon

Uerziger Sonnenuhr 1959
Coffee

XII

Prosciutto with Spiced Artichoke Hearts

Crêpes with Crab and Parmesan Cheese

Asparagus with Lemon Butter

19

Fresh Coconut Custard

Pouilly Fumé 1966
Coffee

XIII

Asparagus Vinaigrette

Broiled New York (Strip) Steaks
Potatoes Lyonnaise

Expresso Café Ice

Chambertin 1959
Coffee

XIV

Eggs à La Russe with Capers

Curried Shrimps with Steamed Rice

Green Salad Vinaigrette

Maple and Walnut Mousse

Côtes de Rhône Red
Coffee

(One is told curry does not "go" with wine but I think it does.)

XV

Asparagus Vinaigrette

Veal Parmigiana
Buttered Zucchini

Soufflé Grand Marnier

Pommard-Epinots 1959
Coffee

XVI

Cucumbers and Mayonnaise

Trout Grenoble
String Beans with Almonds

Port Wine Mousse

Sancerre 1966
Coffee

XVII

Stracciatella

Roast Chicken with Tarragon
New Potatoes with Parsley
New Peas with Green Onions

Persian Melon

Charmes-Chambertin 1957
Coffee

XVIII

Crudities

Pork Chops with Cream
Broccoli with Lemon Butter

Maple Bavarian Cream

Rüdesheimer Berg Rottland 1964
Coffee

XIX

Herbed Tomato Salad

Beef à la Mode with its Vegetables

Fruit Bowl

Fleurie 1966
Coffee

XX

Spinach and Bacon Salad

Curried Eggs
Broiled Tomatoes

Raisins, Figs and Walnuts

Beaujolais
Coffee

And now here are some menus for the small dinner party, for intimate friends or to celebrate an anniversary.

I

Prosciutto with Spiced Artichoke Hearts

Chicken Frances
New Peas with Fresh Dill
Steamed Rice

Mixed Green Salad Vinaigrette

Bananas Flambés au Rhum

Pommard-Epinots 1959
Coffee

II

Smoked Salmon with Capers

Pheasant Roasted with Cream and Brandy
Wild Rice
New Peas, French Style

Apple Tart

La Tâche 1958
Coffee

(When a Burgundian native refers to Richebourg, La Tâche, and Romanée Conti as the Holy Trinity, he implies no blasphemy at all.)

III

Snails, Burgundian Style

Cheese, Seafood and Rice Casserole
Broccoli with Lemon Butter

Limestone Lettuce and
Belgian Endive Vinaigrette

Crême Brulée

Musigny 1955
Coffee

(Because both snails and cheese dishes are so good with red wine, use your oldest and best Burgundy with this menu.)

IV

Celery Victor

Roast Duckling with Chestnut Dressing
New Potatoes
Green Peas with Green Onions

Cherries Gertrude

Chambertin 1959
Coffee

V

Mushrooms à la Grecque

Bourbon Beef Roast
New Potatoes
Broccoli with Hollandaise

Limestone Lettuce and Endive, Vinaigrette

Strawberry Mousse

Fleurie 1964
Coffee

VI

Scallops Seviche

Roast Leg of Lamb
Purée of White Beans and Onions Sautée

Mixed Green Salad Vinaigrette

Pot de Crême au Chocolat

Château La Pointe 1955
Coffee

VII

Oysters Rockefeller

Saddle of Lamb à la Gastronome
Fonds d'Artichauds Gruyère

Mixed Green Salad Vinaigrette

Soufflé Grand Marnier

Château Haut-Brion 1953
Coffee

VIII

Celery Victor

Lobster Newberg
Steamed Rice

Asparagus with Hollandaise Sauce

Strawberries Cardinal

Meursault-Genevrières, Hospices de Beaune 1959
Coffee

Here are some easy, attractive and not expensive regional dinners to give guests and family a change of pace.

IX

A Provençale Dinner:

Onion Soup

Daube of Beef Provençale
Boiled Potatoes
Buttered Carrots
Tomatoes Provençale

Green Salad with Garlic and Olive Oil Dressing

Beaujolais Ordinaire
Coffee

X

A Pleasant Italian Dinner:

Antipasto
Salami   Prosciutto   Mortadella
Tuna with Mayonnaise Pepperoni
Hearts of Artichokes in Oil Eggs
with Mayonnaise

Fettucine Alfredo

Fresh Figs with Cream

Chianti Classico 1964
Cafe Expresso

(The Chianti in the straw-covered *fiaschi* is not expensive. Like Beaujolais it is a wine for large draughts and not for sipping.)

XI

A Simple Greek Dinner:

Tomato Salad

Moussaka Rosalind
Syrian Flat Bread

Iced Canteloupe

Almadèn California Pinot Noir
Greek or Turkish Coffee

(This good quality California varietal wine is better than any Greek wine we have encountered. The finely ground coffee for making the thick Oriental coffee is available at Greek or Syrian specialty shops.)

XII

An Excellent Mexican Meal:

Sopa Albondigas

Mexican Chicken (Gallina Mexicana)
with Rice and Almond Dressing

Mexican Salad (Chunks of Tomato and Avocado
with slices of Green and Red Sweet Peppers,
Dressed with Garlic and Oil)

Pot de Crême au Chocolat

Riojo Red Wine
Coffee

Perhaps a few elaborate menus we have encountered which did *not* please us will be instructive:

Varied Hot Hors d'Oeuvres
Cocktail Sausages in Pastry
Broiled Clam Canapés
Broiled Chicken Liver with Bacon
Melted Cheese Canapés

Prime Roast Rib of Beef
(Excellent meat cooked far too much)
Cauliflower in Cheese Sauce (Overcooked)
Stringbeans with Almonds (Overcooked)
Blueberry Jam
Hot Rolls

Pineapple Sherbert
Richly Iced Yellow Cake (Almost no flavor)

Medium-Grade California Pinot Noir (Served chilled
in elaborate cut glass glasses far too small)

Instant Sanka!

Next a Christmas dinner which had too much food, was
too rich, and had too few contrasts:

Hors d'Oeuvres
Broiled Water Chestnuts and Bacon
Brie and Cheddar Cheeses
Cheese Crackers   Potato Chips
Mixed Nuts

Cream of Mushroom Soup

Roast Turkey   Oyster Dressing
Mashed Potatoes
Spinach Purée
Sweet Potatoes with Marshmallows
Giblet Gravy

Pumpkin Pie with Whipped Cream and Grand Marnier
Mince Pie with Brandy Sauce

Wiltinger Kupp 1959
Coffee
(American style with cream)

(The wine was fruity and altogether lovely, from one of the
choicest vineyards of the Saar. In general a red wine goes
best with the rather strong flavor of turkey, but one of the
charming characteristics of the Rhine and Mosel vintages is
their ability to accompany all sorts of dishes.)

27

Like smaller dinners, ceremonial dinners can be just plain bad. An example is the following annual staff dinner given by a metropolitan hospital. It was half painful and half funny because the hospital administration took such obvious pride in the affair.

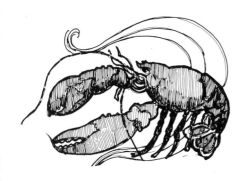

Hors d'Oeuvres
Prawns with Cocktail Sauce
Assorted Canapés
(Made too far in advance and most of them soggy)
Deviled Eggs (They tasted
as if they had been made for patients on a bland diet)

Roast Prime Rib of Beef (At steam
table temperature and much too well cooked)
Frozen Peas and Celery
(Boiled vigorously together)

Yorkshire Pudding (Cold)

Ice Cream Sundae
(Really Ice Milk with a Mincemeat Sauce flamed
with a harsh California Brandy)

Ice Water!
Coffee
(The routine hospital variety and not hot)

This gets us perilously close to the soggy chicken, watery mashed potatoes and hard peas political, business and fraternal "banquets" for which even our leading hotels are infamous and upon which (this being, I hope, a pleasant book) it is just as well to lower the curtain. Let us, in finishing, look at two more ceremonial dinners of a much higher calibre.

A dinner to celebrate a fortieth wedding anniversary:

Fresh Iranian Caviar
Fresh Toast   *Sweet Butter*
Chopped Egg   *Chopped Onion*

Alamaden Blanc de Blanc Champagne 1959

(The more knowing guests avoided the egg and onion.)

Aspic of Foie Gras with Madeira
Fresh Toast
Meursault Goutte d'or 1962

Clear Oxtail Soup with Madeira
Cheese Alumettes

La Iña Sherry
(Lovely and dry, between a Manzanilla and an Amontillado)

Mousseline of Sole Alexandre, Sauce Mornay
Asparagus Points with Butter
Château Haut-Brion Blanc 1964

Contre-Filet of Beef with Truffle Sauce
Potatoes Parisienne
Château Rouget 1929

(This dark ruby Pomerol, more than 38 years old when we drank it, has a penetrating bouquet and a lingering after-taste; it is mature but certainly will live for many more years.)

Salad of Belgian Endive, Watercress and Raw Mushrooms,
Dressed with Neutral Oil and a little Lemon Juice

Imported Brie Cheese
Croutons

Gateau d'Anniversaire
(A fine, rich German Chocolate Cake devised by the Chef as a present for the host and hostess)
Marcobrunner Beeren Auslese, Schloss Schöborn 1959
Coffee

Nothing marred this dinner. The number of guests was few enough and the number of those serving was large enough so that all the dishes arrived before the diners fresh and hot.

A dinner of ceremony given at Château Vougeot by the Confrérie des Chevaliers du Tastevin in the spring of 1966:

Suckling Pig in Aspic with Parsley and Mustard Sauce
Aligoté Magny-les-Villers 1964

Soufflé of Brochet with Truffles in the style of Nantua
Puligny-Montrachet 1964

Fricasée of Young Fowl with Morilles
Côtes de Nuits-Villages 1964

Leg of Young Wild Boar, Royal Hunter Style
Aloxe-Corton 1959

Selection of French Cheeses and Breads

Ice Creams, Assorted Flavors   Cakes
Fruit Basket

Coffee, hot and black
Vieux Marc de Bourgogne
Prunelle de Bourgogne

You will note the contrasting flavors and textures and the progression of the wines from the young and modest (but excellent) Aligoté to the older, heavy, red Aloxe-Corton and the final crowning of the wine list by a 1959 Bonnes-Mares with the cheeses. There was nothing wrong with this feast except that it was served to five hundred persons. Inevitably not all of the food reached every guest as freshly prepared and as hot as would have been desirable.

GETTING ACQUAINTED WITH WINE

3

white bordeaux

Wine, like music, ranges from the simplest of folk songs to the magnificence of string quartets and the floridness of symphonies. Everyone who is not tone deaf is able to enjoy the folk song, but the comprehension and enjoyment of great music requires a minimum knowledge of harmony and musical structure. So it is with wine. The vast majority of the wines made each year in the world are no more complicated than a folk song. They are made, quite literally, by the folk to be consumed and enjoyed with no more ceremony than the simple but usually excellent bread they accompany. But great wines and even good ones, like great music, reward the effort devoted to their study with increased awareness and keener enjoyment.

You will remember, that in my opinion, the wines of France and southwestern Germany constitute the standard by which all other wine is to be judged. The excellence of the better wines from these regions is due, first, to the almost perfect adaptation of soil and climate to the varieties of grapes which, after centuries of experimentation, now grow there; second, to the centuries of tradition and knowledge back of the men who grow and make this wine. I mean in no way to cast aspersions of the wines of California and other localities. I hope you will drink many American wines and will, as we did, grow to love them. Even so, your standards should be based on the traditional French and German vintages.

A word about the arrangement of material in this extremely compressed chapter. If it seems that I jump about in a helter skelter manner from region to region, it is because I am following what seems to me to be an efficient method of introducing you to the various wines of the world, rather than attempting a strictly geographical description. Thus, after introducing the four most important French wine regions, Burgundy, Bordeaux, the Beaujolais and the Rhône River valley, I jump to American wines because I think that is the order in which an Ameri-

red burgundy

champagne

can should most naturally proceed to become acquainted with wines. I then discuss briefly Italian and Spanish wines because in these countries, many moderately good and extremely inexpensive wines are to be found. I feel that we all need to discover wines that will put no unnecessary strains on our purses. I then turn our attention back to France to discuss some of the less important, although still very worthwhile wines, such as those of the Loire Valley and of Alsace. In this part of the chapter, I also discuss, more briefly than it merits, the most glamorous of all wines, those of the district champagne. Most of us are not going to drink champagne most of the time and there are more important things to learn first. The brief discussion of Alsatian wines leads logically into an equally brief discussion of German wines.

More complete discussions of all of these fascinating wines as well as those of South America, Australia and South Africa will have to await the publication of my next book, which is to be devoted entirely to wine.

If you are a novice at wine tasting, start high enough up the scale to learn what truly good wine can offer. On the other hand, the nuances of taste and bouquet of the great wines are so complex and so subtle that first experiences would not justify the cost of such jewels. For a first experience, then, choose some of the following.

Try a good but not great red Burgundy. The wines of Burgundy are full-bodied and generous, more friendly and accessible than the austere wines of Bordeaux. Start with a medium-grade Burgundy from a good but not great year. Buy a *Pommard-Epinots* from the *Côte de Beaune,* the southern part of the famous Golden Slope or *Côte d'Or,* or choose a bottle of Les Amoureuses or Latricières-Chambertin from the northern part of the region, called the *Côte de Nuits.* Select a 1960, 1962, or 1964. These are all now ready to drink, which the 1961s hardly are, but are less expensive than the famous vintages of 1959. Let your bottle rest on its side a few days in a cool place until the agitation from transporting it from the shop to your home has subsided. Then stand the bottle upright in the room in which it is to be drunk for twelve to twenty-four hours so that any sediment may settle down.

Uncork the wine carefully a half hour or an hour before you plan to drink it, unless the temperature is more than 75 degrees, in which case you may want to put the bottle in the refrigerator a *very* short time. In most French dining rooms, *chambrer,* or room temperature, implies somewhere between 65 and 70 degrees. However, I do not feel that any red wine, and more especially any Burgundy, is harmed by temperatures in the 70s and a bottle left in the refrigerator runs the risk of getting too cool. A red wine too cold only *tastes;* it has no aroma and the taste alone is merely somewhat sour—nothing to pay three or four dollars for.

Clear Glasses Preferred

A word about wine glasses. Remember, your glasses should be colorless, clear enough to display the wine, large enough to hold a decent serving, and with a rim curving inward in a tulip shape. The glass should not be filled more than one-third full, so that the wine may be swirled in the glass to release its aroma without danger of spilling. Glasses should hold a minimum of six ounces. Still larger glasses are preferable. In the early years of your wine drinking experiences, one set of glasses will be sufficient, although later you may wish to have more.

Having poured your wine, look at it, both in depth and through the side of the glass. New Burgundy, and a 1962 or 1964 is relatively new, is a dark, bluish-red. Old Burgundy gradually takes on a brownish, slightly lighter color. Both are beautiful. Next, swirl your wine in the glass and place the glass under your nose. Sniff it and then breathe in the aroma with deeper breaths. Both experiences will be rewarding.

Tasting Wine

Take a generous sip. Let the wine slide back over the tongue. Next, swirl it around the mouth. Remember, you are doing this alone, or with a few friends gathered for the purpose of tasting wine. You are learning and need not be on your best behavior, as at a formal dinner party. Move the wine about in your mouth as vigorously (and if need be, as audibly) as you swirl water when you are brushing your teeth. Having gotten every part of your mouth and palate in contact with the wine, take a generous breath of air through the mouth. Now you are really *tasting* the wine. That is to say, all of your taste buds and all of your olefactory receptors are being stimulated. Your sense of touch will tell you that the liquid has a silky, almost velvety, texture. This, then, is the taste of Burgundy.

Now swallow the wine. Continue paying attention to the sensations from your mouth, nose and stomach. Breathe again. You will note a pleasant combination of

33

taste and aroma in some ways considerably different from the taste of the wine while it was in your mouth. This is the aftertaste. Note it well. Its quality is an indispensable mark of a truly good wine. Eat a morsel of cheese, a bit of bread, or take a swallow or two of black coffee to remove the taste from your mouth—to "cleanse your palate." Repeat the process as often as you like.

The next step is to drink a similar bottle of Burgundy with a meal. Convention has it that one drinks Burgundy with steaks, roasts, game, and cheese. In reality, it is excellent with many dishes, not the least of which is chicken. I remain convinced, however, that a benevolent Creator designed this wine most especially for cheese.

Learning the Terms

Now is the time to learn certain terms you will encounter when you read more extensively about wine, or when you listen to wine lovers discussing their favorite topic. These expressions may sound to you a little pretentious or precious. They are not really so, but are, like many technical terms, a sort of convenient shorthand.

You will read, or hear, the wine lover speak of the "nose" of a wine. This means, of course, the fragrance, or bouquet, of the wine, but it also means much more. It describes whether a wine smells fresh or musty, whether or not the wine gives an impression of cleanness, whether or not the bouquet gives itself generously or whether it is small, or gives itself up grudgingly. You will also hear and read of wine's *robe* which is French for dress. What is implied in addition to the depth of color is the wine's clarity and its sparkle in the light. You will read that this or that wine is "soft on the palate." Here, again, "palate" serves as a shorthand description of taste, touch, temperature, and all of the sensations in the mouth.

The difficulty in discussing wine, which is apprehended by so many of our senses, is that it must be done largely in literary terms because neither the French nor the English has suitable sensual terms. The use of "silky" or "velvety" to describe the feel of a wine in the mouth is fairly self-evident, but it is hard to describe exactly what one means when one says a wine is "full-bodied" or "big," or conversely, that it is "small" or "meager." However, as you drink a few bottles of wine, these terms become self-evident and you will find yourself using the same words. Acidity, or the lack of it, is easy to sense. You will soon become familiar with the term "hardness," which

34

describes the presence of tannin, or of excess cream of tartar in the wine. You will discover these qualities the first time you drink a Burgundy, but even more so, a good Bordeaux, when it is too young.

Ready for Beaujolais

You are now ready to try a bottle of Beaujolais. This wine grows a few kilometers south of the Côte d'Or in the valley of the same river, the Saône. Beaujolais is the country cousin of the aristocratic Burgundy. It is made from the Gamay grape, much hardier and heavier bearing than the delicate Pinot Noir which is the parent of all quality Burgundy. (A grape variety is said to be shy bearing when it yields relatively few grapes. It may be taken as a general rule that heavy-bearing varieties of grapes yield less fine, and less delicate, wines than those that produce more sparsely.)

Beaujolais is frank, honest, open and easy to know. It is by far the commonest *vin de table* or *ordinaire* of the Paris and Lyon restaurants. Do not seek age. Beaujolais is best when it is young and fresh. It may be drunk with pleasure a few months after it is made. It most often begins to go downhill after three or four years, or at least to lose the youthful freshness which constitutes its chief charm. Burgundies are for sipping; Beaujolais is a wine for quenching an honest thirst, and for serving with relatively simple meals.

After you have experienced a few bottles of Burgundy and several bottles of fresh, young Beaujolais, you will be ready to sample the white wines from the same regions. Here it will be better to take the wines in reverse order. Find a bottle of inexpensive young white wine labeled *Macon Blanc,* or *Macon Blanc Villages.* Note its clear, pale straw color; enjoy its not very marked, but clean and fresh bouquet. You will find it medium dry, very clean on the palate, with little aftertaste. Now, you are ready for a bottle or two of Pouilly-Fuissé, the crisp, greenish-gold pride of the white wine vineyards between Macon and the Beaujolais. This crisp, exceedingly dry nectar will serve you well with less sweet fish and with all the shellfish at little more than half the cost of the more famous Chablis.

Now, return to the Burgundies and find a bottle of Meursault Goutte d'Or, or Bâtard-Montrachet. You need a good and representative white Burgundy to help form your standards, but you are not quite ready to enjoy the subtlety or pay the price for the queen of them all, *Le*

Montrachet. Choose a 1966, or 1967. Remember that white wines mature faster and do not live as long as the reds. The 1964s are still in fine shape, but are needlessly expensive for your purposes. Only a few 1959s or 1961s are still available, and unless they have lived out their lives in adequately cool cellarage, are probably fading. The wines I have named will tell you about the suavity of the white Burgundies, their perfumed yet absolutely dry character.

Now let us follow the Saône down to where it joins the Rhône at Lyon and some miles further south. Here are grown the Rhône wines to try next. At their best, these are heavy-bodied, richly colored, dark wines with an extraordinary capacity for living long lives. In taste and bouquet, they resemble medium-grade Burgundies, lacking some of the delicacy of the more northern wines, but with a heavy, hearty quality of their own. Because these red Rhônes live so long, they are slow to mature, so search for an older bottle, such as a 1957, 1959, or 1961. I recently opened a bottle of Châteauneuf-du-Pape 1959. It was drinkable enough, but I have no temptation to open more for at least two or three years. For your first sample, try this wine, or a Côte Rotie. Try, too, the Rhône whites. These, again, mature more quickly than the reds, so look for a 1964 or 1966 white Hermitage.

Red Bordeaux

If you have been an attentive student, you are now ready to investigate the red Bordeaux, the wines that Englishmen have for centuries called (incorrectly) claret. These are wines from the Sauvignon and Merlot grapes, both noble breeds, along the banks of the Garonne and the Dordogne rivers and their confluence in another river, the Gironde, which is in reality, a large estuary before the rivers empty into the Atlantic on the southeast coast of France. The important port city of Bordeaux is situated on the Garonne.

The English nearly unanimously, many Americans, and some Frenchmen, think the wines of this region are the most subtle and the greatest produced on the earth. I am not so sure. A great Burgundy from a good year is a thing of joy. Fortunately, we need not make a choice. A word of caution is necessary here, however. Perhaps nowhere in France does the wines produced in a single district vary so widely in quality. For this reason, I suggest that you start with a wine pretty far up the scale of quality, which, unhappily, means pretty far up the scale of prices.

Look for a bottle of Château Lynch-Bages, or Château Batailley or Château Haut-Batailley of the 1960 vintage. The Bordeaux reds take a long time to grow up. The wines of 1960 are of lesser quality than those of 1959 or 1961 or even of 1964. But, they are now ready to drink which the others scarcely are. If you can't find a 1960, then try to find a 1957 in order that you know what *mature* Bordeaux wines taste like. Unready, these reds are hard, even harsh, and give you a misleadingly unattractive impression. You will find your new acquaintance a little more subtly perfumed than the Burgundies, a little more austere. Linger over your sips a little longer than with the Burgundy. This wine takes time to yield its graces, but the time is well spent. Have your Bordeaux reds with somewhat complicated dishes, of veal or chicken.

Next, try a bottle of the white Graves from the Bordeaux district of the same name. It ranges from quite dry and crisp to a little sweet, although still clean and fresh on the palate. It will accompany all of your light meats and most fish, although to my mind, not so well as other whites. You should now be ready to sample a Sauternes, the world-famous golden dessert wine of Bordeaux. Again, for your first bottle, don't pay for a Château d'Yquem. Try, instead, a Château Filhot, Lamothe, or d'Arche, so-called second growths. You would not be shortchanging yourself if you choose a bottle marked simply Sauternes or Barsac. Avoid bottles labeled Haut-Sauternes. The term is meaningless and the dealer may try to charge you more for it.

The sweetness of Sauternes comes from the fact that the grapes are allowed to remain on the vine not only until they are fully ripened, but until they have been attacked by a mold, *Botrytis cinerea,* which produces the so-called *pourriture noble* or noble rottenness. Despite the unattractive appearance of bunches of grapes in this state, really all that has happened is that the filaments of the mold have penetrated the grape skins and allowed most of the water in the flesh of the grape to evaporate. When the concentrated flesh is crushed, it yields a juice (the technical term is a *must*) unusually high in sugar and in the elements which give flavor. This wine continues fermenting until the concentration of alcohol stops the action of the yeasts, and still have from five to ten percent of sugar remaining in the must. The wine usually contains about fourteen percent of alcohol, which is another reason in addition to its sweetness, for drinking it only in small quantities. To be noted are the exceptional bouquet, the liquorous quality of the wine which seems almost thick, and the lingering aftertaste.

German Wines

Before investigating further the less important French wines and the marvelous wines of Germany, let us return to our own country. You are still in process of forming standards and for that reason, should at this point, stick to the wines of California. Even when the wines of New York, Ohio and Virginia are made from European varieties of grapes, they many times soon develop the foxty taste characteristic of native grapes. Viticulturists speak of the *gout de terroir,* the taste of the soil, which may be what causes the native grapes to have this taste.

It is interesting to recall that American grapevines were first responsible for nearly destroying the wine industry of Europe and then, as is only just, for saving the European varieties. American vines are nearly universally infested with a plant louse, *phylloxera.* About 1870, some American root stocks were imported into English and French botanical gardens from which the pest rapidly spread to the European vineyards. Between 1870 and 1900, most French vineyards were destroyed; by 1910, the plague had spread to Spain and to central Europe. After various attempts to disinfect their soil, the French hit on the expedient of grafting their vines to American root stock, which is resistant to the phylloxera. In this way, America saved, after nearly destroying, the world's best vineyards. The last holdout of native French root stocks was at the famous Romanée Conti vineyard in Burgundy, but in the 1950s, the owners admitted defeat, rooted up their vines, rested the land for several years by sowing wheat and replanted with Pinot Noir grapes grafted on American root stock. There is no evidence, in the minds of experts, that the quality of the wine has suffered any diminution.

Before we discuss California wines, let me make the flat statement that the frequently asked question of how California wines compare with French wines is not an admissible question. As the philosophers would say, it is not a real question. The wines are simply not comparable. When a wine drinker of only moderate expertise can differentiate between the wine produced from Pinot Noir grapes in one French vineyard from that produced in another vineyard, frequently separated from the first by the wagon track width of a country lane, how can you compare the wine made from the same grape grown in different soil with totally different climatic conditions 6,000 miles away? France produces a vast quantity of poor wine, much good wine, and small quantities of the choicest wine on the face of the earth. California, likewise, produces much ordinary wine and much excellent wine, with perhaps still more in between. On the whole, the indifferent, inexpensive wine from the California central valleys is not as bad as the worst of the wine from the Midi. On the other hand, we have not succeeded in producing wine which compares with the best that Burgundy and Bordeaux produce in good years.

It is important to know the vintage year of most European wine, because the weather in France and other European countries varies widely. Some years, everything comes together: the ideal amount of rainfall, the one hundred days between blossoming and harvesting have the right proportion of cool and sunny weather, and the harvest season is bright and hot. In such a year, choice vintages will be made. Other years are cold and rainy, and the grapes hardly mature. Or it will rain too much and the crop will be large, but the wine will be watery and the quality poor. In California, there are not such wide swings in the weather, although significant variations do occur from time to time. But in general, the statement that California wines are more uniform from year to year is a fairly safe one. It is desirable, though, that California wines be vintage labeled, if for no other reason than that such information will help guide the purchaser in deciding how long to store them before using. In some cases, the problem is compounded by the fact that the vintner engages in the entirely legitimate practice of blending the wines from different years.

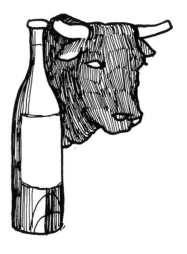

So universal is the recognition that French wine furnish the standard by which others are judged that all over the world where wine growing has developed, the reprehensible practice of naming wines with French names has developed. When you buy a French wine labeled *Musigny* or *Chambertin,* you know it comes from the vineyards of those names in the Burgundy district and from nowhere else. The same is true of wines from other districts of France. But, when you buy a bottle of California or Australian or South African wine labeled Burgundy, you have no possible way of knowing what you get. What you *do* get, in practice, is a wine made from grape varieties inferior to the Pinot Noir which the wine maker at a given vineyard claims will "taste" like a Burgundy. This demonstrates either the wine maker's optimism, or his contempt for the discrimination of his customer.

More recently, the better wine growers of California have adopted varietal labeling. This means that the bottle is labeled with the name of the variety of grape from which it is made. Thus, a Cabernet Sauvignon is made from the juice of grapes of that variety, as is a Pinot Noir, a Chenin Blanc or any other honest varietal name. Recognizing that one hundred percent of varietal wines are not necessarily the best wines (all of the famous château bottled Bordeaux wines are made with varying proportions of Cabernet Sauvignon, Cabernet Franc and Merlot grapes, except for those of Château Mouton), California viticultural authorities prescribe that a wine may carry a varietal label if it contains a minimum of fifty-one percent of the named grape.

Tasting California Wines

The first thing that a perceptive taster, even a comparative beginner, will notice when he tastes a bottle of well-made California Pinot Noir is that here is no Burgundy. It is very fuity on the palate when it is young, has a good deal of tannin, and has a characteristic California nose, hard to describe, but easy, with a little experience, to recognize. Another difference is that most California Pinot Noirs lack the lingering aftertaste which characterizes the better French wines.

The differences are even more marked between most California Cabernet Sauvignons and good Bordeaux. In general, the well-made California wine is a big, rather bold wine, of masculine quality, lacking what might be described as the feminine grace of excellent Bordeaux wines. Actually, most California Sauvignons more closely resemble California Pinot Noirs than they do their French prototypes, although I recently drank several bottles of good California Cabernets ranging in age from twenty-five to nearly forty years. Without exception, these older wines resembled good château-bottled Bordeaux more closely than any California wines I have ever drunk.

Another regrettable fact is that most California varietal wines, especially the serious ones such as we have just been discussing, are sold and drunk much too young. Until the immediate past, California had the policy, extremely unwise in a state desirous of fostering wine growing and making, of assessing personal property tax on wine in a vintner's cellar every year. The California personal property tax is exceedingly high and, obviously, the growers could not continue to hold their wine very many years. The necessary increases in cost would soon drive its price far beyond that of competitive wines. Happily, this mistaken state tax has been repealed. It remains to be seen if the makers will now age their good wines longer before marketing them. The best solution is for the consumer to buy and hold good California wines several years in advance of need, as he does for those from France.

I do not find the California whites quite as good as their prototypes from France. If one drinks a Rocky Hill Chardonnay, or a wine of the same grape from the Livermore Valley, or that made by Almadèn at Pacines with a good fish course, it will be excellent if it is the only white wine taken. But, if it is tasted with a good Meursault or Chablis, it seems a little thin. On the other hand, wines from the Riesling grape, which gives such delicate and highly perfumed wines in the sparse soil and harsh climate of the hillsides above the Rhine and Mosel rivers in Germany, in California produce big, firm, dry wines, which completely lack the grace of the German wines; but, which have instead an attractive forth-rightness of their own. In the summer of 1970, I drank a California Chenin Blanc made at the Chappell winery in the mountains above the Napa Valley which was as dry and crisp as any wine made from the same grape in the Loire Valley, and a lot firmer and bigger. However, most of the California Chenin Blancs I have tasted, have been unattractively sweet and more than a little flabby.

The more modest wines of California, sold under "generic" names–that is, false French or German names–or sometimes called Mountain Red or Mountain White are frequently sold in gallon or half gallon jugs, or in screw top bottles. They have usually been pasteurized. This means the wine is in the same state as canned fruit. The organisms responsible for changes in the bottle have been killed by heat. The wine will remain as good, but no better, than when it was put in the bottle, and therefore, does not improve with age. There is no reason to hold this wine. It should be bought a jug at a time and enjoyed with the majority of simple daily meals, as similar wine has been enjoyed by our fellow men since before the days of our Greek forebears. Most of the wine from the hot, central valleys of California, as well as a large amount made from the commoner, high yielding varieties of grapes in the coastal counties is of this kind.

After you are familiar with California wines, you might like to try a few Italian ones. In view of recent

Understanding Names

scandals regarding the "sophistication" as the authorities put it, of Italian wine, some of which has never been near a grape, one should hesitate to buy the cheapest Italian wines. However, you will find many wines, especially those of northern and central Italy, such as *Barola, Bardolino, Gringnolino, Nebbiola,* the *Chiantis* and *Orvieto,* pleasant, although in general they lack the grace of good French wines. The usual American opinion that Chianti is a "spaghetti wine" is true only for the modest young varieties sold in the straw covered *fiaschi* familiar to everyone. Superior Chiantis come in plain bottles like those of Bordeaux. They are well balanced, full wines which live many years. For completeness, also, try a few bottles of the white wines of Switzerland and of the red and white wines of Austria. You will find them neither outstandingly good nor poor, well worth drinking in their native lands but rarely meriting the cost of importation. The same thing is even more true of Hungarian and Yugoslavian wines, with two exceptions: the *Egri Bikaver,* or Bull's Blood, so named because of its almost truly red, rather than purple color, of Hungary, and that country's charming Tokay (or Tokaj) Aszu, a sweet wine made by the same process of late picking after infestation of the grapes by the *pourriture noble* as Sauternes. Although Greek wine was celebrated throughout classical times and was valued up until a hundred years or so ago, that now produced in Greece is indifferent at best and poor at worst. *Retsina,* the resinated wine, is definitely an acquired taste which does not seem to me worth acquiring.

Spanish and Italian Wines

Wine is produced all over Spain, as it is in Italy. Most of it is quite ordinary, made to be drunk by the grower and his friends and others before the time of the next harvest. But, Spain produces—manufactures rather than grows—sherry, one of the world's famous fortified wines. Sherries range from exceedingly dry wines known as Manzanills, through Finos, to the medium Amontillado and the lush, dark, sweet Olorosos and cream sherries. Another exquisite apértif wine is Montilla, grown around the town of that name and made from the same grapes, and by the same processes as sherry, except that no spirits are added to it. It, therefore, contains fourteen to eighteen percent of alcohol, as against the approximate twenty percent in sherry.

Two Spanish districts produce dinner wine good enough for exportation. In searching for interesting and inexpensive table wines, try those of the Rioja and of Tarragona. The former district is rather high, at the junction of the old kingdoms of Aragon, Navarre, and Castile. The best of the Rioja reds have the style of a good *bourgeois* Bordeaux. The wines of Tarragona, along the Mediterranean coast, do not pretend to be as fine, but are clean and honest, made in great quantity, and shipped all over the world. The reds are strong and dark, with fourteen to sixteen percent of alcohol. The whites are lighter, with an alcohol content of twelve to fourteen percent. Bertràn and Company exports huge amounts of these unpretentious beverages. The company, unfortunately, calls its whites Spanish Chablis. The wine lacks the dryness and the steely quality which characterizes Chablis. It is soft and a little sweet. However, it is sold here for under one dollar a bottle. It is one of the few truly inexpensive white wines that we find satisfactory. Of the excellent whites of the Rioja, the one most commonly seen in the United States is that of the Marquès de Riscal. It is dry and clean, a big, solid wine which is not expensive.

Champagnes

Let us return to France, to the country on the chalky hills around Reims, the farthest north wine-producing region of France. Two varieties of grapes are planted on these hills, the Pinot Noir and the Chardonnay, formerly called Pinot Chardonnay. Most champagne is made from a mixture of these two grapes, but some is made from the Chardonnay alone. When this is the case, the wine is labeled a *Blanc de Blanc* which means a white wine made from white grapes. It is possible to make white wine—really wine ranging in color from golden to pale, almost greenish white—from black grapes. Red wine is made by letting the juice ferment along with the skins of the grapes, which contain all the coloring matter of the fruit. The alcohol extracts the pigment. If the grapes are crushed and the juice pressed out and immediately removed from the skins, a white wine results. Hence, champagnes can be made from black as well as white grapes.

In champagne making, after the usual primary fermentation with various rackings, wines from different locations, and those of the two separate varieties of grapes are thoroughly mixed, in proportions dictated solely by the

judgment of the cellar master, who tries to keep his firm's products uniform from year to year. After blending, the wines are dosed with a weight of sugar calculated to produce the amount of carbon dioxide needed to give the wine its sparkle during a secondary fermentation. The dosed wine is bottled, the bottles are fitted with temporary stoppers, and then put to rest in the cold, deep chalk cellars underlying Reims, Epernay and Ay. Here it matures for two, and more commonly, three years.

At the end of this time, the bottles are placed at an angle in racks with the tops slanted downward. Each day, every bottle is given a sharp twist by a skilled worker and is slanted a little more steeply until finally, all of the yeast cells, mucilage, and the other debris of fermentation is collected on the bottom of the cork, and the bottle is perpendicular, its bottom in the air. The temporary cork is then quickly removed, any wine lost in the process is replaced by the same kind of wine, and the bottle receives a *dosage* of rock candy dissolved in brandy and champagne in quantities to produced the type of wine desired. The variety called *brut* contains about one-half of one percent of sugar, *extra sec* about one percent, *sec* up to three percent and *demi-sec* close to five percent sugar. A sensitive palate can detect the sweetness of a *brut*. *Demi-sec* is a complete misnomer; it is drunk only by rich South Americans, and by the French themselves, who regard it as a dessert wine. A little *natur* champagne, containing no added sugar, is bottled.

Even this brief outline shows that champagne is a necessarily expensive wine. It requires at least five years between the harvest and the time it is marketed, and requires many manipulations. The large French and California plants are marvels of mechanical ingenuity, but many of the processes still depend on the skill of an individual hand worker.

Most champagne is a blend of wine produced in different years, and is sold without vintage designation. But if the harvest is usually good, a manufacturer may declare a vintage year. Of course, any wine bearing a vintage date must be made of grapes grown only during the designated year.

Much sparkling wine is produced in California and labeled California champagne, to the annoyance of the French. But, as Dr. Maynard Amerine, Professor of Enology at the University of California and a consultant to the

French government, has pointed out, the French ought really to subsidize California wine growers. Their keeping French place names alive in America increases the market for French wines. The best of the California products, such as Schamberg Vineyard's Blanc de Blanc, and Almadèn's Blanc de Blanc compares favorably with medium-grade French champagne. But, much California sparkling wine is made by the *Charmât* process whereby the wine undergoes its secondary fermentation in giant tanks. The beverage lacks the lasting sparkle of the wine made by the true *methode champenoise.* Italy also produces a great deal of sparkling wine, much of it sweet. Germany's version, called *Sekt* is economically important because its manufacture calls for a wine of extreme acidity and low alcohol content, just such wine as the Mosel and Rhine vineyards produce in poor years. The *Sekt* industry thus acts as a stabilizing influence in these regions. You should, by the way, drink a bottle or two of *Sekt,* although the excessively high duty that our government places on sparkling wines, makes it not a very good buy. But by all means, drink it frequently if you travel in Germany, where the price is more in keeping with its worth.

France's Loire Valley, with its fabulous châteaux, famous for centuries as the playground of kings and nobles, produces a good deal of wine. Not many of the Loire reds are important, although those of Bourgueil and Chinon are charming when they are drunk in their homelands. Because of their delicacy and low alcohol content, they do not travel well and one never sees them in this country.

But it is for its white wines that we Americans will be grateful to the Loire Valley. The upper Loire in the *département* of the Nièvre produces the first of those readily available in the United States, the *Pouilly-Fumé,* a deliciously soft wine with a faintly smoky taste not to be confused with Pouilly-Fuissé from the valley of the Saône. It contains a legal minimum of eleven percent of alcohol. Further down the river, on the right bank is Sancerre, which produces another attractive wine, crisp and refreshing, and a shade drier than Pouilly-Fumé. More rarely seen but worth buying if you run across it, is Quincy, from the *département* of the Cher. Proceeding down the river to the *département* of Indre et Loire, we find still and sparkling Vouvrays. The still wine is pleasant. So is the sparkling, but it will never give champagne serious competition.

White Wines of the Loire Valley

The next district down the river is Anjou. The Anjou wine most familiar to Americans is the Rosé, which is said by those who like Rosés to be excellent. I have no personal experience. One also sees Anjou *blancs* and sparkling Saumur, which is rather sweet and innocent.

The chief wine of the lower Loire is Muscadet. The wine is exceedingly dry, very light and crisp. Before the days of the *Appellation Contrôlée,* the Muscadets used to be shipped in large quantities to Burgundy to be blended with Chablis. It is not impossible that some of this wine still "extends" the amount of Chablis available for export, despite the *Appellation Contrôlée* laws. I find the wine delightful, and considering the difference in price, prefer it to any but a first-class Chablis with oysters or other shellfish.

Chablis is a Village

Traditionally, the greenish-gold wines of Chablis have been the preferred wine of knowing gastronomes of the world to go with oysters. Chablis is a village of sixteen hundred inhabitants north and west of the Côte d'Or. Close about the village are the vineyards called Bougros, Grenouilles, Les Clos, Les Preuses, Vaudésir, Valmur, and Blanchots, whose wines are classed as *Grands Crus* or great growths. The vineyards producing the next highest quality of wine are Vaillon, Les Fôrets, Montmain, Mont de Milieu, Montée de Tonnerre, Fourchaume, and Séchet, the *Premiers Crus.* The *grands crus* occupy ninety acres, the first growths less than five hundred and twenty acres. Part of the land is always lying fallow, so that the actual surface on which the wine is produced is almost unbelievably small, considering its world reputation.

Alsace and Lorraine, French provinces adjacent to Germany, were annexed to that country at the end of the Franco-Prusian War of 1870. Rather ruthlessly, the Germans insisted that the Alsatian vineyards be planted in heavy-bearing varieties of grapes which they used to blend with, and to supplement, their own production. Since the end of World War I, the vineyards have been much improved and quality has steadily risen. Most of the area is still planted in white grapes. Only in Alsace alone in France, is the wine sold under the name of the grape rather than under the name of the vineyard or town. Alsatian wines in ascending order of quality are the Sylvaner, Traminer, Gewürz-Traminer, and Riesling. All are nice, refreshing wines which are sold in the bottles without shoulders similar to those in which the Rhine wines are marketed. The

Gewürz-Traminer is not necessarily of higher quality than the Traminer; it is more spicy and some wine lovers like the spiciness. An interesting Alsatian wine is the Pinot Blanc. It is fascinating how one can define both the underlying strength of the Pinot grape, and the characteristics of lightness and freshness which seem to inhere in all of the Alsatian wines.

I mention this wine, not because of its intrinsic importance (it is a minor wine), but to make a point. Try this wine after you have drunk the other Alsatian wines and then reflect on the differences between them and the differences between it and a white Burgundy. The Pinots of Burgundy and of Alsace do not compare; they are different. This is an example of what I mean by the inadmissibility of comparing California and French wines. They do not compare; they are different.

We come now to the wines from the Mosel and Rhine rivers of Germany. These are marketed in tall, slim bottles, green for the Mosel and its tributaries, brown for the Rhine and its regions. All of the quality wines of these two districts are made from the Riesling grape. Because of the latitude, with resulting short summers and early winters, good vintages are produced only about three years out of ten; fair wines another two or three times. The remainder of the wine is not worth importing, and such years would be disastrous if it were not for the *Sekt* manufacturers.

Mosel and Rhine River Wines

German wines are usually best when they are young. They are fresh, with a fruity palate and a flowery bouquet which age seems to wither in all but the greatest years, such as 1959.

For your first experience with these wines, buy a bottle labeled *Spätlese* or *Auslese.* The former means "late picked" and the latter "especially selected." Because the grapes are slow to ripen, the grower will sometimes take a chance and leave his crop on the vines to get an additional two or three weeks of sun. If he wins, he produces a superior wine, labeled *Spätlese,* and worth more money. If he loses, and hail or torrents of rain hit his vineyard, his grapes are destroyed and he loses a year's labor. The *Auslesen* also are usually late picked, but not necessarily. If the weather has been kind, a grower can "select out" especially good and ripe bunches of grapes even from those picked at the normal time.

Start with Late Picked and Selected Wines

Chill these wines. But remember that they are delicate, and do not paralyze them by prolonged refrigeration. After you have poured the wine, note its pale, slightly greenish color. In some years, the Mosels, especially, will be nearly colorless. Take time to note the flowery nose. If you are drinking a *Spätlese* you will find it a little sweet, but you will have no trouble distinguishing it from a dessert wine. The *Auslese,* depending on the year, may range from quite dry to as sweet as the *Spätlese.* It will be light and crisp on your palate, without the slightest hint of meagerness. You will know at once that you are drinking an extraordinary wine. These are wines to drink with roast pork, roast goose, delicately herbed omelets, and with the sweeter fish, such as a fresh salmon or trout.

SOME IDEAS ABOUT SHOPPING FOR FOOD AND WINE

If we expect to eat and drink well, we must pay more than the usual attention to selecting our supplies. A conventional American housewife, pushing her cart through the aisles of her favorite supermarket, would undoubtedly tell you that she and her fellow Americans eat better than any other people in the world. She would point to the rows of open bins piled high with all the vegetables in and out of season, the rows of gleaming refrigerator cases crammed with great red roasts and steaks, neatly packaged and covered with cellophane to protect them from germs. She would point to the rows of shelves filled with canned goods and with prepared mixes for everything from soups and pancakes to muffins and cakes, and the piles of beautifully regular loaves of bread which she knows will "stay fresh" practically indefinitely.

How can anyone, she might ask, have better supplies than we? But let us walk down these spotless aisles with our housewife and examine, with a slightly more critical eye, some of the things which so delight her.

First, pick up a package of the lovely precut meat. Tilt the pasteboard or plastic tray. You will see a bloody liquid running from under the roast or steak. This liquid is *juice* which should remain in the meat while you cook it. Next, has it ever occurred to you to question that bright red color? Prime aged beef *looks* aged. It is dark. The surface fat or membrane may be discolored; it might even have a frightening coat of mold on it. But, you will say, you cannot buy prime beef; the meat department of your supermarket doesn't carry it. Supermarkets are in business to sell food. If enough persons demand an article, the markets will stock it.

However, being a sensible person compelled to live on a budget, you don't *want* to buy prime meat all of the time; nor should you. But even when you buy the less

49

expensive cuts of cheaper grades of meat, as most of us should most of the time, you are still entitled to get all of the juice and all of the flavor that you pay for. But when you expect to cook a steak in that most primitive and yet delicious of all ways, broiled, prime beef is worth paying for if you can possibly afford it. The same thing is true when you wish to give family or friends a special treat with a rare filet or rib roast; nothing less than prime meat will do.

Buy Fresh Cut and Fresh Ground Meats

In any case scorn the beautiful precut packages, press the button and insist that the supermarket butcher cut *your* meat while you watch. If he won't do it, the meat man at the next store will. Don't accept meat already ground; you cannot know how long ago and with how much fat it was ground. Select your piece of beef and have the butcher grind it before your eyes. Only in this way can you control the quality of the meat and the amount of fat in it. Another suggestion; try shoulder or chuck when you want ground meat. It is less expensive than round steak and I think it has a better flavor.

Except in emergencies, refuse to buy frozen poultry. If your supermarket won't carry it fresh, you can find specialty shops that do. Or, in most states, you can combine your Sunday drive with buying freshly-killed poultry from nearby farms.

In most parts of our country, the demand for veal is so small that one cannot find the grayish-pink cuts that signify the very young and, therefore, choicest animals. It is also a scandal that one cannot buy mutton in most American cities; a good mutton chop is as superior to a lamb chop as a good beef steak is to a veal cutlet. If you feel that you simply cannot learn to slice bacon properly and therefore must sacrifice part of the flavor, at least buy the precut kind in the smallest possible packages, so that it will not become stale.

Abjure, if you can, the precooked or canned and boned hams.

Unless you enjoy paying cheese prices for milk solids and water, avoid the so-called processed cheeses. These preparations are made only partly of cheese, which is finely chopped and mixed with the much cheaper milk solids and the still cheaper water. I believe the best Cheddar cheese sold in America today is Black Diamond, from a Canadian company which is willing to age its cheese for at least a year before marketing it. If you cannot find it, look for Herkimer County, New York, cheese, which has at least been aged for six months. Yet, every time I go into markets, I see shelves piled with miscellaneous pieces of cheese wrapped in the inevitable cellophane, the label boasting that it has been aged for ninety days.

One of the most dispiriting objects to be found in the American supermarket is the bread, nicely wrapped, quite sanitary and guaranteed to stay fresh, that is, to remain soft, indefinitely. The things that make the loaf stay soft are purely chemical. They make the bread a virtually nondrying sponge. Inasmuch as bread is sold in interstate commerce, I assume that these chemicals are safe insofar as health is concerned. Yet there have been instances in which various additives approved by the U.S. Food and Drug officials have later been found to have long-term ill effects.

Are you old enough to have had a mother who baked bread or energetic enough to have done so yourself? Then you know that honest bread begins to dry out almost immediately; two days after baking it, it is quite dry and a day or so later it is hard. So what? Make more bread before the old becomes stale, or freeze part of what you make. It will not be quite as good as it was when it was first baked but it will still be better than commercial chemical bread. That this stuff stays cotton fluffy does not mean that it is fresh! At least honest bread is fit to eat when it is freshly baked which is more than can be said for the commercial product.

In a few American cities, among which are San Francisco and New York, one can find both sweet and sourdough bread as good as any in Europe. One of the secrets of good French bread is freshness. Even in villages bread is baked twice daily. Paris has four bakings daily and no self-respecting Frenchman would eat last night's bread for breakfast today. Most French bread sold in America should cause them to break diplomatic relations with us.

Freshness is Secret of Bread

Our supermarkets' vegetable bins are piled high with vegetables. But take a look at them! Ears of corn with all the husks stripped off, wrapped in the ubiquitous cellophane and quite without flavor; carrots long, hard and woody; cauliflowers with the white flowerets yellow and sometimes even brown; turnips and eggplants too large; limp string beans; and greens which a boy "freshens" from time to time with a sprinkling can; to say nothing of wilted spinach, peas as big as bullets and nearly as hard, and squash cut in pieces and drying out.

Here again, if shoppers insist on truly fresh vegetables, they will be provided. Buy carrots no longer than six inches and corn only with its husks present. Refuse string beans that are not crisp. Insist on snowy cauliflower and accept no celery with wilted leaves. Select the smallest possible eggplant and Italian squash. American shoppers are defeated when it comes to peas. I find it impossible to buy satisfactorily fresh small peas. With the exception of chopped spinach, peas are the only items which I regularly buy from the frozen food compartments. Both Birdseye and Le Sieur package truly *petits pois,* which taste better than the available fresh peas. I would not buy frozen whole-leaf spinach, but the chopped kind, for soups and purées, seems to me as good as the fresh.

Even when the displays of fresh fruits in the markets appear tempting, it pays to shop with care. Market operators, for understandable reasons, are loathe to discard overripe items if there is a chance that hasty or indifferent customers will buy them. Much fruit is picked too green and never develops its full flavor. The first cherries or the first peaches of the season are poor buys, in quality as well as in price, as you doubtless know. And deny yourself the pleasure of watermelon unless your family is large enough to consume a whole melon or unless you are fortunate enough to arrive at the market just as the man is cutting the melon.

I want to talk especially about tomatoes. Most women shoppers buy them far too ripe. They also tend to select tomatoes which "look pretty." Tomatoes for eating raw or for salads should be definitely firm, with a little green at the stem ends. It does not matter if the fruit is irregular, but it is a handicap if it is too ripe to slice well.

It is just as important not to overbuy as it is to use care in selecting your food items. Although modern refrigerators do a good job in preserving food, the food loses freshness and becomes dehydrated even when tightly enclosed in plastic. Thus, you cannot eat well if you shop only once weekly. Meat keeps it flavor better as part of an uncut carcass than as small cuts in your refrigerator. The yolks of eggs are firmer and the whites beat into a better meringue if eggs have not been stored too long. Try to use only fruits and vegetables that are in season. Quality is better, prices lower and supplies are so plentiful that you can buy fresh daily.

52

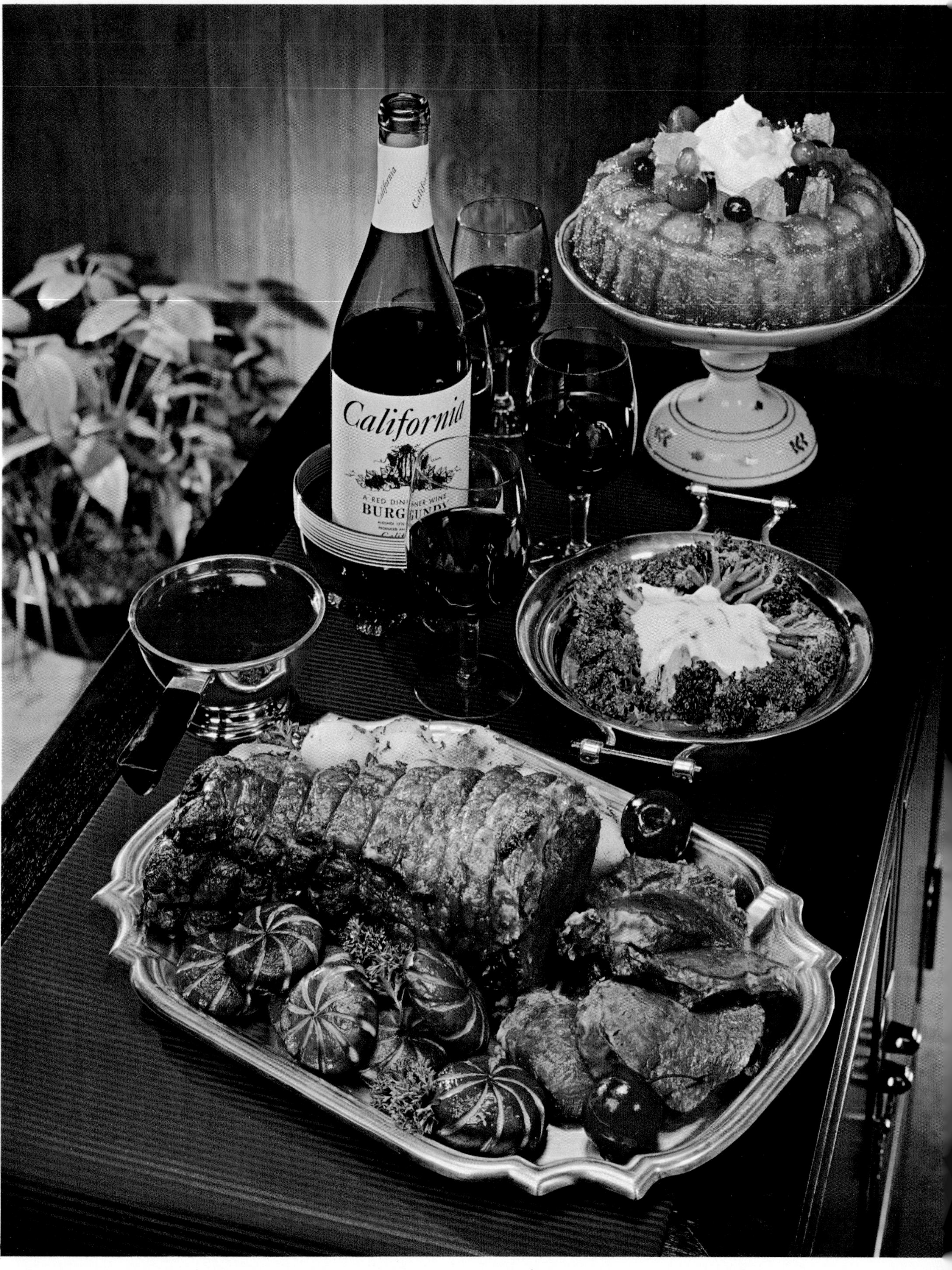

Photo courtesy of: Wine Institute

Care in shopping does not mean paying premium prices. A hasty or indifferent shopper who does not take the trouble to learn the various cuts of meat, the seasons for fruits and vegetables and similar matters, can pay high prices and still get poor foodstuffs. The alternative is to learn these things, watch for the announcement of sales, and then to shop carefully and energetically. But do not be led by special sale prices into overstocking on perishable items.

In the matter of buying wines, the customer, especially if he is a beginner, is not in as good a position to act independently as is the housewife at the supermarket. An honest and knowledgeable liquor dealer can be of great help, but in many sections of the country, such dealers are hard to come by. Many liquor store owners know nothing of wine and are not interested in learning about them.

Buying Wines

At every stage in the art of producing and selling good wines, the ethics of the persons concerned are of great importance. This applies to the producers, the *negociants* in the country of origin (many times these functions are combined in one person), the importers, the distributors, and the retailers. Many department stores, such as Macy's in New York and San Francisco, the City of Paris in San Francisco, and the May Company stores, have good stocks of imported and domestic wines, as of course do many fine food stores in the larger cities throughout the country.

If you do not live near such a store, you will have to work with a small liquor store owner who is willing to learn about wine, or you can order by catalog from a wine seller in one of the larger cities. You will find that your liquor retailer has catalogs listing the names of all the chief importers and wholesalers. Below are two lists, the first of which contains the names of some important growers and shippers in Europe, and the second of some of the reliable importing firms in this country. Neither list makes any claim to completeness, but I know from my experience of nearly four decades of buying wine that all of the firms mentioned are ethical and that my dealings with them, usually through a local retailer, have been satisfactory. Further, you should know the names of three firms which both import and sell to retail customers: Sherry-Lehmann Wine & Spirits Company of New York, the Great Lakes Wine Company of Chicago, and Esquin Imports of San

53

Francisco. During the past two decades, my purchases have been made largely through these firms, especially the latter two.

PRODUCERS AND SHIPPERS

Bordeaux

Barton and Guestier (B. & G.)   Nathaniel Johnson et Fils
Bouchard Père et Fils   Ed. Kressman et Cie.
J. Calvert   Laland et Cie.
Cruse   Alexis Lichine
Louis Eschenhauer   Sichel et Fils Frères
F. Ginestet

Burgundy

Domaine Adrien   Louis Latour
Avery of Bristol   Alexis Lichine
Berthot   J. Monmessin
Bouchard Ainé et Fils   Noirot
Chanson Père et Fils   Patriarche Père et Fils
Marc Chevillot   Poulet Père et Fils
P. Damoy   Ropiteau Frères
J. Drouhin   Société Civile du Domaine
P. Gelin   de la Romanée Conti
Gros-Renaudot   Baron Thenard
Hudelot   R. Thévemom et Fils
Hospices des Beaune   Baron Thorin
Jaboulet Ainé   Comte G. de Vogüe
H. Lamarche

Some American Importers

Atlas Import and Export Corporation, New York
Austin Nichols & Company, New York
Bellows & Company, New York
Bercut-Vandervoort Company, San Francisco
Browne Vinters Company, New York
Canada Dry Ginger Ale, Inc., New York
Esquin Imports, San Francisco
Gambarelli & Davitto (G. & D. Wines), New York
Korb & Company, Inc., New York
Lichine, Alexis, New York

Maynard & Child, Inc., Baltimore
McKesson & Robbins, Inc., New York
Monsieur Henry
G. H. Mumm & Associates, New York
National Distillers, New York
Park & Tilford, New York
Park, Benzinger & Company, New York
Parrott & Company, Seattle
S. S. Pierce Company, Boston
Frank Schoonmaker & Company, New York
Sherry-Lehmann, New York
Mumson G. Shaw Company, New York
Shiefflin & Company, New York
H. Sichel & Sons, New York
Simon Levi, Los Angeles
W. A. Taylor & Company, New York
21 Brands, Inc., New York
Frederick Wildman & Sons, Inc., New York
Julius Wile Sons & Company, New York
Young's Market, Inc., Los Angeles

With these lists you and your local liquor store will certainly be able to select an assortment of wines to fit your growing knowlege and taste. You—and your wine merchant—will gradually learn the names of other sources.

My forthcoming book on wine will go into the subject of identification of wines much more thoroughly, but here are a few facts which will help you to make intelligent purchases at present.

First, French *Appelation Controlée* (Controlled Labeling) laws are strict. In general you can believe the labeling of French wine. In buying wines from Bordeaux you can believe that if the labels say a wine comes from a certain château it really does. But you need to know also that not every château wine is a great one: there are more than 4000 châteaux in Bordeaux. The wine from all of them is likely to be honest but it is distinguished from only about three hundred. German labels are also honest and are the most informative in the world when you learn how to read them.

French Labeling Laws

When you buy California or New York wine you should bear the following facts in mind. To label a wine from any part of the world other than France "Burgundy" or "Sauternes" or any other name is an act of pure fantasy.

At best such a label represents a particular wine maker's idea of how the French wine tastes. Varietal labels on California wine mean, by law, that the wine is composed of at least fifty-one percent of the juice of the named grape. Many times a wine will be composed entirely from the named grape variety. You also need to bear in mind that blending of different varieties is not unethical. All French champagne except that labeled "blanc de blanc," which means that it is made entirely from Chardonnay grapes, is blended from the juice of two varieties, the Chardonnay, a white grape and the Pinot Noir, a deeply colored grape. Also all champagne except that bearing a vintage year is blended from wines produced in different years.

Take Wine on Its Own Merits

A further important fact to note as you drink California wines is that it is not pertinent to ask how they compare to French, or German, or any other wines. A California wine is to be valued for its own merits and not as a substitute for something else.

THE FOUNDATIONS OF GOOD COOKING : HERBS AND SPICES

5

During the Middle Ages the peoples of Western Europe had only salt and a few native herbs to season their food and vary its monotony. At times salt itself was rare and it was always expensive. In seeking control over the routes to the "Spice Islands" huge treasures were expended during the century or more that marked the emergence of our civilization from Medieval into Modern times. Diplomats intrigued and nations waged wars over stations on the route to the ill-known chain of islands in the archipelago extending from the southeast coast of Asia.

It may seem amazing that our forebears attached so much importance to spices that they were willing to expend their treasures and spill their blood for them. Actually, the mystery is simple to explain. Canning was unknown and not for another three-quarters of a millenium would anyone think of preserving food by deep-freezing it. Even salting and smoking were imperfectly understood, and the meat our ancestors were forced to eat most of each year was not always perfectly preserved and at times exceeded even our English friends' tolerance for "gaminess."

The struggle was chiefly for pepper. This pungent berry helped to preserve meat and, perhaps more importantly, to mask the taste of meat not quite successfully preserved. But salt, too, was valuable. During the Middle Ages peasants enjoyed salt only rarely on special feast days. The modern word *salary,* common to all western languages in various forms, springs from the Roman custom of paying troops with measures of salt instead of coins.

There is no doubt that during the Middle Ages food was monotonous even in the castles of aristocracy. Thus, the spices and herbs which could vary the flavor of the same unending round of meat, game and the few common vegetables and fruits, were eagerly sought. Stimulated by

57

the importation of these flavoring items from far places, European peoples began to search out their native herbs. When one notices basil growing in every fence corner of Italy it is easy to see why the taste of that plant has become the typical flavor of Italian cooking.

Sugar, though now an important food, was first brought into Europe by the Crusaders as a flavoring agent and a sweetmeat. The universal use of sugar had to await the discovery of the New World and its sugar cane. Before the introduction of sugar, honey was the universal sweetener.

The peoples who cared most about what they ate and took the most pains with their cooking were the ones who most intensively cultivated the art of using herbs and spices. Pepper and salt became universal condiments. The northern peoples, English, German and Scandinavian used spices such as cinnamon and cloves chiefly in sweet cookery, while it was largely the Latin countries who developed the art of subtly seasoning meats and vegetables.

Should one use fresh or dried herbs?

For most city-dwelling Americans the question is largely academic, but many who live in suburbs or small cities can have satisfactory herb gardens. Even metropolitan apartment dwellers can grow herbs in window boxes.

Onions of varying degrees of potency such as leeks, shallots, and garlic, do not present difficulty. Many American cookbooks advise the substitution of green onions for shallots. Such a substitution is only partly acceptable. The flavors of these two different varieties of the lily family are quite distinct. Furthermore, it is not all that hard to get shallots. If your local grocer doesn't carry them, you will find addresses from which you can obtain the herb by consulting the advertising columns of such magazines as *Good Housekeeping, Sunset, Gourmet,* and *Vogue.* Although it may seem expensive, the amounts used make the cost moderate.

Grocers rarely carry fresh chives, and as one uses the stems rather than the bulbs, they are not available in the ripened state as are the rest of the onion tribe. However, they grow without difficulty—in a small patch of your garden, in a window box, or in the cans in which you can purchase them at any nursery. We transplanted the contents of a small can in our Southern California garden four years ago and the continually spreading patch is now large enough to supply the neighborhood.

Rosemary is hardy. An area in our patio was planted to rosemary as a ground cover. It is quite satisfactory for this purpose, being handsome and fragrant, as well as useful in cooking. Tarragon grows both in the open and in cans. Until a few years ago, the butcher always included several sprigs of parsley with each meat purchase, but, of late, in both the United States and France, one must buy his fresh parsley. It is, however, available the year around. I have never heard of anyone who used fresh bay leaves; but, if you live in Greece where the laurel (which is the source of the victor's wreath and the flavoring leaf) grows, you could do so.

As for the other herbs, you may have to make do with the dried variety. Several reliable producers supply a wide range of herbs, usually as leaves or seeds. Good specialty shops, also, often have the whole dried herbs, especially those such as fennel, which do not grow in this country. Purchase your dried herbs, whether whole plants, seeds or leaves in small quantities in airtight glass containers. The containers should be stored in the refrigerator or in cool places away from sunlight or excessive heat. The containers should be reclosed promptly on removing some of the contents, for the flavors are volatile oils, and will evaporate.

Experience alone can make you skillful in the use of herbs. The strength of individual specimen varies and so does the taste of different people. A sound rule is to use a light touch in employing these aromatics. The purpose of one or a combination of aromatic herbs is to point up or enhance the flavor of the original food. You should never overwhelm it or substitute the flavor of the herb for that of the food. It is easy to add more, impossible to take out too much.

Included with the names and descriptions of the qualities of the various herbs and spices are some general suggestions for their use. But remember, the suggestions are only that: a consensus of what most people who have tried them regard as pleasing combinations. Do not be afraid to experiment. You will doubtless find other combinations that you like. The governing factor is your individual taste; there is no other rule.

NAMES AND QUALITIES

Allspice: This is the berry of the pimento (*Pimenta pimenta*) of the West Indies. The mildly pungent and aromatic spice prepared from these berries is said to resemble a combination of cinnamon, cloves, and nutmeg; hence its name. Called for occasionally.

Anise: An apiaceous plant *Pimpinella anisum,* native to Egypt and cultivated in Spain and Malta for its seeds, which are carminative and aromatic. Used more frequently in making liqueurs and cordials (Anisette) than in cooking; is sometimes encountered in cookies.

Basil for Fish

Basil: The leaves, fresh or dry, are good in soups, stews, meat loaves, lamb, and liver. It is frequently used in Italian vegetables such as eggplant and zucchini and other squashes. Some like it with cabbage and turnips. Indispensable in making tomato sauces for spaghetti. Used in many Italian recipes for halibut, mackerel, and other strongly flavored fish. Cheese, rice, and macaroni dishes benefit from a judicious use of the leaves.

Bay Leaf: Universally used for soup stocks, stews, pot roasts, daubes, and goulash. Can be used in shellfish dishes, and is a must in those prepared Creole fashion. Will enhance boiled onions and squashes.

Caraway Seeds: Used not only in cookies and cakes, but in sauerkraut, noodles, pork, liver, and kidneys. Primarily a Dutch, German, and Scandinavian flavoring agent.

Celery: A widely grown apiaceous plant, quite aromatic, whose blanched stalks are eaten raw as a salad and cooked as a vegetable, but the aromatic characteristics of which make it a useful flavoring agent. A stalk or two of celery is a must in any *bouquet garni;* the leaves are useful, either fresh or dried, in soups, stocks, stews, and casseroles. Celery leaves, together with onions and parsley, flavor any fowl deliciously if cooked in the cavity in place of a stuffing.

Celery Seed: Supplied dry by all reliable spice and herb merchants. Gives a tonic taste to sauces, soups, salads and vegetables. The seeds are not from the same plant that is eaten as a salad or vegetable, but from an oriental plant related to parsley.

Chervil: Another apiaceous plant, *Anthriscus cerefolium,* used in the form of the dried leaves. The English word comes, through Latin, from two Greek words which mean "leaf" and "to rejoice." We should indeed rejoice in this leaf, which adds interest to soups, sauces, herb butters, cheese, seafood, meats, and starchy vegetables such as potatoes or rice, and noodles, as well as to tomatoes, carrots, peas, zucchini and string beans. It deserves to be found on more herb shelves; experiment with it if you do not already know it. It is especially attractive in omelettes and soufflés.

Cinnamon: This tropical bark retains its flavor best as little rolls of bark rather than as powder. The cinnamon sticks can be used to flavor cooked fruits and various hot drinks. Ground, it is the most widely used baking spice. What would an apple pie be without lots of cinnamon? Good with applesauce and apple butter; those who like sweet potatoes will like cinnamon with them.

Clove: Another East Indian spice useful both in sweet cookery and as a subtle hint in certain meats and poultry. For the latter purpose, one can stick cloves in an onion to put inside the cavity of a duck or a roasting chicken, or in a *bouquet garni* for sauces and stews. The favorite American way to bake ham calls for cloves to be inserted in the fat.

Cumin: A dwarf plant, *Cuminum cyminum,* native to Egypt and Syria; has a bitterish, warm taste and an aromatic flavor. Usually supplied in the form of the seeds. Cumin is used in the United States chiefly in Mexican dishes, but elsewhere in the manner of anise and caraway seeds.

Curry Powder: Not a single spice but a mixture of various aromatics, each company making its own from a more or less secret formula. Curry powders are said to be scorned by the natives of India, where each family and each public eating place compounds its own formula. Curry

61

powders come in various degrees of piquancy and are used in the United States and Great Britain to make reasonable imitations of Indian curries. In France, the powders are most often mild and are used sparingly as a flavoring agent, not to make a "curry." Used in this way in soups, poultry, and sauces for meat dishes, they impart a delicate, rather exotic flavor. When you see *à l'Indienne* on a French menu, you can be sure the dish is flavored delicately with curry powder.

Fennel From France

Fennel: An apiaceous perennial, *Foeniculum foeniculum,* always available as seeds but sometimes available as sprigs and small branches, imported from southern France. The latter is the more satisfactory form. The twigs and small branches can be used for an unusual flavor in various stews and daubes. Crush the seed and add to tomato sauce for spaghetti. Crushed seeds make a good herb butter for broiled fish. The seeds crushed with lemon peel and garlic can be rubbed into a pork roast or added to a marinade. Crush a quarter teaspoon of the seeds and add to a meat loaf; add 1/8 teaspoon of the whole seeds to the water for cooking artichokes. Try a few crushed seeds or a sprig when you cook dried beans or lentils. A few whole seeds add an unusual flavor to potato salad. Five or six crushed seeds will give you a new flavor for a crab salad.

Garlic: Indispensable, but you may be surprised to know that it is not widely used in French cooking except in Provence, nor is it heavily used in the north of Italy. Roast lamb is hardly thinkable without thin slices of garlic inserted deeply along the bone; a Mediterranian fish stew would not be authentic without garlic, nor would a spaghetti sauce. For the informal casserole dinner or barbecue, what would a hostess do without garlic bread? But, use a light hand!

Ginger: The hot and aromatic root of species of zingiber, especially the cultivated variety *Zingiber zingiber.* The unscraped root stock is black ginger; the scraped and peeled root is white ginger, which is often candied. Used occasionally in European cooking, frequently in Cantonese and South Seas dishes, and lately popular in this country. It is the flavoring of ginger ale, which some Americans, especially female Americans, still regrettably add to Bourbon whiskey; and of ginger beer, a favorite drink of British children. Used in making ginger snaps and ginger bread, which some of our younger friends tell us is a current favorite as a vehicle for the ingestion of marijuana, masking the taste well, and leaving no incriminating odor, as the smoke does.

Mace: This yellowish white spice closely related to nutmeg (it is derived from the fibrous covering or arillode of the nutmeg) is only occasionally called for. A complete spice cabinet probably should include it, but you won't miss it if you don't have it. You may substitute nutmeg in most cases.

Marjoram: A mild and delicate herb of the mint family, *Origanum majorana,* sometimes specified as sweet marjoram. Used in spinach soup and oyster stew, with any meat stew or pot roast, and to add distinction to gravies. It is good with any broiled fish and with creamed crab or scallops. The vegetables with which it harmonizes are carrots, onions, peas, spinach, and mixed green salads. Marjoram is also good with seafood and chicken salads, and is used in many sauces.

Nutmeg: One of the pleasantest of all spices, nutmeg is the seed of a tree, *Myristica fragrans,* originally grown in the Moluccas Islands but now widely cultivated in the East and West Indies. It is best bought whole and grated as needed. Useful not only in dessert cooking and as a dressing for applesauce and milk shakes, but to enliven sauces. Its subtle flavor enhances many foods, including pork. Try it on cauliflower and spinach.

Onion: Use of onion flakes or onion salt can be interpreted as nothing less than laziness or indifference. Nowhere that food can be bought is the onion unobtainable. It is widely used in stews, soups, and meat cookery. The small white onion is an excellent vegetable, creamed and served with a dash of freshly ground nutmeg; the sweet purple onion can be an important part of several excellent salads.

Orange Flower Water: A distillate of the essential oils of the blossoms of the bitter orange, *Citrus bigaradia,*

63

made in southern France. An elegant flavor for the creams in cream puffs and other pastries. Good in cakes, mousses, and in several drinks.

Oregano: The leaves of a plant botanically similar to marjoram, but more pungent, and with a more decided flavor. Frequently the less delicate flavor is just what is required, as in many Italian and Mexican dishes. It is good in a minestrone, and in other vegetable and tomato soups; try it for an exotic flavor with fried chicken. With melted butter, it goes well with shrimp, lobster, and other shellfish; it will add interest to veal and pork roasts. It is good with mushrooms, stewed tomatoes, and stewed onions. It can be used in green salads, and with potato and seafood salads, or in an Italian sauce to vary your usual omelette.

Paprika: The dried, ripened fruit of *Capsicum annum* and several related species. The best one of several grades is a bright red and is mild but full of flavor. Paprika is valuable both for its flavor and as a pretty garnish for innumerable dishes.

Parsley: An aromatic apiaceous herb, *Petroselinum petroselinum;* one of *the* indispensable herbs of the best French cuisine. In addition to its wide use as a gentle and subtle flavoring agent, it is used, chopped, as a garnish for cold soups, sliced tomatoes and other salads, and in sprigs as a garnish for nearly all meats and fish.

Pepper: The berries of the East Indian plant *Piper nigrum.* It is best purchased and kept in whole berries and ground as needed from a pepper mill at the table, because no container is as effective in preserving the taste and aroma as the skin of the berry itself. The dried berry with its skin is black pepper. To make white pepper, the black skin is removed. To my taste, the flavor of black pepper is markedly superior to that of white, but white pepper is needed for use in making Béchamel and velouté sauces and in such dishes as mashed potatoes where specks of the black skin do not look attractive. Together with salt, pepper is the universal flavoring agent, even among races and individuals who otherwise pay little attention to seasoning.

Pepper, Cayenne: An extremely hot and pungent powder obtained from the fruit of several species of *Capsicum*, the red pepper. Chilis are the dried fruits of the same species. Chili powder is a mixture of chili pepper, cumin, garlic, oregano, salt, cloves, and allspice. Purists among the connoisseurs of Mexican food insist on making their own seasonings, as do the natives of India; but for those of us who like this flavor only occasionally, a good grade of chili powder is quite adequate, in the same way that curry powder is. Tabasco and similar liquid pepper sauces are made from the same fruit. Tabasco is named for the Mexican city of that name.

Rosemary: This small, fragrant, menthaceous shrub (having the characteristics of the plant of the genus Mentha) grows widely in southern Europe and Asia Minor and grows readily in Southern California and other warmer parts of the United States. The needle-like leaves retain their pungency very well in the dried state. Rosemary is one of the characteristic flavors of Italian cooking. It is widely useful in soups, chicken, stews, kidneys, shellfish, scrambled or shirred eggs, and with many vegetables such as cauliflower, string beans, spinach, and turnips.

Rosemary Characteristic of Italian Cooking

Saffron: A species of crocus, *Crocus sativus*, widely cultivated in southern Europe as a dye and as an aromatic. The product used in cooking is composed of the dried stigmas of the flowers of the plant. It has a deep orange color and a pungent, aromatic flavor. Caution: a little goes a long way! If saffron is used to excess, the pungency of its aromatic oils is quite unpleasant. Useful to color as well as to flavor chicken soups; and is sometimes used with chicken, veal, and lamb, as well as various fish; to flavor onions; for deviled eggs, and seafoods. Needed for a good Spanish rice and for making paella.

Sage: The pungent herb which seems to have such a natural affinity for pork and for poultry dressings has nothing to do with the purple sage through which Zane Grey's heroes and the cowboys of other greater and lesser "oaters" of movies and television ride. It comes from a half-shrubby plant of the mint family, *Salvia officinalis*, which is Yugoslavia's principal gift to international cookery.

65

The brush which covers so many thousands of acres of alkaline semidesert in our West is of various species of the genus *Artemisia,* and is not used in cooking. In addition to flavoring pork sausage and poultry stuffings, sage may be used in fish chowders, in cheese spreads, with beans, onions, and tomatoes, and for making Spanish omelettes. Sage lacks subtlety and, if it is used other than in the conventional sausage and stuffing, it should be employed with an extremely light hand.

Savory: An aromatic European mint, *Satureia hortensis,* is also called summer savory to differentiate it from winter savory, which is *Satureia montana*. I have never encountered winter savory. Summer savory is widely used in bean, lentil, and onion soups, with tomato juices, lamb chops and roasts, and in various veal dishes. Many like it with baked beans, lentils, lima beans, and squash. Persons who like sauerkraut say savory is good cooked in this dish. It is good in potato salads, cooked vegetables salads, and with mixed greens. It varies the flavor of deviled eggs and gravies.

Widely Used Aromatic Herbs

Tarragon: An asteraceous plant allied to wormwood and native to Europe; grows well in the United States. Aside from its well-known use in flavoring vinegars, tarragon is one of the most widely used aromatic herbs, both alone and in combinations. It is excellent for soups, cheese spreads, game birds, turkey, veal, and sweetbreads. As the only flavoring agent—except for an onion—placed in the cavity of the bird, tarragon, liberally rubbed into the cavity and over the skin of a roasting chicken, makes this method of cooking fowl one of the most elegant. It is good with any fish or shellfish; and it will point up asparagus, celery (especially as Celery Victor), green beans and peas. It adds distinction to any salad dressing, and together with chives and basil, makes plain sliced tomatoes a delicious salad. It is the most prominent in the mélange of flavors in a Sauce Béarnaise. Used judiciously, tarragon will add to your reputation as a skillful and knowing cook with meat, egg, and cheese dishes. I think it the single best and most useful of the aromatic herbs.

66

Thyme: Any mint of the genus *Thymus;* the common garden thyme is *Thymus vulgaris.* It is derived from the Greek word which means a sacrifice or offering or the incense so used. Thyme was one of the incenses used by the Greeks in their sacrifices. We put it to more practical if not better uses in clam chowder, oyster stew, and cheese spreads; on lamb, mutton, veal, and pork roasts; in sauces for lobster, shrimps and other seafoods; and to liven beets, carrots, onions, and peas. It also adds to aspics, chicken and seafood salads, omelettes, welsh rabbits, and all Creole dishes. Try it with mushrooms.

Extracts and the Real Thing

Vanilla: Use the long, discouraged-looking vanilla bean itself not the alcoholic extract. Vanilla is probably the most widely used sweet flavoring essence in all western cookery for cakes, creams, ices, and all sorts of desserts. While we are on the subject, let me urge you to omit the use of *all* alcoholic flavoring extracts. If you want a lemon flavor, what is wrong with the juice and peel ("zest" in French) of the lemon itself? What can you hope to get from almond extract as compared to almonds themselves? In every case you will find the natural flavor superior to the alcoholic extract.

Zest: This brings us nicely to the end of the alphabet and, at the same time, affords opportunity to call attention to the virtues of the grated peel of good, fresh lemons and oranges as flavors. The French word *zest* expresses exactly what they give to a dish in which they are properly used. Orange and lemon peels are no harder to grate than firm cheese or nutmegs. You just have to remember to do it.

In closing this section, I want to emphasize again that the use of herbs and spices is not only an art, it is a completely individual art. Regard the suggestions for using these materials in this or any other book as completely tentative. You and your family are not only your own best judges, you are your only judges. Do not be afraid to create your own uses and combinations. You can only increase your reputation as a skillful and knowing cook by doing so.

THE FOUNDATIONS OF GOOD COOKING: STOCKS

Basic to good French cooking, and by extension, to all cooking, are good stocks and sauces. Good soups require good stocks. Many sauces demand them. Vegetables gain in appetizing flavor when they are cooked in stock. No self-respecting cook should think of poaching a fish in other than a *fumet,* a fish stock made with fish scraps, aromatics and wine. However, you will use such a *fumet* or *court boullion* only when you poach a fish, so that it is not necessary to keep fish stocks on hand, especially because they are best made from the scraps and skeletons of the fish to be poached. However, the usefulness of meat and chicken stocks is so great that every cook should make her own. They keep very well for considerable periods in a deep freeze.

Simple Beef Stock

Into a large pot put a big soup bone or several cuts of beef shin bone, and a veal knuckle, which you will have had cracked by your butcher when you buy it. Add four or five pounds of beef neck, chuck, rump or other moderately-priced cuts cut into pieces about two inch squares in order to expose as much surface as possible to the water. You may also add a suitable piece of beef brisket to the pot for a dinner of boiled beef, being careful to remove it when it is tender but before it becomes overcooked. Add to the pot two medium-sized scraped carrots, two medium-brown onions and two or three outside stalks of celery. Also use the leaves from a bunch of celery to add a pungent flavor. Make a *bouquet garni* by tying up in cheesecloth two bay leaves, several sprigs of fresh parsley, two large or three small cloves of garlic, a half teaspoon each of tarragon and thyme, and about a dozen cloves. Add to the pot.

69

SIMPLE BEEF STOCK

	big soup bone or several cuts of shin bone and veal knuckle
4 - 5	**lbs. beef neck, chuck, rump**
2	**medium-size carrots**
2	**medium-brown onions**
2 - 3	**stalks of celery**
2	**bay leaves, some parsley**
2 - 3	**cloves of garlic**
1/2	**teasp. tarragon**
1/2	**teasp. thyme**
1	**doz. cloves**

Cover with cold water to a point two inches above the top of the meat and put on a slow fire. When the water starts to boil reduce the heat to a slow simmer; this means that the surface of the liquid should be agitated only very gently. For the first thirty to forty-five minutes of cooking, carefully skim the coagulated protein and as much of the fat as rises to the top.

Leave the lid of the kettle partly off and let the pot simmer slowly for five hours. Add a little water occasionally to replace that lost in boiling. Salt lightly during the simmering.

Strain the stock into a bowl, let it cool sufficiently, and then place it in the refrigerator overnight. Next day remove the congealed fat as completely as possible. This step is important. Use paper towels or blotting paper to get up the last bit of fat; a consommé will not become properly bright on clarification if it is fatty. In many cases, as in making onion soup or minestrone, it is unnecessary to clear the stock; to make an attractive aspic or consommé, it is essential.

To Clear Stock

First, not only the stock but all of the bowls and utensils to be used must be as free from fat as possible. In a mixing bowl, beat up the whites of two eggs with one cup of stock. (If the stock is rich enough to have become jellied, heat it the minimum amount necessary to liquify it.) Heat one or two quarts of the stock, as required, to boiling and, while beating the egg white-stock mixture, pour the boiling stock into the bowl. Put it back in the heating pan and, while continuing to beat it, let it come to a simmer. Reduce the heat so that the mixture barely bubbles for fifteen or twenty minutes and then strain it through several layers of clean cheesecloth.

Chicken Stock

Most markets and poultry houses in these days of selling chicken by the piece have supplies of chicken necks and backs, and my practice is to buy five or six pounds of chicken backs and necks, which will make nearly four quarts of stock. Use exactly the same vegetables and seasonings as for beef stock; start the cooking with cold water, skim, defat, and clear, exactly as in the foregoing recipe.

Brown Stock

Preparing the Stock

Use the same ingredients as for simple beef stock. Brown the meat and the bones and finally the vegetables in a skillet or Dutch oven, either in the oven or on top of the stove. The meat should be evenly and quite darkly browned. Transfer the browned ingredients to the stock pot, drain off as much grease as possible and deglaze the browning skillet or pot with two cups of water, scraping up all of the brown bits and pieces and adding them to the pot. Now proceed exactly as for simple stock.

Brown Chicken Stock

Because brown chicken stock is usually needed only occasionally and then in small amounts, you may make it as required by browning the necks, backs, and giblets of one or more chickens in hot fat, afterward adding two cups of white chicken stock or two cups of canned chicken broth, together with the usual flavoring herbs and vegetables, and simmering the whole gently for one or two hours.

White Stock (Veal Stock)

This variation is more delicate than simple beef stock and is useful in certain velouté sauces and soups.

Use four pounds of veal shank, neck or shoulder and the same weight of cracked veal bones. The proteins of veal are more soluble than those of beef. The boiling liquid will therefore form more scum than the beef, and the stock will need more intensive and longer skimming than is required for simple stock. Except for this fact, proceed exactly as when you are making simple stock.

Emergency Stock

If you find yourself without a required stock you can always make a small supply quickly and easily by reinforcing canned bouillon or chicken broth with several pieces of the appropriate meat, an onion, a carrot, a stalk of celery and a *bouquet garni.* Simmer for two hours.

THE FOUNDATIONS OF GOOD COOKING: SAUCES

7

Speak of French cooking and what comes to the mind of everyone, even the least sophisticated?

Sauces!

Sauces are indeed the characteristic and crowning touches of proper French cooking. There are literally hundreds of these savory preparations. Yet the subject is not as complicated as it may seem, nor as some writers and chefs, not always the best, would have you believe.

The greater part of the whole vast array of sauces are simply variations of one of these five basic kinds: meat juices, sauces made with roux (a thickening of flour or corn starch), purées, emulsions, and flavored butters.

MEAT JUICES

The *jus* of the familiar prime rib au jus served in American restaurants from coast to coast, is an example of this type. It is obtained by diluting the coagulated meat juices and blood in the bottom of the roasting pan with a hot liquid which may be stock, wine or water. The mixture is strained, part of the fat skimmed off and the seasoning corrected with salt and pepper.

The "red eye" gravy obtained by mixing water with the scrapings from the skillet in which old fashioned country cured ham has been fried, is another such sauce. Other familiar examples are the simple sauces made by pouring off most of the fat from the pan in which chicken, duck or other fowl has been roasted and then scraping up the brown particles with wine. The gravies, thick or thin, which the American housewife serves with every sort of roast meat or fowl are further examples, although these latter shade over into the *roux* by reason of the flour used in their thickening.

But this is exactly the point. Most sauces are no more difficult to make than the familiar chicken gravy.

SAUCES MADE WITH ROUX

A roux is a mixture of flour and butter cooked in a saucepan to which other constituents of a sauce are added. A white roux is cooked at a moderate temperature for two or three minutes, and is not permitted to become colored. A blond roux is made by allowing the butter-flour mixture to cook a little longer or at a higher temperature until it turns a golden blond color. To make a brown roux, the mixture is allowed to cook longer, so that it turns brown instead of golden, and then has other items added for flavor, as will be discussed in detail later.

Basic White Sauce

BASIC WHITE SAUCE
2   oz. sweet butter
1/3 cup flour
     hot water
     salt, pepper

This, the simplest of all the sauces, is obtained by making a white roux of two ounces (1/2 stick) of sweet butter and 1/3 cup of flour, and then adding to it, stirring vigorously all the while, hot water to the required thickness. The sauce is then cooked for several minutes to remove the taste of raw flour, and is finished by seasoning with salt and, if you prefer, pepper.

However, for most of the recipes in this book, it is preferable to use a Sauce Béchamel in place of the white sauce. The cost is only slightly greater but the flavor is much richer.

Sauce Béchamel

Sauce Béchamel is made exactly like the basic white sauce, except that you use whole milk in place of water.

Sauce Velouté

To make a velouté (velvety sauce), substitute chicken stock, veal stock, or a fish stock (*fumet* is the technical French word you will encounter in various cookbooks) for the water in a white sauce, according to the food with which the sauce is to be served.

Sauce Mornay

You make Mornay sauce by stirring into one pint of Béchamel sauce 3 1/3 ounces of grated Gruyère cheese, and then thinning the sauce to a proper consistency with essence of mushrooms (see below).

The next step in making sauces is to learn how to enrich Béchamel and velouté sauces with cream, butter, and egg yolks.

Fresh sweet butter stirred into a Béchamel or velouté is in many cases a satisfactory enrichment. Care must be used to beat the butter thoroughly into the sauce, which should then be served immediately. In no case may you reheat such an enriched sauce, or use it in a dish that is to be browned. In such cases the butter will *always* separate and float on top of the sauce.

Sauce Crème

Cream sauce is made by thoroughly beating into a thick Béchamel sauce heavy whipping cream in the proportion of 1/2 cup of cream to 1 1/2 cups of thick sauce.

Sauce Suprême

Suprême sauce is made exactly like a cream sauce, using a velouté in place of a Béchamel sauce.

The most flavorful and elegant sauces require the addition of both cream and egg yolk. Others still are emulsified with egg yolk alone. The secret of making a successful sauce containing egg yolks is to keep the temperature of the sauce below boiling *at all times*. This precaution is as necessary for the true emulsions to be spoken of in the next section as it is for the sauces with a flour base with which we are now dealing. If, during the making of the sauce, you let the water in the double boiler boil, the sauce will curdle. Then you will have on your hands a fancy dish of scrambled eggs instead of the beautiful sauce you intended.

Sauce Allemande or Sauce Parisienne

Escoffier calls a slightly more complicated version of this sauce "Allemande," which means German. More

SAUCE ALLEMANDE OR SAUCE PARISIENNE

2	egg yolks
1 1/2	cup velouté
	lemon juice
1/2	cup whipping cream
	salt, pepper

modern writers refer to it as "Parisienne," which seems a better name. This sauce is quite frequent in good Ill-de-France cooking and is not at all typical of German cooking.

Blend two egg yolks and half a cup of whipping cream in a mixing bowl. Add, a few drops at a time, 1/2 cup of hot but not boiling velouté, beating thoroughly with a wire whisk between additions. Then slowly, but not drop by drop, beat in another cup of the velouté. After this mixture has been accomplished, heat the sauce fairly rapidly to boiling and let boil for one minute, stirring constantly while it is on the fire. After the cooking is finished, season the sauce to taste with lemon juice, salt and pepper.

NOTE: This sauce may be stored in the refrigerator or frozen, if the top is covered with a thin layer of stock or cream to prevent the formation of a scum.

Sauce Bâtarde (Mock Hollandaise)

SAUCE BÂTARDE (Mock Hollandaise)

2	egg yolks
1/3	stick butter
	velouté or Béchamel
	lemon juice

Beat the yolks of two eggs frothy. Then beat into the eggs 1 1/3 ounces (1/3 stick) of butter. Add hot, but not boiling, velouté or Béchamel a few drops at a time until you have one full cup. Beat this mixture into one more cup of whichever sauce you have used, and thicken in the top of a double boiler. Once the mixture is accomplished, you may allow the water to boil. Just before serving, beat in the juice of one lemon.

To make a richer sauce, beat in additional butter just before serving.

Sauce Soubise (Onion Sauce)

SAUCE SOUBISE (Onion Sauce)

1/2	lb. onions
1	oz. butter
3	oz. simple stock
3	oz. white wine
	Béchamel sauce
1	cup heavy cream

Peel a scant half-pound of white or yellow onions, cut in pieces, and cook ten minutes in boiling water. Remove the onions to a sauce pan and let simmer gently with one ounce of butter, a generous three ounces of simple stock, and the same quantity of white wine for twenty minutes. Put the contents of the pan through a colander and add the resulting mixture to one pint of Béchamel sauce. Let cook, covered, for twenty minutes. Beat in one cup of heavy cream and correct the seasoning just before serving. One or two tablespoons of butter may also be beaten into the sauce to enrich it further, unless it is to be used for a *gratin* (a dish to be browned in the oven).

Sauce Nantua

To two cups of Béchamel add three ounces of heavy cream and reduce over a hot fire, stirring with a wooden spoon to avoid burning, until the sauce is fairly stiff. Add three more ounces of cream, two ounces of shrimp butter and the tails of twelve small shrimp. The small dry shrimp of the San Francisco area are ideal, but any small shrimp may be used. In France this recipe is made with fresh-water crayfish. In Louisiana or any other part of the United States where these palatable fresh-water crustaceans are available, use the real thing. For the rest of us, the use of small shrimp is entirely satisfactory.

SAUCE NANTUA

2	cups of Béchamel
6	oz. heavy cream
2	oz. shrimp butter
12	tails of small shrimp

Sauce Bordelaise

Make a blond roux by cooking two tablespoons of flour with three tablespoons of clarified butter or mild cooking oil until it turns a golden blond color. Gradually add with constant stirring one pint of simple stock.

Meanwhile, chop one medium onion finely together with one clove of garlic and one *cepe* (a special variety of mushroom; if you cannot find them, one medium-size brown fresh mushroom will do adequately). Cooked the chopped mixture gently in two tablespoons of high-quality olive oil for thirty minutes. Add a glass of red Bordeaux wine and turn the contents of the skillet into the blond sauce. Cook for five minutes, stirring to avoid burining. You may need to cook the sauce a little longer to thicken it, or you may have to thin it with a little more wine.

SAUCE BORDELAISE

2	tablesp. flour
3	tablesp. clarified butter or mild cooking oil
1	medium onion, chopped
1	clove of garlic
1	cepe (mushroom)
2	tablesp. olive oil
1	glass red Bordeaux wine
1	pt. simple stock

BROWN SAUCE
A Simplified Version of the Sauce Espagnole of Escoffier and Other Classicists of the Old French School

Make a brown roux by cooking two tablespoons of flour with three tablespoons of clarified butter or cooking oil until it turns an even brown color. Away from the heat add one recipe of Sauce Mirepoix (see below under Purées), three cups of boiling brown stock, a tablespoon of tomato paste and a *bouquet garni*. This should include a bay leaf, a stalk of celery, 1/2 teaspoonful of tarragon, thyme, and a few pepper corns, tied up in a cheesecloth bag. Mix the

BROWN SAUCE

- 2 tablesp. flour
- 3 tablesp. clarified butter or cooking oil
- 1 recipe of Sauce Mirepoix
- 3 cups of brown stock
- 1 tablesp. tomato paste and *bouquet garni* salt, pepper

TOMATO PURÉE

- 4 lbs. tomatoes
- 1 - 2 onions and *bouquet garni* water salt, pepper

SAUCE MIREPOIX

- 3 oz. carrots, sliced
- 3 oz. ham, diced
- 1 medium onion
- 2 shallots
- 2 oz. butter thyme, parsley, bay leaf

MUSHROOM FUMET AND DUXELLES

- 1/4 lb. mushrooms or stems alone
- 2 oz. butter juice of one lemon

ingredients thoroughly with a wire whip. Simmer slowly, partially uncovered, for two hours or more, skimming fat and scum as necessary. (Escoffier's directions call for a minimum of eight hours boiling the first day with more cooking the second day.) Add more brown stock if the mixture becomes too thick.

After two or more hours of cooking, strain the sauce through cheesecloth, squeezing all of the juice possible out of the ham and carrots, and correct the seasoning with salt and pepper. The finished sauce should be quite clear, and should be of a consistency to coat a spoon.

Tomato Purée

With little trouble, you can make a tomato purée far better flavored than the canned varieties. Cut four pounds of tomatoes, well ripened, into large pieces. Add one large or two small onions and a *bouquet garni.* Use the minimum amount of water that will keep the contents of the pan from sticking, and simmer gently for forty-five minutes. Remove the *bouquet garni,* season to taste with salt and pepper, and force through a fine colander or sieve. This sauce may be frozen in large or small containers, according to the size of your family, without loss of flavor.

Sauce Mirepoix

Slice three ounces of carrots in thin rounds and dice three ounces of ham. Cut up one medium onion and two shallots. Cook gently in two ounces (1/2 stick) of butter, seasoning with thyme, parsley and a bay leaf, for ten minutes. The mirepoix can be used to intensify the flavor of a plain Béchamel or velouté served with vegetables or over meat.

Mushroom Fumet and Duxelles

After washing and cutting off the earthy ends of the stems, chop 1/4 pound of mushrooms, or use stems alone, and cook them gently in a covered pan with two ounces (1/2 stick) of butter and the juice of a lemon for ten minutes. In certain sauces you will wish to add both the mushrooms and the juice, but for making essence of mushrooms and other purposes, you will separate the liquid from the chopped mushrooms by straining it through cloth. Twist the cloth to extract as much of the juice as possible. The liquid is the *fumet* and the squeezed-out mushrooms are the *duxelles*.

EMULSION SAUCES

Sauce Mayonnaise

This is the definitive sauce of the emulsion type. Even if you feel satisfied with the product you buy, you should make it at home at least once. You may find, as our family has, that the homemade kind is significantly better as well as fresher.

Beat the yolk of one egg creamy and then add, a few drops at a time, a mild, neutral-flavored oil. (We use either a safflower or a corn oil. Olive oil has too distinctive a flavor for most tastes.) Add as much oil as can be incorporated into the emulsion, which will usually be about 1 1/2 cups. When the emulsion is stiff, add two tablespoons of a good white wine vinegar or lemon juice and salt to taste, again beating it in a little at a time.

Mayonnaise Fines Herbes

Finely chop parseley, chives, tarragon, and chervil—1/2 teaspoon or more of each will be about right—and add to the recipe for Sauce Mayonnaise. It is desirable that the parsley and chives be fresh. Dried and crumbled leaves of the others are fairly satisfactory, although of course, fresh are preferable.

Green Mayonnaise

Add to fresh mayonnaise finely chopped capers and sour pickles in the quantity desired, together with a few finely chopped spinach leaves.

Mayonnaise Mousseline

To the recipe given above for fresh mayonnaise add the white of one egg beaten until it is stiff but not dry.

SAUCE MAYONNAISE
1	egg yolk
1 1/2	cups neutral-flavored oil
2	tablesp. white wine vinegar or lemon juice
	salt

79

SAUCE BÉARNAISE

1/4	cup dry white wine
2	tablesp. tarragon wine vinegar
1/2	teasp. dried tarragon
	juice from garlic
	chervil (optional)
2	tablesp. soft butter
3	egg yolks
1/2	cup butter

SAUCE RÉMOULADE

1	hard-boiled egg yolk
1	raw egg yolk
1 1/2	teasp. Dijon mustard
1	oz. tarragon vinegar
1/2	cup or more olive oil
	salt, white pepper
	parsley and
	chives (optional)

Sauce Béarnaise

For each cup of sauce desired, put in a saucepan 1/4 cup of dry white wine, two tablespoons of tarragon wine vinegar, 1/2 teaspoon of dried tarragon and the juice from a small clove of garlic. You may add a little chervil if you like the flavor. Simmer until the mixture is reduced to about two tablespoonsful. Strain and combine with three lightly beaten egg yolks. Put in the top of a double boiler. Be careful that the water in the lower part does not boil. Add two tablespoons of soft but unmelted butter, one tablespoon at a time, beating the sauce continuously. Then, a few drops at a time, add another 1/2 cup of butter, beating continuously. Serve warm, with tournedos or other steaks.

Sauce Choron

To make this interesting variation of Sauce Béarnaise, beat two tablespoons of tomato paste into each cup of Sauce Béarnaise and correct the seasoning with salt. If the tomato dilutes the tarragon flavor more than you like, heat the tomato paste with additional tarragon before mixing it.

We have liked the plain Béarnaise better for steak, but the Sauce Choron is interesting with fish or chicken. Also try it with scrambled eggs or sliced hard-boiled eggs.

Sauce Rémoulade

Here is a variation of the mayonnaise emulsion which employs mustard and deliberately draws on the characteristic flavor of olive oil.

Mash the yolk of one hard-boiled egg and mix it with the yolk of a raw egg, a generous 1 1/2 teaspoons of Dijon mustard, and one ounce of tarragon vinegar. Beat the mixture to a smooth paste. Add, a few drops at a time, 1/2 cup or a little more of a good olive oil, with vigorous beating after each addition until the sauce has the consistency of a firm mayonnaise. Season with salt and white pepper and, if you like, a teaspoon or so of finely chopped parsley and chives.

Sauce Rémoulade is used mixed with shredded raw celery root to make one of the standard French first courses, Celeri Rémoulade. It is excellent also with cold beef or cold ham.

Sauce Hollandaise

Here butter is the fat emulsified with egg yolk. Melt 1 1/2 sticks butter in a saucepan and set aside. In another saucepan beat the yolks of three eggs until they are creamy. Add to the beaten yolks one tablespoon of lemon juice and 1/2 ounce (1/8 stick) of soft but not melted butter. Place over hot, but *never* boiling, water in a double boiler. Stir with a wire whip as the yolks thicken, and gradually beat the mixture until it is creamy. Now add the melted butter, a few drops at a time, beating energetically. If, during the making of the sauce, you let the water boil, the sauce will curdle; that is, you will have lemon-flavored scrambled eggs. On the other hand, keep the sauce warm or it will separate.

If the finished sauce begins to separate, beat into it a tablespoon of cold water and it will again emulsify. Or put a teaspoon of lemon juice and a tablespoon of the sauce into another mixing bowl and beat. Unless you have curdled the yolks with too much heat, this will reform the emulsion and you can add the rest of the thinned or separated sauce to the new emulsion and save it.

Professional cooks sometimes add a tablespoon of a Béchamel or velouté to a Hollandaise that must be held for a longer period than usual.

SAUCE HOLLANDAISE

1 1/2	sticks butter
3	egg yolks
1	tablesp. lemon juice
1/2	oz. soft butter

Sauce Mousseline

Whip 1/2 cup heavy cream in a chilled mixing bowl, and fold into it 1 1/2 cups of Hollandaise sauce just before serving.

Aïoli (Ailloli)

This pungent preparation is much valued along the Mediterranean coast of France, in Provence, where it is stirred into fish sauces, eaten on boiled fish and boiled potatoes, and used as a dressing for snails.

For each two persons, pound four normal-size peeled garlic cloves in a mortar until they are thoroughly pulverized, and then pound the yolk of one egg into the crushed garlic. (If you are making the aïoli for more than two persons, empty the contents of the mortar into a mixing bowl and repeat the process until you have the required amount.) Add olive oil in small amounts, beating

AÏOLI

4	cloves of garlic
1 1/2	cups olive oil
1	tablesp. water (if necessary)
	salt, pepper
	lemon juice
1	egg yolk

81

between each addition. Add a tablespoon of water if the mixture becomes too thick. You can usually beat about 1 1/2 cups of oil into the garlic and yolk mixture for two persons. Season with salt, pepper and lemon juice. The finished sauce should be fairly stiff—about like a good mayonnaise, which, in fact it is—with Provençale overtones.

Sauce Vinaigrette

This is the universal French dressing for a green salad. The classical proportion is three parts of oil to one of a good wine vinegar, which makes a very acid dressing. Our guests seem almost universally to like our proportion, which is eight to ten parts of oil to one of a good tarragon-flavored vinegar. We use either a good safflower or corn oil. In the Ile de France most vinaigrettes are made with the same neutral oils used in this country. In the Midi, or south of France, olive oil is usual. We use olive oil and garlic only if the rest of the dishes are Italian or Provençale.

Sometimes small amounts of green or dried herbs are added, such as chives, tarragon, parsley, or basil. A little dry mustard is permissible.

Sugar is absolutely forbidden, as are ketchup, Worcestershire sauce, or chili sauce. If you use these things you obviously have a dressing of some sort but it is not a vinaigrette, nor in the remotest sense of the word a "French dressing." If you like, there is no reason not to engage in the deplorable habit of adding blue cheese to your dressing, although a Roquefort or any other cheese flavor is much better imparted by adding the crumbled cheese directly to the salad.

The vinaigrette belongs among the emulsions because it is a true emulsion although not a stable one.

Sauce Ravigote

Mash the yolk of one hard-boiled egg in a mixing bowl with two tablespoons of tarragon flavored wine vinegar and mix well. Beat into it as much oil as it will accept, usually six to eight tablespoons added a little at a time. Then add a teaspoon of one of the following: chopped capers, chopped parsley, chopped tarragon, or finely cut chives. You may vary the sauce by using mixtures of these

SAUCE RAVIGOTE

1	yolk of hard-boiled egg
2	tablesp. tarragon wine vinegar
6 - 8	tablesp. oil
	tarragon, chives, capers, parsley (optional)
	salt, pepper

various herbs, to the total amount of one teaspoon full. Finish by seasoning to your taste with salt and freshly ground pepper. This sauce is good with hot or cold beef and with various vegetables.

FLAVORED AND OTHER SPECIAL BUTTERS

Maître D'Hôtel Butter

Work into one stick (four ounces) of softened unsalted butter, two teaspoons of chopped parsley and the juice of three lemons. Season with salt and pepper.

Excellent for sautéed fish and such vegetables as asparagus, broccoli and cauliflower.

Beurre Noir

In spite of being called "black butter," this flavorsome finish for eggs, poached or sautéed fish, and other light colored meats should be a nice nut brown and not black. It *must* be made from *clarified* butter.

To clarify butter, melt over gentle heat in a small saucepan one stick (four ounces) of butter. Skim off the foam and pour the clear yellow oil into a skillet. Be sure that all of the white milk particles are left behind.

Heat the skillet until the clarified butter turns a clear brown. Remove it from the skillet and keep it melted while you put four tablespoons of vinegar in the skillet and reduce it to one ounce by rapidly boiling it, stirring occasionally. Stir in the brown butter and season with salt and pepper. Some cooks like to stir into the butter a tablespoon of chopped parsley. This may be done during the cooking process, or afterward, according to your preference for the flavor of cooked or fresh parsley.

Beurre Manié

The easy way to thicken gravies and other sauces without risk of their turning out lumpy. Mix thoroughly one tablespoon of softened butter with two tablespoons of flour. Stir into the liquid to be thickened and bring to a boil.

MAÎTRE D'HÔTEL BUTTER

4 oz. unsalted butter
2 teasp. chopped parsley
   juice of three lemons
   salt, pepper

BEURRE NOIR

4 oz. clarified butter
4 tablesp. vinegar
   salt, pepper
   parsley (optional)

83

Beurre Blanc

BEURRE BLANC
- 1 teasp. chopped shallots
- 6 tablesp. wine vinegar
- 2 oz. soft butter

Put one teaspoon chopped shallots in a small saucepan with six tablespoons of good wine vinegar. Reduce by boiling to about 1 1/2 tablespoons. Cool and work into the cooled liquid 1/2 stick (two ounces) softened butter. Good with poultry, veal, and fish.

Anchovy Butter

ANCHOVY BUTTER
- 4 oz. butter
- 4 tablesp. anchovy paste or
- 4 filets of anchovy, pounded

Mix together one stick (four ounces) butter and four tablespoons anchovy paste. Or pound four filets of anchovy in a mortar and mix with butter. Put through a fine sieve and chill.

Almond Butter

ALMOND BUTTER
- 1/2 cup almonds
- 1/2 cup softened butter

Blanch 1/2 cup almonds in boiling water and remove skins. Pound to a paste in a mortar and mix with 1/2 cup of softened butter. Rub the mixture through a fine sieve. For use in cream sauces.

Chivry Butter

CHIVRY BUTTER
- 1 teasp. each of chopped parsley, chives chervil, shallots tarragon
- 4 oz. butter

Mix together one teaspoon each of finely chopped parsley, chives, chervil, shallots, and tarragon. Mix with one stick of softened butter.

Lobster Butter

LOBSTER BUTTER
- 1 tablesp. lobster meat
- 1 tablesp. coral
- 2 oz. butter

Pound together in a mortar one tablespoon of lobster meat, one tablespoon of the coral, and mix with two ounces of butter.

Marchand De Vin Butter

MARCHAND DE VIN BUTTER
- 4 shallots
- 6 oz. red wine
- 2 oz. butter
- 1 teasp. chopped parsley

Chop finely four shallots and add to six ounces of red wine. Reduce to one-quarter its volume in a small saucepan; cool and add two ounces of butter (1/2 stick) creamed with one teaspoon of chopped parsley. For broiled steak.

84

Meunière Butter

Clarify four ounces of butter, and heat in a skillet until it is nut brown. Add the juice of one or more lemons, according to taste, and a teaspoon of finely chopped parsley. One of the better dressings for sole and other fish.

Smoked Salmon Butter

Rub in a mortar one or two ounces of smoked salmon until it is thoroughly disintegrated. Mix with four ounces of softened butter to make a smooth paste. Chill.

Shrimp Butter

Put twelve small cooked shrimp through the finest blade of your food chopper and then rub into a pâté in a mortar. Mix into a smooth paste with one stick (four ounces) butter. Chill.

Snail Butter

Peel and put through a garlic press ten medium cloves of garlic, or, if you have no press, chop them finely. Mix with a tablespoon of finely chopped shallots and one tablespoon of chopped parsley. Mix with four ounces of softened butter. Chill.

MEUNIÈRE BUTTER

4	oz. clarified butter
	lemon juice
1	teasp. parsley

SMOKED SALMON BUTTER

1 - 2	oz. smoked salmon
4	oz. soft butter

SHRIMP BUTTER

12	cooked shrimp
4	oz. butter

SNAIL BUTTER

10	medium cloves of garlic
1	tablesp. chopped shallots
1	tablesp. chopped parsley
4	oz. butter

85

From the Deep

THE FOUNDATIONS OF
GOOD COOKING :
BREADS & PASTRIES

8

If you live in any French town, however small, or in New York or San Francisco, you won't have to make bread; you can always buy good (and good always means fresh) bread every day. But most of us aren't living in France or in one of the few American cities where one can get good bread daily; so if we want it, we have to make our own. And, really, to do so is no great trouble. It requires some minimum effort and some attention to detail. However, no cooking that you do will prove so rewarding as the creation of your own oven-fresh, delicious bread, free of the chemicals which commercial bakeries put in their loaves to "keep them fresh."

French Bread

Moisten the yeast and mix thoroughly in 1/2 cup of the water. Mix the moistened yeast, salt, sugar and the rest of the water. Gradually add flour, mixing with a heavy spoon or in a Mix-master until the dough becomes too heavy to beat. Scrape all of the dough out of the bowl onto a floured board and knead with great vigor for a minimum of six minutes, adding a little more flour if required. Continue kneading until the dough is satiny and smooth. Put the dough in a greased mixing bowl, cover with a clean towel and set in a warm place. The ideal temperature is 80 to 85 degrees Fahrenheit. You can easily attain this temperature by placing a pan of hot water in a gas oven without a pilot light or in the electric oven with the current turned off. Put the dough bowl on a shelf above the pan of hot water.

Let the dough double in bulk, which will require about two hours. Punch it down and let it rise in the same warm place until it again doubles in bulk. This will require about forty-five minutes.

FRENCH BREAD
(*Pain Ordinaire*)

- 1 pkg. or cake of yeast
- 1 tablesp. sugar
- 2 teasp. salt
- 2 cups lukewarm water (105 to 110°F.)
- 4 - 5 cups all purpose or (better) unbleached flour
- 1 egg white, slightly beaten

Turn the dough out on a floured board and knead again for several minutes. The more you knead, the finer grained your bread will be. Divide the mass into halves and let it rest on the board for ten minutes. Shape into long, pointed loaves. Butter a cookie sheet and sprinkle it with corn meal. Shake off the surplus corn meal and place the loaves on the sheet. Put them back into the warm place and allow to rise until they double in bulk, for forty-five minutes to an hour. About halfway through this last rising, cut diagonal slashes in the top of the loaf about one-half inch deep. Brush the top of each loaf with a little egg white which has been beaten with a tablespoon of water, and place in an oven preheated to 450 degrees for five minutes. Then lower the heat to 375 degrees and continue baking for thirty-five minutes or until the tops of the loaves are a golden brown. Placing a flat pan of boiling water in the bottom of the oven will make the crust thicker.

To make American-type bread for sandwiches, put the dough in ordinary loaf pans, filling each pan about half full and do not put a pan of boiling water in the oven.

A More Elegant Version

Adding shortening and milk makes the bread somewhat richer and fuller in flavor. It also protects it from drying out quite so rapidly.

Soften one package of yeast in 1/4 cup of warm water. Scald 1/2 cup of whole milk. (Scalding is to kill the enzymes in milk which might interfere with the action of the yeast. Milk is sufficiently scalded when small bubbles appear at the edges of the saucepan in which it is being heated.) Cool somewhat and and add to the milk a tablespoon of butter or leaf lard. Let the mixture cool to about eighty degrees and stir the moistened yeast into it. From this point proceed exactly as in the recipe for oridinary bread.

Sourdough French Bread

When it is good, this is *the* San Francisco Bread.

Moisten the yeast in 1/2 cup of water. Dissolve the sugar and salt in the rest of the water. Place in a crock or large mixing bowl, and add two cups of flour, beating it in well. Cover the crock with a clean cloth or a plate to avoid aerial contaminants and let stand in a warm place for 36 to 72 hours, depending on how sour you like the bread. Start with the shorter period and increase until you attain the degree of sourness you wish. Stir at least once daily. When you remove starter to make bread, add an equal quantity of flour and warm water. After the original fermentation, the starter crock may be kept in the refrigerator. With care to avoid contamination by molds from the air the crock may be kept going indefinitely.

To Make the Bread

Moisten the yeast as usual in 1/2 cup of warm water. Cool the scalded milk and add the shortening, sugar and salt. Put the milk mixture, the moistened yeast and the starter in a mixing bowl and gradually add enough flour to make a stiff dough. This will be about 3 1/2 cups or a little more.. Turn the dough onto a floured board and knead vigorously for ten minutes or longer, until the dough is very smooth and satiny. Place in a greased bowl, cover with a clean cloth and let double in bulk, a process which will require an hour or more. Press a finger into the dough. If the indentation remains, the dough has risen adequately. Knead it down and allow to double in bulk again. Turn out on a floured board and knead for two minutes or longer, divide in half and let the halves rest ten minutes. Shape either into long, slender loaves or round ones. The former yields more crust, the latter less. Let the loaves rise to double their bulk, gashing the tops and brushing with egg white or melted butter as in previous recipes. Bake on a cookie sheet dusted with corn meal in a preheated 400 degree oven for forty-five to fifty minutes.

If you like a still more sour flavor, mix the starter and the other ingredients as before, but use only two cups of flour. Do this in the afternoon, cover the bowl and let it sit in a warm place overnight or longer before completing the dough.

French Rolls

Either the standard French bread dough or the sourdough variation may be shaped into the small rolls pointed at each end. In order to assure the hard crust these rolls traditionally require, be sure to have a pan of boiling water sitting under the cookie sheet while the rolls are baking.

SOURDOUGH FRENCH BREAD
The Starter

1	pkg. yeast
1	tablesp. sugar
2	teasp. salt
2	cups unbleached flour (or use all-purpose flour)
2	cups lukewarm water

To Make the Bread

4	pkg. yeast
1/2	cup warm water
1/2	cup scalded milk
2	tablesp. sugar
1	tablesp. butter or lard
2	teasp. salt
1	cup starter
3 1/2	cups (more or less) unbleached or all-purpose flour

BASIC PASTRY (La Pâte Brisée)
FOR PIES AND TARTS

Nothing is simpler than making good pastry if you follow the simple rules. Nothing is easier than achieving a tough, leathery crust if you ignore them.

The first rule is that the flour and shortening must be finely mixed without actually being incorporated one into the other. One accomplishes such mixing by chopping the *cold* shortening into the *cold* flour in a *cold* mixing bowl with a pastry cutter or with two silver knives and *not* by mixing them with your *warm* fingers, and by finally forming the dough with the minimum amount of ice water that will hold it together.

The second, and only other, rule is that the completed dough be allowed to chill thoroughly and to rest in the refrigerator a minimum of half an hour and preferably longer.

Other things being equal, the colder you manage to keep your ingredients and the longer you let the dough chill, the flakier your crust will be. Pie crust keeps very well in the deep freeze.

The Recipe

Sift flour and salt into a mixing bowl that has been chilled in the refrigerator. Chop in the shortening taken directly from the refrigerator. If the day is hot, do not hesitate to return the bowl and its contents to the refrigerator to rechill as often as necessary. When the flour and shortening are properly mixed, you will have a rather dry appearing mass of particles smaller than peas.

Sprinkle ice water over the top of the mixture while you stir with a cold spoon from the bottom. Keep your warm fingers out of the dough! When more than half the mixture has been moistened, gather it into a ball and put it into the refrigerator while you continue to moisten the rest. Form the latter into another ball and press the two balls of dough together. Cover with waxed paper and allow to rest in the refrigerator at least half an hour.

With American hard wheat flour, an all-butter crust is likely to be too crisp. *Cuisine Pour Tous,* a standard in French households, recommends two parts flour, one part butter and 1/2 part shortening even when French flour, made of soft wheat, is used.

THE RECIPE

2	cups sifted all-purpose flour
2/3	cup leaf lard or butter
1	teasp. salt
	ice water

Butter will give you a richer but less flaky crust.

Puff Paste

Dissolve the salt in 1/2 cup of ice water. Sift flour into a chilled bowl and form a crater in the center. Pour in the salted water and mix, first with a spatula and then with the fingers to obtain a dough firm but not hard. This will require a little more ice water but not much. Knead the dough vigorously for twenty minutes or longer until it is truly smooth, satiny and elastic. Form it into a ball and let it rest in the refrigerator fifteen minutes or longer. Then roll it out on a lightly floured board to about 1/4 inch of thickness. Shape the butter, which should be worked with a spatula or the fingers until it is of the same consistency as the dough, into a cake about one to 1 1/2 inches thick. Place the cake of butter in the center of the sheet of dough and fold first one side of the dough and then the other over it.

Press the folded sides of the dough completely together and replace in the refrigerator to chill for one-half hour. Replace on the floured board and roll out as thinly as possible. Then fold the rolled out sheet of dough on itself once from each side. Repeat the chilling and again roll out and fold the dough once from each of its four sides. The rolling, folding and chilling are to be repeated six times. It is in this multiple folding that the leaves referred to in the French name of the dough are formed.

To recapitulate: There are four important points. First, you *must* knead the dough until it is really satiny and smooth. Second, the butter must be of the same consistency as the dough. Third, you must chill between each rolling. The final point is to use as little flour on your rolling board as will prevent sticking and to brush off excess flour at each turning.

Patty Shells

Roll the worked and refrigerated puff paste out to a thinness of one-eighth inch. For the bottom of the patty shell, cut out a round of dough with a three-inch biscuit cutter. To make the sides, cut out additional pieces with the three-inch cutter and cut out the center of these pieces with a smaller cutter. Use as many of the three-inch rims as are needed to build up the shell to the required height. Brush the top of the bottom piece and the top of each ring

PUFF PASTE
(La Pâte Feuilletée)

4	cups sifted all-purpose flour
1/2	lb. sweet butter
1	teasp. salt
	ice water

91

with the white of an egg which has been beaten with a tablespoon of water. The shells are to be baked on a cookie sheet at 450 degrees for five minutes and then at 375 degrees until they are well browned.

You may make other patterns, such as diamonds, hearts, etc., as you wish. Boat-shaped shells built up in this manner are the *barquettes* of classical French cooking. The shells in any of their forms may be filled with creamed sweetbreads, preparations of mushrooms and dozens of other good things.

Vol-Au-Vent

A vol-au-vent is, in essence, a larger patty shell with a cover. Make a pattern of cardboard about eight inches in diameter and lay it on the puff paste rolled to a thickness of one-eighth inch. Make a series of rings each a little smaller than the preceding one, until you have built up the shell to the desired height. The top is a circle a little smaller than the last ring without the inside of the ring being cut out. Brush the top of the bottom layer, of each ring, and the top itself, with the diluted egg white and bake as with an ordinary patty shell.

Croissants

Roll out puff paste into a circle ten to twelve inches in diameter and about one-quarter inches thick. With a floured knife, cut pie-shaped wedges from the circular layer of paste and roll them up, starting at the wider side and finishing with the point. Shape into crescents, brush the tops with egg white and water and bake on a lightly floured cookie sheet for five minutes at 400 degrees. Reduce the heat to 350 degrees and continue baking until the croissants are golden brown.

There are other methods to make croissants, using a yeast raised dough. However, this is the way to make the rich and flaky breakfast rolls that one remembers so fondly from the better Parisian *patisseries*.

Brioche

Moisten the yeast in the lukewarm water and dissolve in the same water one tablespoon of the sugar. Mix thoroughly with one cup of flour, cover the bowl with a clean cloth, and set it in a warm place to rise.

Blend the remaining flour and sugar with the salt and add three unbeaten eggs. Beat vigorously until the dough is smooth while gradually adding the melted butter. Add the last three eggs, beating well after each one. If the dough appears stiff, add another egg, or even more. The more eggs, within reason that you incorporate into your dough, the richer will be the brioche.

When you have beaten all the eggs into your dough and the yeast sponge has doubled in bulk, mix thoroughly. Place in a well-buttered bowl, cover with a cloth and set to rise in a warm place. When the dough doubles in bulk, punch it down and set the bowl in the refrigerator overnight. The next day beat the dough down again.

If you are using a large brioche mold, pinch off one-sixth of the dough for the top and put the rest in the well-buttered mold. I prefer small brioches made in special molds or simply in muffin tins. In either case, the dough should fill the mold not more than half full. Form the reserved one-sixth of the dough into a ball or balls. Press a slight depression in the top of the larger mass in the mold and put the ball into the depression.

Let the mold or molds stand until the brioches have doubled in size, brush the tops with egg white beaten with a little water and bake at 425 degrees for ten minutes. Reduce the heat to 375 degrees and continue baking until the brioches are nicely browned.

BRIOCHE

1	pkg. of yeast
1/2	cup lukewarm water
2	tablesp. sugar
4	cups all-purpose flour
1	cup melted butter
6	eggs (or more)
1 1/2	teasp. salt

Cream Puff Paste

If you intend the puffs to be filled with a savory cheese or other mixture for hors d'oeuvres, add one teaspoon of salt to the above list of ingredients.

If the paste is intended for cream puffs, éclairs or other desserts, reduce the salt to a pinch and add a few drops of orange flower water, of vanilla extract, or of Grand Marnier liquer according to the flavor of the cream filling you intend to use in the puffs.

Cut the butter into pieces and heat in a heavy sauce pan with the cup of water and the appropriate amount of salt and sugar according to the intended use. When the water boils and the butter is completely melted, add the flour *all at once* and beat as hard as you are able in order to mix thoroughly. Return to heat for a moment or two until the mass forms a ball and begins to leave the side of the pan. Again remove from the fire, and beat in the eggs one at a time. Add the selected flavoring if the paste is for desert puffs.

Although its use is not absolutely essential, you will be able to make better looking puffs, éclairs, and hors d'oeuvres if you use a pastry bag. Spoon the mixture, still warm, into the bag.

For cream puffs, spread out on a buttered baking sheet mounds about one inch thick and two and one-half inches in diameter, leaving at least two inches of space around each puff to allow for its expansion in baking. For éclairs, squeeze out the typical long shape, remembering that they enlarge in baking. For the small appetizer puffs, use a small nozzle and swirl the paste into fancy shapes.

In all cases, bake in an oven preheated to 425 degrees for ten minutes, then reduce heat to 375 degrees. Bake until the puffs are brown and dry, usually about forty-five minutes. Remember that the paste is likely to be still moist inside the puffs. Remove the puffs from the oven, make a tiny hole in the tops of the small ones and a slit with a knife in the side of larger puffs. Return to the oven at 200 degrees for ten minutes. If the insides of the larger puffs are still moist, slit them open and remove the interior, partly baked paste.

Fill the puffs with the desired filling and decorate by dusting with powdered sugar for cream puffs, chocolate icing for éclairs or paprika for savory puffs.

CREAM PUFF PASTE
(Pâté à Choux)

4 oz. sweet butter
1 cup water
1 cup sifted all-purpose flour
4 eggs

Gnocchi with Potatoes

Boil the potatoes and put through a ricer. Beat the cream puff paste and the grated cheeses into the potatoes. With your floured hands, form the mixture into balls a little larger than a walnut, then, on a floured board, flatten them into little rolls about twice as long as they are wide.

Poach the floured rolls in a skillet of gently simmering water, uncovered, until they rise in the liquid and swell to about twice their original size. At this point, they may be used in any recipe calling for gnocchi. Here is an attractive one:

Arrange the gnocchi in a shallow, well-buttered baking dish and barely cover them with a Sauce Mornay. Sprinkle additional Gruyère or Parmesan cheese, or a mixture of the two, over the top. When the dish has

GNOCCHI WITH POTATOES

4 lb. white potatoes
1 recipe Cream Puff Paste
1 teasp. salt
2 tablesp. Parmesan cheese
2 tablesp. grated Gruyère cheese
white pepper to taste

cooled somewhat, dot the surface with butter and run under the broiler for about ten minutes until the sauce bubbles and the top is browned.

Quenelles

These are mixtures of puréed fish, chicken, or veal, with the puff paste, usually with added cream, shaped into ovals about two inches long and one inch wide, and poached in an approapriate liquid: chicken broth, a fish *fumet,* or a veal stock. A blender is the ideal instrument for puréeing the meat or fish, especially the latter.

Popovers

Beat the eggs in a mixing bowl until they are foamy but not lightened in color. Add the milk and salt; then add the flour all at once, continuing to beat briskly with a wire whisk until the batter is thin and smooth. This will require about two minutes. Divide evenly among six well-buttered six-ounce custard cups. Set the cups, some distance apart, in a large shallow pan. Bake in a preheated 400 degree oven for fifty minutes or until the popovers are puffed and brown.

If it is necessary that the popovers wait a few minutes, slit a small vent in the sides of each for escaping steam.

POPOVERS
1	cup sifted all-purpose flour
1	cup milk
3	eggs
1/2	teasp. salt

Onion Popovers

Follow the recipe for plain popovers but add one tablespoon or more of grated onion to the beaten eggs.

Cheddar Cheese Popovers

Follow the recipe for plain popovers but add to the batter one cup of grated sharp Cheddar cheese, then bake as before. My family like these for a Sunday evening supper with a bottle of good Burgundy red wine.

Parmesan Popovers

Follow the recipe for plain popovers, adding to the batter 1/2 cup each of grated Parmesan and Gruyère cheeses.

Savory Crêpes

BATTER FOR SAVORY CRÊPES
(La Pâté à Crêpes Salées)

1   pint milk
2   oz. butter
2   eggs
8   oz. flour
     pinch of salt

This is to make the unsweetened crêpes or thin French pancakes which the thrifty Gallic housewife fills with bits of leftover chicken, ham or seafood and dresses with a tomato or cheese sauce as an entrée.

The easiest way to make this batter is to put all of the ingredients into a blender and blend at high speed for a minute or so. Scrape remaining dry materials from the side of the blender jar and blend a few seconds longer.

If you do not have a blender, sift flour and salt in a mixing bowl, make a hollow and break the eggs into it. Beat the eggs into the flour, then the butter; finally the milk, adding a little at a time.

By either method, the batter should be a thin cream, just coating the wooden spoon which you should use to do the beating. If the batter is too thick, add a tablespoon of water at a time, beating it well into the mixture until it is of the required thinness.

It is absolutely necessary that the batter rest in the refrigerator at least two hours before it is used.

Dessert Crêpes

BATTER FOR DESSERT CRÊPES
(La Pâté à Crêpes Sucrées)

4/5   stick of sweet butter
      juice of 1 lemon
5   eggs
1   cup warm water
1   cup milk
3   oz. powdered sugar
1   cup (8 oz.) flour
1   pinch of salt

If you have a blender, melt the butter, strain the lemon juice, and blend all the ingredients at top speed for one minute or more.

In the absence of a blender, melt the butter, squeeze and strain the lemon juice, and separate the yolks and whites of the eggs. Beat the whites until they just hold a peak.

Sift the flour into a mixing bowl and beat into it the milk and the water to which has been added a pinch of salt. Let this batter rest an hour and then beat into it the egg yolks and sugar. Next incorporate the melted butter and lemon juice. Finally, add the beaten egg white and beat vigorously with a wooden spoon until the batter is smooth and shining. Let it refrigerate for two hours before use.

A small skillet is convenient for cooking the crêpes. The consistency of the batter should be such that one tablespoon of it spreads over the bottom of a five-inch pan. Cook with butter at a fairly high temperature but without burning. It is acceptable to cook either of these crêpes several hours before they are to be filled. Stack them and keep covered in the refrigerator.

Yorkshire Pudding

Sift the flour and salt into a bowl and add a good grind of black or white pepper and as much nutmeg as you wish. Make a crater in the flour and break the eggs into it, one at a time, beating well before each egg is added. After the eggs are well mixed with the batter, add the milk little by little with constant beating.

With the drippings from the pan in which your beef roast is cooking, fill a shallow pan to a depth of one-quarter inch. Heat the pan in a 400 degree oven and then pour into it the batter. Bake at 400 degrees for twenty minutes, then lower the temperature to 350 degrees and continue baking for ten or fifteen minutes until the top is brown and puffy. Cut into squares or diamond shapes and place around the roast for serving. If the roast is served from the kitchen, place a portion of the pudding on each plate and moisten with a spoonful of drippings from the pan.

YORKSHIRE PUDDING

1	cup sifted flour
1	cup scalded milk
3	eggs
1/2	teasp. salt
	freshly ground pepper
	freshly grated nutmeg
	drippings from beef roast

Egg Noodle Dough

Because homemade noodles taste so much better than the dried prefabricated ones, it is desirable to make your own. Because you must have the fresh dough available if you wish to prepare cannelloni, it is *essential* to make it.

Sift the flour and salt into a mixing bowl and make a crater in the flour. Break the whole eggs into the hollow and then add the yolks. Mix thoroughly, first with a wooden spoon and then with your hands. Form the dough into a ball and place on a floured board. Knead until the dough is smooth and all the crumbly particles have been worked into it. Roll dough out on a floured board and let it stand one-half hour. Gather it up and knead again for two or three minutes. Divide it into convenient sized pieces. Roll out each piece as thinly as possible. Cut into pieces of a suitable size for cannelloni, or roll the dough up in the fashion of a jelly roll and with a floured knife, cut noodles to your favorite width. Let stand an hour or more before using.

EGG NOODLE DOUGH

1	lb. (3 cups, all purpose flour)
1	tablesp. salt
2	eggs, whole
5	additional egg yolks

FRITTER BATTERS

The French Batter

THE FRENCH BATTER

1	cup flour
1	pkg. or cake of yeast
1	egg white
1	tablesp. oil
1	pinch salt
	warm water

Here are two recipes for fritter batters. The French version uses yeast; the American one, baking powder.

Sift the flour and salt into a mixing bowl. Make a well in the mixture and add the yeast which has been softened in 1/2 cup of warm water. Then add the oil and beat well. Add enough water to make a batter that pulls out into a ribbon. Beat the egg white until it peaks and then stir it into the batter, adding a little more water, if necessary, to keep it at the proper consistency. Let stand in a warm place two hours or more before using.

The American Batter

THE AMERICAN BATTER

1	cup flour
1	teasp. baking powder
1/4	teasp. salt
2	eggs, separated
2/3	cup milk
1	teasp. salad oil

Sift together flour, salt and baking powder. Add egg yolks to the oil and milk and stir into the flour mixture, beating only enough to moisten the flour. Beat egg whites until stiff and add to flour mixture.

If the batter is to be used to make apple or other fruit fritters, you may add two teaspoons of sugar, one tablespoon of orange flower water, or a tablespoon of Cognac, Grand Marnier or other liqueur as you please for flavor.

98

HORS D' OEUVRES

9

While the French and Italians make desserts as delicious as any in the world, it is safe to say that most Frenchmen care more about how a meal begins than how it ends. Or rather, they find it perfectly satisfactory for a meal to end with fresh fruit or with cheese and no sweet at all, but feel that something is very wrong, indeed, if there is not a little something with which to begin; *une petite chose pour commencer.* In general, I agree with this attitude; this is why this chapter and the two following are extensive.

Most Americans limit the majority of dinners to three courses. In such a case, one will not want hors d'oeuvres, soup and salad, but will make a choice from one of the three. As I look over the record of our dinners for the past several years, I find our choice has most frequently been from among the savory or spicy preparations in the category of "outside the work." Frequently this is a misnomer; some of these dishes are among those with which one takes the most trouble. On the other hand, none more richly rewards you for the trouble you do take. Salads, we find, are our second choice with which to begin the meal, with soups a rather distant third. Nevertheless, a sparkling chilled jellied consommé Madrilène or an ice-cold gazpacho is an attractive way to begin dinner on the terrace on a warm summer evening, and a good onion soup, fragrant with Parmesan cheese, is a comforting beginning on cold winter nights. And then, there are the more formal occasions when a delicate consommé or a clear turtle soup is the proper second course of a more elaborate dinner.

In addition to the dishes with which one starts a meal at the table, I have included in this chapter some of the dips and canapés usually served to family or friends with drinks before dinner.

Aspics are appetizing preparations in a cold jellied base, which may be a beef or chicken stock or a tomato or other vegetable juice. The variety of such dishes is limited only by the ingenuity of the cook. Here are some of our favorites. In all of the aspics, be sure either that your stock is rich enough that it solidifies by its own content of gelatin, or add gelatin to the stock. With the vegetable juice bases, of course, the addition of gelatin is essential.

Poached Eggs in Aspic

POACHED EGGS IN ASPIC

    rich chicken stock
    eggs poached, cooled and
        trimmed neatly to fit molds
1   pkg. gelatin to each qt. of
        stock
    tarragon leaves, fresh
        or preserved in vinegar

Line molds (six-ounce glass or other custard cups) with a thin coating of gelatin-strengthened stock. Cool over cracked ice or in freezing unit until aspic solidifies. Arrange two or three tarragon leaves in a decorative pattern and add another thin layer of aspic to fix them in place. Place one poached egg in each mold. Fill with gelatin-strengthened stock and chill for several hours. Immediately before serving, unmold on a lettuce leaf on a chilled plate.

Aspic with Soft-Boiled Eggs

ASPIC WITH SOFT-BOILED EGGS

1 1/2   pts. chicken stock
    1   pkg. gelatin
    3   oz. dry white wine
    6   eggs
    3   oz. pâté de fois gras
        terragon leaves

Lower eggs at room temperature into boiling water. Take off heat, cover, and let stand five minutes. Pour off hot water and hold eggs under cold water tap to stop further cooking and to make the eggs easy to shell. Shell them carefully.

Dissolve the gelatin in the rich chicken stock and add the wine. Cool and line bottom of custard cups or other molds with stock to a depth of about one-eighth inch. Let solidify in the cold refrigerator while you slice the pâté de fois gras about one-quarter inch thick and then cut out fancy shapes—diamonds, clubs, etc. First, fix a pattern of tarragon leaves in the mold as in the previous recipe, and then, with another shallow layer of aspic, fix the fancy shapes of foie gras. When this layer of aspic has cooled, carefully place one soft-boiled egg in each mold and fill it with the thickening jelly. Chill for several hours. Unmold and serve on lettuce on a chilled plate.

Aspic of Liver with Wine

A first-course dish much less expensive than those made with imported foie gras, and very good in its own right, can be made as follows:

Sauté very lightly in butter, twelve chicken livers cut in pieces. Put them through the finest blade of your food chopper and mix the ground livers thoroughly with the liverwurst and enough butter to make an easily moldable mass. Season quite highly with freshly ground black pepper, tarragon, and a little chervil. Chill, shape, and proceed as in the recipes for foie gras, using whichever wine you prefer.

Tomato Aspic with Cucumbers

Make an aspic by mixing according to the package directions commercial gelatin and tomato juice. In order to be sure of an aspic firm enough to last through its serving and yet not be unpleasantly hard, I prefer to use 1 1/2 packages of gelatin for each package called for. You may substitute vegetable juice, such as V-8, or a highly seasoned tomato cocktail to get a spicier aspic. Chop bits of cucumber into the aspic as it begins to thicken. Fill your mold or molds half full and let become firm in the freezing compartment of the refrigerator. Put a thin layer of sliced cucumbers over the aspic and fill the mold. As the last addition begins to harden, add another layer of thinly sliced cucumbers. Just before serving, unmold and garnish with mayonnaise and a sprig of parsley.

Tomato Aspic with Celery

Proceed exactly as in foregoing recipe, using thin slices of celery in place of the cucumber. You may also like an aspic with celery and cucumbers.

Boiled Egg and Ham in Aspic

Prepare enriched stock as in previous recipe. Prepare molds with tarragon leaf decorations as in previous recipe. Place one-half hard-boiled egg in each mold, cut side up. Add cold aspic to cover egg and chill until firm. Add one slice of boiled ham. Fill the mold with stock and refrigerate until required.

ASPIC OF LIVER WITH WINE

12	chicken livers
1/2	lb. liverwurst
	butter
	black pepper, tarragon
	chervil
	wine

BOILED EGG AND HAM IN ASPIC

1 1/2	pts. rich chicken stock
3	oz. dry white wine
1	pkg. gelatin
3	hard-boiled eggs
6	slices boiled ham, cut to fit molds
	tarragon leaves

101

Aspic of Foie Gras Au Madère

ASPIC OF FOIE GRAS AU MADÈRE

8   oz. can pâté de foie
      gras, chilled
2   pts. rich chicken stock
1   cup Madeira wine
2   pkg. gelatin
      tarragon leaves
      truffles (optional)

This may be made in individual molds or in a ring mold. It is perhaps a little more impressive made the second way.

Chill the ring mold and fill it with a good chicken stock to which has been added 1/2 cup of Madeira wine for each pint and one package of gelatin for each pint. Salt it well, and chill on cracked ice. I like the flavor of the driest of the Madeiras, called Sercial; if you prefer the richer and sweeter varieties, use them.

When a one-quarter inch layer of aspic has solidified over the inside of the mold, pour out the remainder and reserve it. If too thick a layer has formed, scoop it out with a spoon heated in hot water. Remove your can of pâté de foie gras from the refrigerator, open it, and with your hands, form the contents into a ring to fit inside the jellied ring mold. Place thin slices of truffle on the pâté, if you are using it. Now fill the mold and chill for several hours. Immediately before serving, turn out on a chilled plate decorated with tarragon leaves. Fill the center of the ring with watercress.

If you make this preparation in individual molds, place the slice of truffle in the mold and fix with a thin layer of jelly, so that when you turn the contents out of the mold onto the serving plate, the truffle slice will be on top.

Aspic of Foie Gras Au Porto

Proceed exactly as in the recipe above, substituting a good ruby port for the Madeira.

Aspic of Foie Gras Au Xérès

Substitute a good sherry for the Madeira, preferably a full-flavored but not sweet sherry, such as a good Amontillado.

Avocado with Crab

Pick over crab meat, removing all membrane. Heap the meat in the center of half an avocado from which the seed has been removed. Serve with mayonnaise, lemon, or a mustard-flavored dressing.

Avocado with Shrimp

Use small shrimp or pieces of larger ones as in avocado-crab recipe above.

Asparagus Vinaigrette

Select tender young stalks of asparagus and break off tough ends. Wash thoroughly and tie in bundles. Place in cooking vessel upright so that stalks will cook in boiling water but the points only in the steam. Cook until the stalks are barely tender, remove from vessel, and run cold tap water over the spears to stop cooking.

When the asparagus is cold, arrange neatly in a shallow glass dish and squeeze the juice of 1/2 lemon over each pound of asparagus. Cut the peel of one whole lemon in thin strips and arrange under and between the stalks. Barely cover with your standard vinaigrette, and marinate overnight in the refrigerator. Drain well and remove the lemon peel before serving. Decorate each serving with two filets of anchovy and strips of pimento.

Avocado

A good ripe avocado, either the thin-skinned Fuerte available most of the year or the thicker- and darker-skinned varieties, is excellent simply halved and served in its shell with a wedge of lemon. Have salt and pepper mill available.

Avocado Dip (Guacamole)

Mash a sufficient number of ripe, peeled avocados with half their quantity of ripe, peeled tomatoes. Season to taste with grated onion, salt, chili powder and one or two cloves of garlic, liquified in a garlic press or finely chopped. Use as a dip with corn chips or potato chips, preferably the former.

Seafood Cocktails

Ice-cold boiled crab, lobster, shrimp, or chunks of canned tuna may be served in chilled cocktail glasses with either a suprême sauce, or a red cocktail sauce. Oysters may be similarly served, but I do not recommend it. You can get better and fresher oysters on the half shell. I deplore the habit of many restaurants of mixing chopped celery or other fillers with their seafood cocktails. This is clearly done only to dilute the more expensive seafood.

CANAPÉS

Strictly speaking, canapés are small pieces of toast covered with various savory preparations. In current American usage the term applies to taste-ticklers prepared with various crackers, and either homemade or ready-prepared pastry cups of various shapes. Canapés can be as simple as a small round of toast spread with a seasoned butter, or as complicated as one's ingenuity and desire suggest. Do not let canapés sit uneaten. The toast becomes soggy. Make up a few at a time.

Small rounds of toast spread with any of the seasoned butters described in the chapter on sauces are excellent and simple to prepare.

Egg and Olive Canapé

Spread toast with Chivry butter and place on it a slice of hard-boiled egg. In the center of the yolk place a slice of pimento-stuffed olive. Dust with paprika.

Egg and Caviar Canapé

Prepare as above, centering the yolk with black or red caviar. The red caviar (which is the roe of salmon) is much less expensive than the black.

Chopped Chicken Liver Canapé

Spread rounds of toast with anchovy butter and heap on them small mounds of chopped chicken livers.

Anchovy Canapé

Spread toast shapes with anchovy butter and center with a rolled filet of anchovy and a caper.

Canapé of Foie Gras

Spread toast shapes with a mousse or a pâté of foie gras. Decorate with a slice of pimento, or a slice of sour pickle. The mousse is less expensive than the pâté. Dust with paprika.

Roquefort Canapé

Mix equal parts of Roquefort and cream cheeses with enough cream so that the mixture spreads easily. Spread on toast shapes and dust with paprika.

Beau Monde Canapé

Mix cream cheese with enough cream so that it spreads easily, and season highly with Beau Monde salt, thyme and marjoram, the amounts of each depending on your taste. Spread on toast rounds or crisp crackers.

Smoked Salmon Canapés

Spread toast shapes with salmon butter. Cover with thin slices of smoked salmon, and decorate with three capers and a little freshly ground coarse black pepper.

Smoked turkey, thin slices of prosciutto, and salami may be treated similarly. For the turkey, spread the toast rounds with Chivry butter. For the others, use a garlic butter.

Cheese and Caviar Canapés

Mix cream cheese and cream to make a mass that spreads easily, and season mildly with Beau Monde salt. Spread on toast rounds and top each with 1/4 teaspoon of caviar.

Shrimp Canapé

Spread a toast shape with either shrimp or anchovy butter and place one whole shrimp on each shape.

Tomato Aspic with Shrimp

Preferably use small whole shrimp; if larger ones are used, cut them in pieces. Add the tomato-gelatin mixture in at least four layers so that the shrimp will stay in place. Unmold and garnish with two or three small shrimp or pieces of shrimp and top with mayonnaise.

Cheddar Cheese Canapé

Toast bread shapes on one side only. On untoasted side, place thin slices of sharp Cheddar cheese cut a little smaller than the bread shape, and moisten with a tiny drop of Tabasco sauce. Run under broiler until cheese is just melted. Serve at once.

Celery Rémoulade

For each two persons to be served peel one large or two small celery roots (celery-rave) and either shred it or cut it into fine julienne strips. Mix with a rémoulade sauce (see sauce chapter) and serve mounded neatly on chilled plates and dusted with paprika.

Celery Victor

Select small hearts of celery. Trim just below the leaves and at the base, leaving only enough of the latter to hold the stalks together. Halve the hearts lengthwise and cook in chicken stock to which have been added the juice and peel of 1/2 lemon for each four hearts, with 1/2 teaspoon each of basil and tarragon. Cook until barely tender and let cool in the cooking liquid. When the hearts are cold, drain well and put to marinate overnight in a vinaigrette to which has been added the juice and peel of 1/2 lemon for each four hearts. Drain well and serve on cold plates, garnished with filets of anchovy and strips of pimento.

Stuffed Celery

Select tender inside stalks of celery, wash and trim. Divide each stalk in half and stuff.

Caviar

Fresh caviar *must* be served cold. To that end it is placed in its original container, or in a crystal bowl, in a larger bowl of cracked ice or in a hollowed out space in a block of ice.

Accompany caviar with freshly made toast. Some people also serve with it finely chopped egg white and egg

---

STUFFING FOR CELERY

Cream cheese to which has been added enough cream to make it workable, mixed with salt, freshly ground pepper, Beau Monde salt, dried tarragon and dried chervil.

Cream cheese similarly diluted and mixed with chopped walnuts, the whole mixture lightly salted.

A mixture of Roquefort and cream cheese, thinned with cream as necessary.

A similar thinned cream cheese mixed with caviar and seasoned with lemon juice.

Red caviar (salmon roe).

yolk and grated onion. In the opinion of many, including myself, the onion serves only to destroy the delicate flavor of caviar. Others, among whom is numbered my wife, insist that the onion is a desirable addition.

With caviar, serve champagne or *ice-cold* vodka.

Salted Caviar

Here, the chopped egg and onion are permissible because of the more assertive flavor. Here, also, one may substitute thinly sliced pumpernickel for the fresh toast.

Caviar and Cucumber Aspic

Line a ring mold with one-quarter inch of jellied chicken stock as described in the section on aspics. Distribute either fresh or salted caviar down the center of the half-filled mold. Add a layer of thinly sliced cucumbers. Fill the mold with aspic, and refrigerate for several hours. Unmold on a chilled plate and fill center of ring with watercress. Serve immediately.

Caviar and Cream Cheese

Mix a package of cream cheese with salt, a little dill weed and freshly ground pepper. Add enough cream to make it workable. Form into a ball or pyramid and coat the outside with caviar. One may substitute the salted caviar, or the much-less-expensive black fish roe. Refrigerate and serve with thin toast.

Red Caviar or Salmon Roe

Russian or Iranian caviar is the roe of the Black Sea sturgeon. Our own Pacific Coast salmon produce a red roe which is only a little less attractive than the eggs of the sturgeon. Red caviar is particularly adaptable to the preparation of canapés.

Roquefort Cheese Balls

Mix together equal portions of cream cheese and Roquefort cheese with enough cream to make it workable. Add for each 1/2 pound of the mixture three tablespoons

ROQUEFORT CHEESE BALLS

	cream cheese
	Roquefort cheese
	cream
3	tablesp. chives
3	tablesp. parsley
3	tablesp. onion
	salt, pepper
	almonds
	paprika

107

each of chopped chives, chopped parsley, and grated onion, with salt and pepper to taste. Form into balls about the size of walnuts. Roll the balls in blanched, toasted almonds which have been finely chopped and mixed with a little paprika. Chill for at least one hour before serving.

Minted Cheese Balls

MINTED CHEESE BALLS

1   cup cream cheese
3   tablesp. chopped mint
3   tablesp. brandy
       chopped almonds

Mix one cup of cream cheese with three tablespoons of finely chopped fresh mint and three tablespoons of brandy. Form into a ball and roll in finely chopped toasted almonds. Refrigerate several hours before serving with toast shapes or crisp crackers.

Cheese Balls Madère

Make a mixture of cream cheese and mint as described above. Instead of brandy, use three ounces of Sercial Madeira. Form into walnut-size balls. Roll the balls in finely chopped walnuts and refrigerate before serving.

Clams on the Half Shell

**CLAMS STUFFED
NEW ENGLAND STYLE**

12   clams
1/2   cup garlic-flavored
       toasted bread crumbs
       clam juice
       tarragon, dill weed,
         black pepper and salt

Either littleneck or cherrystone clams are excellent served on the half shell on a bed of cracked ice. Instead of burying their flavor in a ketchup-like red sauce, try eating them with nothing except salt and a dash of lemon juice.

Clams Stuffed New England Style

For each twelve clams, make a dressing of 1/2 cup garlic-flavored toasted bread crumbs moistened with clam juice, and seasoned to taste with tarragon, dill weed, freshly ground black pepper and salt. Place the dressing around and over freshly opened clams on the half shell, and run under medium-hot broiler until the edges of the dressing begin to brown.

**CLAMS STUFFED CAFE DE LA
MOTTE STYLE**

12   clams
2   oz. hazelnuts
2   oz. butter
1   teasp. chopped parsley
1   teasp. chopped shallot
       juice of 1 clove of garlic

Clams Stuffed Cafe de la Motte Style

In an excellent small restaurant near the École Militaire in Paris, we used to eat the delicious thick-shelled clams called *praires* cooked in this fashion. I have adapted the recipe to littleneck or cherrystone clams with good results.

For each twelve clams, scald two ounces of hazelnuts and remove the brown, bark-like covering. Put the nuts through the finest blade of your food chopper and then make them still finer by blending or by grinding in a mortar. Mix the pulverized nuts with two ounces of soft butter, one teaspoon of finely chopped parsley and one teaspoon of finely chopped shallot. Add the juice of one clove of garlic. Mix all ingredients thoroughly and place around and over the clams in the half shell. Run under broiler until the butter bubbles and the nuts brown a little. Much superior to the bread stuffing!

Eggs Mayonnaise

Cut one hard-boiled egg in half, lengthwise, for each serving. Place cut side down on chilled plate. Dress with mayonnaise, add a few capers, and dust with paprika before serving.

Stuffed Eggs

The variety which you can give this introductory dish is limited only by your own imagination. Try these to start.

Two halves of eggs, filled with any of these preparations, served on a lettuce leaf, and dusted with paprika, will make a suitable serving.

FRIVOLITIES

Escoffier used this term to characterize a diverse group of hors d'oeuvres. Our list is much shorter, but it will give you an idea of the possibilities open to you.

Cheese Fritters (Beignets)

Make a batter with the flour, salt, oil, and egg, beating the beer into it gradually. Let the batter stand for one hour, then fold in the cheese and the beaten egg white. Drop small portions, about one teaspoon each, into hot fat and fry until brown. Remove with slotted spoon, drain on paper towels and serve quickly.

STUFFING FOR EGGS

Mash yolks and add finely chopped dill pickle. Season with a *hot* mustard and a little cayenne pepper, as well as salt. Add enough mayonnaise to make a smooth paste and heap into the cut whites.

Mix the mashed yolks with salmon, trout, or any other bits of leftover fish, and season highly with cayenne, mustard, and salt. Make into a paste with mayonnaise and fill the white halves.

Vary the procedure directly above by using curry powder in place of mustard.

Sauté some chicken livers, mash them with a fork, and season with salt, thyme and cayenne. Mix with the egg yolk and mayonnaise, and fill the hardened egg halves.

Mix equal parts of cream and Roquefort cheeses with a little cream. Season with salt and fill the egg halves with this mixture. Sprinkle the mashed yolks over the filled eggs.

109

STUFFING (continued)

Mix egg yolks and chopped black olives as a filling. This mixture will require salt and a dash of cayenne or Tabasco sauce.

Mix as much anchovy paste as you like with the mashed yolks. This filling will require no extra seasoning.

Fill the egg halves with flaked crab meat, either alone or mixed with a part of the yolks, and a little ketchup or cocktail sauce.

Mix finely chopped cold boiled ham with the yolks and a generous amount of capers to make a zesty change.

CHEESE FRITTERS (Beignets)

3/4	cup flour
1/4	teasp. salt
1	tablesp. salad oil
1	egg
1/2	cup stale beer
1	egg white, stiffly beaten
1	lb. grated Gruyère cheese
	fat for frying

CHEDDAR CHEESE PUFFS

3/4	cup flour
1/4	teasp. salt
1/2	stick melted butter
1	egg beaten
1	cup grated sharp Cheddar cheese
1	egg white, beaten
	dash of tabasco or cayenne

SHERRY CLAM PUFFS

8	oz. pkg. cream cheese
7	oz. can minced clams
1/4	cup dry sherry
	bacon slices
	toast rounds
	salt, pepper, black and cayenne

Cheddar Cheese Puffs

Mix the first three ingredients, then add the cheese, the beaten whole egg and the additional egg white. If mixture is not stiff enough to hold its shape, add a little more flour. Drop by teaspoonsful onto a greased cookie sheet and bake about fifty minutes in a 400 degree oven.

Sherry Clam Puffs

Drain clams and reserve juice for another use. Mix clams with cream cheese and sherry, and season to taste with salt, pepper, and cayenne. Spread on toast rounds, cover with small slice of bacon and broil on a cookie sheet until bacon is crisp. Serve at once.

Chicken Livers and Bacon

Clean chicken livers, removing all green and black spots, and cut in half. Wrap each half liver in 1/2 slice of bacon, fixing it with a toothpick. Season with salt and a little sweet basil. Broil until the liver is cooked and the bacon is crisp. Serve hot.

Water Chestnuts and Bacon

Wrap water chestnuts with 1/2 slice of bacon, salt lightly, and broil as with the chicken livers.

Hot Sausage Rolls

Roll out a good, short pie crust to a thickness of one-eighth inch. Cook pork sausage meat, rather strongly flavored with sage and a dash of cayenne pepper or tabasco sauce, with a minced onion. Drain off most of the fat and then spread the cooked meat over the rolled-out pastry to about one-quarter inch thickness. Roll up the pastry jelly-roll fashion, wrap it in wax paper and refrigerate until it is firm. With a sharp knife, cut the roll into slices about one-quarter inch thick, and bake on a cookie sheet until the pastry is brown.

Feta Cheese Pastry

Combine by hand, or in the small bowl of your mixer, the two cheeses, the egg and the stick of butter, beating until the mass is smooth. Roll the pastry one-eighth inch thick and cut two-inch squares. Brush each square with melted butter. Toward one corner of each square put one teaspoon of the filling and fold the pastry over it in a triangle. Arrange the folded triangles on an ungreased cookie sheet and bake in a preheated 350 degree oven until a deep golden brown, about twenty minutes.

Camembert Fritters

Work the butter, flour, and cheese seasoned with cayenne pepper into a smooth dough with the two egg yolks. Wrap in waxed paper and chill in refrigerator several hours. Roll out one-half inch thick, and cut in various shapes. Dip first in beaten egg and then in bread crumbs and fry in hot oil. Dust with paprika and serve hot.

Cold Lobster à l'Indienne

Serve bite-size pieces of cold boiled lobster together with a sauce made by flavoring mayonnaise with enough curry powder to taste. The aim here is not "curried lobster," but the more delicate and subtle flavor of the spices in the curry powder. I like to add a little cayenne pepper to the curry powder.

Broiled Pork Sausages

Buy the smallest little pig sausages you can find. Sprinkle lightly with pulverized sweet basil, a little additional sage, and a dusting of cayenne pepper. Broil close to the heat source and serve immediately on toothpicks.

This list of "frivolities" should suggest the possibilities. Amuse yourself by devising others.

Marinated Mushrooms

Select small-to-medium fresh white mushrooms. Trim off soil end, wash thoroughly, and slice thinly. Marinate three to four hours in your favorite vinaigrette to which has been added the sliced rind of a whole lemon and the juice of 1/2 lemon for each half pound of mushrooms. Remove from the marinade with a slotted spoon and serve on a chilled plate, dusting with fresh black pepper.

FETA CHEESE PASTRY

2	8 oz. pkg. cream cheese
1/2	lb. Feta (Greek) cheese
1	egg
3/4	stick sweet butter
	pie crust pastry
1	cup melted sweet butter
	cayenne pepper

CAMEMBERT FRITTERS

6	oz. Camembert cheese
4	oz. sweet butter
1	cup flour
2	egg yolks, beaten
1	whole egg, beaten
	cayenne pepper
	garlic-seasoned bread crumbs
	oil for frying

Mushrooms and Radishes

Prepare mushrooms as in foregoing recipe. One hour before serving, clean and slice thinly, without peeling, such a number of radishes as will equal the volume of mushrooms, and add them to the marinade, mixing well. Serve well drained, on chilled plates, dusted with freshly ground black pepper.

Mushrooms à la Grecque

Make a court bouillon by putting all of the ingredients except the mushrooms in a saucepan and simmering ten minutes. Wash and trim the mushrooms. Leave the small button mushrooms whole or cut the large sizes in halves or quarters, if you have to use them. Add the mushrooms to the boiling court bouillon and simmer ten minutes longer. Remove the mushrooms to a serving dish and rapidly boil down the liquid in the saucepan until the volume is reduced to 1/3 to 1/2 cup. Strain over the mushrooms and when the dish cools, refrigerate overnight before serving.

Artichoke Hearts à la Grecque

Use frozen artichoke hearts and save yourself all the trimming and basic cooking these have undergone. Prepare a court bouillon from exactly the same ingredients as in the recipe for mushrooms and, after thawing the hearts, cook in the court bouillon ten minutes. Remove the artichoke hearts, concentrate the bouillon and pour over the artichoke hearts exactly as with the mushrooms.

Cucumbers, Celery, Belgian Endive and Onions à la Grecque

Peel the cucumbers, halve lengthwise, and scrape out seeds. Cut into strips one-half by four inches and soak in salted ice water an hour. Drain thoroughly and proceed as in the recipe for mushrooms. Simmering time will be ten minutes.

Fresh celery hearts may be split lengthwise and prepared in the same bouillon. Simmering time will be thirty to forty-five minutes, or until the hearts are just tender.

MUSHROOMS À LA GRECQUE

1	lb. small button mushrooms
2	cups water
1	cup olive oil
1/3	cup lemon juice
1	tablesp. minced shallot
1	clove garlic, finely chopped
6	sprigs of garlic
1	small branch fennel or
1/4	teasp. fennel seeds
1/2	teasp. dried thyme
1/2	teasp. dried rosemary
1	stalk celery
12	pepper corns
6	coriander seeds
1/3	teasp. salt

Belgian endive is to be halved or quartered according to size and treated the same way. The cooking time in the court bouillon will range from thirty to forty minutes.

Bell peppers, both green and red, string beans and other vegetables treated the same way will offer further variety in interesting low-calorie introductory courses.

Mushrooms with Savory Meat Stuffing

Remove the stems from the mushrooms and save for making essence or other use. Clean the caps well, and brush lightly with butter.

Put the bacon through the finest blade of your food chopper, mince the onion, and mix all of the other ingredients into a dressing. Fill the caps of the mushrooms with the mixture and place them in a lightly buttered pan. Bake until the dressing is done in a 375 degree preheated oven. Serve at once.

Mushrooms with Clam Stuffing

Prepare mushroom caps as in previous recipe. Make the stuffing by draining a 7-ounce can of minced clams, reserving the juice, and mixing the minced clams with two beaten eggs, two tablespoons of mayonnaise, the juice of two lemons and 1/2 cup of bread crumbs. Bake as in the previous recipe.

Mushrooms with Other Stuffings

Other attractive stuffings for mushroom caps.

Oysters on the Half Shell

Universally liked wherever it is found, this succulent bivalve is at its best served in the simplest possible way: fresh oysters, freshly opened and served in their own shells on a bed of ice accompanied only by a lemon wedge, a little salt, and perhaps a light grinding of black pepper.

To insist on eating oysters with one of the red cocktail sauces or with horseradish is to sacrifice a great deal of their delicacy.

By long gastronomic tradition, oysters are best with champagne or Chablis. But the former is always expensive

MUSHROOMS WITH SAVORY MEAT STUFFING

2	lbs. large mushrooms
1/4	lb. fresh sausage meat
3	slices bacon
1	medium onion
1	cup bread crumbs
1/4	cup chopped green olives
2	eggs, beaten
1	tablesp. fines herbs
	salt to taste
	freshly ground black pepper

STUFFINGS FOR MUSHROOMS

Mince and sauté in butter the mushroom stems and mix with bread crumbs. Season with either tarragon or fines herbs, and moisten with sherry or Madeira.

Make a mixture of the chopped stems with ground ham and season with tarragon.

Make a similar mixture with ground chicken.

To either the second or third stuffings above, add Gruyère or Parmesan cheese.

Make a mixture of sharp Cheddar cheese, bread crumbs and chopped onion, flavored with tarragon and moistened with cognac.

and the latter, with increasing demand, is becoming hard to find and not at all cheap. We find that a good, young, crisp Muscadet is equally delightful with oysters—and a lot less expensive.

Oysters Bouquiniste

Wash and open five oysters for each serving. Chop finely one shallot and 1/4 stalk of celery for each serving. Leave the oysters in the deeper of its half shells and divide chopped vegetables among the five shells, distributing about the oysters. Put in each shell a generous dollop of snail butter (see chaper on sauces) and cover each oyster with a thin slice of bacon cut to fit it. Place the oysters on a bed of rock salt in an ovenproof dish, and place under the broiler until the bacon is crisp and the edges of the oysters begin to curl. Serve immediately.

Oysters Rockefeller

There are many variations of this dish, which is said to have been originated at Antoine's in New Orleans for the original John D. Here is a variation we have liked. I have no idea if this is the original recipe or a later modification.

Put all the vegetables through the finest blade of your food chopper, sending the fennel seeds through along with the vegetables. Heat the butter in a skillet, add the greens, and cook gently for three minutes. Now add all of the other ingredients and purée in a blender, or put through a food mill.

Clean and open four large or five small oysters for each serving, leaving them in the deeper half shell. Put about one tablespoon of the mixture on each oyster, spreading it to the edge of the shell. Place the oysters on a bed of rock salt and put in an oven preheated to 450 degrees until the sauce bubbles. Do not leave in the oven too long or the sauce will dry out. Serve promptly.

Oysters in Champagne Aspic

One cup of aspic will coat a dozen oysters. Make the aspic by dissolving one package of gelatin in four tablespoons of champagne. When it has softened, add to the remainder of one cup of the wine and heat gently until

OYSTERS ROCKEFELLER

1/3	cup finely chopped spinach
1/3	cup finely chopped parsley
1/3	cup finely chopped celery
3	finely chopped shallots
1/2	clove garlic
1/4	teasp. fennel seeds
1/3	cup bread crumbs
1/3	cup Pernod liqueur
1/4	cup grated Parmesan cheese
1	teasp. anchovy paste
1/2	teasp. salt
	dash or two of tabasco sauce
4	oz. fresh butter

the gelatin dissolves. Set the wine-gelatin mixture aside while you clean and open four oysters for each serving. Keep the oysters on cracked ice in the refrigerator.

When the aspic begins to thicken, carefully lift each oyster and put a spoonful of the aspic in the shell, replacing the oyster and putting another spoonful of the aspic on it. Return to the refrigerator until the layer of aspic hardens and then add further coats. Try to finish by having a coating at least one-eighth inch thick of the champagne jelly on each oyster.

Let remaining aspic harden in a layer about one-quarter inch thick. Serve the oysters on chilled plates garnished with watercress and a few cubes of the aspic.

Incidentally, a good-quality California champagne will be entirely adequate for this dish.

Pâté of Veal and Pork, Country Style

Have the butcher grind together veal, lean pork, and fresh pork fat. Also have him cut salt pork in thin slices, and veal and ham in strips.

Cook the onion gently in the butter until it is clear but not browned. Transfer to a mixing bowl. Add the ground meats, eggs, brandy and seasonings. Beat until the mixture is light.

Blanch the salt pork slices by boiling for ten minutes in clear water to remove the salt. After it cools, line a tureen or loaf pan bottom and sides with the slices of blanched pork. Put about one-third of the stuffing mixture in the bottom of the lined pan, packing it down firmly. Next, place on the mixture alternating slices of veal and ham, slipping thin slices of truffle between the two sorts of sliced meat. Now, pack another one-third of the stuffing into the pan, and on top of it arrange the remaining sliced veal, ham, and truffles. Fill the terrine with the rest of the ground stuffing and cover with more strips of blanched salt pork.

Cover with aluminum foil and set in a pan of boiling water which reaches about halfway up the side of the tureen. Bake in an oven at 450 degrees for one and one-half to two hours, or until the juices run clear.

Remove from the oven, and over the foil covering the pâté, place another pan or a board cut to fit. Put a heavy object, such as an iron or a couple of washed bricks,

PÂTÉ OF VEAL AND PORK, COUNTRY STYLE

3/4	lb. ground lean veal
3/4	lb. ground lean pork
1/4	lb. ground fresh pork fat
1/2	lb. veal in strips 1/4 x 1 inch
1/2	lb. ham in similar strips
1/2	lb. salt pork sliced
2	oz. butter
2	eggs, slightly beaten
1/2	cup minced onion
1	bay leaf
2 - 3	truffles
3/4	cup brandy
1/2 - 3/4	teasp. thyme
1	tablesp. minced shallot
1	clove garlic
	salt
	freshly ground pepper
1/8	teasp. allspice

on the board to exert pressure on the pâté while it cools.

Serve plain in fairly thin slices, or with thin rings of sweet purple onion as a first course.

Game and Other Pâtés

Using the basic veal, pork, onion, egg and brandy stuffing, one can make pâtés with slices of wild duck, dove, quail, venison, or other game. If you are making a game pâté, prepare a stock of the tough and otherwise undesirable portions of the game and boil it down into a concentrate to give the stuffing more of the game flavor.

Slices of chicken breast and ham may be incorporated in a pâté in which the basic stuffing has been modified by substituting ground chicken meat for the ground pork. In this case, increase the proportion of fat and butter a little or your pâté will be too dry.

Your pâté will not suffer a great deal if you leave out the truffles. But, if you do, grind a half pound or so of mushrooms and cook them in butter to add to the mixture. You may also use the white Italian truffles in place of the more expensive French black truffles.

Other ways to vary your pâté are to use sherry, Madeira or a Calvados brandy in place of cognac.

Actually, I suggest that you use these two recipes only to familiarize yourself with the general principles of making a pâté. After that you should experiment with variations in ingredients, liquors, and most especially, in herbs, until you create your own special pâté, your veritable *pâté de la maison*.

Pâté en Croute

Use a rich pie crust pastry to line your terrine, being sure that there is at least one-half inch margin of surplus pastry at the top of the terrine. Fill the terrine with the pâté mixture exactly as described in the basic recipe. Cover with a top crust to fit the size of the terrine, and pinch the edges of the crusts to seal the two together. Make a hole about one-half inch in diameter in the center of the top crust to facilitate the escape of steam; this may be kept open by inserting a little cone of light pasteboard. Brush the top crust with butter, and bake in a pan of hot water as directed in the basic recipe.

Pâté of Chicken Livers

Pick over the chicken livers, cutting out all green or black spots, and cut them in two. Cut the veal liver and the salt pork in pieces of about the same size. Chop the shallots finely, add to the meat, and grind black pepper liberally over the meat. Also grate nutmeg liberally over the meat. Salt lightly and pour the Madeira over the meats and let marinate overnight.

Next morning, put everything solid through the finest blade of your food chopper and then, if you like, through the blender, a little at a time. Add the marinade and mix thoroughly. Pack into a terrine or small loaf pan, cover with foil and bake in a pan of water as described in the basic recipe. The pâté is done when a knife blade inserted in the middle comes out clean.

PÂTÉ OF CHICKEN LIVERS

1/2	lb. chicken livers
1/2	lb. veal liver
1/2	lb. salt pork
2	eggs
1	cup Madeira (Sercial)
2	shallots
	salt
	freshly ground black pepper
	freshly ground nutmeg

Shrimp Pâté

Devein the shrimp and put through the finest blade of the food chopper twice. Mix the softened butter and the ground shrimp into a paste and add the other ingredients.

Pack firmly into a lightly buttered mold and let stand in the refrigerator overnight. Unmold on a cold plate and garnish with watercress. Freshly made thin toast goes well with this pâté.

SHRIMP PÂTÉ

2	lbs. shelled cooked shrimp
4	oz. sweet butter
1/2	cup mayonnaise
2	tablesp. Madeira or an Amontillado sherry
1	teasp. mace
1	teasp. salt
1	tablesp. lemon juice
1/4	teasp. fresh black pepper
4	dashes tabasco sauce

Pâté of Smoked Trout

Carefully remove the skin, and also any smoke-darkened edges of the flesh. Remove the flesh from the bones and put the flesh through the finest blade of the food chopper twice. Proceed as with the shrimp recipe, but add 1/4 teaspoon of allspice in addition to the mace. With the smoked trout, I prefer a dry sherry, but you may like the richer and somewhat sweeter taste of the Madeira better, so try both.

You may like to try other smoked, fresh, or salt-water fish prepared in this fashion, although I have found none but smoked salmon as delicate as the smoked trout and the salmon is far too good in its native state to treat in this manner.

117

Prosciutto

Prosciutto, or Parma ham, and the Westphalian ham from Germany are the only hams normally eaten uncooked in this country. In France, you can also find the hams of Bayonne, with an individual flavor of their own. My personal preference is for the Bayonne ham, then Parma ham or prosciutto, with Westphalian ham a distant third.

All of these are served in paper-thin slices. Many American hostesses have a bad habit of serving these hams with melon slices or ripe figs. I do not regard these fruits as good companions for the spicy flavor of these hams.

We serve prosciutto alone and pass a pepper grinder with it, or accompany it with artichoke hearts which come in a spicy marinade.

Smoked Salmon

The finest smoked salmon is prepared from fish caught in the icy fjords of Norway or on the Scottish coast, and the next best from the equally cold waters of Nova Scotia. Most of that available on the Pacific Coast is from our Pacific salmon, which is cut too thick, and comes in a not particularly attractive oil. However, if the oil is carefully blotted off with paper towels, the Pacific Coast smoked salmon is much better than no smoked salmon at all.

Smoked salmon may be served plain, or dusted lightly with a few grains of freshly ground black pepper and a few drops of olive oil. On the Queen Elizabeth, it came with capers, which I found very good. My wife and I have a running debate over whether the smoked salmon is better with rings cut from a sweet purple onion or with capers—she favors the onion rings.

Seviche of Sea Scallops

Cut two pounds of scallops into bite-size pieces. Marinate for six hours in two cups of lime juice, or one cup of lime juice and one cup of lemon juice, to which has been added one grated medium-size onion, one crushed garlic clove and two or three dashes of tabasco sauce, together with salt and freshly ground pepper to taste. Serve well chilled in a little of the marinade.

Seviche of White Fish

Marinate the fish, which may be any firm-fleshed white fish, cut into small cubes, in the lime juice for four hours.

Make a sauce of the other ingredients, mix well, and chill in the refrigerator at least one-half hour. Serve the marinated fish with the sauce in cocktail glasses, all very cold.

Snails Burgundian Style

In most larger cities, one can find snails from France frozen in packages of twelve, already stuffed with the appropriate garlic butter. As neither of the two brands I have encountered had quite enough garlic in the snail butter, I did a little experimenting and found that putting three or four cloves of garlic through a garlic press and dividing the resultant juice among the twelve snails, made the butter exactly right. It is not necessary to thaw the snails. Add the extra garlic juice and put in a 450 degree oven until butter bubbles and the edges of the shells begin to brown.

A more economical way is to buy the canned snails. Remove from the can and wash the snails thoroughly in a strainer. Put about one teaspoon of snail butter (see chapter on sauces) in each shell and then insert a snail. Add more butter. Place in the convenient snail cooking pans with a depression for each snail, or in shallow pie tins, and heat in the oven as in the method for frozen snails.

Snails in Mushroom Caps

Select twelve large mushrooms, remove stems and reserve them for essence or other use. Clean the caps thoroughly. Melt a little snail butter in a skillet and coat the mushroom cap, inside and out, with the snail butter. Place one or two canned snails in each mushroom cap and cover them with the snail butter. Arrange in the depressions of a snail pan, in a coquille, or a small ovenproof serving dish and bake in an oven preheated to 375 degrees for fifteen minutes.

SEVICHE OF WHITE FISH

1 1/2	lb. firm white fish
1	cup lime juice
2	large tomatoes, peeled and cut in pieces
1/2	cup minced onion
2	canned green chilis, chopped
1/4	cup olive oil
1	teasp. salt
1/4	teasp. oregano
	freshly ground black pepper

119

Tomato Stuffed with Shrimp

Peel large, firm tomatoes, one for each person. Cut into six equal segments but leave the bottom half inch undivided. Place on a lettuce leaf, and pull the segments apart, inserting between each two segments one cold boiled shrimp. Sprinkle with finely chopped fresh or dried basil and dress with either a vinaigrette or mayonnaise to which you have added one teaspoon of Dijon mustard and two dashes of tabasco sauce.

Zucchini Appetizer

Select two small, firm Italian squash for each serving. Wash, trim off both ends, and boil until barely tender in water containing the juice and rind of one-half of a lemon and 1/2 teaspoon of basil. Cool in the cooking liquid. Split lengthwise and marinate in a vinaigrette to which you add the juice and rind of one-half of a lemon. Drain and serve on a cold plate, each half garnished with one filet of anchovy and two strips of pimento. Dust with paprika.

SOUPS 10

Albondigas

Fry the minced onion and garlic in oil and scrape into the soup pot. Add the stock and heat.

While the stock is heating, mix the ground meats, the raw rice, and the other ingredients; form into balls about the size of walnuts. Drop the balls into the pot, cover, and boil thirty minutes. Add a sprig of mint and cook ten minutes longer. Serve with the rest of the mint chopped finely and sprinkled on the surface of each bowl.

Generous bowls of this soup with plenty of crisp French bread, followed by a salad, then cheese and a bottle of inexpensive red wine, make a fine Sunday evening supper. Use Zinfandel or other California red, or an inexpensive Beaujolais.

ALBONDIGAS
3/4	lb. ground pork sausage
3/4	lb. ground beef
1	egg, beaten
1	large onion, minced
1/3	cup raw long-grain rice
3	qts. beef stock
1/4	cup oil
2	oz. tomato sauce
1 1/2	teasp. salt
1/4	teasp. black pepper
1	clove garlic, finely minced
2	sprigs fresh mint

Cream of Avocado

For each three persons, mix in a blender the flesh of one large or two small ripe avocados with two cups of cold chicken stock and one cup of thick cream. In the absence of a blender, you may put the avocados through a wire strainer and then beat into the other ingredients. Add one teaspoon of grated onion and season to taste with curry powder, freshly ground black pepper and salt. Use great discretion with the curry powder. What is desired is an extremely delicate flavor, hardly identifiable, but still present.

CREAM OF AVOCADO
1 - 2	ripe avocado
2	cups cold chicken stock
1	cup thick cream
1	teasp. grated onion
	curry powder, black pepper, salt

Serve well-chilled, sprinkling chopped chives on the surface, then dusting with paprika.

Black Bean Soup

Soak two cups of black beans overnight. Next morning, drain the beans and put into a soup pot together with a ham bone containing some meat, one-half pound of salt pork, an onion stuck with two or three cloves, and 1/4 teaspoon mace. Add one quart of water and simmer until beans are bursting. Purée the beans and add one quart of beef stock. Bring mixture to boiling point. Add a dash of cayenne and one-half cup dry sherry. Serve at once.

Boula Boula

Here is one of the rare occasions for which I recommend the use of canned soups. Canned, clear turtle soup is readily available; whereas, in most parts of the United States, turtle meat is not. Also, there are several brands of split pea soup on the market which are quite satisfactory.

Boula Boula is made by mixing equal parts of clear turtle soup and split pea soup and heating together. Top with lightly salted whipped cream.

Chicken Soup with Rice

Take the required amount of chicken stock, and for each quart add 1/3 cup of long-grained rice. Cook until the rice is tender and serve, being careful to stir the soup so that each portion receives its share of the rice.

For families of two or three persons, an economical way to make this soup, or the following one, is to reserve from a roasted chicken, the carcass, neck, giblets, legs and feet, from which the claws have been removed. Cover with water, add one scraped carrot, one stalk of celery and one bay leaf, and simmer for two hours. Remove the skeleton. You will find quite a lot of meat which can be picked off the skeleton. Cut this in julienne strips and add it to the stock together with 1/3 cup of long-grained rice; cook until the rice is tender.

BLACK BEAN SOUP

2	cups black beans
1/2	lb. salt pork
1	onion
2 - 3	cloves
1/4	teasp. mace
1	qt. water
1	qt. beef stock
1/4	cup dry sherry
	dash of cayenne

CHICKEN SOUP WITH RICE

	chicken stock
1/3	cup long-grained rice
	chicken flesh
	water
1	carrot
1	celery
1	bay leaf

122

Chicken Soup à la Reine

To one quart of chicken and rice soup, prepared in either of the ways directed above, add (while it is hot but not boiling) two egg yolks beaten with 1/4 cup of whipping cream, stirring all the while. Do not let the soup boil or it will curdle. Correct the seasoning and serve.

Consommé Bellevue

Add equal parts of clam juice to chicken stock, bring to a boil, and serve with each portion topped by one tablespoon of whipped cream, lightly salted.

Consommé with Celery

To one quart of chicken stock which has been degreased, add one tablespoon of grated onion and two stalks of thinly sliced celery. Cook until celery is very tender.

Consommé Double

Boil two quarts of beef or chicken stock down to one quart. Clarify as directed in chapter on stocks, correct the seasoning, and serve hot as Chicken or Beef Consommé Double.

Jellied Consommé with Herbs

To one quart of double consommé, add one table-spoon finely chopped parsley, one tablespoon chives, and either one teaspoon fresh chervil or 1/2 teaspoon of the dried herb. Cook a few minutes and strain through cheese-cloth to remove the herbs. To make sure that the con-sommé jellies, cool a cup and moisten one package of gelatin in it. Dissolve the moistened gelatin in the hot consommé. As soon as it is dissolved, remove from the heat and, after cooling, add 1/2 cup Sercial Madeira or a good Amontillado sherry. Cool in the refrigerator. Serve, broken up a little, in chilled consommé cups and sprinkled with chopped chives or finely chopped almonds.

JELLIED CONSOMMÉ WITH HERBS

- 1 qt. double consommé
- 1 tablesp. chopped parsley
- 1 tablesp. chives
- 1 teasp. fresh chervil or 1/2 dried chervil
- 1 pkg. gelatin
- 1/2 Sercial Madeira or Amontillado sherry chopped chives or chopped almonds (optional)

123

Consommé Madrilène

To one quart of double consommé, properly cleared, add two cups of tomato purée concentrated to half its volume and, if you like, a little red vegetable coloring (1/3 cup of beet juice will serve nicely). Chill in shallow pans and serve with lemon wedges in chilled consommé cups.

CUCUMBER SOUP

1	cup chicken stock
1	cup light cream
2	large cucumbers
1	tablesp. grated onion
1	sprig chopped parsley
1	tablesp. arrowroot or cornstarch
1	tablesp. lemon juice
1/4	teasp. dill weed

Cucumber Soup

Peel and slice cucumbers. Cook the cornstarch or arrowroot in a little stock until it is clear. Cool, then combine all ingredients in blender, whirling until vegetables are thoroughly puréed. Put through a fine strainer and refrigerate. Serve in chilled bowls, with a dash of dill weed and lemon slices floating on the soup.

Gazpacho

As with most dishes of Spain, recipes for this cold soup are nearly as numerous as the Spanish families who make it. Here are two versions. In our family, we have liked them both.

Grind all vegetables in food chopper, using the finest blade; blend with the tomato juice, oil and seasonings. Chill overnight in refrigerator. (The soup will be nicer if you remove the seeds from the cucumber.) Before serving, whirl for a few seconds in the blender.

Serve in chilled bouillon cups, with a slice of parsley-covered lemon floating on top. Alternately, the soup may be garnished with croutons, made by frying one-half inch stale bread cubes in garlic and oil, and a few dices of cucumbers of the same size. In either case, decorate the plates on which the soup is served with a little watercress.

GAZPACHO I

1	can Italian tomatoes, no. 2 1/2
2	cups tomato juice
1	cup dry white wine
2	stalks celery
1	cucumber
1/2	bell pepper
1/2	onion
1/2	cup olive oil
3	tablesp. chopped watercress
2	tablesp. lemon juice
1	clove garlic
1	teasp. salt
1/4	teasp. freshly ground pepper
3	dashes tabasco sauce
6	thin slices of lemon
	finely chopped parsley
	sprigs of watercress

Peel the tomaotes. Peel the cucumber, remove seeds. Dice tomatoes, cucumber and onion. Rub inside of blender jar with the clove of garlic and put in the tomatoes, onion, and one cucumber. Whirl for one-half minute at moderate speed, then add oil, lemon juice and vinegar. Whirl at high speed for one minute and chill thoroughly. Before serving, add the second cucumber and the green pepper cut into small dices, and season to taste with salt and pepper. Serve over one ice cube.

GAZPACHO II

6	large, fresh tomatoes
2	cucumbers
1/2	medium onion
1/3	cup olive oil
3	tablesp. wine vinegar
	juice of one lemon
1	small clove garlic
1/3	green pepper
	salt, freshly ground pepper

124

Lobster Bisque

Parboil the lobster or the lobster tails in their shells in the chicken broth for two minutes. Remove from stock, cool, and cut meat out of shells and into bite-size pieces.

Melt two tablespoons of butter in a skillet and gently cook the onion and carrot until the onion is clear. Add one-half the cognac and ignite. When the flames die down, scrape the contents of the skillet into the soup pot, and add the bay leaf, marjoram, and stock. Mix the flour with the remaining tablespoon of butter and add this *beurre manié* along with the lobster shells, which have been broken into convenient-size pieces. Simmer, half-covered, for one-half hour, adding the tomato paste after fifteen minutes.

Line a colander with several layers of cheesecloth and strain the mixture, pressing as much liquid as possible out of the shells. Add the lobster meat and milk, and heat nearly to boiling. Add the cream, season with salt and white pepper, and serve at once.

Minestrone

Except for the string beans and peas, put all of the vegetables into the stock together with the bacon cut into small cubes, and the macaroni; cook for thirty minutes. Cut the string beans in one-half inch lengths. Add the beans and peas and simmer for an additional one-half hour. Just before serving, add the basil and garlic. Accompany the soup with a bowl of freshly grated Parmesan cheese.

Essence of Mushrooms

Clean and cut off the earthy ends of one pound of mushrooms. Put the cleaned mushrooms through the finest blade of your food chopper. Mince one medium or two small shallots and cook gently in one tablespoon of butter until the shallots are clear. Add the mushrooms and continue the gentle cooking for three minutes. Pour into the skillet, one quart of chicken stock and simmer gently, with the lid ajar, for one-half hour. Strain through several layers of cheesecloth, pressing the ground mushrooms to extract all of their essence. Reheat and add a wineglass of Amontillado or other dry sherry, or if you prefer the flavor, Sercial Madeira.

LOBSTER BISQUE

1	boiled lobster or 2 9-oz. pkg. lobster tails
3	cups chicken stock
1 1/2	cups milk
1	cup heavy cream
1/2	cup cognac or other brandy
1/4	cup chopped carrots
1/4	cup chopped onions
3	tablesp. flour
3	tablesp. butter
1	tablesp. Madeira
1	teasp. tomato paste
1/8	teasp. marjoram
1	bay leaf
	white pepper, salt

MINESTRONE

1	qt. beef stock
1/2	small cabbage, shredded
1	small potato, cut in pieces
1	carrot, in pieces
1	turnip, in pieces
1 - 2	stalks celery
2	tablesp. peas
2	oz. lean bacon
2	small leeks
1 1/2	oz. macaroni
1	clove garlic
1/2	teasp. sweet basil
2	tablesp. string beans
1/2	teasp. salt

ESSENCE OF MUSHROOMS

1 - 2	shallots
1	tablesp. butter
1	qt. chicken stock
1	lb. mushrooms

125

Cream of Mushroom

CREAM OF MUSHROOM

1 1/2	pt. beef stock
1/2	pt. heavy cream
1/2	lb. fresh mushrooms
1	finely chopped onion
6	tablesp. butter
3	tabelsp. flour
1	teasp. meat essence
1	bay leaf
1/8	teasp. white pepper
	salt

Clean and grind mushrooms with the finest blade of your food chopper. Melt all but one tablespoon of the butter and cook the chopped onion in a skillet until clear. Add the mushrooms and continue the gentle cooking for five minutes. Scrape into the soup pot.

Blend the remaining butter and the flour and stir into the mixture. Add the meat essence, then the stock, and then the bay leaf, stirring constantly. When the mixture starts to boil, reduce heat and simmer slowly for five minutes. Season to taste with salt and pepper, remove bay leaf, and stir in the cream. Serve at once.

Onion Soup

ONION SOUP

2	brown onions
2	oz. sweet butter
1	qt. rich stock

This classic dish, so often poorly made in our restaurants, is easy to prepare well, and when correctly done, is one of the best of soups. It is a favorite of ours for a Sunday night supper. Generous bowls of onion soup, crusty bread, cheese and fruit—all accompanied by a not-too-elegant red wine—will satisfy everyone.

The quality of onion soup is directly dependent on the quality of your beef stock. If you want to make a double stock by boiling two quarts of your already-rich stock down to one quart, you will find yourself well rewarded for the sacrifice.

Slice two brown onions fairly thin and separate the rings. Cook gently in two ounces of sweet butter until clear and golden. Stir often enough so that none of the rings becomes brown or black. Pour into one quart of rich stock and simmer at least one-half hour to blend the flavors—voilà, your onion soup!

Serve this soup with croutons which have been made by frying in butter, or by toasting, one-half inch squares of garlic bread. A generous bowl of freshly grated Parmesan cheese should be left on the table so each diner may help himself.

Onion soup is also frequently served gratinéed. Toast small slices of French bread. Put the soup in oven-proof bowls; place a round of the toasted bread on the surface; sprinkle both the soup and the toast generously with Parmesan cheese; run under the broiler until the cheese melts and begins to brown.

Onion Soup à la Casey

Ask your butcher to halve, lengthwise, two beef shinbones and one large veal knuckle. Bake all pieces in a medium oven until the bones and marrow are brown, but be careful that they do not burn. Cut at least four pounds of beef rump or round into pieces and brown thoroughly in a skillet.

Place the browned bones and meat in a soup pot; add one medium onion cut in half, with a clove stuck in each half; two scraped carrots; two stalks of celery, together with a *bouquet garni* of thyme, two bay leaves, tarragon, and a handful of fresh celery leaves. Add to the kettle one gallon of water and simmer gently for eight hours the first day, skimming the fat and coagulated protein carefully from the surface during the first few hours.

At the end of the first day's cooking, make a *beurre manié* with 1/2 stick (two ounces) of butter and two tablespoons of flour. Add gradually to the stock pot. Simmer eight hours daily for the next two days, skimming as needed, and replenishing the volume from time to time. At the end of three days of boiling, strain, refrigerate overnight and degrease. Take a little of the carrot and part of the onion and purée them in the blender. At this point, you have an elegant stock, which, if it were thicker, would be a veritable Sauce Espagnole.

Slice two cups of onions for each 1 1/2 quarts of the brown stock and brown delicately in butter. Add to the stock with the puréed vegetables and simmer for one-half hour to amalgamate the flavors.

Whereas the usual onion soup is a hearty dish—practically a meal in itself—this one is elegant enough to serve as the soup course at a formal dinner, especially if one strains out the onion rings before serving it. In this fashion, it goes very well with sherry or Madeira.

ONION SOUP À LA CASEY

2	shinbones
1	large veal knuckle
4	lbs. beef rump or round
1	medium onion
2	carrots
2	stalks celery
	bouquet garni
1	gal. water
2	oz. butter
2	tablesp. flour
2	cups sliced onions for each 1 1/2 qt. brown stock

Stracciatella

Make a thin batter by beating one tablespoon flour, the grated rind of one-half of a lemon and 1/4 cup freshly grated Parmesan cheese with two eggs. Pour the batter very slowly into one quart of either beef or chicken stock, beating the stock vigorously.

STRACCIATELLA

1	tablesp. flour
1/2	lemon for grated rind
1/4	cup Parmesan cheese
	beef or chicken stock
	salt, pepper

If you do this correctly, you will have a fragrant soup with a network of whitish-yellow strands throughout. Correct the seasoning with salt and freshly ground pepper. Set on the table a bowl of freshly grated Parmesan cheese for the guests to add as they please.

Sorrel Soup

SORREL SOUP

1/2	lb. sorrel, finely chopped
1	pt. chicken stock
1	pt. light cream
1	tablesp. butter
4	egg yolks
	white pepper and salt

Wilt the chopped sorrel by heating very gently with the butter. Bring the chicken stock to a boil. Beat together the egg yolks and cream. Remove stock from the heat and beat into it the egg-cream mixture, add the sorrel and butter, and reheat in the top of a double boiler. Correct the seasoning with salt and white pepper.

This soup is excellent hot; it is also good refrigerated and served in chilled consommé cups.

Cream of Spinach

Proceed exactly as if making sorrel soup. However, it will be necessary to add a little water and to cover the pan in which the spinach is heating. Cook for five minutes. Cream of spinach soup is excellent hot; but at our house, we have not liked it cold.

Cream of Romaine

CREAM OF ROMAINE

1/2	medium onion, chopped
1	medium head romaine
1	pt. chicken stock
	rind and juice of 1/2 lemon
4	egg yolks
1	pt. light cream

Chop finely, one-half of a medium onion and cook in one tablespoon of butter until clear. Break a medium-size head of romaine in fairly small pieces, discarding all of the coarse ribs. Put the cooked onion and the romaine in the soup pot and add a pint of chicken stock. Simmer for ten minutes or a little longer, until the romaine is tender. Add the grated rind and the juice of one-half of a lemon.

Beat four egg yolks into one pint of light cream. Remove from the heat and beat this mixture into the stock. Good either hot or cold.

Vichyssoise: also termed by Escoffier
Leek and Potato Soup à la Bonne Femme

One does not find this soup on French menus because it is an American creation, although a French chef,

Louis Diat, first made it. (Some say Diat merely followed a recipe well known to his own mother and many other French housewives.)

Slice thinly the leeks and the potatoes. Cook the leeks in butter until they begin to brown, and turn into the soup pot with the potatoes. Add the salt and broth and boil until the potatoes become very tender. Put through a sieve, add the milk, and let simmer a few minutes. Again run through the sieve. Correct the seasoning and add a little freshly ground white pepper if you like. Chill in the refrigerator. Just before serving, beat in the cream with a mechanical egg beater. Serve in chilled bowls and sprinkle the tops with chopped chives.

Watercress Soup

Peel and quarter the potatoes. Trim coarse stems from the watercress and chop the leaves. Place the watercress in a soup pot together with the potatoes, salt and water, and cook until the potatoes are very soft. Purée in a blender or run through a food mill. Reheat, stir in the pepper and, without letting the mixture boil, beat in the cream. Serve garnished with chopped egg and dusted with paprika.

VICHYSSOISE

1 1/2	pts. rich milk
1	pt. heavy cream
1	qt. chicken stock
4	leeks, white parts only
3	potatoes
1	teasp. salt
	chopped chives

WATERCRESS SOUP

1 - 2	bunches watercress
4	medium-size potatoes
7	cups water
1	cup light cream
1	tablesp. salt
1/8	teasp. white pepper
1	chopped hard-boiled egg

SALADS

There are three occasions when salads are useful: to begin a simple three-course dinner; as an interlude for refreshing the palate between heavier courses, usually the entrée and the dessert; at more formal dinners; and as the principal course of a luncheon or, less frequently, a supper.

VEGETABLE SALADS

Mixed Green Salad

This is the type of all salads. Its goodness depends on your greens being fresh, chilled and crisp, and on applying a good dressing immediately before serving it.

Any crisp leafy vegetable may be used. By varying the vegetables, you can vary the salad enough that you never grow tired of it. We usually use at least three lettuces: iceberg or head lettuce, romaine, and one of the soft lettuces such as Boston or butter lettuce, or the bronze edge variety. Limestone lettuce, more expensive and less often available, is always a special treat. Tender leaves of spinach may be included; but cabbage, because of the heavy texture of its leaves and its strongly individual flavor, is excluded. And, while you may like grated carrots and other vegetables (we do), they have no place in a green salad. We also prefer tomatoes as a separate salad. Leaves of Belgian endive and raw mushrooms add further variety. A ripe, but still firm avocado may be sliced into the salad. Its flavor blends nicely; however, because of its softness, it is best added after the salad has been mixed and the dressing applied.

In the chapter on sauces, you will find the recipe for the vinaigrette which should, with your personal modifications, become the standard salad dressing. Let me urge you to try a vinaigrette with less vinegar and more oil than is usually used. We add a touch of garlic and use olive oil only if the rest of the menu is Provençale, Italian, or Mexican. You may add other herbs but sugar should be absolutely excluded. If you like blue cheese in your salad, you will find that crumbling the cheese directly into the salad tastes better than incorporating it in the dressing.

Always break your salad leaves by hand; do not cut them with a knife. Be sure the leaves are dry. Mix with the vinaigrette immediately before serving; or, even better, first put in the oil, then the vinegar and, finally, the salt, mixing well between each addition. Be sure your salad plates are chilled.

LETTUCE SALAD À LA WOHLFORD

6	heads Bibb lettuce
3	oz. caviar (fresh or salted)
3/4	cup olive oil
1/4	cup fresh lemon juice
3	tablesp. dry vermouth
2	tablesp. sherry
1 1/2	teasp. Beau Monde salt
1/2	teasp. salt
1	teasp. grated lemon
1	hard-boiled egg

Lettuce Salad à la Wohlford

Wash and shake dry the inner halves of six heads of Bibb lettuce and spread open like a rose on chilled plates. Place one teaspoon of caviar in the center of each lettuce "rose" and strew a thin line of caviar around the outside of each head. Border the line of caviar with a line of chopped egg yolk and then a line of chopped egg white.

Make a dressing from the other ingredients, shake vigorously and dress the salad just before serving.

Cabbage Salad

Select young, crisp heads of cabbage. Quarter them and cut out the hard center ribs. Then make a julienne of the leaves, or grate on a coarse grater. Dress with a vinaigrette, with mayonnaise, or with mayonnaise to which you have added a little mustard. Serve in neat mounds on chilled plates, with the scarlet of paprika playing a counterpoint to the green of the cabbage.

Caesar Salad

Prepare croutons one-half inch cubes of stale bread, by frying to a golden brown in olive oil.

Sprinkle salt in salad bowl and rub with the peeled garlic clove. Discard the remnants of the garlic. Put the chilled greens, either all romaine or mixed greens as you prefer, in the bowl and add the olive oil. Toss to coat all leaves thoroughly with the oil. Add the lemon juice and toss again. Now, break the egg into the center of the salad, add two dashes of tabasco sauce and toss until all traces of the egg have disappeared into the coating of the leaves. Chop the anchovy filets; add the filets and the croutons, mixing gently into the salad just before serving.

Grated Carrots

Select baby carrots if you can find them. Wash, scrape and grate the carrots. Salt lightly and mix with a vinaigrette. On a chilled plate, serve portions neatly rounded on lettuce leaf. Dust with paprika.

Cucumber Salad

Peel cucumbers, make scallops by drawing a sharply tined fork down them lengthwise, and slice thinly. Soak at least one-half hour in water to which you have added two tablespoons of salt and several ice cubes. Drain, dry, and serve generous portions with one of the dressings.

Cucumber and Onion Salad

Prepare cucumbers as in the foregoing recipe. Peel and slice as thinly as possible, one or more sweet Bermuda onions. Place a layer of onion slices and then a layer of cucumber slices in a chilled bowl. Spread lightly with mayonnaise and salt. Repeat until both vegetables have been used. Finish with a light layer of mayonnaise and let stand in the refrigerator at least two hours before serving.

Cucumber and Tomato Salad

Alternate slices of cucumber with thin slices of tomatoes which are firm and not too ripe. Sprinkle with dill weed or with sweet basil and tarragon; dress with your vinaigrette.

Lemon (Chinese) Cucumbers

Try these small round cucumbers with the yellow skin. They are best, I think, by themselves, but they may

CAESAR SALAD

	Greens as for mixed salad, or romaine only
	salt
3	tablesp. olive oil
	juice of one lemon
1	raw egg
	tabasco sauce to taste
1	clove garlic
6	anchovy filets
1/2	cup croutons

DRESSING FOR CUCUMBER SALAD

Sour cream to which you add salt, freshly ground black pepper and 1/2 teaspoon of dill weed.

Mayonnaise, either plain or with dill.

Your standard vinaigrette.

A dusting with paprika helps make each serving pretty.

133

be used in all of the other recipes, and will give your family a change in flavor.

Kohlrabi with Sauce Rémoulade

Wash the kohlrabi and cut into julienne strips the size and length of kitchen matches. Chill and serve dressed with Sauce Rémoulade.

Potatoes in Oil

POTATOES IN OIL
2   lbs. or more sliced potatoes
4   tablesp. dry white wine
2   tablesp. beef stock
2   tablesp. dry vermouth
      vinaigrette
      black pepper

Use Red Rose or other boiling potatoes—new Red Rose are ideal. Cook two pounds or more, because the salad will remain attractive for more than one day. Boil until done but still firm. Peel the potatoes as hot as you can handle them and cut into slices one-quarter inch thick. Pour over the sliced warm potatoes, four tablespoons of dry white wine, or two tablespoons each of beef stock and dry vermouth. Mix gently and let cool. The potatoes will absorb all or most of this liquid.

When the sliced potatoes are cold, add the standard vinaigrette and a light grind of black pepper. Toss lightly to coat each slice. Or you may make a special vinaigrette of two tablespoons of lemon juice and six tablespoons of oil.

Russian Salad

When you cook carrots, celery, cauliflower, asparagus, or broccoli, add a little extra, and reserve small portions in closed containers in the refrigerator until you accumulate three or four varieties. Similarly, if without planning you find you have small portions of these or other vegetables left over, reserve them. Cut in small cubes and mix with green peas either saved or cooked for the purpose, in proportions of one part peas to three parts of the mixture of other vegetables. Dress with mayonnaise and serve in neat mounds on chilled plates, with a decorative 1/2 teaspoon of mayonnaise and a dusting of paprika on top of each mound.

String Bean and Onion Salad

When you are serving string beans as a vegetable, cook twice the usual amount. Reserve half, and after dinner, when the reserve beans have cooled, put them in a bowl with chopped slices of Bermuda onion, in proportions of two parts of string beans to one part onions. Add the juice of one-half to one lemon, depending upon the quantity, and slice the rind into the salad. Cover with your standard vinaigrette and allow to marinate until dinner time the next day. Drain off most of the vinaigrette; dish up portions of the salad with a slotted spoon after you have removed the lemon peel.

Spinach and Bacon Salad

This is maximally simple, but is one of our family's favorite salads with which to begin a meal.

Select young and tender leaves from two or more bunches of fresh spinach, wash, dry, and break as for a green salad. Chill thoroughly. Just before serving, dress with the usual vinaigrette and a dash or two of tabasco sauce. Crumble two slices of crisp fried bacon on top of each serving.

Tomato Salad

Select firm tomatoes, not too ripe. It does not matter if the ends are a little green or if the shape is a little irregular. Chill and slice thinly. Dust with fresh or dried sweet basil and chives, or with fresh or dried tarragon and chives, or with one of these together with chopped parsley, or with mixtures of all four herbs. By varying the herbs and their proportions, you can achieve a surprising variety of flavors. If you use fresh herbs, follow the usual rule of putting on a vinaigrette immediately before serving. If you use dried herbs, mix your herbs, sprinkle on the tomato slices, and put one teaspoon of the vinaigrette on each tomato slice. This will serve to soften the dried herbs and blend the flavors.

Flavor With Herbs for Variety

Raw Vegetables (Crudités)

Carrot sticks, stalks of celery cut in half, cucumbers peeled, quartered and cut in pieces about three inches long, peeled or unpeeled zucchini, wedges of green or red cabbage, red and white radishes, the flowerets of uncooked cauliflower, and red or green sweet peppers cut in strips,

135

served well chilled in not-too-large a variety, together with ripe olives or the brown, ranch-style olives, make an interesting and—for a change—low-calory first-course for informal meals or serve as a plate of hors d'oeuvres at a buffet supper or cocktail party. Sometimes, we accompany the plate with a dish of mayonnaise, sometimes with a boiled dressing to which a good deal of mustard has been added. Although both styles of ripe olives go well with such a plate, green olives seem to introduce a discordant note, probably because they are sharp while the rest of the items are bland.

More Substantial Salads

Here are more substantial salads, suitable for the main course at lunch or for one of the dishes at a buffet supper.

Chef's Salad

Make somewhat larger than usual portions of green salad. After it has been dressed with its vinaigrette, arrange on salad plates in neat mounds. On top of the mounds, arrange julienne strips of ham, smoked or fresh tongue, chicken or turkey breast, or any other cold meat available, and processed cheese (one of the *very* few occasions when it seems to me that processed cheese is worth using). Add a little more vinaigrette to moisten the julienne and top with one-half hard-boiled egg and, if you wish, a few black olives or cooked spears of asparagus.

Chicken Salad

Cut both the light and dark meat of leftover fowl into small cubes and mix with an equal volume of cubes of crisp celery. Add one tablespoon of sliced almonds for each cup of the mixed ingredients; marinate for several hours with a vinaigrette to which you have added one or two tablespoons of grated onion. Press out all of the vinaigrette possible and mix with mayonnaise. Top each serving with 1/2 teaspoon of unmixed mayonnaise and dust with paprika.

Lobster Salad

Cut cold boiled lobster into bite-size pieces and marinate for several hours in lemon juice and a little oil.

Drain off the marinade and mix with an equal volume of chopped celery. Moisten with mayonnaise and serve on chilled plates with 1/2 teaspoon of unmixed mayonnaise on top. Finely chopped parsley will contrast well with the red of the lobster meat. For a special taste treat, mix a little curry powder—just enough to taste—with the mayonnaise.

Salade Niçcoise

A dish from the Mediterranean coast of France, the recipe varies from household to household and restaurant to restaurant. Like a piece of Baroque music, the written notes may be filled in with as much harmony and ornamentation as you please. Here is a good basic recipe.

Prepare a bed of whole lettuce leaves in your handsomest bowl. In it, arrange the ingredients in separate piles, except for the filets of anchovy which are used to garnish the various piles. Chill the salad well and send to the table with the vinaigrette in a separate container. After everyone has admired the creation, pour in the vinaigrette and mix thoroughly. Or mix only partly and pass the bowl, letting each guest select the portions he prefers.

SEAFOOD AND MEAT SALADS

Shrimp Salad

Mix equal portions of small whole shrimp, or if larger shrimp, cut in half, with cubed celery. Dress with mayonnaise or with a boiled dressing to which has been added a strong dash of mustard. One can use shredded lettuce in place of celery, but the celery makes a far finer salad.

Tuna Salad

Break up into not-too-small chunks one or more cans of the best-quality white-meat tuna and mix with equal quantities of cubed celery or shredded lettuce. Dress with mayonnaise. Here, too, celery makes a much better salad than the shredded lettuce.

SALADE NIÇCOISE

1/2	head of lettuce
4	quartered tomatoes
1	cup or more of potatoes in oil, described in previous recipe
1	7-oz. can tuna
1	cup cooked string beans
2	quartered hard-boiled eggs
1/2	small Bermuda onion, sliced
10	pitted black olives
1/2	strips of green pepper
8 - 10	filets of anchovy, each cut in three pieces
1/2	cup vinaigrette with garlic

137

Cold Meat Salad

You may stretch out leftover bits of cold roast beef, lamb, or other meat by cutting it into thin julienne strips, either by itself or mixed with such things as bologna or salami; mixing it with equal amounts of chopped celery or lettuce; and dressing it with mayonnaise.

FRUIT SALADS

Of the entire class of fruit salads, I have found only two which I consider worthy of our table.

Avocado and Grapefruit Salad

Select grapefruit juicy and somewhat tart. The best are the pink grapefruit from Arizona. Peel a fully ripe but still fairly firm avocado and cut in thin slices. Peel the grapefruit and separate into sections, being careful to remove all of the bitter-tasting white membrane. Arrange alternate slices of grapefruit and avocado on chilled plates and dress with a vinaigrette. Dust each serving with paprika.

Waldorf Salad

For each person, cut into small cubes 1/2 cup of tart red apples such as Winesap or Jonathan and mix with an equal quantity of similarly diced celery and 1/4 cup of broken walnut meats. Mix thoroughly with mayonnaise and serve in neat mounds on chilled plates.

Cottage Cheese and Tomatoes

For each person, select a fine ripe tomato and cut sections nearly through the tomato. Spread the sections apart and stuff with chilled cottage cheese. It is almost equally attractive to mound the cottage cheese and surround it with sliced tomatoes. Dust with freshly ground black pepper and paprika.

Other Fruit Salads

If your tastes are at all like mine, you will not like any other mixtures of canned or fresh fruits, or mixtures of canned fruit with cottage cheese.

It is my firm opinion that such dismal mixtures as a dollop of cottage cheese on half of a canned Bartlett pear or a limp half of a canned peach, or surrounded by limp, sticky apricot halves ought to be forbidden—by law, if necessary.

You find no recommendations for wine in this chapter because wine and vinegar (*vin*=wine and *aigre*=sour) mutually kill each other. Wine should never be served with salad when the salad is the initial course. When the salad comes between two other courses, the wine glasses are always put aside.

FISH AND SHELLFISH

12

Now that one of the major religious branches of our culture has modified its dietary rules, and so freed its members from a certain compulsion, I hope that many more of us will happily explore the delights that sea, stream and shore offer to those willing to try them. Our family has always liked what the Italians call the fruits of the sea and has marveled that others did not share our enthusiasm.

Beginning with this chapter, every recipe, unless specified will be given in terms of a dish adequate for six normal portions.

ABALONE

Grilled Abalone

Nearly everyone who has visited California has seen the handsome shell of this large mollusk, which lives in the shallow coastal waters from Monterey south to the tip of Baja, California, in Mexico. Only the foot muscle, a solid mass of tissue ranging in size from a small orange to a large grapefruit, is eaten. The muscle is extremely tough, but, properly prepared and cooked, it can be cut with a fork and is deliciously sweet. Your fish dealer slices the muscle and pounds each slice into little steaks about one-quarter inch in thickness. The usual serving for each diner is two of these thin slices.

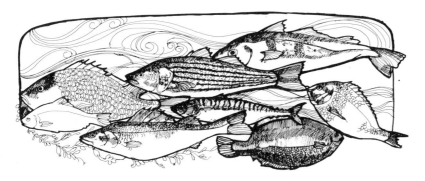

Dip twelve pounded slices in milk and dredge with flour. Cook sixty to ninety seconds on each side in hot, but not smoking, butter. Salt and pepper lightly and serve quickly. Overcooking causes the meat to regain its toughness.

A dry, light, white wine such as a Pouilly-Fuissé or a Sancerre is best with abalone.

BASS

The striped sea bass is a game fish found on both coasts. White sea bass range from a few pounds to thirty or more pounds in weight. Much of the fish sold in American markets is from the black bass, which may attain a weight of several hundred pounds. The same or closely similar species are found in the Mediterranean. Smaller subvarieties weighing up to three or four pounds are among the bottom fish taken near the coast.

Baked Stuffed Striped Bass

BAKED STUFFED STRIPED BASS

1	3 to 4 lbs. bass
1	cup bread crumbs
1	cup oysters
1/2	cup chopped onion
1/2	cup chopped celery
1/2	stick butter (2 oz.)
2	slices bacon
2	tablesp. minced parsley
1/8	teasp. dried marjoram
1/8	teasp. dried tarragon
2	dashes tabasco sauce
	salt
	freshly ground black pepper

This recipe may also be used for the small calico bass or other bottom fish if there are no sportsmen in your family to bring home the stripers.

Melt the butter and cook the onions and celery until the onions become clear. Add the bread crumbs and brown a little. Mix with the other seasonings and one-half the oysters, each cut in two pieces.

Stuff the fish and arrange the rest of the oysters in a line down the belly of the bass. Place in a buttered baking dish and cover with the bacon slices. Cook in a 400 degree oven for forty to fifty minutes, until the fish flakes.

A Macon Village Blanc, a Pouilly-Fuissé, or a dry California white wine will be suitable with this bass.

Bass Poached with Fennel

Mix the wine and water; slice the carrot, the onion, and the celery into it. Make a *bouquet garni* of the last five items, and add to the water-wine mixture. Let the mixture simmer for thirty minutes. This is your court bouillon.

142

Poach the fish filets in the court bouillon until they flake with a fork—ten to twelve minutes. Drain, melt butter, and pour over the filets; dust with paprika. Serve with lemon wedges.

The wine you used to make the court bouillon could also serve as the accompanying wine for this dish. A Pouilly-Fuissé or a California Pinot Chardonnay will be fine.

Bass Baked with Fennel

Arrange six sea bass filets in a generously-buttered shallow baking dish. Place over the filets one-half of an onion, thinly sliced and covered with two strips of bacon or salt pork. Pour into the dish enough dry white wine to cover the fish but not the bacon, and add several branches of fennel or 1/2 teaspoon of fennel seeds. The herb itself will give you a superior flavor. Cover with a lid or with foil for ten minutes in a 400 degree oven, then uncover so that the bacon may brown a little.

The wines listed above for the poached bass will be good with the baked bass also.

Bass Mediterranean Peasant Style

Prepare fish stock by boiling the head and skeleton of a fish, or buy an extra filet for the purpose. Make a *bouquet garni* by enclosing in cheesecloth one bay leaf, 1/4 teaspoon each of marjoram and tarragon, and either a few small sprigs of fennel or 1/4 teaspoon fennel seeds.

Arrange the filets in a well-buttered baking dish; cover with the mushrooms, cleaned and thinly sliced with the chopped onion and shallots. Add the fish stock, wine and the *bouquet garni*. Poach gently until the fish can be flaked. Remove the filets to a hot serving platter and concentrate the liquid to about one-half cup. Sprinkle the parsley into the juice and add three tablespoons of butter, a little at a time, mixing well. Spoon the sauce over the fish.

The red wine and the herbs used call for a red wine to accompany this fish. Use an inexpensive Côte-du-Rhône or a California Zinfandel.

BASS POACHED WITH FENNEL

6	sea bass filets
1	pt. water
1/2	bottle dry white wine
1	carrot
1	medium onion
1	stalk celery
1/2	lemon
1	bunch celery leaves
2 - 3	small branches of fennel or 1 teasp. fennel seeds
1	bay leaf
2	sprigs parsley
2	sprigs thyme or 1/2 teasp. dried thyme

BASS MEDITERRANEAN PEASANT STYLE

2	lbs. sea bass filets
1/2	lb. fresh mushrooms
1/2	cup red wine
1	cup fish stock
1/2	small onion
2	shallots
1	tabelsp. minced parsley
	bouquet garni

143

Bass with Vermouth

BASS WITH VERMOUTH

6	sea bass filets
6	oz. dry vermouth
1	tablesp. chopped onion
1	chopped shallot
	dried or fresh marjoram
	salt to taste
	freshly ground black pepper

Arrange the filets in a well-buttered shallow baking dish. Strew as topping, the chopped onion and shallot, with as much fresh or dried marjoram as you think proper. We like about 1/4 teaspoon of the dried herb. Srpinkle with salt and freshly ground black pepper. Add to the dish four ounces of good French vermouth, cover the dish, and bake in a 400 degree oven until the fish flakes easily—about twelve to fifteen minutes. Remove top and turn up the heat until the onions and the tops of the filets get a little browned.

Remove to a hot serving plate and add two more ounces of vermouth to the baking dish, scraping up all the brown particles. Heat until the vermouth and the cooking liquid have reduced to about one-half their volume, strain, and pour over the filets. Serve with lemon wedges if you like. I prefer this fish without the lemon flavor.

A dry white wine, such as a Pouilly-Fuissé, a Muscadet, or a California Pinot Chardonnay, is the proper wine to serve with this dish.

CODFISH

Brandade de Morue
(Salt Cod with Garlic, Oil and Cream)

BRANDADE DE MORUE
(Salt Cod with Garlic, Oil and Cream)

1	lb. salt codfish
3 1/2	oz. olive oil
3 1/2	oz. whipping cream
2	cloves garlic
1	lemon
	salt
	freshly ground pepper

Soak the salt cod overnight, changing the water at least once. Break the meat into flakes, discarding skin and bones. Mix in a mortar with the olive oil, grinding the fish quite fine. When all of the fish has been ground with the oil, heat gently in a saucepan and add the cream a little at a time, beating vigorously between additions. Add lemon juice, salt, and freshly ground pepper to taste.

This recipe is excellent served with crusty French bread, toasted or freshly sliced, and is also good cold. It is a dish much liked along the Mediterranean coast of France.

Incidentally, try it with an inexpensive red wine. It will demonstrate that the so-called rule of white wine with fish can have exceptions. A Châteauneuf-du-Pape, or a good California Pinot Noir, or a Côte-du-Rhône will be fine.

Codfish Cakes

Break the fish in several pieces and soak in water until bedtime. Drain off the water, cover with milk, and soak in the milk until the next day.

Flake the fish, removing all skin and bones. Beat the eggs until they are light yellow, stir in the flaked fish, and add the mash potatoes. Season to taste and form into cakes. Fry until golden brown in hot oil.

More often than not, we drink a red Beaujolais or Côte-du-Rhône *ordinaire* with codfish cakes. Try one or the other in place of the conventional white wine.

CRAB

All of the following recipes call for the meat of the Pacific Coast Dungeness crab except when the Alaska King crab is specifically requested; in general, the King crab is inferior. The smaller East Coast crab may be substituted for the Dungeness crab with excellent results.

Creamed Crab Dungeness

Pick over the crab meat and remove all membrane. Wash the mushrooms, slice thinly, and cook gently in two tablespoons of the butter until done—about fifteen minutes.

Make a rich Béchamel sauce with the other two tablespoons of butter, the flour, and the cream. Season to taste with salt, pepper, and, very lightly, with marjoram. Cook until the mixture is smooth, then add the mushrooms and the crab meat. Heat through and spoon into six individual shells. Sprinkle heavily with Parmesan cheese, and set under the broiler until the cheese melts. Dust with paprika; garnish each shell with a sprig of parsley; serve at once.

The flavors are delicate and merit a richer wine—a good Meursalt, a Sancerre, or Pouilly-Fumé, or your very best California Pinot Chardonnay.

Crab in the Style of Britanny

Chop the cleaned mushrooms and the onion and sauté gently in the butter. Add the tomato paste and brandy; season with salt, pepper, and, very lightly, with

CODFISH CAKES
1	lb. salt cod
2	cups mashed potatoes
2	eggs
1/4	cup cream
1	tablesp. chopped parsley
1	tablesp. chopped chives
	thyme to taste
	nutmeg to taste
1 - 2	dashes tabasco sauce

CREAMED CRAB DUNGENESS
1	lb. Dungeness crab meat
1	lb. white mushrooms
1	cup whipping cream
4	tablesp. butter
2	tablesp. flour
2	oz. dry sherry
	finely grated Parmesan cheese
	fresh or dried marjoram
	salt
	freshly ground pepper

CRAB, BRITANNY STYLE
1	lb. crab meat
1	box mushrooms
1	medium onion
2	tablesp. butter
2	oz. tomato paste
1	oz. brandy
1 - 2	oz. white wine
	bread crumbs
	curry powder
	salt
	freshly ground pepper

145

curry powder. (Here is an example of the French use of curry powder as a subtle seasoning rather than as a strong one.) Simmer for a few minutes until the vegetables are cooked. Add the crab, correct the seasoning, and thin with one or two ounces of wine. Fill six individual scallop shells, sprinkle with bread crumbs, dot with butter, and set to brown under the broiler.

A white wine, light and crisp, from the nearby Loire Valley, such as a Muscadet, or a Sancerre, sets this dish off to advantage.

Deviled Crab

In two ounces of butter, sauté gently the finely minced onion and shallots until they are soft and clear. Add two or three teaspoons Dijon mustard (start with two and use more if you wish) and a dash or two of tabasco sauce. Add the brandy.

Make a Béchamel sauce with the rest of the butter, the flour and the cream. Add the sauce to the cooked and flavored vegetables and stir in the crab. Distribute among six scallop shells, sprinkle with bread crumbs, dot with butter and bake in a 350 degree oven until the contents of the shells are heated through—about twelve to fifteen minutes.

A Muscadet or Sancerre is our wine of choice here.

Crab Sauté with Almonds

Melt two ounces of butter in a skillet and gently sauté the crab meat, turning frequently. Blanch and split the almonds into three or four pieces each. Melt the remaining butter and brown the almonds. Add the crab meat and then the cream. Simmer gently for two minutes; correct the seasoning with salt and freshly ground black pepper. Serve with steamed long-grain rice.

A California Pinot Chardonnay or a Pouilly-Fuissé seems just right with this dish.

Crab Soledad

Pick over the crab meat, discard all membrane and flake well. Mix with the chopped chives, sour cream, and mayonnaise; season with salt, pepper, and paprika. Add

DEVILED CRAB

1	lb. crab meat
2	cups light cream
4	oz. butter
1	medium onion
2	shallots
	bread crumbs
3	tablesp. flour
1	oz. brandy
2 - 3	teasp. Dijon mustard
	salt to taste
	freshly ground pepper
	tabasco sauce

CRAB SAUTÉ WITH ALMONDS

1	lb. crab meat
2/3	cup almonds
1/2	cup whipping cream
3	oz. butter (3/4 stick)
1	oz. dry sherry
2	tablesp. chopped parsley
	salt
	freshly ground black pepper

146

enough good, dry sherry to moisten the mixture. Heap on six scallop shells and bake thirty minutes in a 300 degree oven.

Then place two or three crab legs on top of each shell, border the shell with thin slices of lemon, sprinkle generously with Parmesan cheese, and run under a hot broiler until the cheese melts. Dust with paprika, garnish with sprigs of parsley, and serve at once.

We usually drink a young Muscadet with this dish.

CRAB SOLEDAD

1 1/2	lb.	crab meat
1/2	lb.	crab legs
4	oz.	sour cream
2	oz.	Amontillado sherry
1	tablesp.	chopped chives
		freshly grated Parmesan cheese
		salt
		freshly ground pepper
		paprika

King Crab Provençale Style

Put the crab, cut into bite-size pieces, to marinate in the wine overnight. Peel, seed, and chop the tomato. Melt the butter in a skillet, and heat the clove of garlic with the chopped green pepper, the chopped onion, and the rosemary until all are soft, about five minutes. Discard the garlic, add the tomato, and season with salt and pepper to taste.

Add the crab meat and the red wine. Then add the cream, a little at a time, stirring between each addition. As soon as the crab meat is heated through, correct the seasoning and serve.

Clearly the tomato, onion and garlic call for a not-too-delicate red wine. We have found a Beaujolais *ordinaire* or a Zinfandel, quite satisfactory.

KING CRAB PROVENCALE STYLE

2	lbs.	Alaska King crab
3/4	cup	red wine
1		large tomato
1/2		medium chopped onion
1/2		small chopped green pepper
1	cup	thin cream
2	tablesp.	butter
1	tablesp.	flour
1		clove garlic
1/4	teasp.	rosemary
		salt
		freshly ground pepper

Soft Shelled Crabs Amandine

The recipe is for individual serving.

Sauté flour-dredged crabs in most of the butter, turning once. Total cooking time should be six to eight minutes. Remove to a hot plate, add the remaining butter, and brown the almonds. Scrape the almonds, with the butter remaining in the skillet, over the crabs; season with salt and pepper; garnish with a sprig of parsley; serve with lemon wedges.

A Muscadet, Pouilly-Fuissé or a dry California white wine will all be suitable with soft shelled crabs. If you have fresh, rather than frozen crabs, they will merit a good Meursault or Chablis.

SOFT SHELLED CRABS AMANDINE

2		soft shelled crabs
1	tablesp.	blanched sliced almonds
2	tablesp.	butter
1	teasp.	flour
		salt
		freshly ground pepper
		lemon wedges

SALTON SEA CROAKER

The croaker is a small fish that is caught along the shoreline and in the surf from San Francisco to the tip of Baja, California, in Mexico. Nature has developed a curious subspecies of this fish in the Salton Sea, at the north end of the Imperial Valley of California, which was formerly connected with the Gulf of California but is now cut off. Like the Dead Sea, the Salton Sea will probably in time grow too salty to support any life. Meanwhile the croakers that live in the saltier-than-the-sea waters have a uniquely delicious flavor. These small fish may be baked whole, using the recipes for small bass, or the fish may be fileted, the filets dipped in milk, dredged in flour and sautéed gently in butter.

In either case, a modest dry white wine is the best accompaniment. I suggest a California Pinot Blanc or a Muscadet.

FLOUNDER

This mild, white-meated fish rarely appears in American markets under its own name. It is usually fileted and sold as "filets of sole." For many purposes, it provides a fair substitute for sole although it is far from being as sweet or as firm. All of the recipes for filet of sole may be used for filets of flounder. Thicker filets, or cross-cut steaks may be baked in any of the ways suggested for bass. Use the wine suggested with the recipe you are using.

Filets of Flounder Thermidor

See under Lobster Thermidor for the two sauces. Make one recipe of each. Roll the filets and fasten with toothpicks or string. Arrange in a well-buttered baking dish and pour the butter sauce over the filets. Cover with foil and bake in a 375 degree oven until the fish flakes easily, about twenty-five minutes. Now pour the thermidor sauce over the fish, sprinkle generously with Parmesan cheese and set under the broiler until the cheese melts and the sauce bubbles.

A Pouilly-Fuissé or even one of the white Burgundies, such as a Meursault or a Chassagne Montrachet, will not be better than this delicious dish deserves.

FILLETS OF FLOUNDER THERMIDOR

4   small or 6 large flounder filets
Parmesan cheese
salt
thermidor sauce
butter sauce
pepper

148

HALIBUT

Halibut à la Parisienne

Select either filets or steaks of halibut, allowing one-half pound per person. Follow the procedure which will be given in detail for sculpin, which is cooked in the same manner.

Grilled Halibut Steaks

Wipe steaks, dip in milk, and then dip in flour seasoned with tarragon, marjoram, salt and pepper. Grill over moderate heat until lightly browned; serve with lemon wedges.

A Sylvaner from Alsace or an inexpensive Petit Chablis will set off this fish nicely.

FINNAN HADDIE

Steamed Finnan Haddie

Put the finnan haddie, cut into serving pieces of one-half pound each, into a skillet with one cup of milk and enough water to cover. Simmer gently until the fish flakes.

Melt butter in a saucepan, blend in the flour, and cook until clear. Add the remaining three cups of milk and simmer, stirring constantly until the sauce thickens. Add the seasonings and cook two minutes longer. Chop the eggs finely and mix into the sauce. Spoon over the finnan haddie, dust with paprika, and garnish with parsley. Serve with a boiled potato.

A not-too-dry white *ordinaire,* such as a California Pinot Blanc, an inexpensive Riesling, or a Spanish "Chablis" is an entirely suitable partner for this modest but good dish.

STEAMED FINNAN HADDIE

3	lbs. finnan haddie
4	cups milk
	water
4	hard-boiled eggs
2	oz. butter
6	tablesp. flour
1/2	teasp. salt
1/4	teasp. freshly ground white pepper
1/4	teasp. marjoram
1/4	teasp. freshly grated nutmeg
1	

LOBSTER

All of the recipes are applicable to the northern Atlantic clawed lobster called *homard* and the large salt-water crayfish or Pacific Coast lobster, found also in the Mediterranean, called *langouste*. The claw meat of the homard is probably a little sweeter than the meat of the Pacific Coast lobster and the tomalley is present in larger quantities. Both species, however, are to be treasured.

Broiled Lobster

All lobsters come to your kitchen either alive or already boiled. If yours is alive, it can be killed by plunging it quickly into a large kettle of boiling water for ten minutes, or until the green shell turns a brilliant red and you can pull out one of the long feelers over the eyes easily.

Split the lobster and remove the intestines, washing and draining them thoroughly.

The traditional way to broil a lobster is to brush the cut surfaces generously with lemon butter and place under the broiler until the edges of the shell turn slightly brown. As a matter of fact, we have found that this procedure always makes the surface of the meat tough. We find it much more satisfactory to brush with lemon butter and then place the lobster halves in an oven at 350 degrees until hot throughout. Serve garnished with parsley and lemon wedges, or pass a heated sauceboat filled with maître d'hôtel butter.

Lobster is always worthy of your best white Burgundy—a Meursault of a good year, or even Montrachet.

Lobster Newberg

This dish is old enough to have become a cliché. What you should remember, however, is that expressions become clichés because they are so true, so good, that they get overused. And I doubt that many of us have eaten Lobster Newberg so often that it has become boring.

The recipe is for each two persons served.

Remove meat of lobster tail (and claws if you are using Eastern lobsters), and cut into regular slices. Put the slices in a liberally-buttered pan and heat until outside of the meat turns rosy. Pour 1/2 cup or more of Madeira wine (have the lobster slices almost covered) and heat gently. Remove the lobster slices and arrange in the two halves of

LOBSTER NEWBERG

1	1-lb. lobster
2	cups whipping cream
2	egg yolks
	butter
1/2	cup (or more) Madeira
	salt
	freshly ground white pepper
	cayenne pepper

150

the shell, keeping the meat warm. Reduce the contents of the pan about three-fourths.

Turn the contents of the pan into the top portion of a double boiler and add the cream. Heat, being careful not to let the water boil. Gradually beat in the yolks of the two eggs. Season to taste with salt and white pepper and just a hint of cayenne pepper, and pour over the lobster slices. Serve at once, with the shells surrounded by parsley or watercress.

This dish deserves your very best white Burgundy, up to and including the best vintages of Montrachet.

Lobster Thermidor

Use one small or one-half of a large lobster for each person.

Cut the lobster meat into bite-size pieces. Make a butter sauce by cooking the minced onion and lemon juice in 1 1/2 ounces of butter, adding one or two dashes of tabasco sauce. When the onion is soft and clear, add the lobster meat and cook until the surface is rosy red.

Make the thermidor sauce by mixing in a saucepan the remaining butter with the flour, adding the mustard, paprika, salt, chervil, and tarragon. Add the wine and simmer gently, stirring constantly until the flour begins to clear. Add the light cream and stir over moderate heat until the sauce is smooth and begins to thicken, Remove from heat.

Beat egg yolks and cream together; add a little of the heated sauce, beating thoroughly. Gradually add more of the sauce until all is added. This is best done in the top of a double boiler. Now, heat the mixed sauce for two or three minutes in the top of the double boiler without letting the water boil.

Divide the lobster meat among the shells and add any of the butter sauce which remains. Divide the cream sauce among the lobster-filled shells, sprinkle the surfaces with Parmesan cheese, and set under the broiler flame until the cheese melts and becomes delicately brown. Garnish with parsley or watercress and serve at once.

Lobster Thermidor is also worthy of your best Burgundy Blanc. Try it also with a good white Graves, such as Château Carbonnieux, or a good Auslese from the Rhine or Mosel.

LOBSTER THERMIDOR

6	small (or 3 large) boiled lobsters
4	oz. butter
1	cup light cream
1/2	cup whipping cream
2	slightly beaten egg yolks
1/2	cup Parmesan cheese
1	tablesp. flour
1 1/2	oz. dry white wine
1/4	teasp. dry mustard
1/4	teasp. paprika
1	teasp. salt
1	teasp. minced onion
1/4	teasp. chervil
1/4	teasp. tarragon
2	tablesp. lemon juice
	tabasco sauce

151

Lobster Curry

LOBSTER CURRY

1/2   boiled lobster for
       each person
    Béchamel sauce
    butter
    chopped onion
    curry powder
    cayenne pepper
    salt

For six persons, gently cook a medium onion, finely minced, in one ounce of butter until the onion is soft and clear. Cut the meat from three large lobsters or six small ones in bite-size pieces. Turn the cooked onion into a sufficient quantity of Béchamel sauce to cover the amount of lobster meat you have and add curry powder to your taste. Let the Béchamel with the onion simmer gently for two or three minutes to amalgamate the flavor; add the lobster meat. Continue on the fire until the lobster is heated through.

In order to accommodate varying tastes, make the curry just strong enough to satisfy the person who likes his curry the mildest. Others can add cayenne pepper to their portions and make them more spicy without spoiling the dish for those who prefer a milder flavor.

Traditionally, it is said that wine does not accompany curry, which is supposed to require beer or Gimlet cocktails. All curries are good with these two drinks, but we have found that we like curry dishes also with coarse red wine. In France, we use a red from Provence; in California, the Santa Tomas, made from the Mission grape in Mexico's Baja, California, is just right. Also suitable are the inexpensive red wines from the central valleys such as Gallo's Hearty Burgundy.

MUSSELS

The common mussel, found on both coasts of the United States and along the Atlantic and Mediterranean coasts of Europe is good and can be had for the gathering. Be careful not to harvest them close to a sewer outfall, or in otherwise contaminated water. Also, along the Pacific Coast, be sure to observe the posted laws regarding the months in which mussels can be taken. (Because mussels during the summer months ingest large quantities of a plankton, which is for them, nourishing food but which is a severe toxin for human beings, it is forbidden to gather mussels during the months in which the offending plankton is present in coastal waters.)

It is essential, if you wish to enjoy your mussels, to scrub them thoroughly to get rid of the sand, which not only adheres to the shells, but is present inside the shells. I shall not repeat the directions to scrub the mussels in each recipe, but you will regret it if you do not.

Moules Marinière

Melt one-half of the butter in a deep pot and cook the garlic and chopped shallots until they are soft. Add the seasonings and the mussels, and barely cover the mussels with water. Boil until all the mussels are open. Add the wine and bread crumbs; correct the seasoning. Let simmer for two more minutes. Serve in deep bowls, with fresh French bread and a green salad.

Supply empty bowls for the shells, and, when the course is finished, napkins moistened with warm water.

Mussels cooked in this fashion call for a simple dry white wine such as a Muscadet or a Pouilly-Fuissé.

Moules au Chablis

It would be silly and needlessly extravagant to use a good Chablis for this dish. On the other hand, an inexpensive California or Spanish "Chablis" would be completely lacking in authenticity because the wine would lack crispness and would be too watery. Use either a Petit Chablis or a young Muscadet.

Sauté the shallots and garlic in a little of the butter. In a deep pot, make a *bouquet garni* of the carrot, celery, celery leaves, and the herbs, tied in cheesecloth. Add the *bouquet garni* and the mussels to the pot, with enough water barely to cover. Simmer until the mussels open. Add the wine and the rest of the butter and simmer two minutes longer. Serve as in previous recipe, with a bottle or two of chilled Muscadet or Petit Chablis.

OYSTERS

It is my opinion that to do anything to an oyster beyond opening and eating it with a little salt and a squeeze of lemon is to deteriorate it. In the chapter on hors d'oeuvres, I have given two good first-course oyster recipes. Here are two good ways to serve oysters as a main course for those of you who want oysters and still feel that the main course should be a hot dish.

MOULES MARINIÈRE
- 1 qt. mussels per person
- 4 oz. butter for each four qts. of mussels
- 1/2 bottle dry white wine
- 1 cup toasted bread crumbs
- 2 cloves garlic
- 2 shallots for each four qts. of mussels
- salt
- freshly ground pepper

MOULES AU CHABLIS
- 1 qt. mussels per person
- 1/2 bottle Muscadet
- 4 oz. butter
- 1 carrot
- 1 stalk celery
- handful of celery leaves
- salt
- 1 bay leaf
- 2 cloves garlic
- 2 finely chopped shallots
- 1/2 teasp. marjoram
- 1/2 teasp. tarragon

Baked Oysters

BAKED OYSTERS

1/2	doz. oysters per person
	olive oil
1	clove finely chopped garlic per dozen oysters
	chopped parsley
	salt
	cayenne pepper

Open the oysters and keep in deeper half of shell. Mix one or more ounces of olive oil with the finely chopped garlic and heat. Put the oysters in a shallow pan in a medium oven. When the edges begin to curl, put one teaspoon of the garlic-flavored oil on each oyster and set under broiler flame until the oil sizzles—one or two minutes. Season with salt and a dash of cayenne pepper, and garnish with parsley. Serve at once.

This dish needs a bottle of first-rate Chablis, or, if this is too costly, a young Muscadet.

Hangtown Fry

As is true of many dishes allegedly originating in San Francisco, the name of this one is picturesque, but the dish is neither new, nor Californian. It is an oyster omelet. The French usually poach the oysters; the Hangtown recipe calls for frying them. Both ways are quick, easy, and good.

Dust the drained oysters first with flour and then with bread crumbs. Fry in the butter, browing on one side. Make an omelet mixture with the eggs, two teaspoons of water for each two eggs; add salt and pepper to taste and a dash of tabasco to lessen the eggy taste.

When the oysters have browned well on one side, turn them over and pour over the omelet mixture. Cook in the usual way, lifting up the edges of the cooked egg to allow the uncooked portions to slide underneath. When the egg mixture is still slightly runny in the center, fold over and slide onto a heated plate; garnish with parsley.

Or try the French method. Poach the oysters in water to which a cup of dry white wine has been added. As the edges of the oysters begin to curl, pick the oysters out of the poaching liquid with a slotted spoon and put in the melted butter in the omelet pan. Pour in the egg mixture and proceed in the normal way.

A Sancerre or Pouilly-Fumé, inexpensive Loire white wines a little less dry than Muscadet, seem to us, preferable for this dish. Or try a Traminer or Gewürz-Traminer from Alsace.

HANGTOWN FRY

6	oysters per person
2 - 3	eggs
1	tablesp. butter
	bread crumbs
	flour
	salt
	freshly ground pepper

154

PERCH

Ocean perch is not one of the greatest delicacies of the sea. But is is inexpensive, plentiful, and always available in the frozen form. Split it up the center, remove the backbone, and pan fry it. Better still, filet the perch, dip the filets in milk and then in flour seasoned with tarragon and marjoram, and fry until the outside is crisp. Serve with lemon wedges.

Select a dry California Pinot Blanc or a Muscadet to accompany this unpretentious fish dish.

Pompano au Papillote

If your taste agrees with that of our friends, you will find this one of the high points of your fish-eating experiences. The recipe can be used, although the results will not be quite as good, with any other delicately flavored white-meated fish. It is very nearly as good with Dover sole as with Pompano.

Sauté first the chopped onion and then the fish filets, browning lightly and turning once. Use care not to break up the filets. When the cooking is nearly done, add the chopped parsley.

Remove the filets to a heated plate. In the skillet still containing the oil and fish juices, melt the butter. Slice the mushrooms thinly and sauté gently for a few minutes. Remove the pan from the fire and add the shrimp, leaving them whole if they are small, but cutting them in pices if they are large.

Add to the pan, which should not be cooling, the anchovy paste, the mace, and as much lemon juice as you like. We find, in our family, that the juice of a whole lemon is too much. Add the sliced truffles and heat the pan gently.

Again, remove the skillet from the fire and allow it to cool. While the pan is cooling, carefully distribute your filets among the squares of vegetable parchment or oiled paper. When the pan is cool enough not to burn the wrist, add the beaten egg yolk and heat very gently, stirring constantly. Warning! If you overheat the pan, the sauce will curdle.

POMPANO AU PAPILLOTE

12	pompano filets
4	oz. butter
1	cup dry white wine, preferably the wine you will serve
1/2	lb. white mushrooms
1/2	cup cooked shrimp
1/4	cup sliced truffles
3	well beaten egg yolks
2	tablesp. first-quality olive oil
1	medium onion, chopped
1	teasp. chopped parsley
1/4	teasp. anchovy paste
1/4	teasp. mace
	lemon juice to taste
	salt
	freshly ground white pepper
6	sqs. of vegetable parchment or oiled paper

155

Pour equal portions of the sauce over the filets. Fold the papers and pin into square shapes. Heat in a 350 degree oven for six to eight minutes and serve.

This fine dish deserves your best white Burgundy. If you prefer a wine a little less dry, use a good white Graves, such as a Château Olivier.

Alternate Version

Here is an alternate version, simpler and also less full of calories.

Omit the shrimp and truffles. In place of the egg yolks, thicken the sauce with one tablespoon of flour. If you do this, be sure to cook the sauce long enough to avoid a raw, floury taste.

With the simplified version, a California Pinot Chardonnay, or a Traminer or Gewürz-Traminer from Alsace will go well.

Red Snapper Provençale

Soak the dried mushrooms overnight. Next day, drain them, reserving the liquid but leaving the last of it so as to avoid any sand which may be present. Cut the mushrooms in small pieces and sauté in one-half of the butter for ten minutes. Peel and quarter the tomatoes. Add them and the chopped onion, garlic, and chives to the mushrooms. Add the liquid in which the mushrooms soaked, and cook until the volume is reduced by one-third.

In the remaining butter, gently sauté the filets of red snapper on both sides and then arrange in a well-buttered shallow baking dish. Pour the tomato-mushroom mixture over the fish, sprinkle with the cheese, dot with butter, and brown under the broiler. Serve at once.

Clearly the tomato-onion-garlic sauce and the relative coarseness of the fish call for a red wine, not a white. A Côte de Provence from France, or a Zinfandel from California will serve admirably. This dish is an example of bourgeoise cooking and it would be as foolish to expend one of your fine wines on it as to deny yourself any wine.

RED SNAPPER PROVENCALE

6	red snapper filets
4	oz. butter
1 - 2	pkgs. dried Italian mushrooms
2	medium tomatoes
1/2	small onion, chopped
1	oz. red wine
1	teasp. chopped chives
2	cloves garlic, chopped or put through a garlic press
	freshly grated Parmesan cheese
	salt
	freshly ground pepper

SALMON

Baked Salmon

Wipe the six steaks or filets dry and arrange in a well-buttered baking dish. Sprinkle the grated onion and other seasonings over the top of the fish, then pour over all of the cream. Bake in a 350 degree oven until the fish flakes easily with a fork—for twenty-five to thirty minutes. Serve sprinkled with chopped parsley and lemon wedges.

The sweetness of the salmon will support a slightly sweet wine from Alsace or a Spanish "Chablis." However, I suggest the modestly-priced young wines from the Loire, such as a Muscadet or Sancerre.

BAKED SALMON

6	salmon steaks or filets
1	cup heavy cream
2	tablesp. grated onion
1 1/4	teasp. dill weed
1	tablesp. butter
	salt
	freshly ground pepper

Grilled Salmon

Select steaks or filets according to your preference and the availability of the fish in the market. Wipe the pieces dry and sprinkle with salt and freshly ground pepper. Let stand a few minutes, brush with butter; grill, turning once. Try to finish with the fish flaking easily but with the surfaces only lightly browned. Sprinkle with chopped parsley and serve with lemon wedges.

I generally choose a dry Loire wine but, it you like one slightly sweeter, one from Alsace or a Spanish "Chablis" will be suitable.

Salmon in White Wine

Wipe steaks dry and season with salt and pepper. Melt the butter in a heavy skillet and sauté the steaks, turning them once. When nicely browned, pour the wine over them, cover the skillet, and simmer until the liquid is reduced to one-half of its original bulk. Remove the steaks to a hot serving dish, sprinkle with the parsley and pour the sauce from the pan over them.

Drink the same wine you used for cooking the salmon: by preference a Muscadet, a Macon Blanc, or a Pouilly-Fuissé.

SALMON IN WHITE WINE

6	salmon steaks
2	oz. butter
1 1/2	cups dry white wine
2	finely chopped shallots
1	tablesp. chopped parsley
	salt
	freshly ground pepper

Poached Salmon with Hollandaise Sauce

For poaching it is preferable to buy all or part of a salmon in one piece, although there is no reason not to poach thick steaks or filets if your family is small.

Make a fish *fumet* by boiling the head, tail, bones, and other waste parts of your salmon (or of portions of a cheaper fish if you are using steaks) in enough water to cover. Then make a court bouillon by mixing equal volumes of the *fumet* and a cheap, dry white wine to which you have added a *bouquet garni* composed of a carrot, a stalk of celery, a handful of celery leaves, one-half of a small onion, two cloves, one bay leaf, and 1/4 teaspoon marjoram. Let the court bouillon simmer for ten to fifteen minutes to amalgamate the flavors, then lower the fish into it in a piece of cheesecloth. You will thus be able to remove the fish without danger of breaking it when it is done enough to flake.

Serve dressed with hollandaise sauce and garnished with sprigs of parsley or watercress.

The lemony flavor of the hollandaise sauce is delicious, but it would interfere with a too-delicate wine. Therefore, I recommend an inexpensive Alsatian wine, such as a Traminer or Riesling.

Poached Salmon with Sauce Mornay

Poach the salmon exactly as in the foregoing recipe. Make a mornay sauce as described in the chapter on sauces. Arrange the poached salmon in a shallow buttered baking dish and cover with the sauce. Sprinkle the top with a little freshly grated Parmesan cheese; run under the broiler until the sauce bubbles and the cheese is browned.

Fish is Sweet

Because the fish is sweet and there is no acid flavor from the lemon, you will enjoy this dish with a good Rhine or Mosel Spätlese or Auslese.

Smoked Salmon, Eggs and Cheese

Melt the butter in a heavy skillet and sauté the onion and shallots until they are clear. Add the smoked salmon and cook over gentle heat, shredding the salmon. Beat the eggs with the cream and the Parmesan cheese. Add to the skillet and stir until the eggs are barely firm. Season with salt and pepper and turn into an ovenproof serving dish. Lay the slices of Gruyère cheese on top and run under the broiler until the cheese melts. Serve at once.

We usually have this dish for a Sunday evening supper and find it worthy of a good Rhine or Mosel Spätlese or Auslese.

SCALLOPS

Coquilles St. Jacques Gratinées

Slice the scallops in pieces one-half inch thick and simmer three minutes in enough salted water to cover. Melt two ounces of the butter in a heavy skillet and cook the shallots gently for two or three minutes. Add the cleaned and sliced mushrooms and cook until they are done—five or six minutes. Mix the other two ounces of butter with the flour and add to the skillet, mixing well and thinning out with the wine and, if necessary, with some of the water in which the scallops were cooked. Cook the sauce and beat the egg yolks into it. Add the scallops and divide among six scallop shells. Sprinkle with the bread crumbs and run under the broiler until the crumbs are browned a little.

The scallops are quite sweet. A good Mosel or Rhine Spätlese or Auslese will show the dish off to its maximum advantage. I have also liked a Gewürz-Traminer from Alsace with it.

Coquilles en Sauce Mornay

Cook scallops in boiling salted water as directed in the foregoing recipe. Slice one-half pound of fresh mushrooms and cook gently in two ounces of butter for five or six minutes. Mix the mushrooms and scallops and divide among six scallop shells. Cover with Sauce Mornay. Sprinkle the top with grated Parmesan cheese and run under the broiler until the sauce bubbles.

Again, a good Reisling Spätlese or Auslese will give you pleasure while it displays this dish to its best advantage.

SMOKED SALMON, EGGS AND CHEESE

3/4	lb. smoked salmon
8	fresh eggs
1/2	lb. Gruyère cheese in thin slices
1/4	lb. grated Parmesan cheese
2	oz. butter
1/2	cup whipping cream
2	tablesp. chopped onion
2	chopped shallots
	salt
	freshly ground pepper

COQUILLES ST. JACQUES GRATINEES

1 1/2	lbs. scallops
1/2	lb. fresh mushrooms
4	oz. butter
4	tablesp. flour
1/2	cup dry white wine
2	egg yolks
2	minced shallots
	bread crumbs
	finely chopped parsley
	lemon juice to taste
	salt
	freshly ground pepper

159

Scallops and Shrimps

SCALLOPS AND SHRIMPS

1	lb. scallops
1	lb. shrimp
1/4	lb. mushrooms
3/4	cup heavy cream
3/4	cup dry white wine
2	oz. butter
1/2	cup grated Parmesan cheese
3	tablesp. flour
2	egg yolks
	juice of 1/4 lemon
1	bay leaf
	cayenne pepper
	freshly ground white pepper
	salt

Cut the scallops in one-half inch thick pieces. Clean and devein shrimp and split in half, lengthwise, unless you have the tiny West Coast shrimp, which may be left whole. Put the shrimp and scallop with a bay leaf in a saucepan with water to cover. Simmer until cooked, ten minutes or less.

In one-half of the butter, sauté the mushrooms, thinly sliced, until they are done, about five or six minutes.

Into another saucepan put the remaining butter. Melt it and then mix thoroughly with the flour. Add the wine and enough of the water in which the seafood had cooked to make a sauce of the right consistency. Cook until it is smooth and of the right thickness, either concentrating it or adding more of the broth as needed. Add the lemon juice and remove from fire.

Beat the egg yolks into the cream. Add a little of the cooled sauce to the egg and cream mixture, beating well between each small addition. Then, add the mixture to the rest of the sauce and reheat in a double boiler without allowing the sauce to boil. Add mushrooms, shrimp and scallops and stir until they are heated. Divide the mixture among six scallop shells or ovenproof dishes, sprinkle with Parmesan cheese, and run under the broiler until the cheese is melted.

We have enjoyed this dish with all of the wines discussed with previous recipes. Because the shrimp constitute such a large part of the flavor, a drier wine is also in order, such as a Pouilly-Fuissé or a California Chardonnay.

SCULPIN

The sculpin is a white-meated fish taken in medium-deep waters along the California coast and is the nearest thing we have yet discovered to the North Atlantic turbot. This recipe was used by our Bretonne cook in Paris, for turbot for which it is perfect. It is nearly as good with sculpin.

Sculpin à la Parisienne

Have the sculpin fileted, making sure the dealer gives you the heads, skeleton and all the scraps for making the *fumet.* You will get one filet from each side, the two being just right for each serving when the fish is the main course. One filet is the correct serving for the fish course of a multicourse dinner.

Make a *bouquet garni* of all of the items after the Parmesan cheese and add to a saucepan with the fish skeletons and scraps and enough water to cover. Simmer for thirty minutes. During the last five minutes add the wine. Strain and use the liquid as a court bouillon for poaching the filets.

Poach the filets gently until they just begin to flake with a fork. Remove from the court bouillon and lift carefully into a well-buttered baking dish. Concentrate the court bouillon to one cup and remove from the fire to cool.

In a saucepan, melt half the butter and stir in the flour until the *roux* is well blended but without allowing it to color. Slowly add the concentrated court bouillon, beating all the while. Then add the milk and cook for five minutes.

Blend the egg yolks and the whipping cream in a mixing bowl and gradually add the hot sauce, at first just in drops, beating constantly. As the sauce cools, it may be added in larger amounts. When all the sauce has been added to the cream egg-yolk mixture, set the bowl over gentle heat and allow it to thicken slightly, being careful not to let it boil. Adjust the seasoning with salt, pepper, and lemon juice, adding the juice a few drops at a time, with thorough mixing between additions.

Cover the filets in their baking dish with the sauce and sprinkle the cheese on it. Run under the broiler until cheese melts and the surface becomes golden brown. Dust with paprika and serve at once.

Our Bretonne cook would sometimes bring to the apartment a dozen écrivisses (fresh-water crayfish) or scampi (small Mediterranean shrimp) or even a dozen Portugais or Belon oysters to place over the filets before covering them with the sauce. A quarter pound or so of fresh white mushrooms, sliced thinly, sautéed in butter, and distributed over the filets dresses the dish up in still another way.

This dish, made either with sculpin or turbot, is good enough to deserve a bottle of your very best white Burgundy; a fine Meursault or a choice Montrachet will not be too good if you can afford one of these. But the dish is good with a less expensive dry white wine.

SCULPIN À LA PARISIENNE

6	sculpins
1	cup dry white wine
4	oz. butter
3	tablesp. flour
3/4	cup milk
1/2	cup (or more) of whipping cream
3	egg yolks
1/4	cup freshly grated Parmesan cheese
	juice of 1/2 lemon
	salt
	freshly ground white pepper
1	handful celery leaves
1	stalk celery
1	carrot
1	bay leaf

SHRIMP

Shrimps Albert

SHRIMPS ALBERT

2 lbs. raw shrimp
2 oz. butter
1 cup whipping cream
3 oz. Sercial Madeira
1 tablesp. cognac
   lemon juice
   salt
   freshly ground black pepper
   tabasco sauce

Shell and devein the shrimp. Melt the butter in a heavy skillet and add shrimp. When they become pink, add the brandy and ignite, mixing the flaming liquor well with the shrimp. Then lower the heat, add the Madeira, and season with salt and pepper. Cook gently, covered, for ten minutes. Take off the fire and add the whipping cream a little at a time, mixing well between additions. Finish with a few drops of lemon juice to taste and a dash or two of tabasco sauce. Correct the seasoning and serve garnished with sprigs of parsley. Steamed and buttered rice is the accompaniment of choice.

Shrimps Albert deserves a good white Burgundy—a Meursault or a Bâtard-Montrachet of a good year, but can do with a more modest wine.

Shrimps à l'Americaine

SHRIMPS À L'AMERICAINE

1 lbs. raw shrimp
3 tablesp. olive oil
3 finely minced shallots
3 oz. dry sherry
1 - 2 oz. brandy
2 tablesp. butter
1 teasp. flour
1 teasp. tomato paste
   crushed peppercorns
   tabasco sauce

Shell, devein and dry the shrimp. Heat the olive oil in a heavy skillet and cook the minced shallots for two minutes, until they become soft. Add the shrimp and cook until they turn pink, about five to seven minutes. Dust the shrimp with the flour, stir well and add the sherry. Stir in the tomato paste—there is supposed to be only enough to color the sauce well—add six to eight peppercorns, salt to taste, and add a dash or two of tabasco sauce.

Cover the skillet, lower the heat, and let cook gently until the shrimp are done. This will require about ten minutes. Adjust the sauce by adding more sherry if it is too thick or too scarce, or by mixing thoroughly a tablespoon of butter with the same quantity of flour and adding it if the sauce is too thin. Just before serving, stir in one or two ounces of good brandy—a sound cognac preferably. Serve garnished with parsley and accompanied by steamed long-grain rice.

The seasoning should be definitely spicy but not excessively so. Vary the number of crushed peppercorns and the amount of tabasco sauce until you find the combination that suits you.

This dish is perhaps a little too heavily seasoned to require one of your best wines. A good young Muscadet or a California Pinot Blanc fills the bill perfectly.

Shrimps with Dill

After shelling and deveining the shrimp, melt the butter in a heavy skillet. As soon as it foams, add the shrimp and half the dill weed. Cook for five or six minutes over low heat until the shrimp turn pink. Add the remaining dill, dust lightly with cayenne pepper, stir a little and serve at once with sprigs of parsley for garnish. As with most shrimp dishes, steamed rice should accompany shrimp with dill.

A fresh young Muscadet is our wine of choice for shrimp cooked with dill.

Shrimps with a Cream Dill Sauce

In a saucepan, melt two-thirds of the butter and stir in the flour, mixing well until it is free of lumps. Heat the milk and just as it begins to boil, add all at once to the butter-flour mixture. Cook a few minutes with frequent stirring and then add the cream, a little at a time, beating with each addition. Season to taste with salt and freshly ground white pepper.

In a heavy skillet, heat the rest of the butter and sauté the shallots until they are clear. Add the shelled, cleaned, and deveined shrimp and cook gently for five minutes. Add the sauce to the shrimp and cook gently for another five minutes. Garnish with parsley, and dust with paprika. Serve steamed rice with the shrimp.

A good, crisp dry white wine is what is wanted here. We have liked all of the Loire whites, the Pouilly-Fuissé and both Almadèn's and Wente Brothers' Pinot Chardonnay.

The next two shrimp recipes will afford you an opportunity to break the so-called rule regarding the necessity of serving white wine with seafood. Tomatoes and herbs in both dishes definitely call for red wines.

Shrimps Creole

Mince the garlic and chop the onions. Cook them in a heavy skillet with the olive oil until the onion is soft and golden. Add the herbs and tomatoes and continue cooking until most of the liquid from the tomatoes has evaporated.

SHRIMPS WITH DILL

2	lbs. raw shrimp
4	oz. butter
2	tablesp. dill weed
	juice of 1/2 lemon
	salt
	freshly ground pepper
	cayenne pepper

SHRIMPS WITH A CREAM DILL SAUCE

2	lbs. raw shrimp
4	oz. butter
2	cups light cream
1	cup milk
1 1/2	cups dry white wine
6	tablesp. flour
2	tablesp. chopped shallots
1 1/2	teasp. dried dill weed
	salt
	freshly ground pepper

SHRIMPS CREOLE

2	lbs. raw shrimp
1 - 2	onions
1	can (1 lbs. 12 oz.) tomatoes
2	oz. olive oil
1	clove garlic
2	bay leaves
2	teasp. thyme
1/4	teasp. marjoram
	freshly ground black pepper
	salt

163

Clean, shell, and devein the shrimp. Add to the skillet, cover, and cook until the shrimp are just done—about ten to twelve minutes. Serve over steamed rice.

An inexpensive young Beaujolais, or California "Burgundy," or a California Gamay will give great satisfaction with this dish.

Shrimps Marinara

SHRIMPS MARINARA

2	lbs. raw shrimp
4	tablesp. olive oil
6	large tomatoes, peeled and chopped or 1 large can Italian tomatoes
1/4	cup chopped celery
	handful celery leaves
	fettucine or spaghetti
2	cloves garlic
1	teasp. oregano
1	teasp. sweet basil
6	sprigs parsley
1	teasp. salt
1/4	teasp. cayenne pepper
	freshly ground black pepper

Heat the olive oil in a heavy skillet and cook the chopped celery and garlic until the celery is soft. Add the tomatoes. Make a *bouquet garni* with the celery leaves, oregano, parsley and basil, and tie in cheesecloth. Add to the tomato mixture and cook gently until it thickens—about thirty minutes.

Clean, shell, and devein the shrimp. Add them to the thickened tomato sauce and remove the *bouquet garni.* Simmer until the shrimp are pink and tender—less than ten minutes. Serve over fettucine (Italian noodles) or spaghetti.

A Côte de Provence, a Barbera or Bardolino, or a Zinfandel from California, all will provide the hearty, forthright wine suitable for this delicious peasant dish.

Shrimps Majestic

For this dish, try to find the tiny Pacific Coast shrimp or the little shrimp of the Carolina coast.

Break the fusilli (a thin spiral-shaped macaroni product obtainable at Italian shops) in pieces one-quarter to one-half inch in length. Cook it in several times its volume of boiling salted water until it is barely tender—twelve to fifteen minutes. Wash in hot water several times and keep warm in a serving bowl.

Next, melt one-third of the butter in the top of a double boiler, and heat the shrimp in it. Mix the heated cooked shrimp with the pasta. In the same double boiler, without washing, melt the rest of the butter. Beat the egg yolk and the cream together thoroughly and add slowly to the butter in the top of the double boiler, beating constantly and not letting the water boil. Mix well with the pasta and shrimp together with the Parmesan cheese. Pass a bowl of freshly grated Parmesan cheese at the table so that each diner can help himself if he desires more.

SHRIMPS MAJESTIC

1	lb. cooked shrimp
2	cups fusilli
4	oz. butter
3/4	cup light cream
1	egg yolk
1	cup freshly grated Parmesan cheese
	salt
	freshly ground pepper

This dish was delicious with a Piesporter Gold-tropfchen from the Mosel. On another occasion, we found a young Traminer from Alsace to be delightful with it.

Shrimp and Filet of White Fish

For this dish we use the filets which are commonly sold in the United States as "filet of sole" but which are in most cases, filet of flounder.

In a heavy skillet heat the oil together with half of the butter. Add the marjoram and the cleaned and sliced mushrooms. Sauté for five minutes. Set the mushrooms aside. Add more butter as needed and sauté the shrimp until they are pink. Set them aside. Remove pan from heat. Add the cream, pepper, paprika, and salt to taste, and stir until the cream is blended with all the juices in the pan.

Arrange the filets in the bottom of a well-greased baking dish and distribute over them the shrimp and mushrooms mixed together. Pour the sauce over all. Mix the cheese and bread crumbs and sprinkle over the contents of the dish. Bake in a 350 degree oven for twenty-five minutes. The top should be well browned but not over-browned.

Serve with a Chilean or California Riesling or a wine of the same species of grape from Alsace.

SHRIMP AND FILET OF WHITE FISH

2	lbs. fish filets
1	lb. peeled and deveined shrimp
1/2	lb. fresh mushrooms
1	pt. sour cream
1/2	cup fine bread crumbs
1/2	cup freshly grated Parmesan cheese
2	oz. butter
1/4	cup cooking oil
1/4	teasp. marjoram
	paprika
	salt
	freshly ground pepper

SOLE

This small fish from the bottom of the English Channel and adjacent waters, which the English call Dover Sole and the French *la bonne sole de la Manche,* is without doubt the most delicate and best eating of any of the many delicious gifts which the seas offer us. Unfortunately, this species is not found on our side of the Atlantic. The fish sold in the United States as filet of sole can be filets cut from any number of reasonably sweet white fish; the most common is perhaps the flounder. The Pacific Coast offers sand-dabs and Rex sole, two closely related species, the meat of which is nearly as white but not as firm or sweet as that of the true sole. The lemon sole from farther out in the North Sea is another white fish, less expensive, but also somewhat less good than true sole.

165

We have our fish dealer obtain for us frozen Dover sole several times each year as a special treat. Most of the time, however, for preparing sole meunière or other simple ways of cooking fish, we are quite satisfied with sand-dabs or Rex sole, whichever is at hand in the market. For dishes calling for filets, we use whatever is offered as "filet of sole" which turns out mostly to be flounder, but is sometimes another Pacific fish known as a Petrale sole.

You can use any of the fish discussed in the recipes which follow or, for that matter, any mild white fish such as pike, shad, haddock or trout. Haddock and cod are not as fine-grained as the others and will give you somewhat different results. Nevertheless, they, too, will be good.

Sole Meunière

Clean the fish according to the variety. True sole should have the top, dark side skinned. After cleaning, pat dry and dust with flour. Melt enough butter in a skillet to cover one side of the fish and sauté gently, turning only once. Remove to a warm plate and add one ounce of butter for each fish to the pan, heating until it is nut-brown. Sprinkle the fish with finely chopped parsley and then pour over it the browned butter added to that in which the fish were cooked. Serve immediately with lemon wedges.

A good white Loire—Pouilly-Fumé or Sancerre—or a good California Pinot Chardonnay is called for here.

Sole with Vermouth and Cream Sauce

Poach the filets in the vermouth until they barely flake; five minutes is usually enough. Remove filets to a shallow, buttered baking dish and keep warm. Reduce the vermouth until there is only a tablespoon or two in the poaching pan. In the top of a double boiler, melt the butter and beat into it, the egg yolks. As usual in making such a sauce, avoid letting the water under the mixture boil. Add the cream and the reduced vermouth, beating all the while, and cook until the sauce is smooth and of the required thickness. Season with a little salt. Pour the sauce over the filets, sprinkle lightly with freshly grated Parmesan cheese and slip under the broiler until the cheese begins to brown. Garnish with parsley and serve at once.

SOLE MEUNIÈRE

1	sole per person or
	2 small sand-dabs or
	2 Rex sole
	butter
	finely chopped parsley
	salt
	pepper
	flour

SOLE WITH VERMOUTH AND CREAM SAUCE

12	sole filets
2	cups dry vermouth
1 1/2	sticks butter
4	egg yolks
1/4	cup heavy cream
	salt
	pepper
	freshly grated
	Parmesan cheese

This dish deserves a good white Hermitage or one of your better Meursaults.

Filets of Sole Amandine

Poach the filets in the wine and water mixture, to which has been added the onion and a little salt. When the fish flakes, remove it to a baking dish buttered with part of the butter. Make your velouté by melting in a double boiler the butter and adding the flour, cooking and stirring until it is smooth and the flour turns a little golden. Beat the egg yolks into 1 1/2 cups of the cream and gradually add a little of the hot fish stock. Keep adding the fish stock until you have used one and one-half to two cups of it, and cook in top of double boiler until it thickens. Again, do not let the water in the double boiler boil. Stir into the sauce the toasted almonds, reserving a few. Pour over the fish in the baking dish. Whip the remaining cream and salt it slightly. Put on top of the sauce and decorate with the reserved almonds. Place under the broiler until the cream browns slightly.

We like this one well enough to offer our best white Burgundy with it; also it is good with a Spätlese or Auslese Rhine or Mosel.

Filets of Sole Bonne Femme

Arrange sole in shallow baking dish. Sprinkle with salt and a good grind of white pepper. Lay on top the sliced onion, bay leaf, and marjoram. Add the wine. If the filets are not quite covered, add a little water. Bake in a 350 degree oven until fish flakes with a fork. Remove the filets, without breaking, to another baking dish and strain the stock in which they have poached.

In a saucepan, melt the butter and add the flour, stirring until smooth. Gradually, add 1 1/2 cups of the fish stock, bring to a boil, and cook until smooth and thickened. This should require about three to five minutes. Correct seasoning, add a dash of cayenne and pour sauce over the filets.

Sauté the mushrooms in the rest of the butter, add lemon juice and another dash of cayenne and salt to taste. Put the mushrooms over the fish. Now, cover all with

FILETS OF SOLE AMANDINE

12	sole filets
1 1/2	cups dry white wine
1 1/2	cups water
1	stick butter
1	tablesp. chopped onion
1	pt. whipping cream
4	egg yolks
1/2	cup split toasted almonds
	salt
	freshly ground white pepper
4	tablesp. flour

FILETS OF SOLE BONNE FEMME

12	small or 6 large (3 lbs.) sole filets
1	stick of butter
3/4	cup dry white wine
1	small onion
3	tablesp. flour
3/4	cup sliced button mushrooms
3/4	teasp. salt
	freshly ground white pepper
1	bay leaf
1	teasp. lemon juice
	cayenne pepper
1/2	cup light cream
1/4	teasp. marjoram
	hollandaise sauce

167

hollandaise sauce and slip under the broiler until browned and glazed—two to three minutes. Garnish with thin slices of lemon and parsley and serve at once.

A Pouilly-Fuissé, a good California Pinot Chardonnay, or a Traminer or Gewürz-Traminer from Alsace will partner this dish to everyone's satisfaction.

Filet of Sole with Mustard and American Cheese

FILET OF SOLE MUSTARD AND AMERICAN CHEESE

3	lbs. sole filets
3	cups fish stock
3	cups light cream
4	egg yolks
1 1/2	cups grated, sharp American cheese
3	tablesp. flour
4	oz. butter
1/2	cup chopped green onions (use some of the green stems)
3	tablesp. chopped parsley
3	tablesp. Dijon mustard
1/3	cup dry sherry
	salt
	freshly ground white pepper

To make fish stock, get the heads, tails, and other fresh fish scraps from your fish market, or buy an extra filet or two. Cook for half an hour together with salt, a large pinch of marjoram and another of tarragon, and a chopped shallot in a mixture of half dry white wine and half water. Use a cup of each. Strain and cook down to one and one-half cups to concentrate the flavor.

Melt one-half stick of the butter in the top of a double boiler and add the flour, stirring vigorously until it is smooth. Beat the egg yolks into the cream. Remove the roux from the fire and add a little of the egg-cream mixture, beating vigorously. Gradually add the rest beating all the while. Cook until thick and smooth in the top of a double boiler without letting the water boil.

Sauté the filets in the other half stick of butter until they are golden brown. Combine the mustard, green onions, and parsley with the sauce and pour over the sole, after having sprinkled the grated cheese over the filets. Place under the broiler until the sauce bubbles and the surface browns.

Medium-quality white Burgundies, best-quality California Pinot Chardonnay, or good, comparatively dry Rhines or Mosels will go well with this dish.

Sole with Herbs in Cream

SOLE WITH HERBS IN CREAM

3	lbs. sole filets
6 - 8	finely chopped shallots
1	box sliced button mushrooms
1 1/2	cups dry vermouth
	lemon slices
3	tablesp. chopped parsley
1	pt. heavy cream
	salt
	freshly ground white pepper

Clean and slice mushrooms thinly. Arrange in bottom of a large skillet—or distribute between two skillets because the fish should not overlap—together with the chopped shallots and parsley. Arrange the filets over the vegetables. Add the wine and bring to a boil. Reduce heat and simmer until fish flakes easily. Remove fish to a hot serving dish and keep warm. Pour cream into skillet and, stirring constantly, boil it until the contents of the pan are reduced to a fairly thick consistency; it will be about right when it coats a spoon evenly. Pour over filets after adjusting seasoning. Serve at once, garnishing the dish with thin slices of lemon and sprigs of parsley. Again, consume a medium to fine white Burgundy or California Chardonnay with the dish.

Sole Mornay

Poach the sole in the usual way in 1 1/2 cups of wine and an equal part of water. If you have a sauce Mornay already made, use it; if not, make such a sauce, using the *fumet* in which the fish was poached as the liquid (see chapter on sauces). Coat the bottom of an ovenproof serving dish with the Mornay sauce; put in the poached filets and cover with the rest of the sauce. Sprinkle the top with the grated Parmesan cheese and run under broiler until the sauce bubbles and the cheese begins to brown.

For our family, this way of enjoying sole calls for a fine white Burgundy.

SOLE MORNAY

3	lbs. sole filets
1 1/2	cups dry vermouth
2	cups sauce mornay
1/2	cup freshly grated Parmesan cheese
	Parmesan cheese

Filets of Sole au Champagne

Put the champagne, mushrooms, onion, bay leaf and parsley in a saucepan and boil until the volume is reduced by half. Remove from heat and, after removing the bay leaf, stir in the heavy cream.

Salt and pepper the filets and arrange in a shallow baking dish. Pour sauce over the filets and sprinkle the Parmesan cheese over all. Bake in a 375 degree oven until done, about twenty-five minutes.

A good dry Meursault or Montrachet will be best with this dish, but other dry whites are good with it.

(Note: Usually I cannot bring myself to opening a bottle of fine champagne to prepare this recipe. Once, however, there happened to be champagne left over after another occasion. We corked the bottles firmly, kept them in the refrigerator, and used them the next night for this dish. It did, although I was skeptical, taste somewhat better than on other occasions when we prepared the dish with California "champagne." However, do not hesitate to use the latter; it makes a fine dish! So does a nonsparkling wine— see following.)

FILETS OF SOLE AU CHAMPAGNE

3	lbs. sole filets
12	oz. champagne
6	tablesp. grated onion
2	tablesp. chopped parsley
2	tablesp. butter
1/3	cup Parmesan cheese
1 1/2	cup thinly sliced mushrooms
1	bay leaf
1/3	cup heavy cream
	salt
	freshly ground white pepper

169

BAKED SOLE WITH HERBS

3   lbs. fish filets
1   stick of butter
2   garlic cloves
1/3 cup chopped onion
2   chopped shallots
    juice of one lemon
2   teasp. chopped parsley
1/4 teasp. dried tarragon
1/4 teasp. dried marjoram
1/8 teasp. freshly grated nutmeg
1/8 teasp. mace

TROUT GRENOBLOISE

6   fresh trout (or 12 if
      fish are small)
3   lemons
    milk
    flour
    salt
    freshly ground white pepper
1/2 cup cooking oil
2   sticks butter
1   tablesp. capers
    parsley

TROUT MEUNIÈRE

6   fresh trout (or 12 if
      fish are small)
4   oz. butter
    flour
    milk
    lemon
    chopped parsley
    salt
    freshly ground white pepper

Sole au Chablis, au Meursault, au Muscadet, etc.

By following the recipe above and substituting any good white wine, one may prepare a variety of sole dishes, each of which will have a subtly different taste. In the case of these other wines, I serve the same wine as I have used to prepare the dish. Such a procedure guarantees perfect harmony between food and wine.

Baked Sole (or other fish) with Herbs

Arrange the filets in buttered baking dish. Melt the rest of the butter in a skillet; cook the garlic, onion and shallots gently until the onion is transparent but not brown. Discard garlic, add other herbs and the spices. Add lemon juice. Cook a minute longer and spread over the fish. If you like, sprinkle bread crumbs or Parmesan cheese over top and bake in a 375 to 400 degree oven until fish flakes easily—fifteen to twenty minutes.

We enjoyed an inexpensive Sylvaner from Alsace with this dish; it, however, will easily support a more elegant wine.

TROUT

Trout Grenobloise

After cleaning trout, dip in milk and shake in bag with seasoned flour. Grate the rind of the lemons. Heat the oil and one stick of butter in a skillet and add lemon rind. Sauté the fish gently until they flake, turning only one. Remove fish to heated plate and add rest of butter to cooking pan, browning as for the Meunière style (see below). Sprinkle capers over the fish and add the browned butter. Garnish with sprigs of parsley and serve at once.

Again, our palates tell us the simple, young dry whites are best here. Our favorite is a young Muscadet.

Trout Meunière

Clean trout and pat dry. Dip in milk and shake in a bag with a tablespoon or two of flour seasoned with salt and white pepper. Melt two ounces of butter in a skillet and, as soon as it foams, add the trout. Reduce heat and cook without letting butter blacken. Turn when brown, about five minutes to each side. Remove to a hot plate, sprinkle with lemon juice and parsley. Melt a tablespoon of butter for each trout in the same pan the fish were cooked in and let it turn golden brown. Pour over fish and serve with lemon wedges and a garnish of sprigs of parsley.

A simple, crisp dry white wine seems to suit this simple—but good—dish very well; we drink either a Muscadet or a Pouilly-Fuissé with it.

TUNA

Grilled Tuna or Swordfish Steaks

Make a marinade of the herbs, chopped onions, lemon juice and olive oil. Arrange fish in a pan just large enough to hold them and add the marinade. Marinate for several hours or overnight, turning the steaks and basting with the marinade. Remove the steaks, drain off the marinade and dry on paper towels.

Heat more olive oil in skillet and sauté the steaks gently for four or five minutes, turn and repeat. If necessary, turn again to complete cooking. Sprinkle with chopped parsley and serve with lemon wedges. Boiled potatoes with plain melted butter is a good accompaniment for these steaks.

A modest dry white wine, such as a Pouilly-Fuissé or a California Pinot Blanc will form a suitable accompaniment to tuna or swordfish steaks.

Creamed Tuna

Break up the tuna—we prefer the best white-meat tuna, called albacore—into chunks, not too small. Add enough Béchamel sauce to cover. Either heat to boiling on top of stove or turn into a buttered baking dish and sprinkle the surface with bread crumbs. Heat in a 350 degree oven for fifteen minutes or until the bread crumbs are browned.

A variation which makes a new dish is to add a few tablespoons of grated Parmesan cheese and one cup of cooked shrimp to the Béchamel sauce and to sprinkle the top of the dish with a mixture of grated Parmesan and bread crumbs.

A simple Sylvaner or Traminer, or inexpensive Rhône or Mosel, or a California Pinot Blanc will do very well with either variation.

GRILLED TUNA OR SWORDFISH STEAKS
6	tuna or swordfish steaks
1/2	cup olive oil
3	tablesp. lemon juice
1/2	cup chopped onion
1/4	teasp. dried tarragon
1/4	teasp. dried marjoram
12	cracked peppercorns
	salt

CREAMED TUNA
2	7 1/2 oz. cans tuna in oil
1 1/2 to 2	cups Béchamel sauce
	bread crumbs
	freshly grated Parmesan cheese

171

FOWL

As in the other chapters, only recipes for chicken, turkey, duck, goose and wild fowl we have liked ourselves are presented. You will not find directions for cooking Chicken Maryland because we do not find Chicken Maryland good. I have eaten many dishes of fowl more complicated than those given here. They have not seemed better than the dishes I have chosen, or they have been too complicated to be worth the trouble.

CHICKEN

Roast Chicken

Many people think that a capon is the fowl of choice for roasting. I am not sure that this is true. Most capons are too fat. On the whole, I prefer a good, reasonably fat hen. The meat is less greasy, the flavor seems equally good, and the cost is less.

Most of the time we do not bother with a dressing. We clean the fowl thoroughly, dry it inside and out, season it with salt and put in the cavity a quartered onion stick with three or four cloves, and a handful of celery leaves. We set the trussed fowl, breast side up, on a rack in a shallow roasting pan and cover it loosely with foil.

Roast all fowl in a slow oven, allowing two and one-half to four hours, depending on size. The fowl is done when the leg joint moves easily and the juice which runs out when the skin is pricked is only faintly pink. About one-half hour before roasting is complete, remove the foil and turn up the heat to brown the skin nicely. Remove the bird to a warm platter and let it stand in a 200 degree oven for fifteen to thirty minutes.

Pour all the fat out of the roasting pan and then replace two tablespoons of it for each cup of gravy that you wish. Add the giblets which have been boiled in a little water and minced finely. Stir into the pan about two

SAUCE FOR CHICKEN

Pour off all the fat from the pan. Add one cup of dry red wine and scrape all of the brown bits from the pan. Bring the contents of the pan to a boil, correct the seasoning and let the wine and chicken juice mixture concentrate for a minute or two. Send to the table in a heated sauceboat.

STUFFING FOR CHICKEN

Use stale bread crumbs or half bread crumbs and half cornbread to which you may add chopped celery, thyme, tarragon, half an onion chopped and cooked gently in a little butter until it is soft; and, if you like the flavor, a little sage. Allow four cups of dressing for a four pound fowl, less if the bird is smaller. Stuff loosely.

tablespoons of flour, scraping up all the browned bits adhering to the pan. Thin out the gravy to the consistency you like with some of the stock in which the giblets were boiled, and correct the seasoning with salt and pepper. Most of the time, we prefer a gravy without the giblets. If you like the idea, thin the gravy with a little water.

Sometimes, especially if we are not serving potatoes with the chicken, we make a sauce in place of the traditional gravy. If you like a stuffing, I suggest this one.

Roast Chicken with Tarragon

Select a good fat roasting chicken, clean well and rub insides thoroughly with chopped fresh tarragon leaves or crushed dried leaves mixed with a little brandy and butter. Stuff the cavity with onion and celery leaves. Mix brandy, butter, and a generous amount of tarragon and rub plentifully on the outside of the fowl. Brown at 425 degrees, reduce to 350 degrees and baste frequently. If the butter and juices from the bird are not sufficient, add more butter, brandy and tarragon, painting the breast and legs and letting the mixture melt and flow into the pan.

Remove bird to heated platter, add a tablespoon of cognac to the pan and scrape up all browned bits. Warm another tablespoon of cognac and light, pouring the flaming liquor over the fowl. Heat the pan juices until there remain only two or three tablespoonsful. Pour this over the bird just before serving.

Your best red Burgundy is worthy of chicken cooked in this manner.

Chicken Roasted with Cream

Rub the cavity of a plump roasting chicken with salt, pepper, butter, and a tablespoon or two of brandy; introduce into the cavity a small onion stuck with three or four cloves. Truss as usual and rub outside of fowl with soft butter. Roast breast side up in a shallow pan for fifteen minutes at 425 degrees and, when the breast is beginning to brown, turn heat down to 350 degrees and roast for an hour, basting with pan juices and butter. Then begin basting with two tablespoons of heavy cream every five minutes until you have used a half pint of cream. Continue basting with the mixed cream and pan juices, which will look curdled, until the fowl is done, as determined by easy mobility of leg joint.

Remove the bird to a hot platter and add half a cup of strong chicken stock or, failing that, canned chicken broth, to the roasting pan. Mix well, scraping all of the browned bits, and bring contents to a boil. Strain and serve the sauce at the table in a heated sauceboat.

Because of the cream, you could, if you wish, drink a white wine with this food, however, I would recommend a red.

Southern Fried Chicken

This dish is still one of the very good ways to cook chicken, especially with a country cream gravy and fluffy rich mashed potatoes. It deserves a place in every discriminating family's repertory.

Cut up young fryers, or in most urban markets, buy only the pieces you like. Clean, dip in milk, then shake in a bag containing one-half cup of flour seasoned with salt and pepper. If you do not drain all the milk from the pieces, you can coat them quite thickly with the seasoned flour, which will give you a better crust.

Brown chicken in an iron skillet in a mixture of one-third butter and two-thirds cooking oil, one to one and one-half inches deep, hot but not smoking. When the pieces are brown on all sides, cover and cook for fifteen minutes. Then remove cover and finish cooking with the lid off until pieces are tender. Depending on the age of the chicken, it will require twenty-five to forty minutes to cook. Chicken is not a meat to serve rare.

Cooking Time for Chicken

Remove chicken to paper towels to drain excess fat; then put in an aluminum foil-lined pan; keep hot in the oven. Drain off all but about two tablespoons of the cooking fat, stir in two tablespoons of flour until smooth and add rich milk or cream, scraping all of the browned pieces in the skillet. Simmer for a few minutes to make the gravy smooth and of proper consistency. Serve with fluffy, rich mashed potatoes.

Either a good red wine or a full-bodied white complements fried chicken. We have liked Côte de Beaune wines such as Pommard; regional Bordeaux, for example, a

175

mature Pauillac or St.-Emilion; or a good white Burgundy. Similar California wines may also be served. You may find the reds preferable.

Chicken Sauté with Shallots and Herbs

CHICKEN SAUTÉ WITH SHALLOTS AND HERBS

2	3-lb. fryers or chicken pieces to serve 6
1 1/2	cups dry red wine
1 1/3	cup chopped shallots
2/3	stick butter
3	teasp. minced parsley
1	teasp. chopped fresh tarragon or 2/3 teasp. dried tarragon
1 1/2	teasp. chervil
1 1/2	teasp. salt
	freshly ground black pepper

Sprinkle the chicken pieces with salt. Melt the butter in an iron skillet and brown the chicken pieces on all sides. Make an empty space in center of the pan and put in the shallots and herbs. Turn fire down and cook gently for five minutes or so, until the shallots are soft but not brown. Add the wine, cover and let simmer for half hour or so until the chicken is done. Remove chicken to hot serving dish and skim fat from pan. Boil down the contents until only a few tablespoons are left. Pour over chicken and serve at once.

Steamed rice with freshly ground black pepper and lots of butter seems to us the only possible accompaniment to this dish, although, obviously, this is not a matter of statute.

We like red Burgundy with this dish or sometimes, to vary the flavor, a good Bordeaux, or one of the better California reds.

Chicken Sauté with Tarragon

CHICKEN SAUTÉ WITH TARRAGON

2	fryers or chicken pieces to serve 6
1	cup flour
1/2	stick butter
1/4	cup olive oil
2	tablesp. fresh tarragon or 3 teasp. dried tarragon
1 1/2	teasp. salt
1	cup dry white wine
	freshly ground black pepper

This method of preparing a frying chicken combines the best of southern frying with the more subtle taste of two of the world's most agreeable herbs—tarragon and freshly ground black pepper.

Season the flour with the salt. Shake the chicken pieces in the bag without moistening in milk. Heat the butter and oil in an iron skillet and brown all the chicken pieces. While you are doing this, steep the tarragon in a little of the wine. After all of the chicken is nicely browned, add the wine with tarragon and then the rest of the wine, cover and simmer until tender—another twenty to twenty-five minutes. Skim off some of the fat, concentrate the pan juices by boiling and pour over the chicken pieces. At the table, grind black pepper over the chicken.

Serve a wine similar to that you used to prepare the dish, but better if possible.

Deviled Chicken

Mix all ingredients thoroughly and then marinate the chicken pieces in the mixture for several hours, turning occasionally so that every part of the chicken is marinated.

Line a shallow roasting pan with foil and place the pieces of chicken in it, skin side down. Cook thirty minutes in the oven at 350 degrees, basting frequently with the marinade. Turn the pieces over; cook for another thirty minutes; continue basting.

Because of the high flavor of mustard, ginger, and hot pepper, this dish goes best with a red wine. The flavor of the chicken is not subtle. Therefore, it would be foolish to use one of your good Burgundies or Clarets with it. An inexpensive young Beaujolais or California Gamay or Pinot Noir fits the bill exactly.

DEVILED CHICKEN

	chicken pieces for 6, or 3 broilers split in two
2/3	cup soy sauce
1/2	cup Dijon grey mustard
3	tablesp. olive oil
4 - 5	good dashes tabasco sauce
1	teasp. dried thyme
1/2	teasp. ginger
1/4	teasp. freshly ground black pepper

Chicken with Lemon

Reserve two tablespoons of the olive oil. Crush garlic with salt, blend in the rest of the herbs and onion. Add the oil and lemon juice, shake vigorously and let stand overnight.

Brown the chicken pieces in a mixture of butter and the reserved olive oil, turning frequently. When the pieces are browned, transfer to a casserole, discard the cooking fat, pour the mixture of lemon juice, oil and herbs over the chicken and bake at 350 degrees for one hour.

A dry white wine, not too elegant, may be drunk with chicken prepared in this manner instead of the red which is more often suitable for chicken.

CHICKEN WITH LEMON

2	fryers or chicken pieces to serve 6
1/2	cup fresh olive oil
1/2	cup lemon juice
3	tablesp. chopped onion
2	tablesp. butter
1	teasp. salt
1/2	teasp. dried thyme
1/2	teasp. dried marjoram
1/2	teasp. freshly ground black pepper

Chicken in Champagne

Rub the chicken inside and out with salt and freshly ground black pepper together with the tarragon. Roast in a 450 degree oven a half hour or until the breasts are browned, basting frequently with the butter. Reduce heat to 350 degrees and roast until done, as determined by easy movement of the first joint. Remove fowl and keep warm.

Clean and slice the mushrooms. Pour part of the drippings from the roasting pan and add the mushrooms, sautéing for five minutes. Add champagne, or a dry white wine, scraping all the browned particles. Dissolve the curry

CHICKEN IN CHAMPAGNE

1	large or 2 small roasting chickens
5	oz. champagne
1/2	lb. small mushrooms
2	oz. butter
1	pt. whipping cream
2	oz. cognac
1/2	teasp. tarragon
1/2	teasp. curry powder
	salt
	pepper

powder (what is desired is just a delicate hint of flavor so do not use more than one-half of a teaspoon), mix with the pint of cream and add to the roasting pan. Simmer until the sauce thickens; correct seasoning if necessary.

Either carve the birds in the kitchen and pour the sauce over them or carve at the table. Place the sauce in a heated sauce dish on the table. The latter is perhaps a little more elegant, but unless the man of the house is a skilled carver, you will detract from the dish by allowing it to cool.

Serve with steamed rice and lots of freshly ground pepper and melted butter.

Your best Montrachet or Meursault or a rich, slightly sweet Spätlese or Auslese from the Rheingau would be ideal here.

Coq au Vin

Originally, this was a method of cooking old roosters to make them palatable. However, in urban markets, it is difficult to find an old rooster; one is lucky to find a stewing hen. At least in Southern California, the markets offer chiefly young chickens weighing two and one-half to five and one-half pounds. This is just as well. Coq au Vin is a palatable dish and making it with tender, young chickens can only make it more so. Besides, it shortens the cooking time—no small consideration in our culture, where time is often short.

Fry the bacon in a casserole until it is light brown. Remove the bacon, and in the fat, brown the chicken on all sides. Reduce heat, season the chicken with salt and pepper, return bacon to casserole and cook for several minutes, turning the chicken pieces occasionally. Douse with the cognac and ignite, shaking the vessel so that the burning liquid comes into contact with all of the meat. Add the wine and enough stock to cover all of the chicken, together with the garlic and herbs. Simmer for twenty to thirty minutes until the chicken is tender.

Meanwhile, sauté the mushrooms in part of the butter. Remove, and cook the onions in the same fat, adding a little more if needed. Allow the onions to brown only slightly. Return the chicken pieces to the casserole; continue simmering until the chicken is done. Remove it to

COQ AU VIN

2	roasting chickens, quartered
8	oz. bacon, cut in strips of 1/4 by 1 inch
1/2	lb. mushrooms
1/3	lb. small onions
1/2	bottle young Beaujolais (any full-bodied red wine will do, but poor wine will make the dish poor)
1/2	cup cognac
4	tablesp. flour
1	stick butter
2	cups brown chicken stock or condensed canned bouillon
	salt
	freshly ground pepper
2	cloves garlic
1/2	teasp. thyme
2	bay leaves

a hot plate and keep it warm. Mix the flour and the rest of the butter thoroughly (beurre manié) and beat it into the cooking liquid.

Return the chicken to the cooking liquid, add the mushrooms and onions, heat to boiling and serve immediately from the casserole.

This dish, even when the wine used in cooking is a Beaujolais, merits a good Burgundy, such as a Pommard, or a Charmes-Chambertin, if possible.

Chicken Cacciatore

Wash chicken and pat dry. Heat oil and butter in a casserole and brown chicken on all sides. Remove chicken pieces as they brown and set aside.

Add onion and garlic to the casserole and cook until onion is soft and beginning to brown. Add tomatoes, salt and other seasonings. Simmer uncovered until sauce begins to thicken—twenty to thirty minutes. Now add the wine and return chicken to the casserole. Simmer, covered, until chicken is tender—about forty to fifty minutes. Serve with some of the sauce over the chicken; pass the rest in a heated sauceboat.

A good young Beaujolais, a Zinfandel from California or, if you want to be consistently Italian, a bottle of Barbera or Bardolino will go well, along with crusty bread and a green salad with garlic in the dressing.

Chicken in Cream à l'Indienne

Melt butter in an iron skillet and add oil. Heat, but do not let it smoke. Brown the chicken pieces, getting them evenly and quite deeply browned. In another pan cook the onion, sliced very thinly, and the shallots until the onion is glazed. Scrape into the skillet with the chicken, season with salt and pepper and pour into the skillet a cup of cognac or other good brandy. Dissolve a teaspoon of curry powder in a little water and add to the mixture as it begins to simmer. The intention here is to achieve a delicate flavor.

Cover the pan and let simmer gently until the chicken is tender. When it is almost done, add a full cup or more of thick cream, scraping all of the brown scraps from the pan. Lower the heat and let cook until the combined

CHICKEN CACCIATORE

3	broiler-fryers, cut up, or chicken pieces to serve 6
3	tablesp. olive oil
2	tablesp. butter
1	large or 2 small onions
1	large can tomatoes (preferably Italian)
1/2	cup red wine
1	clove crushed garlic
2	tablesp. chopped parsley
1	teasp. dried sweet basil
1 1/2	teasp. salt
	freshly ground black pepper

CHICKEN IN CREAM À L'INDIENNE

2	broiler-fryers cut up or chicken pieces to serve 6
1	oz. salad oil
4	tablesp. clarified butter
1/2	onion, thinly sliced
6	shallots
1	cup cognac
1	teasp. curry powder
1	cup (or more) whipping cream
	salt
	freshly ground black pepper 179

chicken juice-brandy-cream sauce has begun to thicken and get a little gummy. Serve immediately. Add a little more cream to the pan and cook down if necessary in order to have a tablespoon or more of sauce to garnish each serving.

Chicken cooked in this fashion merits a Meursault or Montrachet, or a château-bottled white Graves. Steamed rice, garnished with chopped parsley and gleaming with lots of melted butter is a worthy accompaniment. (You can fast the next day to make up for this elegant dish and the fine wine.)

Suprême of Chicken with Brandy

SUPRÊME OF CHICKEN WITH BRANDY

4   suprêmes
1   stick butter
1/2 cup Madeira (Sercial)
1/2 cup cognac
     salt
     freshly ground black pepper

French cooks refer to the boned, skinless breast of the chicken as suprêmes. If the first joint of the wing is left attached to the breast half, the suprême becomes a côte-lette. Frequently, breast of chicken is presented to the diner dry and hard. This is a result of overcooking. Always cook this part of the chicken with very gentle heat and be careful not to overcook it.

Here are two recipes using the suprêmes, and one which calls for the cutlet.

Clarify the butter by melting in a saucepan. You will find that you have a golden colored oil floating on top of some watery material containing white particles. Pour off the golden oil. The water and the white material are the ten percent of butter that is milk and that burns easily. Pour the clarified butter into an iron skillet and sauté the salted and peppered breasts until they are golden, turning from time to time and being careful not to let the heat get too high. Pour the cognac over the chicken and ignite it, shaking the pan to be sure that all of the meat is in contact with the brandy. When the flame extinguishes itself, cook for five minutes over low heat and remove the chicken to a heated serving platter. Add the Madeira to the pan and scrape up all the brown particles. Let the sauce boil a little until its volume is reduced by one-third and pour over the chicken. Serve at once.

This dish is too delicate for a red wine. It calls for a full-bodied white Burgundy, such as a Meursault; a white Hermitage from the Rhône is also good with it, as is a good rich Spätlese from the Rhine. An excellent California Chardonnay will also do it justice.

Suprême of Chicken à la Frances

Clean and sauté the mushrooms in one-third of the butter, leaving them whole. Cook the artichoke bottoms in chicken broth unless you are using canned ones.

Clarify the rest of the butter and gently sauté the suprêmes in a heavy skillet until they are golden. Pour cognac over the chicken but do not ignite it. Add sherry and shake the pan. Simmer, then add the sautéed mushrooms and the artichoke bottoms and continue cooking gently.

When the chicken is tender, remove it, together with the artichokes and mushrooms, to a covered pyrex dish and keep hot in a low oven. Add one-half pint or less of whipping cream to the pan juices, scrape the brown particles and let thicken. Remove from fire. Beat two egg yolks in a little of the thin cream and add some of the hot sauce from the pan, beating constantly. Then add the egg yolk mixture to the pan and heat gently, adjusting the thickness of the sauce by adding more thin cream if necessary. Warning! Sauce will curdle if it overheats.

Arrange one suprême and one large or two small artichoke bottoms on each heated plate. Put four mushrooms on the large artichoke bottom or two on each of the two small ones, stir half a teaspoon of chopped chives into the sauce, adjust the seasoning with salt and a grind of pepper, and spoon over the chicken. Garnish with parsley sprigs or watercress and serve at once.

This preparation merits a bottle of your best white Burgundy, a fine Auslese or Spätlese from the Rhine or Mosel; however, it is excellent with lesser wines.

SUPRÊME OF CHICKEN À LA FRANCES

6	suprêmes
2	oz. butter
6	large or 12 small artichoke bottoms
24	button mushrooms
2	tablesp. cognac
1/2	cup medium-dry sherry
1/2	pt. whipping cream
1/2	pt. (or less) half and half
2	egg yolks
	salt
	pepper
	chopped chives

Chicken Kiev

Classically, this dish consists of chicken cutlets (one-half of the breast of a chicken with the first joint of the wing still attached). The meat is pounded thin and rolled around cold butter, then dipped in bread crumbs and deep fried. I have not found the original dish especially interesting; but with slight modifications, it becomes very good indeed.

Pound the chicken cutlets between sheets of waxed paper with a cleaver or mallet until they are thin. Season

181

CHICKEN KIEV

6	chicken cutlets
2/3	stick of butter
3	tablesp. blanched almonds finely ground
	flour
1	tablesp. chopped chives
2	eggs, slightly beaten
1	cup fine bread crumbs
1/4	teasp. dried tarragon
	salt
	freshly gound black pepper
	freshly grated nutmeg
	oil for frying

the thinned-out cutlets with salt, dried tarragon and a light grating of nutmeg. Then sprinkle evenly over them the almonds and chives.

Cut the butter into six equal-size strips and place one in the center of each cutlet. Bring the two sides of each cutlet together so that they overlap and roll so that the wing bone protrudes from one side.

Dredge in flour, dip in beaten egg, and roll in bread crumbs. Put the rolled-up cutlets in the refrigerator for a time. It is a good idea to do this part of the preparation in the morning so that the rolled cutlets may refrigerate for several hours.

Heat fat until just below the smoking point; fry the cutlets preferably in a basket to avoid excessive handling, until they are well browned. Drain on paper towels. Keep the fried cutlets hot in the oven. Serve with pepper in a pepper mill at the table.

Parsleyed new potatoes garnish this dish very well. A luscious Spätlese or Auslese from the Mosel or Rhine, or a good red Bordeaux match this dish well.

Gallina Mexicana (Mexican Chicken)

A representative example of authentic Mexican cookery, with little resemblance to the greasy, overspiced dishes one encounters along the border.

Clean bird thoroughly and pat dry. Mix the cooked rice, almonds, onion, tomato purée, herbs and salt, together with the slightly beaten egg. Stuff the fowl with this mixture rather loosely because the stuffing will expand as it cooks. Sew the cavity and place the fowl in a kettle of boiling water. Simmer until it is tender. This will require one and one-half to two hours. Remove from the pot, drain carefully. Rub the surface of the fowl with butter, flour, salt and, if you like, freshly ground pepper. Place breast up in a shallow pan in a 400 degree oven until the skin browns nicely, basting occasionally with the liquid from the pot in which the chicken has been boiled. The browning will require about thirty minutes.

We do not serve any vegetables with the fowl cooked in this way. The dressing appears to be all the accompaniment needed. The taste is very good but not at all sophisticated, so that an inexpensive Beaujolais *ordinaire* or a California Zinfandel or Mountain Red wine is a suitable and enjoyable drink with this dish.

GALLINA MEXICANA
(Mexican Chicken)

1	large hen
1	cup cooked rice
1/2	cup tomato purée
1/2	cup minced onion
1/4	cup blanched almonds
1	egg
2	tablesp. flour
2	tablesp. butter
1/2	teasp. oregano
1	teasp. minced parsley
	salt

Squab Chicken with Prosciutto

Do you remember when these youngest of marketable chickens were first seen in the stores and were sold under the name of "Cornish Game Hens"? They actually are routinely reared commercial chickens sold at two months of age. However, putting aside the business about a special breed of "game hen," these little birds are succulent and elegant, just right for one serving. They are tender and juicy although, like veal, they lack a little in flavor.

To make the dressing, sauté a tablespoon of chopped onion and one chopped shallot in three tablespoons of butter until the onion is soft and translucent. Add the ground veal, cooked rice, and finely minced parsley. Beat the eggs and mix all these ingredients thoroughly, adding the marjoram, tarragon, salt to taste, and a good grind of black pepper. Stuff six squab chickens; sew cavities; truss the little birds and wrap each in a slice of prosciutto. Heat three tablespoons of butter in a casserole or the Dutch oven and brown the prosciutto and birds on all sides. Add two ounces of warmed cognac and set ablaze. When the brandy has burned itself out, add one cup of good medium-dry Madeira, cover and braise gently for one-half hour.

Serve with glazed onions, whole stuffed mushroom caps, or small new potatoes.

For economy's sake, I have tried making this dish with ordinary American ham, but the lack of flavor does not warrant the economy.

A good Médoc, such as Château Pontet Canet or Château Haut Batailley, or a rather light Côte de Beaune such as a Volnay is preferable to any white wine with squab chicken prepared in this way.

Squab Chicken with Cheese and Rice

You will get very different flavors with this recipe.

Sauté onion and garlic until onion is soft and golden. Add rice and continue to sauté, stirring rice until it is well coated with butter and yellow in color. Add chicken stock and saffron; simmer, covered, until the liquid is absorbed. Mix cottage cheese, tomato, olives and herbs with the cooked rice.

Salt and pepper, inside and out, six squab chickens and stuff loosely with the cheese-rice mixture, sewing the cavities and trussing the birds. You will have surplus rice-

SQUAB CHICKEN WITH PROSCIUTTO

6	squab chickens
1	cup ground veal
1	cup cooked rice
1/2	cup minced parsley
2	eggs
6	large (or 12 small) slices prosciutto
6	tablesp. butter
2	oz. cognac
1	cup Madeira
1/2	teasp. dried marjoram
1/2	teasp. dried tarragon
	salt
	pepper

183

SQUAB CHICKEN WITH CHEESE AND RICE

6	squab chickens
1	medium onion, chopped
1	clove garlic
2	tablesp. butter
2	cups uncooked long-grain rice
4	cups chicken stock
	(or canned broth)
1	scant teasp. saffron
1	lb. small curd cottage cheese
1	large tomato, peeled
	and chopped
1/2	cup ripe pitted olives, sliced
1/4	cup grated Parmesan cheese
6	strips bacon
1/2	teasp. thyme

cheese mixture which may be cooked in the oven in a casserole.

Place a slice of bacon over the breast of each chicken and set, breast upright, in a shallow baking pan. Brown the birds in a 450 degree oven for thirty minutes; reduce heat to 350 degrees and continue roasting until the birds are done—about one-half hour.

Serve with portions of the extra cheese-rice mixture and garnish with parsley.

The presence of the cheese makes a red wine even more appropriate with fowl prepared in this manner than in the foregoing recipe. However, a *light* red wine is indicated, such as one from the Médoc in France, not a dark, rich Burgundy or a Pomerol.

TURKEY

Roast Turkey

I include a recipe for roasting turkey only reluctantly; and because the force of tradition in America seems to dictate that we eat this rather coarse and somewhat strongly flavored bird at least twice a year, at Thanksgiving and at Christmas. Sometimes, when one is unlucky, he will also be confronted with one of these enormous creatures on New Year's Day.

For your next holiday dinner, I urge you to vary your menu and serve one of the really good roasts of beef which I shall detail in the following chapter; or try pheasant or guinea fowl if you feel that chicken is too pedestrian for you. Although we frequently enjoy chicken prepared by all of the recipes I have described in this chapter, the general feeling at our table is that no bird—or no way of cooking a fowl—is as delicious as an expertly roasted chicken seasoned with a bit of tarragon and basted frequently and copiously with butter. But if you feel that Christmas is not Christmas without a turkey, here is one of the best ways to prepare one of the biggest of all of our edible birds.

Clean the bird carefully inside and out. Before stuffing, rub inside with a mixture of softened butter, salt and several tablespoons of cognac. Stuff rather loosely with one of the stuffings given, sew cavities and truss the bird by tying legs closely together to the tail and the wings closely to sides across back, or by holding them closely to the body with a large skewer. Rub the skin generously with butter. Cover breast with bacon slices and set on a rack in a roasting pan, breast side up.

Place in an oven at 425 degrees for thirty minutes, then reduce heat to 375. Test doneness by observing the color of juice running from a prick in a drumstick; the bird is done when the juice runs a clear yellow. It will require about twenty minutes per pound. Remove the bacon slices; turn heat to 400 degrees for a little while at the end to brown the breast.

Baste frequently with a mixture of butter and dry red wine.

Turn the heat to 200 degrees and place the turkey on a platter in the oven. Pour off most of the fat from the roasting pan, add one cup of strong chicken stock or canned condensed chicken broth, one-half cup each of red wine and cognac to the pan. Stir into the liquid, two tablespoons of flour and cook until smooth and of the proper thickness, scraping all of the brown particles from the pan. Strain the gravy into a heated sauceboat and pass at the table.

Chestnut Dressing

Cut open the shells of two pounds of chestnuts, or less good, but more convenient, use canned chestnuts and heat in hot fat. Peel and cook until soft in strong chicken stock. two cups of bread crumbs.

Cook a large onion in butter until soft and golden; add a few chopped shallots. Slice thinly, two ounces of truffles and add to the onion. Next, add one teaspoon each of dried thyme and dried tarragon, together with salt and freshly ground black pepper to taste. Mix all with the chopped sausage and chestnuts; moisten with one-half cup each of cognac and Madeira. Stuff both upper and lower body cavities loosely with this mixture just before roasting.

Onion and Sage Dressing

Using a larger proportion of cornbread to ordinary bread helps to make this dressing lighter than an all-bread dressing.

Cook onion and celery in butter until the onion is soft and golden. Mix all the ingredients and correct season-

CHESTNUT DRESSING

2	lbs. chestnuts
	chicken stock
1	large onion
2 - 3	chopped shallots
2	oz. truffles
1	teasp. dried thyme
1	teasp. dried tarragon
	freshly ground black pepper
2	cups pork sausage
2	cups bread crumbs
1/2	cup cognac
1/2	cup Madeira

185

ONION AND SAGE DRESSING

6	cups crumbled cornbread
4	cups stale bread crumbs
1	cup finely chopped celery
1/2	cup finely chopped onion
1	stick butter
1/2	cup red or white wine
1 1/2	teasp. sage
1 1/2	teasp. salt
1/2	teasp. dried marjoram
1/2	teasp. dried thyme
	freshly ground black pepper

ROAST DUCKLING WITH CHESTNUT STUFFING

2	"Long Island" ducklings
3/4	lb. ground veal
1/2	lb. ground pork
1 1/2	lbs. French chestnut puree (large can)
3/4	cup chicken stock or canned chicken broth
1	large or 2 small onions
3	tablesp. chopped parsley
4	tablesp. Madeira wine
1/2	cup dry red wine
	salt
	freshly ground black pepper

ing to taste. You might prefer more sage than the recipe calls for. If the dressing seems too dry, add a little cognac or more wine.

Turkey has always seemed to me to be a case in point regarding the old fallacy of "red wine with meat, white wine with fowl." The flavor of this bird is definitely full and rich enough not only to support, but demand a rather full-bodied red wine. I would serve it with a good red Hermitage or other Rhône, a medium-quality Burgundy, or the best California Pinot Noir.

DUCK

Roast Duckling

The usual duck available on the American market is a domestically reared variety, the white Pekin. Not all "Long Island Ducklings" appearing on restaurant menus were hatched on that populous island; nor can I think of any reason why they should have been. What is necessary to know is that domestic ducks found in the United States are extremely fat. No larding is necessary in their cooking; on the contrary, it is always advisable first to pull out all the loose fat one finds about the openings in the body cavity and then to prick the skin on the back, the sides of the breast and the legs in order that surplus fat may drain away during the cooking. Only true ducklings—that is to say, birds six months old or younger— should be roasted. There is much less meat on a duck than on a chicken of the same size; for six persons, it is advisable to have two ducklings.

Thaw the ducks, preferably in the refrigerator, if it is frozen. Clean and dry cavities and season inside and out with freshly ground black pepper and salt. Put the ground meats, chestnut purée, onion and parsley through the finest blade of the meat chopper. Add the Madeira, the chicken broth, and salt to taste. Stuff the ducks loosely and sew cavities. Truss the birds neatly and prick skin with fork at one inch intervals along the back, lower breast, and legs. Brown for one-half hour or so in a 450 degree oven and then reduce heat to 350 degrees. Cook until juice from a prick with a fork runs slightly pinkish (about twenty minutes per pound).

Remove to a heated serving platter, pour most of the fat out of the roasting pan and add one-half cup of dry red wine. Swirl in a tablespoon of butter. Let sauce boil and pour over duck.

A good roast duckling rates a rich, heavy Burgundy, such as a Chambertin; or, if you prefer a Bordeaux wine, select a good Pomerol or one of the full-bodied California reds.

Duckling Braised with Olives

Clean a duckling; season with salt and pepper; put an onion and a handful of fresh celery leaves in the body cavity. Roast at 450 degrees, breast side up, until it is well browned, about thirty minutes. Remove duckling to hot plate, pour off all the fat possible from the roasting pan and add one cup each of chicken stock and good, dry red wine, first stirring a tablespoon of flour into the hot pan juices. Cook until sauce is smooth but not too thick and add a *bouquet garni* of one stick of celery one carrot, one bay leaf and 1/2 teaspoon each of dried thyme and dried tarragon. Return duck to pan and braise it, covered, until it is tender (about twenty minutes total cooking to the pound). Desalt 24 pitted green olives by heating them for five minutes in water. Drain and add to the sauce.

Carve and pour sauce, including olives, over the sliced duck. If the bird is to be carved at table, have platter, sauceboat, and duckling extra hot so that the sliced portions will arrive before the diner still hot. Domestic duckling is fat enough that it becomes unappetizing when even slightly cooled.

A full-bodied Château-Neuf-du-Pape or other Rhône wine, a medium-quality, rather heavy Burgundy or California wine will prove satisfying with a duckling presented in this manner.

Use Rhône Wine with Braised Duckling

Roast Domestic Mallard Duckling

The finest ducks that I have ever eaten in my life were a series of young domestic mallards reared by a patient and sold to me for several seasons.

We cleaned and dried the body cavities, salted them and put into each cavity one quartered onion and a few

187

celery leaves. The ducklings were placed upright on a rack in a shallow pan and browned in the oven at 450 degrees for one-half hour and then cooked another one-half hour at 350 degrees without pricking the skin and with no seasoning other than a little more salt.

These birds lacked the gaminess of their wild progenitors. Their tenderness and sweetness resulted from their having been grain fed and having never flown.

If you are fortunate enough to find such birds, try to pour as a libation to them a Chambertin or Clos Vougeot.

Wild Duck

There is a widespread convention—superstition, one could almost say—that wild ducks should be cooked for fifteen minutes in an extremely hot oven and then promptly eaten. I have been presented with numbers of wild ducks by grateful patients and I have tried on many occasions to cook them in this manner. My testimony is that a duck carcass doesn't even get warmed through in that period of time and that it is not cooked at all. Further, although I have heard numerous hunters tell of cooking and eating ducks in such a fashion, I have never actually seen one doing it. If you have a husband or friend who boasts that he likes wild duck roasted for fifteen minutes in a hot oven, my earnest counsel is to have nothing to do with the proceedings; tell the mighty hunter that you will furnish the roasting pan and the oven, but that he will have to do the cooking—and the eating—and otherwise assume all responsibility for his game.

I have found wild ducks edible—and even moderately palatable—when they are treated in one of the following ways.

Clean and dry the carcass and season with salt and pepper. Put a quartered onion and some cup-up celery and celery leaves inside the body cavity. Rub the outside of the carcass with a mixture of salt and softened butter and have quite a lot more butter available for basting. Cover the breasts with two slices of bacon or salt pork. Cook for thirty minutes at 450 degrees, reduce heat to 350 degrees and cook until juice from a prick runs nearly yellow. Baste frequently, first with the butter and then with the pan juices. During the last twenty minutes, remove bacon and let breast brown.

The second way to make this game palatable is to make a marinade of 1/2 cup cooking oil, a finely chopped onion, a clove of garlic, and 1/2 teaspoon each of dried thyme, tarragon and marjoram, with a bottle of inexpensive red wine. I usually use a young Côte du Rhône. Marinate the carcass overnight, turning occasionally. Remove from the marinade, dry, season and roast for one-half hour in a hot oven to brown. Put in a casserole with a tight lid and pour in the rest of the marinade. Braise slowly until thoroughly tender. Strain and thicken the liquid with butter and flour. Boil the sauce until it is smooth and thick enough to coat a spoon. Serve over slices of the duck.

In my opinion, an inexpensive young Beaujolais or California red wine is quite adequate for wild duck.

Roast Goose

In the Northwest, where winter temperatures frequently fell to thirty degrees below zero and summer heat attained ninety-eight to one hundred degrees, the climate was much too harsh for growing turkeys. Further, most of the ranchers in our section were German immigrants, or first-generation descendants of such immigrants. Consequently, I grew up thinking of roast goose rather than turkey as the festive bird for holiday eating. For many years, I did not eat roast goose because the size of the bird was too great for a family of two or three persons. Of late years, however, poultry producers have developed the so-called "junior goose," a bird weighing between six and eight pounds. Thus, this delectable main dish again becomes available to those with small families and small ovens.

You may stuff goose with any stuffing suitable for chicken or turkey, or you may make a sweet stuffing using apples or prunes or both. Because I disapprove of sweets with meat, I give no such recipes. They are easily available in standard cookbooks.

Because the goose is so extremely fat, I prefer not to stuff it, but merely rub the inside of the body cavity with salt, freshly ground pepper and dried tarragon, and then place into the cavity a whole onion quartered and a handful of celery leaves. Be sure to prick the skin along the back, the lower part of the breast, and the drumsticks, as with domestic ducks, in order to allow as much fat to escape during the cooking as possible.

German Immigrants
Festive Bird

189

I prefer the high temperature method for roasting goose because of the high fat content. Place the bird, breast up, on a rack well above the bottom of a roasting pan and put it in a 450 degree oven. After thirty minutes, turn the heat down to 425 degrees. Begin basting with red wine and a little butter. As fat appears in the bottom of the roasting pan, siphon it off with a baster and continue basting with the wine mixture.

Serve Goose Without Gravy

Because of the excessive amount of fat, I think goose is better without gravy. For the same reason, it should be served as hot as possible. Either a full-bodied red, such as a good Rhône, or a semisweet Spätlese from the Mosel or the Rhine will increase your enjoyment of a good roast goose.

SQUAB

A squab taken at the proper time can be among the most delectable of eatables. The proper time is when the young bird has not quite fully developed all of his adult feathers, but still has many pin feathers and much baby down. Such a bird has never flown; if his parents are well fed with good grain, he will be fat and extremely tender.

One of the sadder facts of life, however, is that commercially obtainable squabs are seldom of this age or quality. I suppose that it is because growers get paid by the pound and wish to maximize their profits; but most squabs from the market weigh well over a pound, are fully feathered, and are just plain tough.

If you are lucky enough to find a supply of the first kind, all you need to do is to clean them, wipe the carcasses dry inside and out, apply judicious amounts of salt and pepper to both the in and outsides of the birds and roast them in a hot oven until they are nicely browned and the little drumsticks move freely. Baste once or twice during the cooking.

Such a bird is worth opening a bottle of your best Chambertin, Clos de Vougheot or other fine Burgundy, but a lesser wine will do.

If you feel you want squab but can only find the common market variety, somewhat too old, try the following method.

Make a marinade with one-half of an onion, a shallot, a stalk of celery and 1/2 cup cooking oil added to one-half of a bottle of inexpensive Beaujolais or California red wine. Add a *bouquet garni* of one bay leaf and 1/2 teaspoon each of dried marjoram and tarragon. Let the birds lie overnight in the marinade. To cook, take them out of the marinade, dry well, tie a couple of strips of bacon across the breasts and brown the birds all over in a casserole in a couple of tablespoons of butter. When they are brown, add enough marinade to cover one-third of the carcasses, cover tightly and braise in a slow oven for at least one hour, until they are (if that is possible) fork tender.

Actually, even rather tough "squabs" yield pretty well to this treatment and make a palatable pièce de résistance (although if you do not braise them long enough, there will be more resistance than you will like).

Drink a modest red wine (generally the same wine you use in making the marinade) with squabs prepared in this manner.

PHEASANT

Roast Pheasant

A good deal of experimenting with this species of fowl, obtained both as gifts from my brother and other hunting friends, as shot wild specimen and domestically reared on game farms, has convinced me that Escoffier was absolutely right when he said that pheasant served fresh was dry and, he might have added, not especially interesting meat. He asserts that hanging for at least three days is necessary; that the bird must be a little "high" to make it tender and to bring out the full delicacy of its flavor. Each person will have to judge the question for himself. However you decide, here is a recipe which will insure maximum succulence and minimum dryness.

Clean the bird carefully and wipe body cavity dry. Rub inside with salt and freshly ground pepper and moisten with cognac. Then stuff either with freshly ground pork fat, as Escoffier recommends, or more conveniently, with sweet butter in which you put two or three sliced truffles. Cover surface of the body with slices of bacon and roast in a 350 degree oven for about forty-five minutes to an hour—until the thigh moves easily and the juice from a fork hole is not pink. Remove bacon and turn oven heat up to brown the bird.

When a pheasant is young and well cooked, it merits wild rice as its accompaniment. When you can, choose one of your better bottles of château-bottled Bordeaux, such as a 1952 Château Margaux or Château LaTour to serve with pheasant.

ROAST PARTRIDGE OR GROUSE

Clean the birds well and pat the cavities dry. Rub the interiors with salt, freshly ground black pepper, and a generous pinch of dried tarragon. Add a teaspoon or two of butter. Rub outside of bird well with butter; wrap in two slices of bacon, truss neatly. Set, breasts up, on a rack in an oven preheated to 400 degrees and baste frequently, using at first butter and then the pan drippings. The birds are done when the little drumsticks move freely and the juice runs clear from a prick, usually forty to fifty minutes. Remove bacon to allow breasts to brown.

Cooking Livers Separately
Serve on croutons made by slicing white bread, removing crusts and frying in butter. Alternately, you can be a little more elaborate and cook the livers of your little birds gently in a little butter and then grind them with the finest blade of your food chopper. Fry the croutons as above, spread with the liver and place under broiler for a couple of minutes just before taking the birds out of the oven.

Pour most of the fat (which will be chiefly butter and bacon grease) off and discard. Add a couple of ounces of dry red wine and one ounce of cognac to the remaining pan juices and heat to boiling, scraping all of the browned particles. Stir in a tablespoon of butter as the sauce boils and serve in a heated sauceboat.

Sautéed whole mushroom caps and, if the game is tender, wild rice will complement the roast partridges or grouse with grace.

If the birds appear old and not very tender, content yourself with an inexpensive Beaujolais or California Gamay; if they are young and fat, they will merit one of your better Burgundies or a good, aged, regional Bordeaux.

GUINEA FOWL

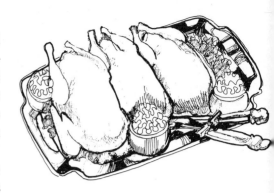

This handsome, dark-meated fowl is found as wild game only in South America, chiefly in Brazil. Those available in American and French markets are reared on game farms. In France, the guinea fowl is known as a *pintade* and is quite popular. Even the domestically reared birds are tough enough that they are usually braised rather than roasted.

Clean the bird and pat the body cavity dry. Rub with salt, freshly ground black pepper and a generous quantity of dried tarragon leaves. Fresh tarragon will be better still, if you can obtain it. Mix the seasonings with a tablespoon of butter before rubbing inside the cavity. Truss the bird; tie a couple of bacon strips across the breast; brown in a heavy casserole or Dutch oven in two tablespoons of butter. Add to the casserole 3/4 cup of strong chicken stock or condensed canned broth and the same amount of dry red wine. Add a *bouquet garni,* of one bay leaf, several fresh celery leaves, a chopped shallot, a teaspoon of chopped parsley or several sprigs of parsley and another 1/2 teaspoon of dried tarragon or a sprig of fresh tarragon. Cover the casserole and cook in a 350 degree oven until the bird is nearly tender. Uncover the casserole, remove the bacon and turn up the oven heat a little so that the breast of the *pintade* will brown nicely.

Remove the *bouquet garni,* skim off most of the fat and boil the liquid in the pan down until there is not more than three-quarters of a cup left. Add an ounce or two of cognac or, if your family likes a faintly sweet taste, the same amount of Grand Marnier liqueur.

Wild rice cooked in chicken stock (or if you want to make the relationship more close, in a stock made by boiling the neck, wing tips and giblets of the guinea fowl in 1 1/2 cups of water with a little onion) is a natural partner for a nicely cooked guinea fowl.

We drank a bottle of Latricière-Chambertin 1959 with our last guinea fowl and did not regret opening such a good wine.

WILD DOVE

Two varieties of the wild dove, the mourning dove and the whitewing, somewhat more rare, abound in the

Southwest and are favorite targets of hunters. After trying many ways of cooking these small, dark-meated birds, we have concluded that a simple braising gives the best result of all.

Clean the birds well, allowing two or three per person. Season them inside and out with salt and freshly ground black pepper, and shake in a bag with flour. Brown them gently in a mixture of butter and cooking oil. When the birds are brown all over, add enough chicken stock to cover half the depth of the birds, cover and simmer gently until tender. This usually requires forty to forty-five minutes. Remove birds to a hot platter, skim off some of the fat and stir in a tablespoon of flour. Cook until smooth and well browned and strain over the birds.

Rice, wild rice, or sautéed mushroom caps are good garnishes for a plate of doves.

A bottle of fresh, young Beaujolais, one of your less expensive Burgundies, or a good California Pinot Noir will be adequate as drink with this game.

QUAIL

These gay little crested birds are found widely over Europe and America and are greatly enjoyed for eating. French cookbooks are full of recipes for cooking them on the spit, wrapped in grape leaves and other quite elaborate ways. None of these more troublesome ways, however, turns out to be any more delectable than quail, hunter's style.

Quail, Hunter's Style

Allow two birds per person. Quail should be field dressed (drawn and skinned) because it is almost impossible to remove all of the down and pin feathers from the carcasses. Each bird should be split up the breast and slightly flattened with a heavy cleaver. Shake in a bag with salt, pepper and flour.

Heat cooking oil one-half to one inch deep in an iron skillet; add three to five cloves of garlic and two bay leaves. Cook until garlic browns, discard it, and cook the quail four minutes on one side and three minutes on the other.

194

Serve on croutons made by removing crusts from halves of thick slices of bread and frying them in butter.

We find a dish of tiny green peas cooked with a lettuce leaf and a little green onion a satisfying accompaniment for quail.

The dish is simple and not at all subtle, although very good. For this reason, we have always been reluctant to pull the cork on a bottle of our better vintages; however, a good Beaujolais, California Pinot Noir or Gamay fills the bill nicely.

BEEF

The assertion of nutritionists that the cheaper cuts of meat and the lower grades of beef are just as nutritious as the more uncommon and, therefore, more expensive cuts is perfectly true. However, for certain uses, enjoyment is enhanced if we can afford the best portions of the highest grade meat. This is, I think, especially true with beef.

Steaks cut from well-aged prime beef need no sauces. Anything which conceals their natural flavor is an intrusion. The same thing is true for a fine standing rib roast or one made of a well-hung sirloin strip. But it is a waste of money to buy the best grade of beef and the more expensive cuts where the dish calls for long cooking, for example, by braising or making a stew.

It is also true that while the filet of beef is tender, it is somewhat lacking in flavor. This is why there are so many recipes for cooking this cut, both as steaks and as roasts, in order to add flavor to it.

My guiding principle for the inclusion of recipes are: that you will like the recipes that my family has, that the materials are readily obtainable, and that the recipes do not require more skill than those possessed by a reasonably competent housekeeper. I have also tried to maintain a sensible balance between recipes calling for tender but expensive cuts of beef and those which are, at the same time, more economical and still very good to eat.

Standing Rib Roast

I urge you to buy this cut only in the prime grade of beef. The reason is that when it is properly tender, this meat is most delicious when it is rare and lesser grades often will not become tender enough with minimum cooking.

I also encourage the high temperature method for cooking this roast. It is surprising how little difference in time is required to cook a very large roast as compared to a small one by this method.

Wipe the roast with a damp cloth and rub salt and fresh black pepper into the fleshy parts. Insert a meat thermometer in the thickest part. Set on a rack and put into an oven preheated to 450 degrees for forty-five minutes. For a two-rib roast, this is usually sufficient cooking; for larger roasts, turn off heat and allow the meat to stay in the oven for one hour. Another method, equally satisfactory, is to remove the roast from the oven after the forty-five minutes of high heat and, just before serving, replace it in the oven at 350 degrees for thirty minutes. In any case, the most satisfactory results are obtained by using the meat thermometer. The inside of the roast will be rare when the thermometer reaches 140 degrees, very rare at 120 degrees, and medium at 150 degrees.

No Basting During
Cooking Period

Do not open the oven door during the forty-minutes cooking period. It is not necessary to baste a standing rib. Transfer the roast to a platter which will conserve the juices as it is carved. Cut into thin slices and serve with no other sauce than the roast's own juices. Baked potatoes served with chives (if you like) and lots of butter are a fine accompaniment for a rib roast, as are potatoes roasted in the pan below the rack in which the meat stands.

A good Burgundy—a Pommard, a Charmes-Chambertin, or a good Volnay—or a mature Rhône such as a red Hermitage or the very best California Pinot Noir is our preferred wine with a good roast beef. A good classified château Bordeaux, such as Pontet Canet, a Château Talbot or Château Cantemerle, will also be found delicious, if a trifle more austere than a Burgundy of equal quality. You will note that I recommend for rib roast excellent red wines but not the very best. The reason is that although practically all Americans and English find unadorned beef very much to their taste (and I am one who does) the flavor is not the most subtle and, while it deserves good wine, the fragrance and delicate flavors of the very best wines would be overshadowed by the forthrightness of the meat.

Rolled Rib Roast

Although some housewives like to have their rib roasts cut from the bone and rolled, this practice sacrifices a certain amount of excellence in return for greater convenience, and, therefore, is not recommended. Butchers themselves rarely roll their top quality rib roasts, but reserve this method of presentation for choice or good grades of meat. There are occasions when such a roast will serve your purposes quite well. Use the same high temperature method as described for a standing rib roast.

The rolled roast is especially well adapted to spit roasting over charcoal. If you have a man in your family who likes to "barbecue" and you want beef, the rolled roast is the one to buy. Marinate it overnight in a mixture of olive oil, red wine, chopped onion, garlic and bay leaf, and brush it with the marinade while it is roasting on the spit or grill. A rolled rib roast is too good to paint with the mixture of artificial smoke, sugar and other things that occur in the usual "barbecue sauce." A California Pinot Noir will be more than adequate here.

Rump Roast

Rump or sirloin, of the grade stamped "prime" is about the least expensive piece of meat that one should attempt to roast plain. Allow one-half to three-quarters of a pound of the boneless rump per person. If there is no fat in the roast, have the butcher tie a sheet of suet across the top.

Rub with salt and pepper and insert the meat thermometer into the center of the roast, avoiding any bone. Roast at 450 degrees. Because it is less tender, many persons find they like a rump roast a little more completely cooked than the rib. If you want the interior of the meat to be, at most, medium rare, let the thermometer attain 150 degrees. Do not allow the roast to become hotter than this because the outside portions will be too dry.

Carve a rump roast against the grain in order that each serving will have some of the tender muscles as well as portions of the muscles less tender.

Pour off most of the grease from the roasting pan and stir in two tablespoons of flour. Add water to the pan juices and stir while cooking to incorporate all of the browned particles. A brown gravy should coat a spoon but still pour easily.

Serve with roasted or baked potatoes or glazed onions. One of the lesser Bordeaux or Burgundies, or a California Pinoit Noir will suit this roast admirably.

Sirloin Strip Roast

From this piece of beef, comes those steaks called "New York cut" in the West and "strip steaks" in New York. To our taste, a four to six pound cut of this meat, while expensive, is the most delicious of all roasts. It should be roasted rare. Use the meat thermometer and do not let the temperature rise above 130. It is really better if you stop the cooking when the meat thermometer has attained 120 degrees. Because the cut is not as thick as a standing rib roast, it may not take quite as long to reach the desired temperature so the thermometer should be watched carefully.

This roast, in our opinion, calls for the finest red wine in your cellar—a Chambertin, Richebourg, or Clos Vougeot from Burgundy; or a premier grade Bordeaux such as Château Mouton or Château Lafite Rothschild.

Roast Beef Bourbon

A thick piece of top round steak marinated in a mixture of bourbon whiskey and soy sauce will furnish a roast which is tender and juicy; one with peculiarly excellent flavor without the corresponding disadvantage of toughness.

Marinate the meat at least three hours, preferably four, turning two or three times so that both sides of the meat are soaked equally. Place on a rack in the oven heated to 450 degrees, insert the meat thermometer and roast until temperature reaches 140 degrees. You might like this roast a little more rare and that 120 or 130 degrees on the meat thermometer will be sufficient.

ROAST BEEF BOURBON

4 - 5   lbs. top round, at least four inches thick
1/3   cup bourbon whiskey soy sauce sufficient so that marinade covers one-half the meat
1/2   teasp. dry mustard, dissolved in a little water
1   clove crushed garlic
1   teasp. salt
  a good grind of black pepper

200

Slice thinly and serve on heated plates with roasted or boiled potatoes.

We usually drink a young Beaujolais or an older Rhône with this roast. Both the meat and the wine seem to please our guests very much.

Filet of Beef

The tenderest of all beef is the long, rather thin, muscle cut from the inside of the loin and known as filet, or sometimes as the tenderloin. If all the methods of preparing this tender cut of meat were gathered together, they would fill a large book. As I have said, there are so many ways to prepare the filet because, while it is delightfully tender, it is rather lacking in flavor. The entire filet may be presented in many ways from simple to elaborate, roasted or braised, or it may be cut into steaks. Steaks cut from the center, with the largest diameter and at least three inches thick are the famous Châteaubriands. Steaks from both sides of the center, usually cut about one inch tick, make the filet mignon; those of smaller diameter from the tail end furnish us tournedos; the very tip, with diameters ranging down from two inches to one inch, are the medaillons of beef which one sees on restaurant menus usually served "sauté sec."

We will now deal with several methods of preparing the filet as a roast.

Roast Filet of Beef

Select for six persons, a filet weighing three and one-half to five pounds. Unless your guests are unusually voracious, you will have meat left over. This is good; there is no cold beef quite so good.

A Meal for Six

Because the filet is all lean meat, have the butcher lard it with several strips of fat pork, or tie pieces of blanched fat pork around the roast, or tie over the top a thin layer of suet. Rub with salt and fresh black pepper, insert a meat thermometer and roast in a 450 degree oven on a rack until it reaches the required degree of doneness. Because the mass of the meat is not so great as in a rib roast, you will have good rare meat if you stop the roasting process at 130 degrees instead of letting it cook to 140 degrees. It is a pity to serve this fine meat overcooked, but

201

obviously each family will have to determine by experience at what point to stop the cooking. Caution should be exercised as this meat cooks sooner than one would expect.

Let the roast rest on an ovenproof platter in a 180 to 200 degree oven while you pour one-half cup or so of beef stock or condensed beef bouillon in the roasting pan after pouring off part of the fat. Bring to a boil and reduce the volume to about one-half, stirring with a wooden spoon to incorporate all of the browned particles. Correct the seasoning. Slice enough of the meat thinly for a first serving, arranging the pieces to overlap one another with the last piece overlapping the uncut portion. Pour the sauce over the meat and serve immediately.

Plain roasted filet may be garnished with small roasted potatoes and attractive piles of carrots, peas, cut string beans, boiled onions or other vegetables in contrasting colors. All should be served hot and fresh. If you would like to add a festive touch, tell your family you are serving Filet de Boeuf Bouquetière or Filet Jardinière.

A good, medium-grade Burgundy—Charmes Chambertin, a Beaune Clos de Mouches, a Mercurey, or a mature Rhône—will help make the filet a real feast. If you like the austerity of Bordeaux, choose a Pomerol or St. Emilion rather than the more delicate Médocs.

Roast Filet with Mushrooms and Sherry

Rub the filet with salt and pepper, insert a meat thermometer, and put in a shallow pan in a 450 degree oven. Roast fifteen minutes.

Clean mushrooms and slice them thinly. Melt the butter in a skillet and sauté mushrooms gently until they are done, about five minutes. Spoon the mushrooms over and around the filet and pour over all one cup of a good dry sherry, warmed. A good California sherry may be used, although a real Amontillado, obviously, will be preferable. Reduce oven heat to 375 degrees, baste frequently with the pan juices and cease cooking when the temperature reaches 130 for rare, or 140 for moderately rare. Slice thinly and serve on a heated platter with the mushroom surrounding the meat and the slices of meat overlapping, with the juices spooned over the meat. Provençale baked tomatoes and small roasted potatoes are excellent garnishes. Potatoes Anna is another good accompaniment.

ROAST FILET WITH MUSHROOMS AND SHERRY

4 - 6	lbs. filet, one piece
1	lb. white mushrooms
1	cup dry sherry
1/2	stick butter
	salt
	freshly ground black pepper

Serve with one of the wines discussed in the previous recipe.

Roast Filet with Mushrooms au Madeira

Proceed exactly as in the recipe above, substituting a dry Sercial Madeira for the sherry. I will not say that the dish prepared with Madeira is better, but it is a little richer—to pay for being a little richer, it is also a little sweet. Many persons, of course, like slightly sweet flavors with various meats. Try both ways.

I like tiny peas or buttered carrots better than garlic flavored tomatoes as a garnish for the filet with Madeira.

Also you might find that you will like one of your richer Burgundies with this version.

Beef Wellington

Clarify half the butter and pour into a heavy skillet with the cooking oil, hot, but not smoking. Brown the filet on all sides.

Clean and chop the mushrooms finely. Cook in the rest of the butter. Mix the cooked chopped mushrooms with the liver pâté. Slice the truffle thinly and insert into the browned filet top and bottom at regular intervals. (The more truffles you feel you can afford, the better the dish.)

Roll out the pastry in a size large enough to wrap the filet and about one-quarter inch thick. Place the filet in the middle of the pastry and spread over the sides and top with the mixture of liver pâté, mushrooms and butter. Fold the pastry so that it completely covers the filet, moistening the edges with water and sealing by pinching firmly. Trim off the excess pastry, reroll and use the extra dough to make leaves or other ornamental shapes to place on top of the roll. Brush the top and sides with a slightly beaten egg and place in a 425 degree oven until the pastry is golden brown.

If you are careful to remove the filet from the browning pan as soon as it is brown all over and bake until the crust is nicely browned, the middle will be rare and the edges of the filet only medium well done. If it is too done, try browning the meat more lightly or, if it is too rare for the taste of your family and guests, cook it a little more in the browning skillet.

BEEF WELLINGTON

3 - 4	lbs. beef filet
	pastry dough to enclose filet
4	oz. liver pâté
1	oz. truffles
1/2	stick butter
1	oz. cooking oil
1	egg, slightly beaten
	salt
	freshly ground pepper
1	cup chopped mushrooms

203

We garnish Beef Wellington, cut in fairly thick slices in the kitchen and served on *hot* plates, with tiny fresh vegetables and serve good Burgundy, a mature Rhône, or the very best California Pinot Noir with it.

Filet of Beef Harold

Cut off the thinnest end of the filet and reserve for another use. Make a cut down the center of the filet from the thicker end almost to the other end so in effect, you have a long, thick-walled bag of meat. Slice the truffles thinly. Mix the liver pâté and the almonds, ground as finely as your food chopper will do the job. Moisten this mass with the cognac. If it is not thin enough to go into the pastry bag or a basting syringe, use more brandy.

Fill the incision in the center of the filet with this mixture, pushing down a slice of truffle every inch or so. Sew the upper edge of the incision with a trussing needle and brown the filet in a mixture of butter and oil, turning frequently so that the absolute minimum of cooking will take place in the interior of the filet. Encase in pastry as described in the foregoing recipe and bake on a cookie sheet in a 450 degree oven until the pastry is browned.

This, of course, is merely a richer elaboration of Beef Wellington, but the added flavors make it worthwhile from time to time.

It merits your best red wine from the Côte de Nuits, or at the least, the best Cabernet Sauvignon from California.

Boeuf Strasbourg en Chemise

If you proceed exactly as in the recipe for Beef Harold but use only four ounces of pâté de foie gras and no almonds or brandy, you will have Beef Strasbourg in a Shirt.

All of the recipes given in this chapter thus far have envisioned the use of a meat of a high enough quality to be tender when it is roasted and—usually—roasted a comparatively short time. It is time to consider a way in which the nutritious and flavor-filled tougher cuts can be made attractive. The method for accomplishing this purpose is braising and herewith is the very prince of pot roasts.

FILET OF BEEF HAROLD

3 - 4	lb. filet
2	oz. liver pâté
2	oz. blanched almonds
1	oz. truffles
2	tablesp. clarified butter
1	tablesp. cooking oil
	pastry dough to enclose filet
1	egg, slightly beaten
	salt
	freshly ground black pepper
1	oz. cognac

Beef à la Mode

Cut the bacon or salt pork in four larding strips each. Marinate these in a little brandy. Sprinkle with chopped parsley just before using.

Remove fat from the beef and either trim or tie it into an attractive shape. Lard it with the twelve strips of bacon or pork fat. Slice the onion thinly, scrape and slice one carrot, together with the crushed garlic and herbs and put into a bowl. Pour in the bottle of wine, the vinegar and the brandy. Marinate the meat in this mixture for twenty-four hours in a cool but not refrigerated place, turning the meat from time to time unless it is completely covered.

Next day, remove the meat from the marinade, dry it, and brown in the clarified butter in a Dutch oven or casserole. Add the marinade with the calves feet or veal knuckle and put in a moderate oven to simmer for two hours. Then remove the beef long enough to strain the marinade, replace, and add four carrots, scraped and cut into serving pieces, the onions, the cloves and two more tablespoons of brandy. Cook gently for another hour or more until the meat is tender.

Remove the veal knuckle or the calves feet, slice and serve the beef on heated plates with some of the sauce poured over the slices. If the sauce is too thin, reduce by boiling rapidly without covering.

If you are unable to find the calves feet or the veal knuckle, you will not have spoiled the flavor for serving the dish hot. For serving cold, which is also an attractive way to eat beef á la mode, trim the remaining piece of meat into a regular shape. Pour the remaining sauce around and over it. If you have used calves feet or a veal knuckle, the sauce will become a jelly when it is cold. In the absence of the gelatinizing feet or knuckle, dissolve a package of un-sweetened gelatin in a little hot water or, preferably, beef stock, and add to the sauce. If there is not enough of the liquid, make an aspic by adding gelatin in the proper proportions to a pint of beef stock or a can or two of condensed bouillon and use it.

Use a mold and turn out on a chilled serving plate after an overnight stay in the refrigerator. Garnish with watercress or sprigs of parsley.

A good young Beaujolais or a Rhône has always been more than satisfactory as a partner for beef á la

BEEF À LA MODE

4	lbs. top round or rump, choice or good, one piece
3	slices bacon or salt pork
1	bottle dry red wine
1/2	cup brandy
1	tablesp. clarified butter
3	calves feet or one veal knuckle
2	tablesp. red wine vinegar
5	carrots
1	medium onion
6 - 8	small boiling onions
	several sprigs of parsley
	leaves from a stalk of celery
1	bay leaf
1	clove crushed garlic
1/4	teasp. thyme
1/8	teasp. freshly grated nutmeg
	salt
	freshly ground black pepper
1/4	teasp. tarragon

205

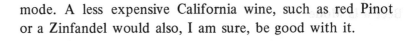

mode. A less expensive California wine, such as red Pinot or a Zinfandel would also, I am sure, be good with it.

Steaks

Beef for steaks, perhaps even more than for roasts, must be of excellent quality if the steak is to be broiled and served without adornment, which is the way the best steaks ought to be served.

Good sirloin, T-bone, and what are known throughout the West as New York cut steaks and in New York as strip steaks, should be cut from well-aged prime or, at the minimum, choice beef.

Depending on the mood I am in, my favorite steak is the strip or New York cut, or T-bone. The strip steak is, in effect, the large side of a boned porterhouse steak, the smaller, inner side being the tenderloin or filet. This seems to me better than the Porterhouse steak because you have only the part which has the best texture as well as flavor and, furthermore, you do not have to struggle with the bone. However, on occasion, I like the T-bone, cut from further down the loin, because it has a highly individual and very attractive flavor. I feel that it is a mistake to cut these steaks too thick. If your steak is much more than one inch thick, you really have a broiled roast, and would do well to cut it vertically.

Good steaks are best broiled on a grill over a bed of charcoals made from good oak or hickory. They should *not* be salted before being broiled because salt tends to draw the juice to the surface.

Do not overcook steak. Try to acquire enough experience that you only have to turn it once. It is better to make a sharp incision into the edge of the meat to test its doneness than it is to risk overcooking it. From six to eight minutes to a side is usually sufficient, depending on the heat of the coals, the distance of the grill from the fire, and the thickness of the steak.

For a good broiled steak, a sprinkling of salt, a good grind of black pepper and a generous dab of soft sweet butter is all that one could wish for in the way of a sauce.

But if the meat is not quite top quality, or perhaps merely for variety, you might like a good steak sauce occasionally.

206

Wine Merchant's Sauce

This is the usual decoration that the natives of Burgundy, Bresse and the Charolaise use when they eat a steak from the beautiful white Charolais cattle, which provide beef of quality equal to the best Herefords or Aberdeen Angus of this country.

In a small skillet, sauté the shallots in half of the butter until they are soft and golden. Add the stock, wine, and lemon juice and boil until the volume is reduced by half. Now add the rest of the butter. Adjust the seasoning with salt and pepper, pour over the steak on a hot platter and sprinkle with chopped parsley.

A Simpler Red Wine Sauce

Cook the wine and chopped shallots together until the volume is reduced by two-thirds. Mix parsley and butter. After the wine and shallot mixture has cooled, combine with the parsley butter. Place a generous dab on each steak as it finishes cooking.

White Wine Steak Sauce

Sauté the shallots in the butter until they are soft and golden. Add the mustard, parsley and wine. Boil until the volume has reduced by one-half. Pour over steaks as they come off the grill.

Chateaubriand

As I mentioned earlier, this steak is cut from the center of the filet, where the diameter is the largest. It should be a minimum of three inches in thickness (enough to serve two) and may be cut even thicker.

As with most cuts of the filet, it is preferable to sauté a Chateaubriand steak rather than to broil it. Use either clarified butter or a mixture of clarified butter and oil. Sauté at fairly high heat for ten minutes, turning constantly in order to brown the meat on all sides. Then cover, reduce heat, and cook fifteen minutes longer. If you like the meat medium rare, it may be necessary to cook even longer. It should be sliced thinly and served with sauce Béarnaise, maître d'hôtel butter, or a mushroom

WINE MERCHANT'S SAUCE

1	tablesp. minced shallots
3	tablesp. beef stock or condensed bouillon
1 1/2	cups dry red wine
1	stick butter
1	teasp. lemon juice
	salt
	freshly ground pepper
1	teasp. (or more) chopped parsley

RED WINE SAUCE

2	teasp. shallots
6	oz. dry red wine
1/2	stick softened butter
1	teasp. chopped parsley
	salt
	freshly ground black pepper

WHITE WINE STEAK SAUCE

1	cup dry white wine (Pouilly-Fuissé or Maconnais)
1	tablesp. chopped shallots
2	tablesp. butter
1	tablesp. Dijon mustard
	salt
	fresh black pepper
2	teasp. chopped parsley

sauce. Sautéed whole mushroom caps or souffléed potatoes make an excellent garnish.

You will like a good medium-grade Burgundy, such as a Charmes-Chambertin or Echézeaux, or Pommard-Epinots or a good Pinot Noir from California.

Tournedos Sautés

Rim With Bacon or Fat

Tournedos are neat round steaks cut usually about one inch thick toward the ends of the filet. Have your butcher rim each tournedo with a slice of bacon or fat pork and tie with string, which will hold the fat pork in place and keep the tournedo nice and round.

Sauté at fairly high heat in clarified butter on both sides. Because of the lesser thickness, the tournedos will probably not need further cooking after they are brown on both sides.

Make croutons by cutting out rounds of white bread one-half inch thick, the same size as the tournedos, frying them to a golden brown on both sides in butter.

Season the tournedos with salt and freshly ground black pepper and place on the croutons, keeping them in a 200 degree oven. Pour one-half cup or so of dry red wine in the skillet, scrape all of the browned particles and as the mixture comes to a boil, stir in a tablespoon of sweet butter. Let cook a minute and strain over the tournedos, which should be served immediately with a garnish of pommes soufflés or pommes frites (freshly made French-fried potatoes).

A medium-grade Burgundy, as a Pommard Rugiens, or a good regional Bordeaux or a California Cabernet Sauvignon, will go nicely with this simplest of the tournedos.

Tournedos with Chestnuts

Marinate the filet mignons in the wine, to which has been added the sliced carrot and onion, for two or three days in the refrigerator.

Drain the chestnuts and cook them in the chicken stock together with two stalks of celery, salt, and a generous grating of nutmeg. Cook until the chestnuts fall apart. Purée them or put them through the blender; keep hot.

Cook the filets in olive oil in a saucepan until they are crisp outside and rare in the center, which will take ten to fifteen minutes, depending on how rare you like them. Remove from the oil, drain on paper towels and keep warm on a heated platter.

To the saucepan in which the filets have been cooked, add the chopped shallots, a stalk of chopped celery, together with the cream and brandy. Boil up and continue cooking until the volume of the sauce is reduced to a rather thick consistency.

Serve the filets on croutons made according to the directions in the preceding recipe, with a pile of the purée of chestnuts on the side. Pour the sauce over the purée.

As with most steaks, the forthright flavor requires a medium-grade Burgundy, a heavy California Pinot Noir or a Rhône.

Tournedos Béarnaise

Cook tournedos in clarified butter or butter and olive oil as described in the basic recipe. Place on fried croutons and garnish generously with béarnaise sauce. Serve extra béarnaise sauce in a sauceboat.

A good accompaniment for a filet prepared in this manner is potatoes cut into olive-size pieces and cooked gently in butter until they are golden on the outside and soft inside. Sprinkle with chopped parsley. The old cookbooks call these Pommes Château.

A sound, medium-grade Burgundy, Rhône, as heavy a California Pinot Noir or Cabernet Sauvignon as you can find is the proper drink with this steak.

Tournedos Henri IV

Only slightly more trouble to prepare than tournedos béarnaise, but considerably more festive.

Sauté one tournedo for each person as in the recipes above. Prepare the croutons as above. On each crouton, place one large (or two small) artichoke bottoms cooked until just done in beef stock. If you use canned artichoke bottoms, heat them through in a little beef stock. Place the steak on the artichoke bottom and then garnish generously with béarnaise sauce and pass extra sauce in a heated sauceboat.

TOURNEDOS WITH CHESTNUTS

1	filet mignon, 1 inch thick for each person
1	small can whole chestnuts, cooked in salt water
3	stalks celery
	olive oil
3	chopped shallots
	salt
	pepper
	nutmeg
1	bottle dry red wine
1	sliced carrot
1	sliced onion
1/8	teasp. dried thyme
1	can chicken broth or 2 cups chicken stock
1	cup brandy
1	pt. cream

Sautéed mushroom caps and a bottle of good, full-flavored and heavy-bodied wine, not too subtle, is our choice here. There is just enough acid in the béarnaise sauce to kill off the most delicate of the bouquet and taste of a fine old château-bottled Bordeaux or even of the best Burgundy.

Tournedos Rossini

Fry the croutons and sauté the tournedos exactly as in the previous recipes. Dredge slices about one-quarter inch thick of pâté de foie gras a little smaller than each tournedo in flour and heat the slices in the skillet the tournedos were cooked in. Place the heated slices of pâté on the tournedos and on top of all, place a slice of truffle. Add to the skillet, 1/2 cup of strong stock or condensed bouillon; scrape all of the browned particles. Then, as the stock boils, add 1/2 cup of Madeira or sherry and cook until it is reduced somewhat. I personally prefer an Amontillado sherry, but you might like the slightly sweeter taste of the Madeira. Strain over the tournedos.

Either the pommes château or pommes soufflés are, I believe, preferable with this rather rich dish to the sautéed mushrooms. Because of the absence of the acid flavor of a béarnaise sauce, you might like a bottle of the best Bordeaux or Burgundy.

Filet of Beef with Tarragon

Melt the butter in a skillet or chafing dish, cook the shallots gently until they are soft and golden. Turn up the heat, put in the beef and tarragon and stir constantly. The cooking will require only two or three minutes. Season with salt and pepper. We like beef cooked in this manner best of all over plain boiled noodles.

It merits a good Burgundy or one of your lesser château-bottled Bordeaux wines.

Beef Sauté à la Parisienne

Make a sauce by pouring ten ounces of boiling water on the two packages of mushrooms and let stand for three hours or, better, overnight. Remove mushrooms from the liquid and chop finely. Pour the water in which the mushrooms soaked carefully into a saucepan, discarding the

FILET OF BEEF WITH TARRAGON

2   lbs. filet for 6 persons. Have your butcher cut the filet into postage-stamp size squares as thin as possible.
1/2   stick butter
2   minced shallots
2   tablesp. fresh tarragon or 2 teasp. dried crushed tarragon
    salt
    pepper

bottom because of possible sand. Add the chopped mushrooms, the unclarified butter and beef extract, and simmer for forty-five minutes. Thicken a little with flour and season to taste with salt and pepper.

Brown the filet slices in a skillet with the clarified butter, cooking about two minutes to each side. Before removing meat from the pan, add 1 1/2 ounces of cognac and ignite. Place, after seasoning with salt and pepper, on a hot serving dish.

Add the rest of the cognac to the heated sauce and pour over the steak as it is served. The serving plate should be liberally garnished with watercress.

A good Burgundy or a fourth or fifth cru château Bordeaux is indicated here.

We have been concerned up to this point with steaks of the best possible beef. It is now time to turn to some of the extremely palatable dishes that can be made from tougher and less costly meat.

Beefsteaks Calvados

Place the steaks between waxed paper and with a mallet or side of a cleaver, pound them as thin as possible. Heat part of the butter in a skillet and cook the minced shallot and garlic until they are soft and golden.

Mix the flour, tarragon and salt in a paper bag and shake the pounded steaks in the bag until they are well coated.

Add the rest of the butter to the skillet, turn the heat up and cook the steak quickly, about two minutes to each side.

Pour the Calvados (or failing that, New Jersey or California applejack) in the pan and ignite. Spoon the flaming liquor over the steaks and when the flame is extinguished, serve on hot plates, straining the sauce over the meat.

We usually have a regional Bordeaux, a Pommard-Epinots, or a Volnay with this dish.

Steak Diane

Have steaks cut about one-half inch thick from bottom round or rump of choice or good grade beef. Place

BEEF SAUTÉ À LA PARISIENNE

3	lbs. filet, one piece, sliced 1/2 inch thick
1	stick butter, clarified
2	pkgs. dried mushrooms
4	oz. cognac
1	stick butter, unclarified
2	tablesp. beef extract
1	tablesp. flour
	salt
	pepper

BEEFSTEAKS CALVADOS

6	round or rump steaks 1/2 inch thick, 1/2 lb. each
2/3	stick butter
2	tablesp. flour
1	clove minced garlic
6	shallots, minced
1/2	teasp. dried tarragon
1	teasp. salt
1 1/2	cups Calvados
	black pepper (on table)

211

STEAK DIANE

1/2	lb. meat per person
2/3	stick butter
	juice of two lemons
1 1/2	cups brandy
	worcestershire sauce
6	chopped shallots
6	teasp. chopped parsley
	salt
	freshly ground black pepper

CUBED STEAK CHEZ NOUS

6	cubed round steaks
2	tablesp. flour
1	teasp. dried marjoram
2	oz. butter
2	tablesp. chopped shallots
4	oz. dry red wine
	salt
	black pepper

POTTED SWISS STEAK

2	lbs. Swiss steak
2	tablesp. flour
2	large onions, chopped
4	oz. (or more) fresh mushrooms
1/2	stick butter
1	cup dry red wine
	salt
	black pepper
1/4	teasp. dried thyme
1/4	teasp. dried tarragon

between sheets of waxed paper and pound them as thin as possible with a mallet or side of a cleaver. Season with salt and black pepper.

Clarify butter and heat in a chafing dish at the table until it is almost smoking. Put the chopped shallots, lemon juice, Worcestershire sauce to taste into the chafing dish and cook for a minute or two until the shallots are golden and soft. Put the steaks in quickly and cook about two minutes on each side (three minutes if you like the meat well done). Pour brandy over the meat and ignite; serve as soon as flames are extinguished.

Serve with dutchess potatoes and a good Burgundy or a sound regional Bordeaux, or the best California Cabernet Sauvignon.

Cubed Steak Chez Nous

Mix the flour, marjoram, salt and pepper and shake in a paper bag with the cubed steaks or with steaks pounded as above.

Melt part of the butter and cook the shallots until they are soft and golden. Add the rest of the butter and keep it just below the temperature at which it turns brown. Cook the steaks about three minutes on each side. Add the wine and cook for another two minutes. Remove the steaks to a hot platter and concentrate the sauce about fifty percent, pouring it on the steaks as they are served.

We usually eat French fries and drink a bottle of Beaujolais or California Gamay with these steaks.

Potted Swiss Steak

Sprinkle the pieces of steak with the flour, salt, a good grind of black pepper and the two herbs. Pound the flour and seasonings into the meat between sheets of waxed paper with a mallet or side of a cleaver. Clarify the butter, put in a heavy casserole and heat briskly. Brown the steaks on both sides. Remove the steaks, add onions and brown them. Replace steak, arrange onions around it and add the wine and an equal amount of water. Cover and bake one and one-half hours or until tender, adding the mushrooms which, in the meantime, have been sautéed in a little more butter, during the last half hour. Serve on hot plates, spooning the sauce over the meat. If necessary, thin it with a little water or beef stock.

A Beaujolais or good California red wine will suitably partner this potted steak.

Swiss Steak Mozzarella

Sprinkle the flour, basil, salt and pepper on the meat, cut into individual serving size. Pound between waxed paper. Melt the butter in a casserole or an iron skillet that can be covered. Brown the meat on all sides. Add the tomatoes and wine. Simmer, covered, for one hour, then add the onion and green pepper. Cook another one-half hour or so until meat is tender. Leave uncovered during the latter period so that the sauce thickens. Top the meat with the cheese and run under broiler until cheese melts and begins to bubble.

This dish will serve as a good reason for investigating one of the moderately-priced Italian red wines such as a Barbera, Bardolino, or a better quality Chianti. Obviously, an inexpensive Beaujolais or a sound California red will do very nicely.

Beef Steak au Poivre

Crack the peppercorns in a piece of cloth with a mallet or break them with a pestle in a mortar. Sprinkle one-half of the cracked peppercorns over one side of the steak and pound them in with the mallet or the side of a heavy knife. Turn the steak over and repeat with the rest of the peppercorns. Let stand for one-half to one hour.

Clarify the butter and brown the steaks on each side quickly. Then reduce the heat and cook a few minutes longer. Remove the steaks to a hot serving plate and deglaze the skillet with the wine. Salt the steaks. Add a tablespoon of butter to the wine which has been reduced to about fifty percent of its original volume; cook a minute longer and pour over the steaks.

Pommes soufflés and a good stout Rhône or California red will do justice to this meat.

London Broil

This is a broiled beef flank. It is amazingly good in spite of the fact that a more unlikely looking piece of meat can rarely be seen in a butcher's showcase. The flank is thin, and is obviously coarsely grained, so that when it

SWISS STEAK MOZZARELLA

2	lbs. beef round or rump 1/2 inch thick
2	oz. butter
1	can (1 lb.) tomatoes (Italian, if possible)
1/2	cup chopped onion
1/2	cup shredded Mozzarella cheese
1/2	cup chopped green pepper
1/2	cup dry red wine
1 1/2	teasp. salt
	pepper to taste
1/2	teasp. dried sweet basil

BEEF STEAK AU POIVRE

6	steaks cut from sirloin, tenderloin or top round, 3/4 inch thick
2	teasp. black peppercorns
1	stick butter
1/2	cup dry white wine
	salt

213

comes to the table tender and juicy, it is not only good eating, but a surprise. We use the following method.

We buy for six persons, a flank steak weighing at least - two and one-half to three pounds and marinate it overnight in the same vinaigrette that we use for green salad. This consists of one part of good red wine vinegar to eight or more parts of a neutral cooking oil, flavored only with salt.

We remove the steak from the marinade, pat it dry with paper towels and broil three inches from the heat source for five minutes on each side. It is then removed to a hot serving platter, doused liberally with sweet butter and a little salt, and carved in thin slices diagonally across the grain.

Flank Steak Remains Juicy Inside

During the broiling, the long thin piece of meat contracts and becomes almost twice as thick. Contrary to expectations, the outside is dark brown and crusty; the inside ranges from pink to red and is extremely juicy.

A baked potato with lots of butter and chives is good with broiled flank steak, which deserves one of your medium-good Burgundies or third or fourth cru château-bottled Bordeaux. This is so because the flavor of this cut of meat is excellent, and there are no extraneous flavors to detract interest from the wine.

Beef Burgundy Style (Boeuf Bourguinonne)

Cut the meat into cubes about one and one-half inches in size. In a Dutch oven or casserole, heat the butter and bacon drippings and brown the meat. Remove the meat temporarily. Slice part of the onions and chop the shallots and garlic. Cook gently in the fat in the pot until the onion is tender and beginning to brown. Add the flour and stir well to make a brown *roux* or thickening.

Return the meat to the pot, together with a *bouquet garni* of the parsley, bay leaf, thyme and marjoram. Add wine and stock to the pot until the meat is well covered. Put on the lid and simmer gently for three or more hours. Replace the liquid as necessary with more wine and stock in equal proportions.

Brown the rest of the onions in a little butter. Do the same with the mushrooms, leaving them whole if they are small or halving or quartering according to size. Scrape and cut the carrots into two inch long pieces.

214

About three-quarters hour before the cooking is completed, add the vegetables. When the cooking is finished, the sauce should not be too plentiful and should be fairly thick. If the sauce is too thin, finish off the cooking without a lid. Just before completing the cooking, add the cognac.

Strain out the vegetables and arrange around the meat placed in the center of a hot serving dish. Pour some of the rich sauce over all and pass any remaining sauce in a heated sauceboat.

A crisp green salad to begin the meal, lots of crusty French bread with it and a fruit bowl after will make as good an informal meal as you could wish for, especially if you add a bottle of young Beaujolais, a good California Pinot Noir or Cabernet Sauvignon to it.

Carbonnades à la Flamande

This is the best known stew of Belgium. In place of wine, beer is used. In Brussels, the tradition is to use a strong, dark beer.

Season the beef, cut in pieces one-by-two-by-one inches, with salt and pepper and brown well in the hot lard. Cut the bacon into small cubes and fry until crisp and brown in the same skillet the meat was browned in. Remove the meat and bacon cubes from the pan and pour off all but two tablespoons of the fat, saving a little for browning the onions.

Heat the reserved fat in another pan and brown the onions and chopped garlic, stirring constantly so that the onions brown but do not burn. Now, turn the onions and meat into a casserole with a lid and add the beer sauce. Add a *bouquet garni* of the parsley, bay leaf and thyme, replace the lid and let simmer until the meat is tender. The length of time needed will depend on the beef selected. Obviously, a piece of neck or flank, graded good, will not cook tender as quickly as a piece of rump graded choice. If you use the cheapest cuts, as you should in this stew, it will take two and one-half to three hours—and well worth it too!

Some cooks like to thicken the sauce by adding a thick slice of bread liberally smeared with mustard. We like it both ways.

Our *ordinaire,* which is an inexpensive young Beaujolais, goes well with this dish, although I suppose that one

BEEF BURGUNDY STYLE
(Boeuf Bourguinonne)

2	lbs. lean chuck, round or rump
1	tablesp. butter
1	tablesp. bacon drippings
1	tablesp. flour
2	slices bacon
~~3~~	~~oz. cognac~~
6	shallots
1	clove garlic
1	bay leaf
~~1-1/2~~	~~teasp. salt~~
1/2	bottle dry red wine
1	cup strong beef stock or condensed bouillon
1/2	lb. small onions
1/2	lb. carrots
1/2	lb. mushrooms
6	sprigs parsley
1/2	teasp. marjoram
1/2	teasp. thyme
	freshly ground black pepper

CARBONNADES À LA FLAMANDE

2 1/2	lbs. chuck, neck, rump or flank
1/4	lb. bacon
1/3	cup lard or cooking oil
2	tablesp. flour
12	oz. beer (preferably dark)
3/4	lb. thinly sliced onions
1 - 2	cloves garlic
	sprigs of parsley
1	bay leaf
1	teasp. thyme
1 1/2	teasp. salt
	fresh black pepper

215

perhaps ought to drink beer with it. On the other hand, the meat does not taste beery at all, and the red wine goes very well with it.

We have now seen how it is done in Burgundy and Belgium; now let us look at a stew as it is often made in the Midi, the sunny south of France washed by the Mediteranean.

Beef en Daube Provençale

This dish may be prepared using round or rump in quite large chunks—about two inches long—or the meat may be left in one piece. It has always seemed to members of my family, better the latter way. Obviously, the cooking time will be shorter if the meat is cut into smaller pieces. Try it both ways and let your family decide for themselves.

Put all of the ingredients into a large crock and marinate at least twenty-four hours, turning the meat several times if the marinade does not cover it.

Cut the bacon into strips and fry it crisp. Dry the roast from the marinade and brown it in the fat from the bacon. Now, place the meat, the cracklings from the bacon, and the marinade in an earthenware or enamel casserole and cook in the oven, covered, at 225 degrees for at least six hours or more, until the meat is tender.

Remove the meat to a hot platter and let the casserole cool. Skim most of the fat from the surface and strain. Serve part of the strained sauce mixed with macaroni boiled until it is tender in salted water. Pass the rest of the sauce in a heated sauceboat or pour over the sliced meat if you elect the method using small pieces. Be sure to make the *macaronnade;* it is simple and is just right for this dish.

Serve with a Côte de Provence, an inexpensive Beaujolais or an inexpensive California red wine.

Now a central European stew, using sour cream.

Beef Stroganoff

Shake the beef, cut into strips one-by-one-half-by-one-half inch, in a paper bag with the flour, salt and pepper.

BEEF EN DAUBE PROVENÇALE

2 1/2	lbs. rump, round or shoulder
3	slices bacon or salt pork
1	veal knuckle
1	bottle dry red wine
1 1/2	teasp. salt
	fresh peel of 1/2 orange
	fresh peel of 1/2 lemon
2	bay leaves
4	large (or more if small) cloves garlic
2	sprigs of fresh rosemary or 1/2 teasp. dried rosemary
1/2	teasp. thyme

Heat the oil and butter. Sauté the onion and garlic gently until the onion is soft and golden. Add the beef and brown well. After browning the meat, add the stock, cover and simmer slowly until the meat is tender.

When the meat seems to be tender, pour off most of the liquid and stir into the meat enough heavy sour cream to cover it, about one pint. Heat carefully until the cream and stock mixture begins to bubble a little, correct the seasoning and serve with noodles or rice. We prefer the noodles. They seem more authentically middle European. This is not really important; actually, we prefer the taste and texture of the noodles. If you prefer rice, there can be no objection.

A Beaujolais, or a modest California red wine has always seemed to us satisfactory with this stew.

And next are the two delicious braises, using beef about as inexpensive as can be bought.

Braised Short Ribs

Mix flour, salt, herbs and a good grind of black pepper. Wipe the short ribs and shake in a paper bag with the flour-herb mixture long enough to coat them thoroughly. Brown the onions in the hot fat in a Dutch oven or casserole; add the meat, browning thoroughly on all sides. Add the stock and cook either in an oven at 225 degrees or simmer gently on top of the stove for two and one-half hours. Add more stock if necessary. Add carrots after one and one-half hours. Skim off some of the fat before serving.

Either boiled potatoes or crusty French bread is good with braised ribs. You will find that a Beaujolais or California *ordinaire* will make the ribs taste better and, happily, the ribs will improve the taste of the wine.

Braised Oxtail

Treat the oxtail joints exactly as you would the short ribs in the foregoing recipe, except that you should add a clove or two of garlic to the onions. We also like a half pound to a pound of mushrooms sautéed in a little butter, added together with the carrots. Another interesting variation is to substitute some leftover dry red wine for

BEEF STROGANOFF

2	lbs. chuck or round
2	tablesp. butter, clarified
2	tablesp. cooking oil
1	pt. (approx.) sour cream
1	small onion, sliced
4	cloves minced garlic
1 1/2	cups strong beef stock or condensed bouillon
	salt
	freshly ground pepper

BRAISED SHORT RIBS

5	lbs. short ribs, cut in serving pieces
6	tablesp. cooking oil or half bacon drippings
3	cups strong stock or condensed bouillon
1	cup carrots, 2 inches long
1	cup chopped onion
4	tablesp. flour
1/2	teasp. rosemary or several sprigs fresh rosemary
	salt
	fresh pepper
1	teasp. thyme

half or more of the beef stock. Still another is to gently brown in butter a dozen small onions in place of the mushrooms—or have carrots, onions, mushrooms and wine all in the dish. It is good in all these ways. Again, you will want to skim off some of the fat by allowing the dish to cool a little and then reheat before serving. A good red *ordinaire* will, again, be fine.

Beef and Kidney Pie I

BEEF AND KIDNEY PIE I

2	lbs. round, rump or chuck
1	lb. veal kidney
	or lamb kidney
3	tablesp. flour
1	teasp. salt
	black pepper
2	oz. cooking oil
	or bacon drippings
1	medium onion, sliced
1 1/2	cups strong beef stock
	pastry dough sufficient
	to line and cover dish

Mix salt, pepper and flour. Cut the beef into one inch cubes. Clean the kidney carefully, removing all membranes and fat. If you are using a veal kidney, save some of the fat and use it in place of cooking oil. Cut kidney in three-quarter inch cubes.

Brown the sliced onion in the fat (or render the suet and use it); sauté the onion slices until they are soft and golden. Temporarily remove onions and brown the mixed kidney and meat after flouring them by tossing in a paper bag with the seasoned flour. Replace the onions and gradually add the stock, stirring so that the cooked flour makes a smooth brown gravy. Cover and simmer slowly until meat is tender—one and one-half to two hours. Line Pyrex or other dish (one quart or more in capacity) with pastry dough rolled to one-eighth inch thick. Let the cooked meat cool and put into the dish. Cover with a top crust. Seal by moistening both edges and pinching together. Make a fairly large central hole in the top crust or several smaller slashes and brush with slightly beaten egg.

Cook in an oven heated to 400 degrees for twenty minutes and brush with the remaining beaten egg. Cook for another five to ten minutes until the crust is nicely browned.

Steak and Kidney Pie II

Proceed exactly as above but clean and sauté, whole or halved, one package (six ounces) of button mushrooms.

Steak and Kidney Pie III

Proceed as above, but use proportions of one-half dry red wine and one-half stock. Add 1/2 teaspoon each of basil and tarragon, dried, and one bay leaf. In place of the mushrooms, use one-half pound of small boiling onions, carefully browned in butter.

A large green salad before the steak and kidney pie and fruit with two or three cheeses after it should satisfy any family's hunger. Your red *ordinaire* and this savory pie will mutually improve each other as you consume them together.

Chili Con Carne with Frijoles

Mix flour, salt and at least two (preferably more) teaspoons of chili powder in a paper bag. Shake the meat, cut in one-quarter to one-half inch cubes in the seasoned flour (attention: not ground beef!!) and sear in the hot drippings to which you have added the garlic in a heavy casserole or Dutch oven. Reduce the heat, add the stock, cover and simmer for one hour. Add the cumin seeds and taste for seasoning. Add more chili powder and salt, according to your taste, and simmer slowly another hour or until the meat is tender. Add more stock if necessary. When the meat is done, there should be a fairly large amount of the dark red gravy.

Soak the beans overnight. Change the water, add a teaspoon of salt and cook slowly until the beans begin to burst.

Serve the chili and the beans together.

This dish should really be consumed with beer. However, if you do not like beer, the coarsest red wine that you can find makes a fine partner. A wine from Provence, a wine made from the Mission grapes at Santa Tomas, or a cheap California central valley red would strike precisely the right note.

There are times when one is in a hurry, or the budget is strained, if not actually fractured and when, for a number of reasons, it seems desirable to have ground meat in one form or another. Here are two recipes which will keep such occasions from being too boring, either for the cook or her family.

First, a tip. Do not buy ground round. Ground chuck (or shoulder) is always considerably cheaper and also tastes better. Actually, I prefer the ground chuck even to ground sirloin which is still more expensive than round. Choose a piece of meat and have your butcher grind it fresh, or do it yourself.

**CHILI CON CARNE
WITH FRIJOLES**

2	lbs. stewing beef, neck, chuck or round
2	tablesp. flour
1 1/2	teasp. salt
4	cloves minced garlic
1	cup pink beans
	chili powder
1	teasp. cumin seeds
2	tablesp. bacon drippings
2	cups strong beef stock

Grilled Ground Round Steaks with Wine

GRILLED GROUND STEAKS WITH WINE

2 lbs. ground chuck
1 cup dry red wine
1/2 teasp. dried thyme
1/2 teasp. dried tarragon
1 1/2 teasp. salt
   clarified butter or cooking oil
   cooking oil

Mix the meat, wine and herbs together and form into six patties—each one inch thick, without pounding the meat down too much. Grill for five minutes on each side, one and one-half inches from heat source, or in a heavy iron skillet with a minimum of clarified butter or cooking oil.

You may vary the flavor of ground steaks by a knowing use of herbs. One seasoned with sweet basil and thyme will not taste like one with tarragon. Rosemary is another herb to use. Use whatever wine you have leftover, providing it is not sweet.

Still another flavor can be had by substituting two or three tablespoons of brandy for the wine and then pressing into the surface of the patties, cracked whole peppercorns, for a less expensive version of pepper steak.

The important thing is to seal the flavor in by searing the surfaces quickly; then reducing the heat; and cooking until it is done to your desire. Overcooking is even more fatal to ground meat than to other kinds.

Your red *ordinaire* should be more than adequate with broiled ground steaks.

Meat loaf is another covenient and economical way to serve beef. There is only one trouble with it; it is so *dull!* However, here is a meat loaf that my family and I have thought not at all dull.

Beef and Cheddar Loaf

Chop the onions and celery finely or put them through the food chopper. Beat the eggs slightly, then mix all of the ingredients except for two ounces of the cheese. Shape into a loaf and bake in a greased baking pan in a 350 degree oven for one hour. Pour off the drippings and sprinkle the remaining two ounces of cheese over the top of the loaf. Return to oven fifteen minutes longer.

This meat loaf is as good cold as hot. Because of the special affinity of good red wine and good cheese, it, unlike most ground meat dishes, merits a good Rhône, a medium-grade Burgundy, or a good California Cabernet Sauvignon or Pinot Noir.

You will encounter recipes now and then which call for mixing ground beef with Roquefort cheese. Let me

BEEF AND CHEDDAR LOAF

2 lbs. ground beef
1/2 lb. old, sharp Cheddar cheese
2 eggs
1/2 cup finely chopped celery
1/2 cup finely chopped onion
2 tablesp. finely chopped parsley
1 teasp. salt
   ground black pepper

220

counsel you against doing such a thing. Roquefort is a delicious cheese and the mold which helps make it good and savory as it is, only makes the beef taste as though it were spoiled. Also, you will encounter a recipe for a French version of hamburgers called Ground Steaks Miremonde which dilutes the beef with bread crumbs and either cornmeal or farina. If you are forced to be very economical or if you like the taste of meat diluted with cereal—fine—this dish may be for you. But, it still tastes like beef diluted with starch.

In general, I am, like most men, a little unenthusiastic about clever ways to use up leftovers. But there will be times when the most skillful cook and careful planner will have leftover meat; in fact, when we have a rump roast, we plan to serve it at least once sliced cold with a mustard or horseradish sauce. Also, when we serve guests a standing rib roast, we do not like to serve the outer, dry and somewhat tough muscle of the cut. While all of this is quite true, the real reason for presenting the next two recipes is simply that they are good—too good not to have once in a while.

Southern Hash

Use the outer, tough layer of muscle from the previous night's standing rib roast, or leftover meat of any kind. Cut—do not put through the food chopper—into one-half inch cubes.

Boil the whole potatoes until they are barely done and cut them into cubes of the same size.

Mix the flour, salt and pepper in a paper bag and shake the meat in the flour even though it has already been cooked.

Heat the fat in a heavy skillet; add the chopped onion and garlic; cook slowly until the onion is soft and golden. Turn up the heat and add the meat. Brown it well and then add the potatoes. Let them brown a little, stirring with a wooden spoon. When the potatoes have browned slightly, add stock and any leftover gravy. Stir until the flour adhering to the pan and the meat thickens into a gravy. Continue cooking five to ten minutes to blend the flavors, adding a little more stock if necessary.

Even though this hash is made from leftover meat, it is of good quality and the dish is so savory that I am

SOUTHERN HASH

3	cups leftover beef cut in 1/2 inch cubes
3	cups potatoes cut in 1/2 inch cubes
1	large or 2 small onions
1/2	stick butter, clarified or 4 tablesp. bacon drippings
1	clove garlic
1	tablesp. flour
1	teasp. salt
	black pepper
1	cup stock or leftover gravy or a combination of both

221

always tempted to open a good Rhône or one of my medium-grade Burgundies instead of contenting myself with the Beaujolais *ordinaire*.

Beef en Casserole

You may use leftover roast, pot roast, or steak. Cut the meat into cubes about three-quarters inch in size or into strips one-by-one-half-by-one-half inches depending on the shape of your leftover meat.

Mix flour, salt and oregano and shake the meat in a paper bag to coat it thoroughly. Heat the oil in a skillet and cook onion and garlic until the onion is soft and golden. Add meat and brown well. Add rest of seasoned flour and stir until the *roux* (the mixture of fat and browned flour) is smooth. Add the meat, wine, stock and pimentos with their juice, and simmer for a few minutes. In a one and one-half quart casserole, arrange the cooked macaroni, the meat mixture and the grated cheese in layers, finishing with a layer of cheese. Bake in a 450 degree oven fifteen to twenty minutes, until the contents bubble and the cheese on the surface begins to brown.

A pleasant variation is to substitute one-half Gruyère and one-half Parmesan cheese for the Cheddar.

Like good hash, this casserole is a fine dish in its own right. As such, it deserves to be partnered with a good Rhône or a better-than-average California red wine. (No one but you need know that the casserole is based on leftovers.)

Beef Tongue

The tongue is the only internal organ that I like except for the kidney, which has been dealt with as beef and kidney pie. But the tongue is not really an internal organ, after all; it is, except for a little fat and the skin covering it, composed entirely of voluntary muscle. It is good fresh, corned, and smoked.

The fresh tongue should be scrubbed vigorously with a brush and all loose fat and connective tissue at the base removed. The smoked or corned tongue should be soaked overnight, then scrubbed and trimmed in the same manner as the fresh tongue.

BEEF EN CASSEROLE

4	cups leftover beef
4	tomatoes, peeled and quartered
4	cups cooked macaroni
2	cups (12 oz.) grated sharp Cheddar cheese
2	large or 3 medium onions
1	clove chopped garlic
1	cup dry red wine
1/2	cup strong stock
1	can sliced pimentos with their juice
6	tablesp. oil or drippings
1 1/2	teasp. salt
1/2	teasp. dried oregano

The cooking should be started with enough cold water to cover. When the water begins to boil, the heat is reduced and the tongue is simmered for three hours, or until it is tender. The smoked or corned tongue may be cooked in plain water. The flavor of the fresh tongue will be improved by adding to the liquid in which it is boiled, one carrot, a stalk or two of celery, a handful of fresh celery leaves and either fresh parsley, thyme and tarragon— several sprigs each—or several sprigs of parsley and a teaspoonful each of dried tarragon and thyme, together with a clove of garlic, a few cloves and some whole peppercorns.

After the tongue is tender, it should be allowed to cool in its broth. Cut off the gristle and small bones at the base and skin it, starting the incision on the under surface at the base and pulling the skin forward. Serve in slices about one-third inch thick, with fresh spinach. Europeans frequently serve mushrooms or lentils with tongue, either fresh or smoked.

Allow to Cool in its Broth

In general, your red *ordinaire,* Beaujolais or California, will be adequate for this dish.

Corned Beef

The brisket is the best cut of corned beef, although beef round is sometimes prepared in this manner.

Wash, cover with cold water, and add for a four to five pound brisket, four bay leaves and a medium-size onion stuck with six or eight cloves, or add pickling spices for a more exotic flavor. Bring water to a boil and simmer gently for three hours or more until the meat is tender.

It is not unlawful to serve other vegetables with corned beef, but cabbage, not overcooked, is both traditional and very good.

Drink Beaujolais or an inexpensive California red wine with corned beef.

OTHER MEATS 15

VEAL

You will sometimes have difficulty in finding good veal in American markets, particularly the mass supermarkets. Veal is not as popular in the United States as it is in western Europe, and you are less likely to find true milk-fed veal. The best veal is from animals three to six weeks old, still nourished entirely on milk. Its flesh is the palest pink; as the animal gets older and begins to eat grass, its flesh gets redder and it begins to look more like beef. As a matter of fact, a good deal of the supermarket "veal" is really baby beef.

Therefore, look for the palest pink when you shop for veal. And remember: if enough customers demand an item, the markets will stock it.

Veal is tender but the flavor is somewhat neutral. For this reason, most of the veal dishes we have found attractive call for the addition of wine, herbs and cheese. It is for this reason that you will find no recipes for roasts of veal in this book.

Blanquette of Veal

This is only a stew, but it is one of the best stews in the world.

Choose at least part of the meat from the breast. It is less expensive, and it has cartilage and small bones which will add flavor to your stew. Have all the meat cut in as

BLANQUETTE OF VEAL

2 1/2	lbs. veal breast, shoulder or leg
6	oz. white wine
2	small carrots
1	egg
1	oz. butter
1 1/2	tablesp. flour
1/2	lb. mushrooms
1/2	lb. small boiling onions
1	*bouquet garni*
	freshly ground white pepper
	salt

uniform a size as possible, about one and one-half inch squares. Put the meat in a casserole with the wine. Cut the onion in two and stick a clove in each half. Make a *bouquet garni* of one stalk of celery, the carrots cut in slices, a bay leaf and 1/2 teaspoon of thyme enclosed in cheesecloth so that it may be removed. Add to casserole and fill with enough water to cover the meat.

Bring the water to a boil, then lower heat and simmer very gently. Because veal has lots of soluble protein, you will have to skim it longer and more frequently than you would with beef. Cook for two hours or until the meat is tender.

Clean the mushrooms, and unless they are small, slice them. Peel the onions and cook the mushrooms and onions together in half of the butter, keeping the heat low enough to avoid browning the butter. Cook for twenty-five to thirty minutes.

When the meat is cooked, remove the *bouquet garni* and strain the broth. Keep the meat warm and reserve the broth.

In a small saucepan, make a *roux* by mixing the flour and the rest of the butter. Cook for several minutes. Gradually add some of the broth to the *roux* and let it simmer for six to eight minutes. Now, turn the thickened sauce and the rest of the broth back into the casserole and let it simmer for ten minutes. Add to it the mushroom-onion mixture.

When you are nearly ready to serve, correct the seasoning (it should be mild) and prepare to thicken the sauce. Beat the egg until it is foamy and gradually add one cup of the sauce to the egg after the sauce has cooled a little, beating all the time. Be sure the sauce is not boiling. You may now safely stir the egg thickening into the sauce without its curdling.

Blanquette of veal is delicate enough and flavorful enough to rate a good commune Bordeaux, such as a Pauillac, a St. Estèpe or a Margaux, or one of the best of the Côtes wines such as a Côte de Bourg. If you select a California wine, let it be the best Cabernet Sauvignon you can buy, which means it will cost as much as the Bordeaux.

Veal Scallops with Tarragon

Have the butcher cut slices three-eighth inch thick from a leg of veal or from boned rib chops across the grain.

Wipe the cutlets clean and place on a board between sheets of waxed paper. Pound with a mallet or the flat side of a cleaver until they are one-quarter inch thick. Shake the cutlets in a paper bag containing the flour, one teaspoon of salt, and a good grind of black pepper. Sauté the cutlets in the cooking oil over a brisk fire about 4 minutes on each side. They should be golden brown.

Remove to a warm serving dish and add to the skillet in which the cutlets were cooked, one ounce of butter, one cup of good white vermouth, and the fresh or dried tarragon. Cook until the volume is reduced by one-half and pour over the cutlets.

Serve a good regional Bordeaux, such as a Médoc.

Veal Scallopini, Roman Style

Pound the scallops as directed in the previous recipe. Season with salt and pepper and let stand while you make the sauce.

Heat one-half of the butter in a skillet and sauté the mushrooms gently until they are golden. Then add onion and garlic either chopped finely or put through a garlic press. Continue cooking until the onion is soft and golden. Add tomatoes, vermouth, salt to taste, and tarragon; simmer, covered, for one-half hour, stirring occasionally.

Heat the rest of the butter and cook the scallops rapidly until they are lightly browned on both sides. Return all veal to the skillet and add the sauce. Let simmer, covered, for five minutes. If the sauce becomes too thick, add a little more vermouth or a little chicken or beef stock.

Sprinkle with the Parmesan cheese just before serving.

Again, I think you will like a good Bordeaux or its California equivalent, Cabernet Sauvignon, better than a Burgundy with this dish.

Veal Parmigiana

Heat the oil and sauté the onion and garlic until golden. Add all of the other items and bring to a boil. Reduce heat and let simmer ten minutes, covered. The tomatoes should be reduced to a pulp and the sauce should be quite thick.

VEAL SCALLOPS WITH TARRAGON

2	lbs. veal scallops
1	cup French dry vermouth
3	tablesp. cooking oil
1	tablesp. flour
1	tablesp. fresh tarragon or 1 teasp. dried tarragon
	freshly ground black pepper
	salt

VEAL SCALLOPINI, ROMAN STYLE

2	lbs. veal scallops
1/2	lb. small mushrooms
2	lbs. fresh tomatoes
1	medium onion, chopped
2/3	cup dry vermouth
1	clove garlic
4	oz. butter (1 stick)
1/2	teasp. dried tarragon
1	cup freshly grated Parmesan cheese
1	teasp. salt
	freshly ground black pepper

227

VEAL PARMIGIANA

6	large or 12 small scallops of veal
2	eggs
1	cup dry bread crumbs
1/2	cup olive oil
8	oz. Mozzarella cheese
1/2	cup freshly grated Parmesan cheese

SAUCE FOR VEAL PARMIGIANA

1	can tomatoes (1 lb.) preferably Italian
1/2	cup chopped onion
2	tablesp. olive oil
2	cloves minced garlic or put through garlic press
3/4	teasp. salt
1/2	teasp. dried oregano
1/2	teasp. dried sweet basil freshly ground pepper

VEAL PICCATA

2	lbs. veal cutlets
2	tablesp. flour
1	teasp. salt
1/2	cup dry white wine or dry vermouth
1	teasp. dried sweet basil freshly ground pepper
3	tablesp. olive oil
1	lemon
2	teasp. butter

Beat the eggs. Dry the scallops and pound as in the other recipes. Dip in egg, then in bread crumbs. Buy seasoned bread crumbs or add 1/4 teaspoon of dried sweet basil to plain crumbs. Heat the oil in a large skillet and cook the scallops until they are golden brown on each side, which will take three or four minutes each. Remove as they are done to make room for more. You may need more oil.

Place the cooked scallops in a shallow baking dish large enough to hold one-half of them in one layer. Cover with half the sauce and half of both sorts of cheese. Repeat with the rest of the scallops and the sauce, ending with Parmesan cheese on top. Bake in a 350 degree oven until the contents of the dish bubble and the cheese begins to brown.

Serve with Barbera, Bardolino or, for a novelty, a frothing Lambrusco, a red wine from the Emilia Romagna district, which foams up almost like a beer when you pour it, but in which the sparkle soon subsides. If your taste is similar to that of my wife and me, you will not want it often, but it is fun occasionally.

Veal Piccata

Pound the cutlets thin and wipe dry, as in all the cutlet recipes; shake in a bag with flour, salt, pepper and basil. Heat oil in skillet and brown each cutlet well on both sides. Slice lemon as thinly as possible and place slices over cutlets. Add the wine, cover the skillet and simmer for five minutes. Remove meat to a hot serving plate. Add more wine (a spoonful or two) to a skillet and scrape all the browned particles. Stir in two teaspoons butter. Let cook for a minute or so, then pour over scallops.

Any inexpensive red wine will suffice. The lemon flavor is not wholly sympathetic to wine.

Osso Bucco

Have your butcher saw the veal shanks into sections two to two and one-half inches long, so that the marrow will not be disturbed. Chop the carrots and celery into fairly small pieces. Heat the olive oil in a casserole and cook the vegetables until they are barely beginning to brown. Add the chopped onion and continue cooking until the onion is soft. Add the pieces of veal and brown, turning them frequently. Cream the flour and butter to-gether and add this mixture to the casserole, stirring well. Cook over medium heat about five minutes. Now, add the wine, the stock and the tomato purée.

Grate one teaspoon of the lemon peel and set aside. Add the balance of lemon peel to the casserole together with your *bouquet garni*. The latter should contain a bay leaf or two, four sprigs of parsley, a teaspoon of dried sweet basil, and 1/2 teaspoon dried thyme, all in cheese-cloth for easy removal.

After the contents of the casserole come to a boil, lower heat and simmer very gently for one and one-half to two hours, until the meat is tender. Stir occasionally to prevent sticking.

Place the meat on a hot serving dish and strain the sauce over it. If the sauce needs thickening, remove the cover and turn up the heat for a time. Sprinkle with the reserved grated lemon rind and parsley mixed together.

The traditional accompaniment for osso bucco is plain boiled spaghetti or a Milanese rissoto.

It goes well with any Italian red wine, but it also goes equally well with a full-bodied white. Try it sometime with a Pouilly-Fuissé or a Wente Brothers Pinot Char-donnay.

Veal Matelote

The name means sailor's stew because it was first cooked by the wives of Breton and Norman fishermen.

Melt the butter in a heavy casserole and brown the pieces of veal, which you have first wiped dry. Sprinkle the flour over the browning meat and turn frequently. Add herbs and spices to taste. For the first time you make the mixture, I suggest that you use 1/2 teaspoon of thyme, six sprigs of parsley, one bay leaf, and a good dash of allspice, together with salt and pepper as you like. After the first time, adjust the seasonings to your family's taste. Stir in the water and wine; cover the casserole and heat until it boils; turn down heat and let simmer gently.

Peel the onions; wash and slice the mushrooms unless they are very small, in which case they are best left whole. Cook the onions and mushrooms together in a little butter in a covered skillet for five minutes or until they are beginning to become soft. Add them to the casserole. When

OSSO BUCCO

6	veal shanks
3	small carrots
2	stalks celery
3	tablesp. olive oil
1/2	cup dry white wine
	peel of one lemon
1	tablesp. butter
1	teasp. flour
1	*bouquet garni*
4	oz. tomato purée
1	teasp. chopped parsley
1/2	cup strong stock

VEAL MATELOTE

3	lbs. veal breast
3/4	lb. boiling onions
3/4	lb. small mushrooms
3/4	stick butter
1	tablesp. flour
4	oz. dry red wine
2	oz. water
	salt
	pepper
	bay leaf
	thyme
	parsley
	ground allspice

229

the meat is tender (approximately two hours) remove the bay leaf and sprinkle the matelote with a teaspoon of finely chopped parsley.

Because red wine was used in the cooking, and because the seasoning and the butter are French rather than Italian, the matelote calls for a nice light red wine; a regional Bordeaux (one labeled Médoc or St. Emilion) or a Beaujolais will do nicely.

Veal Sweetbreads

Allow for Shrinkage in Preparation

One of the most delicate of meats and one which lends itself to many elaborations, almost all of which are good. Here are two, both relatively simple to do, and both excellent. It should be remembered when buying sweetbreads that about one-third of the raw weight will be trimmed off and lost in the preparation. Thus, allow a minimum of one-half pound, raw weight, for each person.

The preliminary preparation for sweetbreads is the same. Soak them in ice water for several hours. Then put them in a court bouillon made by adding two tablespoons of wine vinegar, two or three chopped shallots, one-half of a small onion, a few sprigs of parsley and 1/2 teaspoon of salt to each pint of water. Start them in enough of this cold court bouillon to cover and let come to a boil gradually. Simmer until the sweetbreads are white and opaque. After they have cooled enough to handle, remove the membrane which covers them and cut away the large tubes which connect the two parts, as well as any other unattractive portions. Then wrap in a clean napkin and place them in a plate or other flat utensil. Cover with a cutting board or other small board and put a weight of about five pounds on the board. Let them rest in this fashion for a full hour or longer. They are now ready for whatever recipe you have chosen.

Veal Sweetbreads in Mushroom Sauce

To make the sauce, first clean and slice the mushrooms. Cook them in one tablespoon of butter for about five minutes, until they are golden.

Melt two tablespoons of butter in a saucepan and stir in the flour until all lumps have disappeared. Let this roux cook until it is quite brown. Add the chicken stock and cook gently for one-half hour. About half way through the cooking, add one-half of the Madeira. The sauce should, when it is cooked, be neither soupy nor pasty, but should coat a spoon and be the texture of a good gravy. Correct the texture as necessary by adding more flour or more stock. Add the mushrooms after thirty minutes and continue cooking another ten minutes. Just before pouring over the sweetbreads, add the rest of the Madeira, after correcting the seasoning.

Cut the prepared sweetbreads into regular pieces about one inch in size. Melt the butter in a heavy skillet and sauté gently until the pieces become golden brown. The cooking should be very slow, and should take about thirty minutes. Correct the seasoning and place the sweetbreads in a serving dish rather than in a platter. Pour the sauce over it and, if you like, dress it up either with sprigs of parsley or a sprinkle of chopped parsley.

This dish merits as good a red Bordeaux as you can afford. It is also excellent with a full-bodied white, such as a Meursault or Chassagne Montrachet, or a California Chardonnay.

Sweetbreads and Chicken Breasts in Scallop Shells

Prepare sweetbreads as in basic recipe. Cut into one-half inch cubes. Clean and dry the chicken breasts. Cut them into cubes the same size as the sweetbreads. Mix butter and oil in a saucepan with a heavy bottom over the lowest possible heat. Cook sweetbreads and chicken for five minutes. Try not to let them begin to brown. Add the shallots, mushrooms, and bay leaf and cook three minutes longer. Sprinkle one teaspoon of flour over the contents of the pan and stir thoroughly, cooking all the time. Add all the liquid ingredients and let come to a boil. Turn down the heat and simmer as gently as possible for about one-half hour, stirring occasionally. Season with salt and pepper to taste and divide equally among six warmed scallop shells. Dust with paprika and decorate each shell with a sprig of parsley.

The tiniest possible peas, cooked in the French manner with a few pieces of shredded lettuce and a little green onion, is an excellent vegetable to go with this special dish. For a super gala occasion, you can add one or two truffles, sliced thinly, at the same time as the mushrooms.

VEAL SWEETBREADS IN MUSHROOM SAUCE

3	lbs. veal sweetbreads
1/2	stick butter
	salt
	freshly ground black pepper
2	tablesp. flour
2	tablesp. butter
2	cups chicken stock
4	oz. dry Madeira
6	oz. mushrooms

SWEETBREADS AND CHICKEN BREASTS IN SCALLOP SHELLS

1 1/2	lbs. sweetbreads
1/2	lb. chicken breast
1/2	lb. small white mushrooms
1/4	stick butter
2	tablesp. cooking oil
1/2	pt. heavy cream
2	oz. dry white wine
2	oz. Madeira (Sercial by preference)
1	tablesp. chopped shallots
1	bay leaf
1	teasp. flour
1	teasp. salt
	freshly ground black pepper

231

We enjoy equally with this dish, a bottle of our finest red Bordeaux or a good, full-bodied white Burgundy, such as a Meursault or a Montrachet. It is also delightful with a rich, full Auslese or Spätlese Rhine or Mosel.

Veal Kidneys

While beef kidneys may be eaten—they are especially adapted to a beef and kidney pie—veal kidneys are more tender and milder. It is not only unnecessary to soak kidneys in water, but it is harmful to their texture and flavor; they absorb too much water. When you purchase them, see that the kidneys have a fresh odor with little or no smell of ammonia. Wash them very quickly in cold water, remove the fat and the outer membrane, as well as all the white parts and the tubing at the center. It is preferable to do the preliminary cooking with the kidney whole. In this manner, less of the juice is lost and there is less danger of overcooking, thereby giving the kidneys a tough, rubbery texture. When you slice the kidney, it should still be pink inside.

Veal Kidneys with Mushrooms Flambé

Heat one-half of the butter in a heavy saucepan and cook the whole kidneys over brisk heat for three or four minutes, turning them frequently. Remove the kidneys and keep warm.

Add the rest of the butter and sauté the mushrooms, cleaned and sliced if they are large, but left whole if they are small, for five minutes. Pour off part of the butter and deglaze the pan with the wine, letting its volume reduce by about one-half.

Cut the cooked kidneys in slices about one-eighth inch thick and replace in the saucepan. Pour over half of the cognac and flame, stirring and basting with the flaming brandy. When the flame is extinguished, add the rest of the brandy and let simmer one minute. Add the cream and let cook only long enough for the sauce to thicken a little. Serve garnished with chopped parsley.

A good full-bodied Burgundy is best with kidneys, but failing that, a good stout Beaujolais. The point is that the flavor of the dish is full and it needs a full-flavored wine to partner it.

VEAL KIDNEYS WITH MUSHROOMS FLAMBÉ

2	lbs. veal kidneys
6	oz. mushrooms
4	oz. cognac
2	oz. dry white wine
2	oz. butter
1	teasp. finely chopped parsley
	salt
	fresh black pepper
1/2	cup cream

232

If you cook kidneys exactly this way, but just before you add the cream, mix a teaspoon or two of Dijon mustard with it, you will have Kidneys Dijonnaise style.

Veal Kidneys with Madeira
(Rognons de veau au Madère)

Prepare the kidneys and cook whole in the butter as in the preceding recipe, turning frequently for about four minutes. Remove the kidneys to a plate and keep them warm. Add the flour to the saucepan and stir until the butter-flour mixture is well browned and free of lumps. Add the stock gradually and cook for fifteen minutes until the sauce does not taste raw. Add the Madeira (more or less than is directed) according to the thickness of the sauce. Quickly slice the kidneys and return to the sauce. Let simmer only long enough to reheat the kidneys thoroughly.

This preparation, like the one above, calls for a full-bodied Burgundy, or at least, a good Beaujolais.

Saltimbocca

Properly prepared, these little cutlets live up to their name which means "jump into the mouth." Carelessly prepared or overcooked, they are hardly worth the trouble. So be careful and watch to see that they are barely cooked and, in no case, overdone.

After pounding the cutlets, season with salt, pepper and the two herbs. Cover each cutlet with one or more pieces of prosciutto. Heat the butter, but do not let it smoke. Fasten the two kinds of meat together with pieces of toothpick and put them in the skillet, veal side down. Cook about two minutes and turn quickly. Do not cook the ham side quite as long. Remove quickly to a hot platter. Add the juice of one-half of a lemon and a little more butter to the pan. Scrape browned particles with a wooden spoon, let simmer a moment and pour over the little cutlets.

Your red *ordinaire* will serve very well here.

LAMB

In no market in California during the last several years, nor anywhere in a year's residence in France and

VEAL KIDNEYS WITH MADEIRA
(Rognons de veau au Madère)

2	lbs. veal kidneys
4	oz. butter
6	oz. beef stock or condensed bouillon
6	oz. Madeira
1	tablesp. flour
	salt
	fresh black pepper
	chopped parsley

SALTIMBOCCA

6	veal cutlets, pounded to less than 1/4 inch thick
6	slices (or more) prosciutto same size as cutlets
1/2	teasp. sage
1/2	teasp. summer savory
1/3	stick butter
	salt
	pepper

233

Italy, have we been able to buy mutton. Even in Great Britain, traditionally the home of mutton, we found roast mutton only at Simpson's; even at this traditional British eating place, mutton chops were unavailable.

For all practical purposes, then, lamb seems to have replaced mutton on all Western tables. There is no question but that lamb is milder; nevertheless, I still recall with pleasure, my days as a medical student in San Francisco when we used to get big, juicy, flavorful mutton chops, as different, and as much better than lamb chops, as good beef is different and superior to veal.

Roast Leg of Lamb
(Gigot d'Agneau)

ROAST LEG OF LAMB
(Gigot d'Agneau)

5 - 6	lb. leg of lamb
	onions
	bouquet garni
1/2	cup red wine
	salt
	pepper

Wipe clean. Do not remove the thin, skin-like covering called the fell; it helps preserve juices during the cooking. Choose a leg weighing around five to six pounds. Make tiny slits extending to the bone and insert thin slices of garlic; four or five if you wish a very mild flavor, more if you like a more pronounced flavor. Rub the surface with a mixture of salt and pepper. Put on a rack in a shallow roasting pan. Put into the pan, five or six slices of onion, a small onion, a stalk of celery sliced, and a *bouquet garni* consisting of a bay leaf, several sprigs of fresh parsley, a few fresh celery leaves and a teaspoon of dried thyme and another of dried savory, all in cheesecloth. Add 1/2 cup red wine to the pan. Put in a 450 degree oven for fifteen minutes and then lower heat to 350. Always insert a meat thermometer, avoiding the bone. Roast until the thermometer reaches 145 to 150 degrees, basting with the pan juices occasionally. This will produce lamb which is juicy and pink. If you like it well done, roast until the thermometer shows 160 degrees; but if you do, you run the risk of having dry as well as gray meat. If you do not have a meat thermometer, roast twelve to fifteen minutes a pound for medium rare and up to thirty minutes for well done.

The full flavor of lamb requires a red wine, but the flavor is delicate enough that most of us prefer a good Bordeaux to a Burgundy. If you are using a California wine, choose a Cabernet in place of a Pinot Noir. For a plain roast leg, select a good regional, such as Médoc or St. Emilion; for an extra good roast, choose a wine with a commune name such as Pauillac or Margaux.

Roast Leg of Lamb with Rosemary

Sauté carrot, celery and shallots in the butter for five minutes, stirring to prevent burning. Add 1/2 cup each of water and wine to the vegetables.

Rub the meat, after wiping it clean, with salt, pepper and rosemary, or make incisions and insert little sprigs of the herb in the meat and place a few sprigs in the bottom of the pan. Arrange the sautéed vegetables around the roast and brown for fifteen minutes in a 450 degree oven, then lower temperature to 350 degrees and roast until the meat thermometer indicates the desired degree of doneness—145 or 150 for a pink rareness, up to 160 if you want the meat well done. Baste occasionally with the pan juices and with additional water and wine if needed.

If you wish a gravy, let the pan juices cool after removing the roast to a hot platter and skim off grease. Add remaining water and white wine. Mix a tablespoon each of butter and flour and add to the pan. Scrape brown particles and let cook until the gravy is of the desired consistency.

Try omitting the usual American garnish of mint jelly and serve your roast lamb instead with either green beans or white navy beans as the French do. I suspect you will like it·better.

Again, a good regional Bordeaux is suggested as the right accompaniment.

Leg of Lamb in a Crust
(Gigot d'Agneau en Croûte)

Here is a specialty of Chef Raymond Thulier of the Restaurant Baumanière, one of the ten provincial three-star restaurants of France, which is at Le Baux, at the foot of the Alpilles, between Nîmes and Avignon in Provence. This astonishing little range of miniature mountains has the same steep, jagged peaks as the real Alps, but its peaks are only a few hundred feet in altitude instead of thousands of feet. Incidentally, Le Baux gives its name to bauxite, the richest of the earth's aluminum-containing material, widespread over the earth, but first discovered here.

Select a leg of baby lamb weighing two and one-half to three pounds. Have it deboned by the butcher. Clean the lamb kidneys, remove the fat around them and at their

ROAST LEG OF LAMB WITH ROSEMARY

4 - 5   lb. leg of lamb
2   cups dry white wine
2   cups water
4   chopped shallots
1   tablesp. butter
1   sliced carrot
1   stalk sliced celery
   several sprigs fresh rosemary
     or 1 teasp. dried rosemary
   salt
   pepper

235

LEG OF LAMB IN A CRUST
(Gigot d'Agneau en Crôute)

2 1/2
to 3 lbs. leg of lamb
2 lamb kidneys
6 oz. button mushrooms
  pastry dough for crust
1/2 teasp. salt
1 egg yolk, beaten
1/3 stick butter
3 oz. Madeira
1/2 teasp. dried thyme
1/2 teasp. dried rosemary
1/2 teasp. dried tarragon

middle; cut away all of the tubing and white parts. Rinse quickly in cold water and blot dry with paper towels. Melt one-half of the butter in a skillet and sauté the whole kidneys about four to five minutes, turning frequently. Remove from the skillet and deglaze with the Madeira, to which may be added the powdered herbs. Quickly cube the kidneys, which should still be pink inside, and return to the skillet with the rest of the butter.

Fill the aperture in the leg of lamb left by the bone with the preparation in the skillet, reshape the leg, and close it with three or four stitches of kitchen string.

Place the leg in a 450 degree oven in a shallow pan for sixteen minutes, turning once. In the meantime, roll out a rich pastry dough (Pâte Brisée)large enough to encase the leg. Place the leg in the middle of the dough and cover, moistening and sealing the edges. Cut three or four slashes in the top of the crust to allow the steam to escape. Brush the pastry with beaten egg yolk, and place on a pastry sheet in a 400 degree oven for fifteen to twenty minutes until the crust turns a nice golden brown.

Warning: these directions give you the meat quite rare, which is the way the French eat it, and the way we grew to like it; but, it is definitely rare and if you want your meat only pink or even well done, increase the time in the oven before putting the roast in the pastry.

Chef Thulier serves his gigot with a gratin of potatoes, the recipe for which you will find in the chapter on vegetables.

We drank a bottle of 1952 Châteaux Margaux with the croûte. It was a great extravagance, but well worth it. You will find the dish worthy of the best château-bottled claret.

Crown Roast of Lamb

This is formed by using all of the loin of a spring lamb. Your butcher will separate the two sets of ribs from the backbone and bend them outward in the form of a half circle. The two half circles, each containing eight ribs and, therefore, the meat of sixteen rib chops, are tied together to make the crown. The chops should be "frenched," that is, the meat should be cut away from the end of the bone for about an inch. Be sure that the butcher covers the end of each rib with salt pork. If he does not, you may put a piece of raw potato over each bare end to prevent its burning. There should be strips of bacon or salt pork under the strings tying the two semicircles together, to conserve flavor and add juiciness. Have the butcher trim off all the meat from the inside of the crown and grind it, either for inclusion in a stuffing to fill the crown, or for use as lamb patties. Obviously, a crown roast is a major project, to be undertaken by most of us only for a special grand occasion. I would like to suggest it as an alternative to the traditional Thanksgiving or Christmas turkey.

Rub salt and pepper over the surface of the roast and, if you like, thyme and savory. You may make a stuffing with bread crumbs and butter seasoned with onion, shallot, thyme and savory; or a stuffing of one-half of the ground lamb trimmings and one-half pork sausage, with onion and the same seasoning, together with a little sage. Or try this: place a cup or small bowl in the middle of the crown to maintain its roundness while it cooks. Remove the bowl when cooking is complete, fill the center with creamed mushrooms or creamed veal sweetbreads.

Stuffing is Optional

Start the cooking, as with a leg, at 450 degrees for fifteen minutes, and then lower oven temperature to 375 degrees. Baste with butter and wine, and later with the pan juices. Roast for one and one-half hours for rare, a little longer if you like it less pink. This is the finest meat of the lamb and it deserves to be served rare and juicy. If you use a meat thermometer, be sure it is halfway between two of the rib bones, in the center of the meat.

If you use a stuffing, serve glazed carrots or green tiny peas. If you use the creamed mushrooms, no further garniture is needed. Some French cooks serve buttered Brussels sprouts with a crown roast. These seem to us to have too coarse a flavor.

The crown roast, again, merits your best Bordeaux.

Roast Saddle of Lamb

This cut is the same choicest portion of the lamb carcass as the crown roast, that is, the two sets of loin chops, but this time the meat is left in one piece. Actually, it roasts somewhat better than the rack or crown roast because less surface is exposed from which juice may be lost. Your butcher will bone the loin if you like. It is a little easier to carve but does not look quite as handsome as it comes to the table.

237

ROAST SADDLE OF LAMB

1	double loin or saddle of lamb
1	carrot
1	small onion
3 - 4	shallots
1	stalk celery
4	tablesp. cooking oil
1	cup dry white wine
1/4	cup chopped ham
1	bay leaf
6	sprigs of parsley
1/2	teasp. thyme
1	clove chopped garlic
2	whole cloves
1 - 2	pinch of mace

SADDLE OF LAMB EN CROÛTE CHEZ NOUS

4 - 5	lb. saddle of lamb
1	small onion
4	shallots
1	small carrot
1/2	stalk celery
3	oz. small mushrooms
2	oz. Madeira
	pastry to cover meat
1/2	stick butter
1/4	cup chopped ham
1	bay leaf
3	sprigs parsley
1/2	teasp. dried thyme
2	whole cloves
1/2	teasp. dried savory
	salt
	freshly ground pepper
	a good pinch of mace

238

Heat the oil in a skillet or baking pan and brown all the vegetables and herbs. Add the meat and sear on all sides until the meat is definitely browned. Insert a meat thermometer and transfer the vegetables to a baking pan, laying the loin on top, and add a cup of dry white wine. Roast in a 350 degree oven until the thermometer reaches 150 to 160 degrees, or about eighteen minutes per pound. Again, the meat should be definitely pink. Baste frequently with the pan juices. Serve with mushrooms, pan roasted potatoes, peas, or Brussels sprouts.

To make a special sauce, strain the contents of the roasting pan into a small saucepan and when the liquid cools, skim the fat. Add two tablespoons of tomato paste and thicken with a tablespoon each of flour and butter well mixed. The sauce should boil a few minutes and should be of a consistency to coat a spoon. Correct seasoning and add an ounce each of Curaçoa and cognac, together with the chopped ham. Do not boil after adding the liquors. Serve immediately and pass the sauce in a hot sauceboat.

Your best Bordeaux is called for here.

Saddle of Lamb en Croûte Chez Nous

Clarify the butter. Chop all the vegetables except the mushrooms rather finely and cook them in part of the butter in a casserole. When the vegetables are soft and brown, add the herbs and mace, together with the cloves and bay leaf. Clean and slice the mushrooms and sauté them in another pan in the rest of the butter until they are done—five minutes or so.

Now brown the meat over the browned vegetables as in the previous recipe. Add the Madeira and cover the casserole, turning down the heat somewhat and cooking about ten minutes to the pound.

Meanwhile, roll out a rich pastry dough. Place the browned meat in the center and scrape all the browned vegetables and juices on top of it. Distribute the sliced mushrooms and the chopped ham over the loin and deglaze the casserole with a little more Madeira, letting it reduce by one-half. Add this on top of the mushrooms and encase in the pastry. Moisten the edges and seal well. Make one or two holes in the top to allow the escape of steam. Brush with beaten egg yolk. Bake on a cookie sheet in a 400 degree oven until the crust turns a nice golden color, which should be about one-half hour.

Endive braised in butter with walnuts, or artichoke hearts filled with buttered little peas are worthy garnitures for this truly elegant dish. It also will do honor to your best Bordeaux.

Broiled Butterflied Leg of Lamb

Have your butcher bone a five to six pound leg of lamb. When you get it home, spread it out, skin side down, and make a series of incisions on the inside sufficiently deep that the meat will lie flat, but not risking going entirely through to the other side. Marinate for twenty-four hours in the following marinade.

Slice one medium onion, one stalk celery and one carrot into a crock. Add three or four minced shallots, a teaspoon each of dried oregano and sweet basil, two teaspoons salt, two teaspoons Dijon mustard and a good grind of black pepper. Add one or two minced cloves of garlic, 3/4 cup olive oil and one-half of a bottle of dry red wine. Mix well and immerse the lamb, or, if the lamb is not entirely covered, turn it several times during the twenty-four hours.

Dry the meat with paper towels, grease the grill over your charcoal or electric broiler; grill four inches from the heat for ten minutes on each side. Then increase the distance of the grill from the fire and cook until the meat is done. For juicy pinkness, this will usually be about an hour's total cooking time; if you want the lamb well done, it will take longer. Baste frequently with the marinade.

This method of preparation is particularly well adapted to the hooded barbecue grills which circulate smoke from the charcoal inside the hood where the meat is cooking.

Serve with boiled white beans, or with roasted potatoes and green peas. A hearty Pomerol will add to your enjoyment of the broiled flavor of this meat, particularly if you have the sort of barbecue which subjects the meat to a good deal of smoke. A good Napa Valley Cabernet Sauvignon will also do it justice at somewhat less expense.

Braised Shoulder of Lamb

Have the butcher bone and roll the shoulder. Rub the meat with flour, salt and freshly ground pepper; brown

BROILED BUTTERFLIED LEG OF LAMB

4 - 5	lb. leg of lamb
1	medium onion
1	small carrot
1	stalk celery
3 - 4	shallots
3/4	cup olive oil
1/2	bottle dry red wine
1 - 2	cloves garlic
1	teasp. dried oregano
1	teasp. dried sweet basil
1	teasp. salt
2	teasp. Dijon mustard
	black pepper

239

BRAISED SHOULDER OF LAMB

4 - 5   lb. boned shoulder of lamb
2   tablesp. butter
1   large eggplant
1   lb. fresh tomatoes, peeled
      and chopped, or 1 No. 2
      can of Italian tomatoes
2   large onions
2   cloves crushed garlic
    flour
    salt
    pepper
1   cup dry red wine

in the butter in a casserole, turning so that all sides are well browned. Remove meat temporarily and into the casserole or Dutch oven put the eggplant in large chunks, the tomatoes and sliced onions. Crush the garlic cloves in a press or mince finely into the casserole. Add the wine and place the meat on top of the vegetables. Cover and put into a 350 degree oven; cook until tender. Do not uncover the casserole for at least two hours. It may take three hours before the meat is tender. If the combined juices of the meat and the thoroughly cooked vegetables are too thin, add two teaspoons of flour, well mixed with the same amount of butter and stir well into the mixture; let cook five or ten minutes without the lid.

You will need no further vegetables with this dish. Garnish with sprigs of parsley and serve a good regional claret. Here, I prefer a Pomerol or a St. Emilion, rather than the more delicate Médoc.

Braised Shoulder of Lamb and Beans

BRAISED SHOULDER OF
LAMB AND BEANS

4 - 5   lbs. boned shoulder of lamb
1   large onion
2   cloves garlic
1   cup strong stock or
      condensed bouillon
    flour
    salt
    pepper
1   cup (or more) white beans

In France, one frequently encounters a braised shoulder of lamb with white beans.

Rub the boned and rolled shoulder with flour mixed with salt and pepper. Brown in a casserole with the butter. Remove and reduce heat a little while you cook the onion and garlic until the onion is soft and golden. Replace the shoulder, add the stock and cover. Cook in a 350 degree oven about one and three-quarter hours.

Soak the beans overnight. About two hours before they are to be added to the meat, cover with salted water and simmer gently until they are soft. After the lamb has cooked as described above, skim off most of the fat in the pan. Strain the beans and arrange in the casserole around the shoulder; better yet, lift up the meat, arrange the beans in the casserole and replace the meat on top of them. Cook at least another one-half hour or until the meat is tender.

Obviously, there is no place in these dishes for mint jelly, either real or (as I have seen in supermarkets) imitation.

A good bourgeois or artisan cru of Bordeaux or a young Beaujolais will furnish just the zest needed with this fine dish.

Grilled Lamb Chops

Have your butcher "french" the chops—or do it yourself. This means removing the thin, tough rim of meat that extends to the tip of the chop so that the first inch of the bone is bare. Also, remove part of the fat surrounding the chop. Lamb chops are juicier and more flavorful if they are cut thick and cooked only until they are pink inside. It is better to serve one chop (two ribs) per person than two thin, dried-out ones.

You can increase variety and interest if you use different herbs to flavor your lamb chops.

Lamb Chops with Dill: Rub each chop on both sides with pulverized dill weed and then with a scant teaspoon of bland cooking oil. Stack the chops and let sit for several hours before grilling.

Lamb Chops with Tarragon: One of our favorites. Treat the chops the same way as above, rubbing pulverized dried tarragon.

Lamb Chops with Basil: Use dried basil, but this time, rub the chops with olive oil; basil is a characteristic herb of Italy and Provence, and the flavor of olive oil is equally characteristic of these Mediterranean regions.

Lamb Chops with Garlic: Garlic fits a chop as well as a roast.

Lamb Chops Hollandaise

Trim excess fat from the chops and rub with the dried basil. Cover with a cloth and let sit for four or five hours.

Clean and slice the mushrooms. Grill chops about four inches from heat source. We like them quite pink and juicy. You can achieve this in seven or eight minutes exposure to the heat on each side. If you like the chops completely cooked, grill ten minutes per side. Sauté the mushrooms in the butter.

Arrange the chops on a hot serving tray with the mushrooms in the center. Top each chop with a generous tablespoon or more of the hollandaise sauce and serve immediately.

LAMB CHOPS HOLLANDAISE

6	double loin lamb chops
12	oz. fresh mushrooms
1	teasp. dried basil
2	tablesp. butter
6	oz. (or more) hollandaise sauce
	salt
	fresh black pepper

241

Chops cooked in this manner deserve a good commune Bordeaux, such as a Pauillac or St. Estèphe, or even one of your classified crus, such as a Château Palmer.

Daube of Lamb

DAUBE OF LAMB

4 - 5	lb. leg or shoulder of lamb
1/2	bottle white Rhône wine
1/2	bottle red wine
3	carrots
1	large or 2 small onions
1 1/2	oz. cognac
2	cloves garlic
1	tablesp. red wine vinegar, tarragon flavored
1/4	lb. salt pork
1/2	stick cinnamon
1	teasp. peppercorns
1/2	teasp. whole cloves
1	teasp. salt
1	tablesp. flour
1	tablesp. butter

Like all boiled meat, lamb cooked in accordance with this recipe comes out looking a little gray and unattractive, thus belying its real goodness. I have, therefore, modified the original French recipe, first by browning the meat at the end of the cooking and, second, by thickening the sauce somewhat. Either a leg or a shoulder may be used. The flavor of the leg is perhaps a little better, but not notably so, and the shoulder is a good deal less expensive.

Have the butcher bone your shoulder or leg, but bring the bones home with you. Cut the salt pork into narrow larding ribbons.

Crack the peppercorns in a mortar or with a hammer in a cloth and put in a crock. Put the cloves of garlic through the garlic press or mince them finely. Chop the onion and slice the carrot into fairly thin rounds.

Pound the cracked pepper into the meat, both on the outside and on the bone side. Cut up the half stick of cinnamon and insert it and the cloves into the boned side of the meat. Place with the vegetables and salt pork in a large crock and mix the two kinds of wine. A Côte du Rhône is the least expensive red to use, and a moderate-priced Hermitage will serve for the white. Marinate the meat together with the bones at least twenty-four hours in a cool room, but not in the refrigerator. Turn the meat if the marinade does not cover it all. Next day, take the meat out of the marinade and lard it with the pork strips, which also have been in the wine mixture.

Reshape the leg or shoulder and tie with kitchen string. Place in a pottery or enamel casserole (not in a Dutch oven because of the acidity of the wines) and pour the marinade over it. Cover the casserole closely and cook in a 225 to 250 degree oven for six hours.

Remove the meat from the marinade and let the latter cool somewhat. Keep the meat warm and about twenty minutes before serving, place it in a shallow pan in a 450 degree oven to brown slightly on the top.

Skim most of the fat from the cooking liquor. Strain it and thicken with a beurre manié made by mixing the flour and butter well. Cook for ten minutes or so and skim if necessary. Pour part of the sauce over the meat on a hot serving platter and pass the rest in a warm sauceboat.

A good red Rhône, somewhat better than that used for cooking the daube, matches the meat perfectly. Buttered Brussels sprouts or green peas go well with it also.

Lamb Stew (Ragoût d'Agneau)

Make a *bouquet garni* by putting the bay leaf, celery leaves, thyme and marjoram in a cheesecloth bag, tied with string for easy removal.

Mix the flour with 1 1/2 teaspoons of salt and a good grind of fresh black pepper. Shake up the meat with the seasoned flour in a paper bag to coat it well.

Breast, shoulder, or neck are the usual cuts for making lamb stew. The breast will, as in veal, have much fresh young cartilage which will add flavor and consistency to the stew's liquid. Have the meat cut in pieces about one and one-half inches in size.

Melt the butter in a heavy casserole and brown the meat well. Stir in any of the seasoned flour left over from flouring the meat and add the wine, together with enough water to cover the meat. Simmer gently until the meat is almost cooked. Usually, this will take about one hour. At this time, remove meat to another pan, add the vegetables and strain the cooking liquid over all. Continue the cooking until the vegetables are done. Correct the seasoning and serve.

Garnish with sprigs of parsley. Serve with crusty French or Italian bread and a good regional Bordeaux—Pomerol or St. Emilion will be just right—or a California Cabernet Sauvignon.

Lamb Shanks

The characteristic gelatinous texture and flavor of the comparatively inexpensive shanks of lamb make them worth having occasionally. Here are two ways to braise them (the only possible method of preparation) which will give you quite different end results.

Mix the salt, thyme, oregano and a good grind of black pepper with the flour in a paper bag; shake the shanks in this mixture, or dredge the flour onto the shanks and rub into the meat.

LAMB STEW
(Ragoût d'Agneau)

3	lbs. lamb breast, shoulder, shank or neck
2	cups dry white wine
6	small carrots
6	small turnips
3	tablesp. butter
2	tablesp. flour
1	clove minced garlic
1	large onion
1	bay leaf
1	teasp. thyme
1	teasp. marjoram
1	handful fresh celery leaves
	salt
	freshly ground black pepper

243

BRAISED LAMB SHANKS

6	lamb shanks
3/4	cup chopped onion
3/4	cup chopped celery
3/4	cup chopped carrots
1/3	cup cooking oil
1 1/2	cups beef stock or condensed bouillon
2	tablesp. flour
1	teasp. salt
	freshly ground pepper
1	clove garlic
1/2	teasp. dried thyme

LAMB SHANKS BRAISED IN RED WINE

6	lamb shanks
1/2	bottle red wine
2	tablesp. flour
1/2	teasp. dried rosemary or several sprigs fresh
2	tablesp. olive oil
2	cloves garlic
1 1/2	teasp. salt
	a good grind of black pepper

Melt the oil, preferably not olive oil, and brown the floured shanks on all sides. Transfer the browned shanks to a casserole or Dutch oven and add the vegetables to the skillet in which the shanks were browned. Sauté them gently for about five minutes, stirring to avoid sticking or burning. Put the garlic through the press or mince finely and add to the skillet. Transfer all the contents of the skillet to the casserole over and about the meat. Add the stock, cover tightly and cook in the oven for one and one-half hours at 350 degrees. If the shanks are tough, the time required may be a little longer, but be careful not to overcook or the meat will become stringy.

We have liked a regional Pomerol with this dish better than the more expensive wines. The flavor is excellent, but a merely good wine is right.

Lamb Shanks Braised in Red Wine

Mix the salt, pepper, and flour and either shake in a paper bag with the shanks or dredge by hand. Brown lamb in oil and transfer to a casserole. If you are using the dried rosemary, sprinkle it over the shanks in the casserole; if you are using fresh, put several sprigs in the pan. The garlic is to be put through a press or chopped finely and mixed with the wine, which should cover the shanks to a depth of one-half inch. Cover closely and cook in a 350 degree oven until tender. Here again, be careful not to overcook.

Broiled Lamb Kidneys

Lamb kidneys are the smallest and perhaps the most delicate of all kidneys. They may be used in making steak and kidney pie or kidneys flambé, but it is rather a shame to use them in this way because they are so good simply broiled.

Remove the fat and covering membrane, cut away all of the white material and tubing at the root of the kidney, rinse quickly in cold water and split.

Brush with oil and grill, turning frequently, for four to six minutes. They should be browned a little on the outside but still pink and tender inside.

Another good way with lamb kidneys is to dip them in a vinaigrette—four parts oil to one part good wine vinegar—for a few minutes and then grill without draining the vinaigrette completely from the kidney halves.

A regional claret or young Beaujolais seems right with broiled lamb kidneys.

Lamb Kidneys with Sherry

Prepare three lamb kidneys per person as described above but do not split. Sauté them very gently for five minutes in lots of butter. Then sprinkle either chopped fresh tarragon over them, or 1/4 teaspoon of dried tarragon for each three kidneys. Put into the pan, 1 1/2 ounces of Dry Sack or other slightly sweet sherry, turn the heat down to the lowest possible point, cover the cooking pan and cook for three minutes. Remove the kidneys to a warm plate, salt them and if the wine-butter mixture is too liquid, let it concentrate. Pour it over the kidneys. The difficulty here is to learn just exactly how long to cook the kidneys. They must not be overdone. On the other hand, an underdone kidney is repellent to most persons.

When you have learned to do these kidneys exactly right, they will partner one of your better red Burgundies or perhaps even a château-bottled Bordeaux red wine.

Lamb Curry

The quickest and easiest way to make a lamb curry is to make a good curry sauce and then warm up leftover lamb roast—either leg or shoulder. We use the same basic curry sauce for all curries—lamb, chicken, lobster and shrimp, as well as curried eggs.

Peel and slice two large onions; simmer in a saucepan with a quart of lightly salted water for thirty minutes or longer. The water is then strained off and used to make the basic white sauce; the onions are discarded.

Melt two tablespoons of butter in a saucepan and gradually stir into it two tablespoons of flour, without letting it become colored. Gradually add the onion-flavored water and cook for fifteen to twenty minutes until the sauce is done. The consistency is then adjusted by adding more of the onion-water if it is too thick, or a little more butter mixed with flour if it is too thin. At this point, flavor the white sauce with two or more teaspoons of a good grade of curry powder. If members of your family differ widely in the degree of heat they like in their curry, cayenne can be added to individual servings, thus keeping

LAMB KIDNEY WITH SHERRY

3	lamb kidneys (per person)
	butter
	fresh chopped tarragon or
	1/4 teasp. dried tarragon
1 1/2	oz. Dry Sack or
	sweet sherry
	salt

LAMB CURRY

	leftover lamb
2	onions
2	tablesp. butter
2	tablesp. butter
2	tablesp. flour
2	teasp. (or more)
	curry powder
	cayenne (optional)

245

happy both those who like a mild curry and those whose preference is for a hotter one.

There is a tradition that wine does not go with curry; but because my wife does not like beer, we drink wine with all curries. Any good, fairly coarse red *ordinaire* goes well with these spicy dishes.

Moussaka à la Rosalind

In general, my wife and I have not liked the cooking of the Near East, but the following version of Moussaka, a traditional dish of Greece and other Near Eastern lands, is so good that we couldn't help liking it. It is not hard to prepare and makes a fine dish for a buffet supper when you have lots of guests. We are indebted to Rosalind Wholden for the recipe. Miss Wholden, in addition to being a fine cook, is a distinguished art historian and a perceptive critic.

Peel eggplants and cut into one-half inch round slices. Cover with water and salt and let stand for one hour, or until the slices look limp. Drain, rinse the slices under cold tap water, and dry on paper towels. Mix flour, monosodium glutamate and pepper. Shake a few eggplant slices at a time in the seasoned flour in a large paper bag. Heat the olive oil and fry the eggplant, browning well on both sides. Let drain on paper towels to remove excess oil. Set aside temporarily.

Fry the sausage in a heavy skillet in its own fat until it is medium brown, turning and stirring to keep the ground meat from lumping. Spoon the meat into a saucepan and reserve.

Sauté onions in the remaining pork fat in the skillet, adding a little butter only if absolutely necessary. Add the onions to the cooked sausage and mix well. Transfer one-half of this mixture to a second saucepan.

Season the lamb with salt and oregano and mix well with the monosodium glutamate. Heat in a skillet over a low flame to render the fat from the meat without browning it. Combine cinnamon and lamb, then add all of this to one of the saucepans containing half of the sausage-onion mixture. Stir in the wine and cook over a gentle flame until the wine is absorbed.

MOUSSAKA A LA ROSALIND
Part I - Eggplant
3	large eggplants
2	qts. water
1/2	cup salt
1	cup flour
1	tablesp. monosodium glutamate
1	cup olive oil
	freshly ground pepper

Part II - Pork Sausage Mixture
1	lb. spiced pork sausage
3	cups finely chopped onions

Part III - Lamb Mixture
1	lb. lean ground lamb
1	cup dry white wine
1/2	teasp. cinnamon
	oregano
	salt
1/2	teasp. monosodium glutamate

Fry the minced garlic in the lamb fat remaining in the skillet. Season the ground beef to taste; add the monosodium glutamate; add to the skillet with the garlic. Brown it quickly over a hot flame, stirring. Add the chopped parsley and place in the second saucepan containing the other half of the sausage-onion mixture. Add the tomato purée and the red wine; cook until nearly all the liquid has been absorbed.

Prepare the béchamel sauce according to the recipe in the basic chapter on sauces, but use thin cream (half and half) instead of milk.

Grease a deep twelve by sixteen inch roasting pan and arrange the eggplant slices in such a way that the bottom of the pan is completely covered. Any remaining slices may be used to line the sides of the pan. Place the beef-tomato mixture over the eggplant layer and spread evenly. Now cover the meat mixture with a layer of washed spinach leaves to act as a sieve for the upper layer. Add the lamb-oregano-sausage mixture above the spinach leaves and spread evenly. Cover this layer with the sliced mushrooms.

Pour over all the béchamel sauce and sprinkle the top with a cup of Parmesan or Romano cheese, freshly grated.

Bake one hour at 400 degrees until the top is well browned. Remove from oven and let stand for forty minutes before serving.

Rosalind adds the cautionary note that if you don't have a really deep pan, you had better line your oven bottom with foil because the moussaka bubbles.

The dish is good but the flavors are strong and not subtle. A wine of similar quality is called for. We have liked our Beaujolais or Côte-du-Rhône *ordinaires,* or a California Zinfandel with it.

Shaslik

This is the Russian name for lamb cooked en broche; the Armenians call it shish kebab.

You may use any lean cut of lamb. Because the pieces cook only briefly, the lamb, ideally, should be of good quality. Use a leg if possible. The cubes should be fat free.

Marinate overnight in olive oil and wine, to which the garlic (put through a garlic press), the chopped shallots, and the oregano have been added.

Part IV - Ground Beef Mixture

1 1/2	lb. ground beef
1	cup thick tomato purée
1	cup dry red wine
3	cloves finely minced garlic
	salt
	freshly ground black pepper
	monosodium glutamate
4	tablesp. chopped parsley

Part V - Sauce

2	qts. rich béchamel sauce

Part VI - Baking

10	fresh sliced mushrooms
	fresh spinach leaves
1	cup freshly grated Parmesan or Romano cheese

SHASLIK

3	lbs. lamb cut into 1 1/2 inch cubes
1/2	cup olive oil
1	cup dry red wine
2	cloves crushed garlic
4	finely chopped shallots
1	teasp. dried oregano
	salt
	freshly ground pepper

Place meat on skewers, either alone or alternating with some or all of the vegetables listed below. Broil either under the grill or, better, over charcoal. Turn frequently so that the meat will cook evenly.

Chunks of onion and eggplant, together with mushroom caps work best, as their cooking time coincides closely with that of the cubes of meat. Potatoes are likely to be undercooked; tomato wedges, a favorite with many people, usually are overcooked, collapsed and miserable looking on the broche. Green pepper, often used, adds color and a distinctive flavor.

Season with salt and freshly ground pepper only after the skewers of meat and vegetables have cooked. This avoids drawing juice to the surface of the meat and losing it during the broiling.

A good regional Bordeaux; for example, a Pomerol, or a Côte de Castillon, will suite the shish kebabs. Serve either with a rice pilaf or plain buttered long-grain rice.

Mixed Grill

A fine dish for an occasional informal family meal. For each person, broil one lamb chop, one lamb kidney, two slices of bacon and two "little pig" sausages which have first been parboiled. Serve with a gratin of potatoes and the same sort of wine consumed with the shaslik.

PORK

When I was a youth growing up in the southern part of the United States, there was a superstition that pork was unfit to eat during the summer. Or perhaps it was not wholly superstition. The best of homes had only ice boxes and many homes did not have even those. Another part of the lore concerning pork was that it was safe only if very well done. We now know that trichinae, which is a parasite widely infecting pork both in America and Europe, are killed when the meat reaches a temperature of 137 degrees. Do not cook pork so that that it is gray and dry. However, because it does have the most fat of any edible meat, pork is best cooked more slowly and somewhat longer than other meats. Broiled pork chops are usually too dry to be very good.

248

When you cook a pork roast, use a meat thermometer and stop the cooking when the internal temperature reaches 180 to 185 degrees. (This place is marked on most meat thermometers.) It is best to roast pork at a lower temperature than beef. A good practice is to brown the roast at 450 degrees for fifteen to thirty minutes and then reduce the oven temperature to 325 degrees. It also helps to keep the meat juicy and defatted to roast in a covered casserole rather than in an open pan—in other words, a pork roast is very nearly braised. A loin will, of course, roast faster than a thick leg of pork; this is why the use of the meat thermometer is advisable.

Roast Loin of Pork

Because of the size of our family, the loin is a more practical roast than a fresh leg or shoulder. Most families will find this true. One does not usually serve a roast leg of pork to dinner guests, although this cut of meat, well cooked in a good restaurant, can be delicious. The loin may be boned or not, as you prefer. In estimating the size roast you will need, allow the thickness of two chops for each person.

Rub the meat on all sides with salt, thyme and sage. Put the casserole, uncovered, in a 450 degree oven until the meat browns. (The meat should be placed in the casserole fat side down.) Alternately, brown the meat on top of the stove. After browning, add a cup of white wine to the pan, together with the sliced onion, bay leaf and carrot. Cover and continue cooking at 325 degrees until the thermometer registers 180 to 185 degrees.

About one hour before the estimated end of cooking, you may pour off part of the fat and surround the roast with small potatoes to roast with it. Other good garnitures are mashed potatoes and puréed chestnuts.

It is pork, more than any other meat, that demonstrates the fallacy of the so-called rule, so widely believed in America, that one serves red wine with meat. Pork calls for a white wine; preferably a full-bodied and even a somewhat sweet white wine. It is with roast pork that I best like a good Rhine or Mosel Spätlese or, failing that, the inexpensive white wine exported from Tarragon in Spain under the somewhat misleading name of "Spanish Chablis."

ROAST LOIN OF PORK

3	lb. boneless pork loin
1	teasp. dried thyme
1	medium onion
1	carrot
1	bay leaf
	salt
1/2	teasp. sage

A leg can be cooked in the same way, but being thicker, will require longer time to cook. It is better to remove the skin entirely from a fresh leg of pork before the cooking begins.

Roast Pork Boulangère

ROAST PORK BOULANGERE

4 - 5	lb. pork loin (unboned weight)
1	cup chicken stock or condensed broth
1	cup white wine
12	small new potatoes or 6 large, halved
2	medium onions
1	teasp. thyme
1/2	teasp. sage
2	teasp. salt
2	tablesp. flour
	pepper

Mix salt, thyme and sage. Rub well into the unboned loin. Brown as described above, then place meat thermometer in center of roast, being careful it does not touch any bone. Reduce temperature to 350 degrees and roast in open pan for one and one-half hours. Now, place the meat in a casserole with the cover and arrange the potatoes and onions, peeled and quartered, about the meat. Add the chicken stock and wine; cover. Continue cooking at 325 to 350 degrees until the meat thermometer registers 185. Place roast in the center of a hot platter with vegetables arranged around it. Decorate the potatoes with chopped parsley.

Again, I recommend a good Mosel or Rhine; a full-bodied Graves is also good, as are the better wines from Alsace.

Roast Pork à la Provençale

Wipe the roast dry. Make small incisions along the fatty side, and insert thin slices of the garlic and small mushrooms. Brown the roast by either the hot oven method or on top of the stove; insert the meat thermometer and put in the oven at 325 to 350 degrees, arranged fat side up. Put the stems of the large mushrooms as well as the small ones through the food chopper. Mix with the sausage meat, salt and herbs.

Wash the tomatoes and large mushrooms. Cut the tops off the tomatoes and shake out all the juice and seeds. Stuff the tomatoes and the large mushroom caps with the mixture of sausage meat and small mushrooms. Place the tomatoes and the mushroom caps alternately in a skillet with a cover in the heated olive oil, and sauté over a lively heat for five minutes. Then cover and lower the heat to the gentlest level possible and let the stuffed vegetables cook twenty minutes longer. To know when to begin cooking the vegetables, allow forty-five minutes a pound for the meat to cook.

ROAST PORK À LA PROVENCALE

3	lb. boned pork loin
12	or more large mushrooms
1/2	lb. smaller mushrooms (or use more of the large)
6	tomatoes (nice and round)
1/2	lb. pork sausage
3	cloves garlic
1/2	teasp. sage
1/2	teasp. thyme
1	tablesp. chopped parsley
4	oz. olive oil
1	teasp. salt

Serve the meat on a heated platter with the tomatoes and mushroom caps alternating around it. Pour the juices from the cooking pan over both meat and vegetables.

Because of the garlic and tomatoes, as well as the generally high flavor, you will, I think, like this pork roast best with a good Rhône, an inexpensive Côte de Provence, or a California red such as a Zinfandel, rather than with a white wine.

Pork Chops Breaded and Grilled

This is a typical French housewife's way of cooking "Côtelettes de porc" and illustrates the inadvisability of grilling or broiling pork chops unless you have very young, tender meat. When this is the case, this simple way of cooking them can be very good.

Trim all but about one-quarter inch of fat from the rim of the chop and make two or three cuts in the fat so that the chop will lie flat. Dip each chop in the beaten egg and then in bread crumbs. Grill for seven or eight minutes on each side.

Drink an inexpensive Rhine, Mosel, or Alsatian wine with these chops; or for minimal expense, the slightly sweet "Spanish Chablis."

PORK CHOPS BREADED AND GRILLED

12	thin chops (1 rib)
1	egg, beaten
	finely rolled bread crumbs
	salt
	freshly ground black pepper

Pork Chops with Piquant Sauce

Melt the butter in a skillet with a cover. Brown the chops on both sides, trimming all but one-quarter inch of the fat. When the chops are well browned, remove them to a hot platter and add the onion slices to the skillet. Cook over low heat until the onion is tender.

Add tomato paste; add a little of the vinegar from the capers and drain the rest of it and discard. Add capers, wine, and water to the skillet and stir well.

Replace the chops in the pan with the other ingredients and simmer gently over a low fire, with the pan covered, until the chops are tender—about thirty to forty minutes. Garnish the serving dish with chopped parsley.

Here again, a not-too-subtle red wine will be most suitable. A California red of moderate cost, a young Beaujolais or a Côte-du-Rhône is about right.

PORK CHOPS WITH PIQUANT SAUCE

6	thick loin chops
1	medium onion, sliced
4	oz. tomato paste
1	cup white wine
1	tablesp. butter
1	cup water
1	small bottle capers
1	pinch cayenne pepper
1	teasp. salt
	pepper

251

Pork Chops Charcutière

PORK CHOPS CHARCUTIÈRE

2	lb. loin chops (6 pieces)
1/2	cup chopped onions
2	tablesp. cooking oil (in Paris, one would use lard)
1	teasp. flour
1	cup beef stock
1/2	cup dry white wine
2	tablesp. thinly sliced sour pickles
1	teasp. Dijon mustard
	chopped parsley

A way of presenting côtelettes de porc frequently encountered in Paris restaurants. The sauce makes up for any lack of tenderness resulting from the comparatively brief cooking.

To make the sauce, cook the onions in the oil or lard in a small saucepan until they are soft, without coloring. Sprinkle with the flour while stirring with a wooden spoon. When the mixture turns a golden brown, add the meat stock a little at a time, stirring constantly, then the wine. When the sauce begins to thicken, season to taste with salt, freshly ground black pepper, the mustard and the chopped pickles. Simmer for twenty minutes over the lowest possible heat, skimming two or three times.

Brown the chops in a couple of tablespoons of lard or oil over brisk heat; lower heat; cover the skillet and cook for twenty minutes or so until the chops are tender. Serve the chops on hot plates with the sauce poured over them and then sprinkle all with chopped parsley.

A good Gewürz-Traminer or a rather dry Rhine will go well with these chops.

BAKED STUFFED PORK CHOPS

6	double loin chops
1 1/2	cups fresh bread crumbs
1/4	cup bacon drippings
1	egg
2	large onions
1	clove garlic
3/4	cup dry white wine
3/4	cup strong stock
	butter
1	tablesp. chopped parsley
1	tablesp. chopped green pepper
1/8	teasp. each thyme, mace and fresh nutmeg
1/2	teasp. sage
1	large bay leaf
	several sprigs parsley
1/2	teasp. thyme
3 - 4	whole cloves

Baked Stuffed Pork Chops

Combine the fresh bread crumbs, bacon drippings, sage, thyme, nutmeg and mace; one tablespoon each of chopped onion, chopped parsley and chopped green pepper. Cook this mixture in a buttered skillet for five minutes over low heat and then combine with the beaten egg.

Have the butcher cut pockets in each of the double chops. Wipe the chops clean, remove all but one-quarter inch rim of fat, and fill the pockets loosely with the dressing.

Slice the remaining onion thinly in the bottom of a buttered casserole. Arrange the chops on top of the onions, and add a *bouquet garni* of the bay leaf, the rest of the thyme, the cloves and garlic in cheesecloth. Pour in the stock and wine; bake in an oven at 375 degrees for one and one-half hours.

A good Alsatian, such as Sylvaner or Traminer, is a suitable accompaniment for these succulent chops.

252

Pork Chops with Cream and Brandy

Remove all but a thin rim of fat and nick the edges so that the chops will remain flat. Dip in beaten egg and then in finely rolled bread crumbs. Brown quickly in bacon drippings or oil, turning only once. When the chops are well browned, pour in one-half of the cream, cover, reduce the heat and let simmer under the lowest heat for fifteen to twenty minutes. You may need to add a little more cream during the cooking.

Remove the chops to a hot platter. Add the remaining cream to the pan and scrape all of the brown bits. Allow the cream sauce to reduce until it is quite thick, add the brandy and let the sauce boil up once. Salt the chops and give them a grind of black pepper before pouring the sauce over them. Fresh green peas with a little lettuce and green onion make a good garnish for this rich dish, which merits a good Rhine or Mosel. The wine should be a little sweet, so choose an Auslese or Spätlese.

PORK CHOPS WITH CREAM AND BRANDY

6	thick double chops
1	cup whipping cream
2	eggs, beaten
	bread crumbs
1 1/2	oz. cognac or other good brandy
4	tablesp. bacon drippings or cooking oil
	salt
	freshly ground black pepper

HAM

One has to go to a good deal of trouble to find an old-fashioned country-cured ham, the sort that used to hang in the smokehouse all summer without spoiling. Most "ham" available today has been treated and smoked only long enough to make it taste, more or less, like ham. It must be held under refrigeration. Curiously enough, most of the canned hams also keep only in the refrigerator. A Smithfield or other Virginia-cured ham from peanut-fed hogs is a special case and should be treated according to its own recipes. Smithfield ham is strictly an acquired taste and one that I have never acquired. Therefore, I have no recipes to offer for its preparation. This omission will trouble no one because nearly every cookbook will tell you how to cook this item.

Nor am I going to burden you with a recipe for routine baked ham. Either you already know how to bake a ham or any routine cookbook will tell you. As nearly as I know, the process in most cases consists of no more than heating a precooked ham and smearing the surface with brown sugar and sticking cloves in it to give the illusion of an old-fashioned baked ham. For those of us old enough to remember country-cured hams before the triumph of merchandising whereby packers sell us injected water under the guise of "tenderizing the meat," the illusion vanishes when we put the first forkful in our mouths.

Be that as it may, here is a recipe which will make a genuine cured ham a real treat for Easter or any other occasion. It will even make the modern refrigerated or canned substitute reasonably good.

Braised Ham in Champagne

BRAISED HAM IN CHAMPAGNE

1 ham (preferably real country-cured)
1 bottle champagne (inexpensive)
1 cup brown sugar
3 tablesp. flour
3 onions
6 cloves
3 cloves garlic
1 teasp. thyme
2 stalks celery
2 bay leaves
6 sprigs parsley

If you start with an old-fashioned country-cured ham, begin by scrubbing it with a brush under running water and soaking it for twenty-four hours in three or four changes of water.

Then put the ham in a deep kettle with water to cover. Add three onions, each stuck with two cloves, three cloves of garlic, the thyme, celery, bay leaves and parsley. Cook for three hours, cool, and reserve eight ounces of the strained liquid in which the meat was boiled. If you start with refrigerated ham, omit the soaking and boiling.

Skim the ham and remove most of the fat. Put in an open roasting pan with the stock and a bottle of California champagne. An inexpensive Charmât wine will serve because, obviously, one cooks the bubbles out anyway. Roast for one hour at 350 degrees, basting with the liquid. Drain ham and reserve the liquid. Replace the ham and spread one cup of brown sugar over the surface. Turn the oven to 500 degrees and place the ham in the oven again until it is brown and glazed.

Mix the flour with a little of the wine and stock; add to the liquid, stirring until it boils. Allow to simmer for fifteen minutes. Serve the sauce in a hot sauceboat with the carved ham.

This dish is worthy of your best Rhine or Mosel; it is also delicious with a big, full-bodied white Burgundy such as a Meursault of a good year.

Ham Braised in Cream and Brandy

Sear both sides of the ham slices in a heavy iron skillet. Cover with cream and turn the heat low; let it simmer for fifteen to twenty minutes. Add one-half of the brandy and ignite. When the flames die down, remove ham to hot platter, sprinkle with a dash each of nutmeg and mace and a grind of black pepper. Add a little more cream to the pan and stir up the brown particles. Just before serving, add the remaining brandy, let boil once and pour over the ham.

We like a nice, chilled Mosel with this ham.

Ham with Mushrooms and Cream

Lay the slices of ham, large and thick enough so that each one is a serving, in a casserole with the wine. Cover and let it cook over the lowest possible heat for fifteen or twenty minutes. The modern refrigerated ham does very well here.

Trim and wash the mushrooms and slice them fairly thin. Cook them five minutes in the cream. Season with salt and a little freshly ground black or white pepper. Add the juices from the casserole in which the ham cooked to the cream. Pour a little of the mixture in a small bowl and let cool. Beat the egg yolk thoroughly into the bowl and gradually add more of the warm sauce. Heat the sauce over hot water, without letting it boil. Serve the ham on a hot platter dressed with the sauce and garnished with sprigs of parsley.

We have enjoyed moderately-priced Mosels and Alsatian Traminers with this delicious but easily prepared dish.

Ham and Veal Croquettes

Croquettes are usually thought of as ways to use leftover meat or fowl, and they, indeed, can be used in that way. But I think these croquettes are good enough to merit starting with fresh ingredients bought for the purpose if you don't have leftover meat.

In a tablespoon of butter, gently sauté the chopped onion. Let it become soft but not colored. Mix the onion, parsley, the two meats, salt, allspice and a good dash of cayenne together with the brandy.

Make a sauce by whipping one-half cup of cream, then stirring into it the béchamel sauce in which you have mixed the curry powder. The idea here is to strive for a delicate hint of curry (à l'Indienne), enough to flavor the entire mixture.

HAM BRAISED IN CREAM AND BRANDY

2	ham slices, 1 inch thick
8	oz. light cream
2	oz. brandy
1	pinch nutmeg
1	pinch mace
	black pepper

HAM WITH MUSHROOMS AND CREAM

6	ham slices, 3/8 inch thick
8	oz. dry white wine
6	oz. whipping cream
1	pkg. (6 oz.) white mushrooms
2	eggs
	salt
	pepper
	lemon

HAM AND VEAL CROQUETTES

1/2	lb. ground ham
1/2	lb. ground veal
1	tablesp. finely chopped onion
1	teasp. parsley
2	eggs
1	tablesp. butter
1/2	teasp. (or more) curry powder
1/2	teasp. salt
1/4	teasp. allspice
	dash of cayenne pepper
1/2	cup béchamel sauce
1/2	cup whipping cream
	fat for deep frying
1	tablesp. brandy

255

Now, form cone-shaped croquettes by mixing enough of the sauce into the meat mixture so that it stays together but not enough to make it too soft. Chill the croquettes two hours or more; dip in beaten egg; roll in fine bread crumbs and fry in deep fat until they are golden brown. Dust with paprika and garnish the plate with sprigs of parsley.

A good Sylvaner or Traminer will do very well here. You will note that in recommending Rhine, Mosel or Alsatian wines, I fail to mention California equivalents. This is not forgetfulness, but is due to the fact that I do not believe California Rieslings, Traminers, or Sylvaners resemble the German and French wines closely enough to be used in their place.

Ham and Beans

HAM AND BEANS

2   cups small navy beans
1 - 2   onions, quartered
      ham
      salt
      pepper

Throughout central and southern France, the cassoulet is nearly universal. In those parts of the Midi where many geese are reared for the making of pâté de foie gras, the dish always includes *confit d'oie* or preserved goose. We always suspected that the only purpose of the goose in the mixture with otherwise good meat and white beans, was to dispose of the great surpluses of preserved goose which must accumulate, considering that each goose furnishes a great deal of meat and only one small fat liver. Many of the cassoulets contain lamb and the ones from Provence, contain, naturally, garlic. With all the varied recipes, it never seemed to me that the French dish ever quite came up to our simple ham hocks and beans combination. Nevertheless, I give a recipe for one of the more typical cassoulets after that for ham and beans.

Soak two cups of small navy beans overnight, after picking over and washing. Next day, drain and cover with fresh salted water. Add one or two onions cut in quarters and cook for one hour. Add a piece of ham from the shank end, sufficiently large to provide for six persons, and cook another hour or more until the beans begin to burst and the ham is tender. Season with freshly ground black pepper and salt to taste.

We drink our Beaujolais *ordinaire* with this good American dish.

A Cassoulet
(You could find dozens of other recipes)

Pick over the beans, wash, and soak overnight. Next day, cook them for three-quarters of an hour. Add the garlic, finely chopped.

Cut the pork and the goose meat in pieces about one and one-half inch squares and brown in the goose grease or oil. Take the meat out of the skillet and make a brown roux with the remaining grease and the flour. Turn all of the meat and the roux from the skillet into a kettle with a quart of stock or water and let cook gently for three hours. Add the beans and prolong the cooking one hour. Just before serving, add the cervelat and the small sausages cooked in boiling water. Salt and pepper to taste.

A stout Côte de Provence, a Bordeaux *ordinaire,* or a California red from the central valley are all adequate wines to partner this dish.

A CASSOULET

1	lb. small white beans
1	lb. pork shoulder
1	lb. cervelat sausage
6	small sausages (smoked link or chipolatas will do)
1/2	lb. cooked goose
2	oz. goose grease or other oil
4	oz. tomato purée
3	tablesp. flour
2	cloves garlic

EGGS, CHEESE, MUSHROOMS & CEREALS

16

We have dealt with all of these foods in previous chapters as hors d'oeuvres and as components of other foods. Here, we present for your pleasure, main dishes in which one or a combination of these items form the chief part of the dish. There are said to be more than 1500 ways to cook eggs. While there may not be that many different cheese or pasta dishes, still, there is a legion.

Many of these dishes are what the French term *maigre,* that is, they are meat free, and are suitable as Friday or Lenten dishes for those who still keep the ancient proscriptions. However, I have included no dish for that reason. Every recipe is presented because my family and I like the dish and enjoy eating it. I cannot see how a man eating a fine, feathery cheese soufflé and washing it down with a good Burgundy, or enjoying crêpes filled with crab covered with a fine mornay sauce with a Sancerre or a white Burgundy, can possibly imagine himself sacrificing, or enduring any hardship whatever! Again, while many of these dishes are economical, they are not included for that reason.

The dishes in this chapter are not, for the most part, suitable for formal entertaining. Rather, they are for delicious family meals or for informal suppers with close friends.

Bon apétit!

Eggs with Ham or Bacon

The breakfast par excellence for many Americans; one of these combinations, preceded by a green salad and followed by a bowl of fruit or a warm apple pie, is also a fine and quickly prepared supper for Sunday evening, after the concert or theater, and other such occasions.

The French sauté the ham or bacon and then drop the eggs into the skillet over the meat and let them cook gently until the whites are coagulated. But I still prefer the American way of sautéeing the meat and eggs separately. At whatever meal they are served, ham or bacon and eggs call for hot buttered toast.

They go well with your Beaujolais or California red *ordinaire*.

Shirred Eggs with Black Butter

Melt 1 1/2 teaspoons of butter in each of six ramekins. Break two eggs into each and season to taste with salt and freshly ground white pepper. Cook under broiler at sufficient distance so the eggs will not coagulate too quickly. Baste with another teaspoon and one-half of the butter during the shirring. The cooking should stop when the whites are set and not yet quite opaque. Meanwhile, heat six tablespoons of butter in a small skillet until it turns a dark nutbrown. Sprinkle a scant teaspoon of capers over the surface of each two eggs. Quickly pour into the skillet, six teaspoons of vinegar, stir well with the butter and pour over the eggs. Serve immediately.

Garnish each ramekin with a small sprig of parsley and serve an inexpensive dry red or white wine with the dish, according to your own preference.

Eggs Chimay

To prepare the duxelle, clean and chop finely one pound of white mushrooms. Wring all the juice possible out of the mushrooms in the corner of a clean dish towel. Chop enough shallots finely to make two tablespoonsful. Gently sauté the shallots in butter until they are soft, then add the chopped mushrooms and turn up the heat a little. Sauté until all the juice is evaporated and the mass appears to be dry and brown.

To make a mornay sauce, add a cup of grated Gruyère cheese and three egg yolks beaten into a little cream to one pint of béchamel sauce.

Cut the hard-boiled eggs in two, lengthwise, and remove the yolks to a mixing bowl. Mix them well with the duxelle and enough mornay sauce to make the mass easily workable. Correct the seasoning with salt and white pepper.

SHIRRED EGGS WITH BLACK BUTTER

12 fresh eggs
1   stick butter
6   teasp. tarragon wine
        vinegar
6   teasp. capers
    freshly ground white pepper
    salt

EGGS CHIMAY

12 hard-boiled eggs
1   pt. sauce mornay
1/2 lb. duxelle
3   oz. grated Gruyére cheese
    butter
    chopped parsley
    salt
    white pepper

260

Pile the yolk-mushroom mixture into the whites and lay in a buttered baking dish. Pour over them the remainder of the mornay sauce. Sprinkle the top with grated Gruyère and put in the oven at 400 degrees, until the surface of the sauce is golden and the sauce bubbles. Garnish with chopped parsley and a dash of paprika and serve immediately.

A full-bodied white Burgundy, white Graves or Rhône, all go nicely with eggs cooked in this manner.

Eggs à L'Aurore

Heat the béchamel sauce and melt into it the Gruyère cheese. Cut the hard-boiled eggs in two and put the yolks through a fine sieve. Chop the whites and add them to the béchamel with the cheese melted in it; season with salt and white pepper.

Into buttered ramekins, put alternating layers of the egg-cheese sauce with sprinkled layers of the sieved yolks, finishing with a layer of the yolks.

Place in a 450 degree oven for about fifteen or twenty minutes, until the sauce is thoroughly heated.

We have liked eggs à l'aurore with a white Graves.

EGGS À L'AURORE

- 12 hard-boiled eggs
- 1 pt. béchamel sauce
- 2 oz. grated Gruyère cheese
- 1 oz. butter
  freshly ground white pepper
  salt

Eggs and Tomatoes Provençale

Cut the tomatoes in half and shake out the seeds and most of the pulp. Lay them in a baking dish greased with olive oil and season with fines herbes. Break an egg carefully into the top of each tomato half, season with salt and pepper and bake at 350 degrees for about twenty-five minutes or until the whites of the eggs are thoroughly set. Garnish by sprinkling each egg with fresh parsley or chives chopped finely.

Serve eggs cooked this way with a regional claret such as a Médoc, a Beaujolais, or a California red wine.

EGGS AND TOMATOES PROVENCALE

- 12 eggs
- 6 large tomatoes
- 2 tablesp. olive oil
- 1/8 teasp. each basil, parsley, tarragon and thyme
- 1 clove garlic
  salt
  freshly ground pepper

can line w/ cheese, too

Scrambled Eggs

Break the eggs, which should be at room temperature, into a bowl and beat enough to break the yolks but not enough to mix the whites and yolks thoroughly. Pour into a skillet with a heavy bottom in which the butter has been melted. Cook over low heat, stirring almost constant-

SCRAMBLED EGGS

3	eggs (for each person)
1	tablesp. butter
1	tablesp. cream
	salt
	freshly ground white pepper

ly. *Keep the heat low.* When the contents of the pan are still soft and creamy, remove from the heat and beat in the cream. This will make the eggs light and the heat already present will complete the cooking. Season with salt and a grind of white pepper during the beating in of the cream and serve on hot plates. Dust paprika over the eggs and garnish the plate with a sprig of parsley.

Hot buttered toast or hot, crusty French bread is almost a necessity with scrambled eggs.

You will find recipes for scrambling eggs in a double boiler without butter. Such a procedure gives no improvement whatever in flavor and makes the pan in which the eggs cooked uncommonly hard to wash. It is not recommended.

With scrambled eggs, my family like a nice, semi-sweet, almost water-clear Mosel, such as a Piersporter Lay or an Uerziger Würzgarten.

Scrambled Eggs, My Way

SCRAMBLED EGGS, MY WAY

3	eggs (for each person)
1	tablesp. butter
1	tablesp. cream
1	tablesp. red sweet pepper
1	tablesp. green sweet pepper
1	small clove garlic for
	12 eggs
	salt
	white pepper

Melt the butter in a heavy skillet and gently sauté the chopped garlic and the red and green peppers cut in strips about one-quarter inch wide and one and one-half inches long until they are soft. Let the pan cool somewhat, then put in the eggs in which the yolks have barely been broken. Cook slowly and let some of the white set before stirring so that there will be flakes of both white and yellow in the finished dish. When nearly done, stir in the cream and serve · in a similar manner to plain scrambled eggs.

The mild, very light Mosels seem best with this dish also.

The Basic Omelet

BASIC OMELET

3	eggs (per person)
3	teasp. water
	good dash of tabasco sauce
	salt
	pepper
	butter

Individual omelets are much easier to handle. They can be cooked just right and the whole procedure goes so rapidly that it is much less trouble to prepare six omelets of the proper size than to struggle with one omelet large enough for six persons. Besides, few households have an omelet pan large enough to accommodate eighteen eggs.

Although I have seen cooks in the hash-house type of restaurant make omelets—usually a tough, greasy preparation which they labeled "Spanish omelet"—on top of the grill along with hamburgers and bacon and eggs, it is almost essential to have a pan which is reserved exclusively for omelets.

The omelet pan should be of iron, heavy enamelware or cast aluminum. One with a bottom diameter of seven or eight inches with rounded sides is right for the three-egg individual omelet. If you choose an enamel or cast aluminum pan, all that you have to do before seasoning is clean it thoroughly with soap and water, being careful to rinse all the soap away. If you select the iron pan, work over the inside surface with a scouring powder and fine steel wool.

In either case, after having cleaned the new pan thoroughly, fill it until it is almost full of cooking oil and heat nearly to smoking. Remove from the fire and let stand full of the oil overnight. Next day, pour off the oil (it is still useful for frying and need not be wasted) and wipe it clean with paper towels. If burned butter or bits of egg stick to the pan (which will happen only if you are inattentive), rub the pan with a teaspoon or two of dry table salt. Never wash the pan! If it becomes so soiled with burnt oil, or if it is accidently used to cook something else, scour it and reseason with a panful of hot oil.

To make the omelet, let three fresh eggs stand until they reach room temperature. Break into a small mixing bowl. Add three teaspoons of water, a good dash of tabasco sauce together with salt and freshly ground white pepper to taste. Beat the eggs with a wire whip or a fork about forty times. This will serve thoroughly to mix the whites and yolks but will not raise any foam to speak of.

Heat a generous tablespoon of butter in the omelet pan until it ceases to foam. Tip the pan in all directions so that the sides are coated. The heat should be fairly high, so that the omelet will cook rapidly, but not so high as to burn the butter.

Turn the beaten eggs into the hot butter all at once and swirl about the bottom of the pan so that as much of the egg as possible is immediately cooked. Then, shaking the pan to keep the bottom of the omelet loose, lift edges with a spatula and tip pan in all directions so that the uncooked egg in the center runs to the edges. While the middle of the mass of eggs is still creamy, shake the omelet and, at the same time, tip the pan so that the edge slides up the side of the pan. Work the spatula under the oppo-

263

site side of the omelet and fold the omelet over on itself at the same time that you slide it out of the pan onto a heated plate. Cooked properly, the omelet should be just beginning to show a little golden brown on the surface and should be still creamy inside. Remember that the mass of eggs is a poor conductor of heat, and, therefore, the center will continue to cook for some time after the omelet is folded and removed from the heat.

A Sunday Evening Meal

In our household, we have omelets frequently as a Sunday evening meal with either heated French bread or buttered toast. We serve a light Mosel or Rhine wine with them.

Omelet Fines Herbes

If you have an herb garden, chop chives, thyme, parsley and marjoram extremely fine and use 1/4 teaspoon of the fresh mixture with each basix omelet. Most of the time, I do not have available the fresh herbs, so I use a generous pinch each of fresh chives and parsley and a little larger pinch of the Spice Islands mixture of fines herbes which contains thyme, oregano, sage, rosemary, marjoram and basil. Whether you use fresh herbs or dried, beat them into the eggs at the same time as you put in the other seasonings, and proceed as with the standard omelet. Tarragon, watercress and chervil are other excellent herbs to use.

Cheese Omelets

You can get interesting variations in flavor at very little trouble by using at different times, a good sharp Cheddar, a Gruyère, a Parmesan and, finally, a mixture of equal parts of Parmesan and Gruyère.

Whichever cheese you select, add a heaping tablespoon, well grated, at the moment when the bottom of the omelet is well set, but before you are ready to turn it.

Mushroom Omelet

Here again, you can get different dishes by varying the manner of cooking the mushrooms, either sautéeing them or preparing them in a cream sauce. In general, I like an omelet made by sautéeing two tablespoons of thinly sliced mushrooms gently for about five minutes in butter and adding them to the omelet at the same moment you would the cheese in the recipe above.

Bacon Omelet

Fry three strips of bacon crisp, set aside to drain on paper towels and proceed with the preparation of the omelet. When the bottom of the omelet is set, crumble the bacon in the center and proceed in the usual manner.

Omelet Paysanne

Make a peasant-style omelet like the bacon omelet; but, after frying the bacon, put 1/2 cup of boiled potatoes into the skillet with the bacon drippings and cook until barely soft and brown them delicately on all sides. At the proper moment, add both crumbled bacon and the salted and peppered potatoes to the omelet.

Spinach and Other Vegetable Omelets

Chop cooked spinach fine, heat and add to the omelet. Cooked celery, asparagus tips, fried onions or mixtures of these vegetables make still other omelets. The one with onions is an omelet Lyonnaise.

Crab Omelets

For each individual omelet, heat well picked-over crab meat in a tablespoon of butter with a pinch of dried tarragon. When it is heated through, add one tablespoon of béchamel sauce and one teaspoon of sherry. Incorporate into the omelet in the usual way. You may use filets of anchovy, chopped lobster meat, shrimp cut into small pieces and leftover fish flaked and highly seasoned to make still other omelets.

All the omelets up to this point call for a light Rhine, Mosel or Alsatian wine.

Omelet with Chicken Livers (Omelette Chasseur)

Cook the shallots, chopped finely, in the butter in a small skillet until they are soft. Add the mushrooms, cleaned and sliced thinly, and the chicken livers, each cut into three or four pieces. Cook very briefly, about one or

OMELET WITH CHICKEN LIVERS
(Omelette Chasseur)

For six 3-egg omelets:

3	chicken livers
3	mushrooms
2	teasp. shallots
1 1/2	teasp. flour
3	tablesp. dry white wine
	chopped parsley

SPANISH OMELET SAUCE

3/4	cup chopped onions
1	large green pepper, sliced
1	large red pepper, sliced
1/2	stick butter
	salt
	pepper
2 - 3	cloves garlic
3	cans (8 oz.) tomato sauce
1/2	teasp. chili powder or
	several pinches of cayenne
	or several dashes of tabasco

one and one-half minutes, until the liver pieces are lightly browned. Stir in the flour and add wine. Mix well.

Make six individual basic omelets. At the proper moment, add one-sixth of the sauce to each omelet, finish cooking and turn onto hot plates. Sprinkle with chopped parsley. Sometimes, such an omelet is served garnished with a few broiled small mushrooms arranged down the middle of the folded omelet.

Good with a white Graves or a white Burgundy.

Spanish Omelet

Sauté the onions and peppers gently in the butter until they are soft but not brown. Add the rest of the ingredients and simmer for fifteen minutes, adding a little stock or water if sauce thickens too much. Adjust seasoning.

Make six individual basic omelets and serve with this sauce over them.

The onion-tomato-garlic flavor calls for a red wine of not-too-subtle flavor—a Côte de Provence, a regional claret, or a hearty California Barbera would all be suitable.

Puffy Omelet

This has quite a different flavor and texture from ordinary omelets, but occasionally is attractive. I always feel a little as though I were cheating when I complete the cooking in the oven, but in this case, if not in college examinations, it is preferable to cheat than to fail. Good luck!

Separate the whites and the yolks of two eggs for each person. Season the yolks with salt, pepper and a dash of tabasco. Beat them until they are thick and lemon colored.

Add an extra egg white for each four eggs and stir in a pinch of cream of tartar. Beat the whites until they peak but are not at all dry. Fold the whites gently into the yolks but do not beat them and do not mix thoroughly. Use an omelet pan with an ovenproof handle. Butter bottom and sides well and cook the omelet until the bottom is delicately browned, as determined by lifting up an edge with the spatula.

At this point, place the pan in an oven preheated to 375 degrees until the top is browned and feels firm when pressed with a finger.

It is at this moment that many conventional recipes call for the folding the omelet out of the pan onto a plate. And at this point, whenever I try to follow such directions, the omelet *always* falls. Therefore, I merely slide it gently —and prayerfully—out of the pan onto a hot serving plate and get it to the table as fast as possible. It usually works.

The flavor of a successful puffy omelet is unusually delicate. Therefore, to my taste, it demands a light German or Alsatian wine.

Frittata

Here is a hearty Italian version, good occasionally for a change.

The usual directions call for using raw spinach and completing the cooking by baking for ten minutes. To my mind, this does not sufficiently cook the spinach and it overcooks the eggs. Therefore, my method is as follows.

Slice the onion thinly. Heat the oil in a large heavy bottomed skillet and sauté the onion and the crushed garlic very gently until the onion is soft, but not browned. At this point, add the one-half pound of *cooked,* chopped spinach from which as much of the liquid as possible has been removed by draining and pressing it in a fine strainer. When the spinach is hot, the eggs, seasoned with salt and pepper and with the cheese beaten into them, are poured into the pan. The mixture is stirred as for an omelet, then its edges are tipped and the uncooked egg allowed to run underneath. The cooking is completed on top of the stove over low heat, but without folding as for the usual omelet.

In this way, one preserves everything good about the dish while avoiding what I feel is the rather unattractive flavor of half-cooked spinach and the wholly unattractive texture of overcooked eggs.

This dish is excellent with a good *secco* from Orvieto, which although white, is full-bodied enough to stand up to the garlic and spinach. It is also good with any light red wine, such as a Beaujolais or Bordeaux regional, or a California Mountain Red.

Pipérade

The name of this Basque dish, not quite an omelet, but not quite scrambled eggs; neither quite French nor

FRITTATA

12	eggs
1	large onion
1/2	lb. chopped spinach
4	tablesp. olive oil
1/2	cup freshly grated Parmesan cheese
1	large or 2 small cloves garlic
1	tablesp. chopped parsley
	salt
	freshly ground pepper

PIPÉRADE

6	ham slices 1/4 inch thick
12	eggs
2	green peppers
1	red pepper
1	large onion
1	large or 2 small cloves garlic
3	tablesp. olive oil
1	teasp. chopped chives
1	teasp. chopped parsley
1	teasp. fresh tarragon or
	1/4 teasp. dried tarragon
	salt
	freshly ground pepper
3	tomatoes
	tabasco sauce

quite Spanish, but *Basque,* refers to the mixture of vegetables, basically tomatoes and peppers. There are many variations. The French, sometimes a little messy with their egg and meat dishes—for example, in the way they drop their eggs into the frying pan over bacon or ham—usually direct that the beaten eggs be cooked into the vegetable mixture. Other recipes call for the vegetables as a garnish around the eggs. I have before me, three recipes: one calls for cooking the eggs into the vegetables, one for spreading the cooked vegetable mixture over and slightly into the eggs, and the third for using the pipérade as a garnish around the eggs. Again, the ham can be omitted, chopped into the eggs, into the pipérade, or, as we do at our house, kept separate.

Slice the onion and peppers thinly. Crush the garlic in a garlic press, or chop finely. Cook the onions, peppers and garlic in the olive oil until they are soft but not browned. Peel and quarter the tomatoes; shake out the seeds. Add to the skillet with the other vegetables, cover and simmer until all are well cooked and most of the liquid has evaporated. Broil the ham and keep warm.

Beat the eggs, season with salt and pepper, and add six dashes of tabasco sauce and twelve teaspoons of water as for an omelet. Cook in olive oil, stirring a moment or two and then lifting edges so that the liquid egg runs underneath the cooked part. Stop the cooking when the eggs in the middle are still creamy, slide the eggs onto a hot serving plate, spoon the vegetable mixture around the eggs and arrange the ham slices around the pipérade and serve immediately. A Côte de Provence, a regional claret, or a similar inexpensive California red wine will make a fitting accompaniment for this hearty luncheon or supper dish.

Quiches

Recipes for these savory pies vary a good deal, but most French writers agree with the Larousse Gastronomique that true *Quiche Lorraine* is composed of a custard of milk and eggs with either bacon or ham, and that the recipes calling for cheese, onions, or a mixture of the two are variants. The question of terminology appears unimportant; to my palate, all the variations except those containing an identifiable quantity of onion are good. But, again, according to my palate, the simplest one of all is the best.

However, do try all the variations. Whether you agree with me or not, you cannot lose. Make the quiches in a straight-sided cake pan.

Line two eight inch, straight sided cake pans or two flan rings on a baking sheet with a good short crust (pâte brisée).

Have the bacon cut into fairly thick slices. Fry crisp and drain on paper towels. Break bacon into fair size pieces and press these pieces into the pastry.

Beat the eggs, cream and seasonings in a mixing bowl. Divide equally between the two pans. Dot the top of each filled pan with generous bits of butter and set the pans in a 375 degree oven for twenty-five to thirty minutes. They will be done when a knife or a straw plunged into the center comes away clean.

Serve with a good full-bodied white Burgundy or a chilled white Graves. A green salad as a first course, French bread with the quiche, and fresh fruit in season will make a fine informal dinner or Sunday night supper. Try substituting one-half cup of diced ham sautéed in butter for the bacon. It is good, although, I think, not quite as good as the bacon.

Other recipes call for eight eggs and four cups of milk. Such a custard sets very well, but is less rich and tastes less good than when the pie is made with all cream. Some cooks also like to slice an onion thinly, sauté it in butter and spread over the ham or bacon. Try it if you must, but I think that neither the flavor nor the texture of the sautéed onion has any place here.

QUICHE LORRAINE WITH BACON

	pastry dough sufficient for 2 8 inch one-crust pies
6	eggs
1/2	lb. bacon
1	pt. whipping cream
1/2	stick butter
1	teasp. salt
2	good pinches fresh nutmeg freshly ground pepper

Quiche with Gruyére Cheese

Omit the bacon and stir into the custard mixture, four ounces of grated Gruyère cheese. Because of the added fat in the cheese, it is acceptable to use either half milk and half cream or even all milk for this dish.

You may make a Quiche au Fromage de Cheddar by substituting a good sharp Cheddar for the Gruyère in this recipe.

A third variation may be made by using one-half Gruyère and one-half Parmesan cheese. In this case, I definitely recommend using all milk. If you use thick cream, the quiche is likely to turn out to be too oily.

With the cheese quiches, my own preference is for a good red Burgundy or Beaujolais. However, no law governs the subject and if you like a white wine better, there is no reason not to use it.

CHEESE

The world produces countless kinds of cheese. France alone is said to produce regularly on a commercial basis, more than 400 different kinds. In general, the innumerable varieties of cheese fall into five classes: fresh, soft, semihard (or if you prefer, semisoft), hard, and blue. Blue cheeses are those which, as part of the curing process, are innoculated with one of two varieties of the penicillium mold—either *penicillium roqueforti* or *penicillium glaucum.* These molds are closely related to the common bread mold, *penicillium notatum,* from which penicillin, one of our most important life-saving antibiotics, is made. As may be deduced from this relationship as well as from centuries of practical experience in consuming them, the cheeses made with these molds are in no way unwholesome, although in the quantities in which they are ingested, they have no medicinal values. However, we are interested here in the pleasures of the table, not in medical therapy.

Cottage cheese, cream cheeses and the related Italian ricotto are used in cookery. However, most of the soft and semisoft cheeses are eaten without further preparation. In western European and American cookery the three important cooking cheeses are Gruyère in France and Switzerland, Parmesan in France and Italy, and the Cheddar-type cheese (with their local variations such as Cheshire and Wenleysdale in Great Britain) in the British Isles, the United States and Canada. Americans also take full advantage of the merits of Parmesan (and its relative Romano) and of Gruyère. The other principal Swiss cheese, Emmenthaler (the one with large holes) is not frequently used in cooking.

Cheese Soufflé

All of the French recipes—naturally—call for either Gruyère or a mixture of Gruyère and Parmesan cheeses. You can, indeed, make a good soufflé with these cheeses, but what most of us in America have in mind when we think of a good cheese soufflé is one made with a Cheddar-type cheese, preferably a well-aged sharp cheese such as the Canadian Black Diamond.

Your soufflé will rise better if it be cooked in a soufflé mold or a straight sided Charlotte mold. However, while they are convenient, these pans are not absolutely essential. I have made some good soufflés in a round two or two and one-half quart Pyrex baking dish with sloping sides. What is essential is that the bottom and sides of the mold be well buttered. If, after buttering the inside of the pan, you sprinkle finely grated cheese over the buttered surface and then invert and shake the pan, it will be even easier for the soufflé to rise nicely.

Use Mold to Make Soufflé Rise Better

If you already have béchamel sauce prepared, measure out two measuring cupsful, or one pint. If you do not have it, make the sauce by melting 1/2 stick (two ounces) butter and stirring into it 1/4 cup of flour. Beat with a wire whisk until the flour and butter are well blended but do not let it color. Heat 1 1/2 cups of milk to boiling and add all at once to the flour-butter mixture, continue to beat vigorously. Beat in the seasonings and cook ten minutes. Remove from the heat and let it cool somewhat.

Separate the whites and yolks of the eggs. Add the yolks, one at a time, to the hot but not boiling béchamel and beat each one vigorously into the sauce. Do *not* try to save work by using a Mixmaster or even a rotary eggbeater. Every time my cook or I have done so, the soufflé has failed to rise.

Add one extra egg white to the four. Beat, again with the whisk and not with a mechanical beater, the five whites until they peak but do *not* beat until they become dry. Stir into the sauce about one-quarter of the egg whites, then beat in the grated cheese. Now cut the rest of the egg whites into the sauce; again do *not* mix too thoroughly. There should be little mounds of unmixed white on the surface of the mixture when you turn it into the baking dish.

Put the mixture into the center of an oven preheated to 400 degrees and immediately reduce the heat to 375 or 350 degrees. Do not disturb for at least twenty-five minutes. In twenty-five or thirty minutes, the top will be nicely browned. The inside will be very creamy, but the soufflé will fall at once if removed. To make it more stable,

271

cook a few minutes more, until a sharp knife slid into the side of the puffed-up soufflé comes out clean. It will stand up at least until it is served and will be light when it is eaten.

A good cheese soufflé is worthy of a bottle of your very best Burgundy because of the natural affinity between cheese and heavy red wine. And I meant it when I said Burgundy; the only Bordelais wine full-bodied enough to do a good cheese dish justice is perhaps a Pomerol of a successful year. Nearly, but not quite, as acceptable is a sound California Pinot Noir.

Salmon Soufflé

Make exactly like the cheese soufflé but use Gruyère in place of Cheddar cheese and use only one-quarter pound. Flake one-quarter pound of cooked salmon (preferably poached) thoroughly and add it to the sauce when you have finished beating in the eggs.

Chicken Soufflé

Cook a tablespoon of chopped onion and one or two chopped shallots in a little butter until they are soft and golden.

Put through the finest blade of the food chopper the sautéed onion and shallot and one cup of leftover chicken. Season well with a little powdered thyme and tarragon and stir this mixture into the soufflé when you have finished adding the egg yolks. Again, reduce cheese to one-half and use Gruyère in place of Cheddar.

Ham Soufflé

Season a cup of ground leftover ham, baked or boiled, with a tablespoon of grated onion, salt, white pepper, and 1/4 teaspoon each of sage and thyme. Add to the soufflé after the egg yolks and proceed, again, with reduced amounts of Gruyère cheese.

Cheese Strata

A dish *almost* as good as a good cheese soufflé and ridiculously easy to make. No reader of this book, of

CHEESE SOUFFLÉ

1	pt. béchamel sauce
1/2	lb. finely grated Cheddar cheese
1	teasp. salt
4	eggs
1	extra egg white
	dash of freshly grated nutmeg
	dash of cayenne pepper

course, would ever be caught in the pangs of a severe hang-over, but if you have a friend who does occasionally find himself in such a predicament, tell him about cheese strata, because it is a dish which can be successfully achieved even by someone who does not fully have his wits about him.

Trim crusts from twelve slices of bread, preferably a little dry. Arrange six slices in a buttered baking dish of such size that the six slices of bread nearly cover the bottom. Sprinkle two-thirds of the cheese over the bread, then arrange the other six slices in a new layer, finishing with the remainder of the cheese. Beat the eggs slightly and stir into the milk. Season with the salt and a good grind of white pepper and pour into the baking dish over the two layers of bread and cheese. If you have chosen the right size baking dish, the liquid will come about to the top of the bread. Let stand fifteen or twenty minutes so that the bread absorbs as much of the liquid as possible. Crumble the crisply fried bacon over the top of the strata and bake in 325 degree oven until it is puffy and golden brown— about forty to forty-five minutes. The air in the porous bread acts like a leavening agent; it expands as it is heated, making the dish puffy and light, almost like a soufflé. The strata will rise even better if it is left overnight before baking.

Two Creamed Mushroom Dishes

There is no logical reason why recipes for main dishes of mushrooms should go in this chapter. Both of these dishes are very good. The first one is really a soufflé, so the present chapter seems as good a place as any to present them.

Like all soufflés, this one starts with a béchamel. But because the béchamel sauce here is extra rich—using cream, extra butter and mushroom juice—it seems best to give the recipe in full.

Clean the mushrooms and remove the stems. If you have the small button mushrooms, leave them whole; if you can find only the larger brown ones, slice the caps fairly thin.

Sauté the mushrooms in four tablespoons of butter for five minutes and drain off the butter and juice. There should be about one cup.

CHEESE STRATA

12	slices of bread (preferably stale)
1/2	lb. diced or grated Cheddar cheese (preferably sharp)
4	eggs
3	cups milk
3/4	teasp. salt
6	slices bacon
1 - 2	tablesp. butter
	a good dash of cayenne pepper

MUSHROOM SOUFFLÉ

2	lbs. mushrooms
8	tablesp. butter
4	tablesp. flour
1/8	teasp. mace
1/8	teasp. nutmeg
1	cup half and half (light cream)
4	eggs
1	extra egg white
	salt
	freshly ground white pepper
	dash of cayenne pepper

Melt the other four tablespoons of butter in a heavy bottomed saucepan and stir in the flour, *without* letting it color more than slightly. When the *roux* thus made has cooked a few minutes, add alternately and a little at a time, beating vigorously between additions, the cup of half and half (light cream) and the mushroom butter and juice. Reserve one cup of the resulting mushroom béchamel, together with the stems, for a mushroom soup.

Season the other cup with salt, freshly ground white pepper, nutmeg, mace and a good dash of cayenne. Let cool somewhat.

Separate the whites and the yolks of four eggs. Add the yolks to the warm sauce as you separate them, beating the sauce with a wire whisk as you add each yolk. Beat the four whites with one extra white added until they peak but are not dry.

Stir the mushrooms into the béchamel-egg yolk mixture. Add one-fourth of the egg white, whisking it well into the mixture. Then chop, rather than beat in the remaining egg white, being careful, as with any soufflé, not to mix the whites too thoroughly.

Bake in a buttered and crumbed soufflé or baking dish in a 350 degree oven in a pan of water until a knife comes out clean when slid into the side. This will require forty to forty-five minutes.

This soufflé merits a bottle of the best white Burgundy—a good Beaune, Meursault or even a treasured bottle of Montrachet.

Creamed Mushrooms with Sherry

CREAMED MUSHROOMS WITH SHERRY

1 1/2	lb. mushrooms
3	tablesp. butter
3	tablesp. sherry
1 1/2	cups sour cream
1/8	teasp. mace
1/8	teasp. allspice
	salt
	freshly ground pepper

Again, by preference, select button mushrooms, or at least the medium-size white mushrooms. However, if you cannot get these, accept the large brown ones. Leave the buttons whole but slice the larger ones. In any case, wash them well and chop the stems. In a heavy skillet, sauté gently in the butter until the mushrooms begin to brown, add the sherry—a medium-dry sherry such as Amontillado or its California equivalent is best—and let cook one minute while stirring vigorously. Now, add the sour cream and the seasonings to taste and let simmer until the sauce thickens a little. Serve on toast with a good, white wine.

If you make this dish using a Madeira rather than a sherry, you will have a quite different effect.

We like a nice, crisp Rhine or Mosel with mushrooms prepared with the sherry.

Macaroni and Cheese

A simple dish, but when well made, a lovely one!

Cook the macaroni until it is moderately tender in three quarts of boiling salted water. Choose a size of the elbow-type macaroni that is neither very small nor large. If the pieces are large enough to be ribbed, they are too large.

Drain and arrange in a Pyrex or other baking dish or casserole with alternating layers of grated Cheddar cheese. Reserve enough thin slices of cheese to decorate the top of the casserole. Cover the macaroni and cheese layers with the béchamel sauce and arrange slices of cheese on top. Bake in a 350 to 375 degree oven until the cheese on top bubbles and begins to brown, usually about twenty-five to thirty minutes.

In my opinion, a good dish of macaroni and cheese in which the cheese has not been spared (such as in this recipe) deserves a better-than-average Beaujolais, such as a Fleurie or a moderately-good Côte de Beaune Burgundy, as a Santenay or a Volnay; or a village wine from the Côte de Nuit, such as a Chambolle-Musigny.

Spaghetti with Meat Sauce

Soak the dried mushrooms overnight in two cups of water. Put the ground beef once again through the finest blade of the food chopper. Chop the onion and mince the garlic.

Heat the olive oil in a heavy iron skillet and sauté the garlic and onions until they are soft and golden. Add the salt to the meat and turn into the skillet. So that the ground meat remains light and fluffy, without lumps, cook over fairly high heat until it is well browned, turning and stirring frequently. Pour off the water in which the mushrooms soaked, being careful to avoid any sediment or sand; add it to the skillet; chop the mushrooms and add. Then add the peeled and chopped fresh tomatoes (or the canned ones) together with the basil and rosemary. Cover and simmer at least two hours. The sauce should be cooked

MACARONI AND CHEESE

1	lb. elbow macaroni
2	cups béchamel sauce
	salt
1/2	lb. Cheddar cheese (preferably sharp and as aged as you can afford)

275

SPAGHETTI WITH MEAT SAUCE

1	lb. long spaghetti
1	lb. ground beef
1	large onion
3	cloves garlic
1/2	cup celery
	salt
1/4	lb. (or more) freshly grated Parmesan cheese
1/3	cup olive oil
1	pkg. dry mushrooms
1 1/2	lb. tomatoes (or one No. 2 1/2 can Italian tomatoes)
2	teasp. dried sweet basil
1/2	teasp. dried rosemary

down until none of the vegetables is individually recognizable. If necessary, add beef stock to keep the sauce adequately liquid.

Bring to a rapid boil three quarts of salted water and feed the long bundle of spaghetti into it from one end. Do not break the spaghetti into "convenient" lengths. The proper length is the length the manufacturer furnishes. Boil it until it is as soft as you like. All over Italy, we were served spaghetti "al dente" too chewy for our taste. Drain in a colander and rinse thoroughly at the hot water tap. Serve on heated plates with the sauce spooned over it generously and pass the grated cheese. (The packaged already-grated Parmesan cheese available in supermarkets is so lacking in flavor that its use is not recommended in any case.)

For most Americans, Chianti in straw-covered bottles is the spaghetti wine *par excellence.* This is wrong on two counts. Actually spaghetti wine is whatever the red wine of the district is; second, Chianti in the straw-covered *fiaschi* is very much a *vin ordinaire.* In reality the region around Florence produces quite superior wines—superior, that is, as Italian red wines go. These Chiantis are marketed in bottles of the same shape and size as Bordeaux bottles.

Any drinkable, fairly flavorful, red wine is good with spaghetti with this sauce; a fine wine would be lost amid the sharp flavors of the tomato, garlic and basil.

Here is another version of spaghetti, still authentically Italian.

Spaghetti alla Carbonara

Boil spaghetti twelve or fifteen minutes, according to how firm you like it, in three quarts of salted water. Drain and rinse.

For the sauce, heat the butter and olive oil in a skillet and sauté very gently the ham and bacon, cut into narrow strips about one and one-half inches by one-quarter inch. After cleaning the mushrooms, slice them thinly and add to the skillet. Do not allow any of the items to brown, but cook about five minutes after adding the mushrooms. Remove from the heat and quickly add the freshly grated Parmesan cheese and the eggs, the latter well beaten, and mix well. Season to taste with salt and pepper.

SPAGHETTI ALLA CARBONARA

1	lb. spaghetti
4	tablesp. olive oil
2	tablesp. butter
1/2	cup ham
1/2	cup bacon
3	oz. Parmesan cheese
2	large or 3 small eggs
1/2	cup mushrooms
	salt
	freshly ground black pepper

276

Pass additional freshly grated Parmesan cheese at the table.

This dish merits a good Chianti or Bardolino or a good California Pinot Noir or "Barbera."

Ricotto Pasta

Drain the spinach as thoroughly as possible. Mix well with the Italian ricotto cheese and the Parmesan cheese. Add the basil and salt. Now, knead the sifted flour into the mass. Form into balls about the size of small walnuts, roll in additional flour and cook in boiling salted water for twenty minutes.

Serve with the same meat and tomato sauce as in the first spaghetti recipe.

I would pamper this dish with a wine a little better than an *ordinaire;* say a good Beaujolais or a quality Chianti or a good California Pinot Noir.

Tufoli with Stuffing

To make the sauce: Chop the garlic finely, brown in the oil, and add the other ingredients, first peeling and quartering the tomatoes. Cook at least forty-five minutes.

To make the stuffing: Drain the spinach as dry as possible. Chop the onions and mince the garlic. Cook them until they are tender in the oil. Add mushrooms, herbs, and the beef, browning it well by frequent stirring. Let cool. Cut the Mozzarella cheese into small cubes. Mix the contents of the skillet with the Mozzarella cheese and the spinach together with the beaten egg. If necessary to make the mass easy to handle, use another egg.

Boil the tufoli about twelve minutes in three quarts of salted water. They will be about half cooked. Rinse in cold water and stuff with the mixture above.

Line a baking dish with a layer of the marinara sauce, then a layer of the stuffed tufoli and another layer of sauce. Now, sprinkle a generous portion of freshly grated Parmesan cheese and repeat the layers, finishing with the grated Parmesan cheese on top of a layer of sauce. Bake in a 350 degree oven for one-half hour.

Serve with any good coarse red wine, Italian or domestic. The wine will make the dish better and, happily enough, the dish will improve your wine.

RICOTTO PASTA

2	cups cooked chopped spinach
1	cup ricotto cheese
1/2	cup flour
2	eggs
1/2	cup freshly grated Parmesan cheese
1/2	teasp. dried sweet basil
1	teasp. salt

TUFOLI WITH STUFFING

1	lb. tufoli
1	lb. chopped beef
1/2	lb. mushrooms
1/2	lb. cooked chopped spinach
1/2	lb. Mozzarella cheese
1	egg
4	cups marinara sauce
1	large or 2 small onions
3	cloves garlic
2	tablesp. olive oil
1	teasp. dried sweet basil
1/2	teasp. dried oregano
1/4	lb. (or more) freshly grated Parmesan cheese

MARINARA SAUCE

1/3	cup olive oil
3	cloves garlic
4	cups tomatoes
1 1/2	tablesp. chopped parsley
1	scant teasp. dried basil
2	teasp. salt
1/4	teasp. oregano
4	tablesp. tomato paste

Fettuccine Alfredo

FETTUCCINE ALFREDO

1	lb. dried noodles or an equal quantity of homemade dough cut thin
1 1/2	sticks fresh butter
3/4	cup whipping cream
2	eggs
2	cups freshly grated Parmesan cheese
	freshly ground black pepper

This dish is notably better if you use homemade, freshly-made noodle paste, but it is quite good even with commercially dried noodles. In the chapter on breads and pastries, there is a good recipe for homemade noodles. Cut your noodles to whatever width you like. In Rome, we chiefly encountered quite narrow pasta.

Cook the noodles in a large amount of salted water; drain, rinse, and put in a warmed casserole. Beat the eggs into the cream. Melt the butter. Add alternately the butter, egg-cream mixture and the grated cheese, tossing between each addition and keeping the casserole hot. Salt to taste and finish with a good grind of black pepper. Pass additional freshly grated Parmesan cheese at the table.

This *pasta,* with its rich but gently cheesy flavor, deserves a good Beaune or Pomerol red for its accompanying drink.

Chicken and Ham Cannelloni

CHICKEN AND HAM CANNELLONI

1	lb. egg noodle dough
1/2	lb. cooked chicken
1/4	lb. thinly sliced prosciutto
1/2	cup flour
1	stick butter
	salt
1	tablesp. chopped parsley
1/4	lb. small mushrooms
1	cup whipping cream
2	pts. whole milk
1/2	teasp. nutmeg
1/2	teasp. mace
1/2	teasp. white pepper

Fettuccine is preferably made with fresh dough; for Cannelloni, such fresh dough is essential. Fortunately it is easy to make.

Make fine julienne strips of the chicken and prosciutto. Clean the mushrooms and slice thinly. Cook gently in one-third of the butter for five minutes.

Heat the milk to near boiling. In the top of a double boiler, melt the remaining butter and stir into the flour, working all the lumps out of it. Then, gradually add the scalded milk, beating with a wire whisk until the sauce thickens. Add the cream, the spices, salt and white pepper to taste.

Use about one cup of the sauce to mix together the chicken, ham and noodles.

Roll out the noodle dough into lengths convenient for your baking dish, and four inches across. The usual length of cannelloni is four to six inches. Cook the squares or rectangles of dough in boiling salted water for eight to ten minutes, until they are tender. Drain and spread the pieces of dough on damp cloths. Spread about two or two and one-half tablespoons of the filling in the center of each of the cannelloni and roll firmly.

Arrange in two layers in one or more baking dishes, with a generous sprinkling of Parmesan cheese between the layers. Cover each layer with the sauce. Finish with the sauce, sprinkled with cheese. Bake in a 375 degree oven for twenty minutes.

Like fettucine Alfredo, this dish merits one of your better, full-bodied medium-grade Burgundies or a regional wine from Pomerol.

Polenta with Cheese

The French regard maize as feed for horses and cattle, but Italians, like Americans, know better. The Italians, however, grind their cornmeal, made from yellow corn and called polenta, considerably coarser than American cornmeal. It, consequently, has a different texture—and when it is adequately cooked—better flavor. Combined with a good sharp Cheddar-type cheese, it makes a fine and hearty dish.

Salt the water and boil the coarse yellow cornmeal for at least one hour. Warning: you will have to stir it frequently to prevent sticking. When the polenta tastes fully done, cut the cheese into one-quarter inch cubes and stir into the hot mush. Just before removing from the heat, stir in half a stick of butter.

This dish doesn't taste Italian; it just tastes good. And, like all good dishes with Cheddar cheeese as their predominant flavor, it merits a good Burgundy or California Pinot Noir.

The French have carried the business of making attractive entrées out of odds and ends of leftover food further than the average American housewife, both because the whole business of cooking and eating well is perhaps taken a little more seriously in that country than in ours; but also, because even less than her American sisters, the French woman can ill afford to waste food.

One of the more attractive of the French methods of using up leftover bits of meat, fowl and even vegetables involves the little thin pancakes that the French call crêpes. Most Americans know about *crêpes sucrées,* the sweet crêpes, or at least one of the more notorious of them, Crêpes Suzette, but not all are aware of what can be done with *crêpes salées,* or salted crêpes. Here are some sugges-

POLENTA WITH CHEESE

1 1/2	cups polenta
6 1/2	cups water
1/2	stick butter
1	lb. sharp Cheddar cheese (preferably Black Diamond)
	salt

tions. You will find how to make the crêpes in the chapter on bread and pastry.

Crêpes with Ham and Tomato Sauce

Peel and quarter the tomatoes and cook without water in a covered saucepan for five minutes over a low fire. Chop the carrot and onion finely. Add these to the tomatoes together with the herbs. Make a blond *roux* by melting the butter and stirring the flour into it, letting the mixture cook until it turns a golden color. Stir the stock into the *roux,* beating after each addition and then add the thickened stock to the vegetable mixture. Let simmer for forty-five minutes and adjust the seasoning with salt and pepper.

Either place a thin slice of ham or one tablespoon of leftover ham cut into fine julienne strips in the middle of each crêpe. Sprinkle with grated Gruyère and roll firmly. Arrange in a Pyrex or other baking dish and cover with the tomato sauce. Sprinkle the remaining grated cheese over the sauce and put into a 350 degree oven for about ten minutes, until the sauce bubbles and the cheese is melted. Serve hot.

These ham crêpes call for a light red wine such as a regional Bordeaux.

Stuffed Crêpes

The first recipe could utilize either leftover ham or meat bought especially for making the crêpes. This recipe is notably adapted for using up leftover bits and pieces.

Chop together the veal, ham and mushrooms. Use more or less mushrooms as you have less or more meat. Mix with the bread crumbs which have been soaked in milk. Season with the herbs and with salt and pepper to taste. If the dressing is too dry, moisten with a little béchamel sauce. Put a heaping tablespoon of the dressing in the middle of each crêpe, roll it fairly tightly and arrange in the bottom of a suitable buttered baking dish. Cover with the béchamel sauce and sprinkle with the grated cheese. Cook in a 350 degree oven for about ten minutes, until the top of the sauce begins to take on a golden color.

I have enjoyed these "clean-up-the-kitchen" crêpes both with a light red and with a light Mosel.

CRÊPES WITH HAM AND TOMATO SAUCE

12	small crêpes
12	ham slices cut to fit crêpes (or 2 cups julienne)
1/2	lb. Gruyère cheese
2	cups tomato sauce

TOMATO SAUCE

1	lb. tomatoes
1	carrot
1	onion
1	cup beef stock or condensed bouillon
2	tablesp. flour
2	tablesp. butter
1	teasp. dried thyme
1	bay leaf
	salt
	pepper

STUFFED CRÊPES

12	crêpes
1	cup leftover veal, beef, or lamb
1	cup leftover ham
	a few oz. of mushrooms
2	oz. fresh bread crumbs
1/2	cup grated Gruyère cheese
4	tablesp. butter
5	oz. milk
1/4	teasp. dried tarragon
1/4	teasp. dried thyme
	salt
	pepper
2	cups béchamel sauce

Crab Crêpes with Sauce Mornay

Pick over the crab meat, removing all membrane. Mix with enough sauce mornay to make a mixture that handles well. Season with salt and freshly ground white pepper. Divide between the crêpes and roll them tightly. Arrange in a buttered baking dish, pour the rest of the sauce mornay over the rolled crêpes and sprinkle with grated Gruyère cheese. Place in a 350 degree oven until top begins to be golden brown.

Note: You may substitute any leftover white flaky fish for part of the crab in this recipe with very little damage to its good quality.

My family and I have preferred a crisp light Rhine or Mosel with these, especially when they are made entirely with crab.

Seafood, Cheese and Rice Casserole

Here is another flexible recipe, designed to use up remnants of cheese and seafood around your kitchen. The quantities of each item are flexible, so do not hesitate to make the dish if you have less of one of the items and perhaps more of another than is called for.

Sometime when you notice that you have various pieces of cheese about, cook an extra cup of long-grain rice. The cheese can vary but the rice ought to be light and dry, with the grains not stuck together. Cut your cheese into small cubes except for grating one-half cup of the Parmesan for topping. Cut up the shrimp. Here again, substitutions are permissible, such as pieces of cooked lobster or crab. We have made the casserole with leftover chicken; it was good but lacked the tang that the seafood gives it. If you have a few shrimp available, and a little leftover chicken, they will combine very well.

In any event, butter a casserole, spread in it one-half of the rice, then the mixed cheese and seafood (and/or chicken) and finish with the remainder of the rice. Cover by sprinkling the half cup of grated Parmesan cheese over the top and dotting generously with butter. Set the casserole in a pan of water and bake in a 375 to 400 degree oven for one-half hour or so, until the top is nicely brown.

If your proportions are anywhere near those given in this recipe, a Muscadet or Sancerre will prove enjoyable with it.

CRAB CRÊPES WITH SAUCE MORNAY

3/4	lb. flaked crab meat
1	pt. sauce mornay
	salt
	pepper
12	crêpes
2 - 3	oz. grated Gruyère cheese

SEAFOOD, CHEESE AND RICE CASSEROLE

1	cup long-grain rice
1/2	cup Bel Paese cheese
1/2	cup Provolone cheese
1	cup Parmesan cheese
1/2	cup mild Cheddar cheese
1	cup (more or less) cooked shrimp
	butter

GARDEN VEGETABLES, POTATOES & RICE

17

In shopping for vegetables, it is unwise to look too hard for bargains. Vegetables should be harvested young and brought to market as rapidly as possible. If you have a good green grocer who makes such treasures available to you, cooperate with him by buying frequently and often, and in suitable small quantities. If your marketman has a special sale on some items of green groceries because it is the height of the season and he is overstocked—fine—take advantage of the sale. But, if the sale is because the stock is growing old and wilted, pass it up; your purchases will not be bargains.

Do not overcook vegetables. Braise them at low heat in butter and a little chicken or beef stock whenever possible. When braising is not feasible, use stock for boiling if you can. If you must use water, keep the quantity as small as possible.

ARTICHOKES

There are various recipes for stuffing and otherwise elaborating on the artichoke. None of these methods seems attractive to me when it is a question of the entire artichoke. Only the stalk ends of the leaves can be eaten; stuffings and coatings only get in the way.

Select fresh artichokes of moderate size, take off the coarse outer leaves, trim the spiny tops from all the upper leaves and cut the bottom off smoothly. Tie the artichokes with string and plunge into salted boiling water until tender when the bottom is tested with a fork.

Serve with melted butter or with a dish of hollandaise sauce. Because of its distinctive flavor, the artichoke is best served as a separate course.

Artichoke Hearts

Here, in my opinion, is one of the rare cases in which availing yourself of the frozen food bins of your market is a desirable thing. The frozen hearts have a satisfactory consistency; they are uniformly trimmed; they save a lot of work and waste. We parboil them in a little chicken stock to cover and then arrange in a shallow baking dish and dress with a sauce mornay, over which we sprinkle a little freshly grated Parmesan cheese and bake in a 350 degree oven until the sauce bubbles and browns.

Also Good Braised

The artichoke hearts are also good braised with a generous half cup of butter and the same amount of chicken stock, and seasoned only with salt and freshly ground pepper.

ASPARAGUS

In America, one generally finds the green kind, either thick or thin; in Europe, the white is more often seen.

Use Only Fresh Stalks

In either case, select only fresh stalks. Wash them and snap off the tough ends where breaking is easy. Do not try to save more than this because the part below the break is too tough to be worth eating. Do not discard the broken off lower ends. Cook for one-half hour or longer, retain the cooking liquid and press these ends of stalks through a sieve as the start of a cream of asparagus soup.

In order that the more delicate spears may steam while the tougher stems are boiled, tie the asparagus in bunches and cook in an asparagus steamer, or a tall saucepan with the bunches standing upright. Asparagus requires cooking in slightly salted water two-thirds of the way up the bunches for eighteen to twenty minutes or until the tips are tender. Do not overcook. Limp asparagus even *looks* discouraged.

Serve hot with hollandaise sauce, melted butter and a little lemon, or arrange in rows on a hot platter and sprinkle the heads with Parmesan cheese. Just before serving, cover the cheese-sprinkled tips with brown butter. This is Milanaise style asparagus.

Another way is to lay the asparagus on an ovenproof platter in rows and dress the tips of each row with

284

sauce mornay. Sprinkle with grated Parmesan and brown under the broiler. This is asparagus au gratin.

Arrange asparagus on a hot platter in rows and sprinkle over the heads with chopped egg yolk and parsley. Then, just before serving, cover with a mixture of one-quarter toasted bread crumbs and three-quarters butter. This is Polish asparagus.

Served cold with a simple vinaigrette, asparagus vinaigrette is a fine first course.

Like artichoke, asparagus should be served as a separate course and not as a garnish for another course.

French Fried Asparagus

Dip the cold stalks of asparagus into the egg, which has been beaten with the milk and seasonings. Roll in bread crumbs and fry in deep fat at 370 degrees about two minutes. When it is done, the stalks will rise to the top of the frying kettle and will be delicately browned. Drain on paper towels. Fried asparagus can be served as an accompaniment to steak or other red meat.

FRENCH FRIED ASPARAGUS

2	lbs. cooked asparagus
1	egg
3	tablesp. milk
1	cup (or more) bread crumbs
1/2	teasp. salt
1/4	teasp. marjoram
	freshly ground black pepper
	fat for deep frying

BROCCOLI

Early in the season, one sometimes finds broccoli small enough that it seems best to cook both stalks and flowerets together. But, most of the season, the stalks are so large that it is more satisfactory to cut off the flowerets, retaining enough of the branched stems to hold them together and to buy enough at each purchase for two meals. For the first meal, one has the flowerets; for the second, one can peel and cut up the stalks and prepare them by one of the recipes given below. Some people think the stalks are a more delicate vegetable than the flowerets. Broccoli, like cabbage, requires rapid cooking, uncovered, in a relatively large amount of salted water to lessen odor. Even more suppression of the cabbagy odor can be obtained by putting a slice or two of bread in the boiling liquid. Do not overcook.

At our house, we like the small whole plant; or the flowerets, barely tender, either with salt and melted butter or with hollandaise sauce.

Broccoli Stems with Olive Oil

BROCCOLI STEMS WITH OLIVE OIL

      sliced broccoli stems
1/2 cup olive oil
1   small clove garlic
      juice of two lemons
      salt
      freshly ground black pepper

Cook the stems in salted water, to which a tablespoon of lemon juice or vinegar has been added, until they are tender. (Peel the coarser stems.) Then slice and place in a hot dish. Heat 1/2 cup of olive oil mixed with the crushed pulp of a small clove of garlic and the juice of two lemons. Pour over the sliced stems; add salt and freshly ground black pepper to taste; serve.

Creamed Broccoli Stems Mornay

Slice broccoli stems cooked as in previous recipe into a buttered casserole. Barely cover with a sauce mornay, sprinkle top with freshly grated Parmesan cheese and place in a 375 degree oven until the sauce bubbles.

The stems are also good boiled until tender and dressed either with melted butter or hollandaise.

BRUSSELS SPROUTS

This miniature member of the cabbage family, which to my medical eye, looks like a foetal cabbage, is commonly overcooked.

One quart of sprouts is adequate to serve six persons. Wash, trim stems, and remove old or yellowed leaves. Cook in a large amount of salted water *not* over seven or eight minutes. Serve with melted butter.

Brussels Sprouts au Gratin

While in general, I prefer vegetables cooked and served with maximum simplicity, certain ones are worth a little more elaborate preparation.

After cleaning and trimming a quart of Brussels sprouts, cook for seven minutes in the smallest possible quantity of chicken stock. Drain and arrange in a buttered Pyrex or other baking dish. Cover with béchamel sauce and sprinkle the top with a layer of bread crumbs and Parmesan cheese. Cook in a 375 degree oven until the top begins to brown.

Brussels Sprouts Mornay

A slight variation of the foregoing recipe. Cover the cooked sprouts with a mornay sauce. Otherwise, proceed as in the previous recipe.

CABBAGE

Select a good, firm head of cabbage. Quarter it, cut out the thickest part of the stem and boil rapidly without a cover in a large amount of salted water. Stop the cooking when the cabbage is barely fork tender and while it is still green. Drain in a colander, return to the saucepan and set over gentle heat with one-half stick of melted butter, moving the pieces of cabbage about gently so that all parts are coated with butter without the sections coming apart.

CARROTS

Very small carrots are to be scraped, cut into round slices or split and quartered, according to your preference. Barely cover with water slightly salted; for two pounds of carrots, use one-quarter stick of butter. Cook over low heat until the liquid is almost absorbed and move the carrots about so that they will be well coated with the butter and slightly glazed.

If you are using old and big carrots, parboil them and then carry out the above procedure.

It is the firmly held belief of every member of my household that sugar does nothing for carrots except spoil their flavor. Therefore, I propose no other recipe for this simple and delicate vegetable.

CAULIFLOWER

Wash and trim off leaves and heavy parts of stalk. Like all members of the cabbage family and unlike all other vegetables, cauliflower is to be cooked in a large amount of lightly salted water. A piece or two of bread in the kettle will reduce the odor. Serve with melted butter and a little freshly ground pepper.

287

STEWED CELERY

celery stalks cut into one
    inch pieces
slightly salted chicken stock
melted butter
ground pepper
dill weed (optional)
1   teasp. tarragon (optional)

BRAISED CELERY

1/2   celery heart (per person)
1/2   cup butter
      chicken stock

CELERY

One can either braise celery hearts, or if you are buying the full bunch of celery for making celery victor, for example, you can stew the outer stalks very conveniently.

Stewed Celery

Cut the outer stalks of celery into pieces about one inch long, scraping the strings from any especially coarse stalks. Cover with slightly salted chicken stock and simmer until tender. Serve with melted butter and a little ground pepper. Interesting variations can be had by adding a teaspoon or two of dill weed to the stock; on other occasions, add a teaspoon of dried tarragon. In any of the three cases, save the cooking liquid for adding to a soup stock.

Braised Celery

Trim all of the leafy parts from hearts of celery and also trim the root until just a thin section, sufficient to hold the stalks together, is left. Split the celery hearts, providing one-half heart for each person.

Parboil the hearts for fifteen minutes. Then put in a covered casserole or a skillet which can be covered, together with one-half cup of butter and just enough chicken stock to cover the hearts half way. Cook gently until the liquid evaporates and then sauté slightly in the remaining butter.

Creamed Celery

Sliced, stewed celery may be put in a buttered baking dish and covered with a sauce mornay, or with a sauce béchamel. In the first case, dust the top with grated Gruyère cheese and bread crumbs; in the second, with a rather heavier layer of freshly grated Parmesan cheese and bread crumbs. The dish is then put into a 375 degree oven until the sauce bubbles.

Celery Root

In addition to making a fine salad when it is cut or grated into thin strips and served with a rémoulade dressing, this root is an attractive and somewhat spicy vegetable when it is cooked. We like it two different ways.

In the first, it is peeled, cut into cubes about three-quarters inch in size and simmered until it is tender in a minimum quantity of chicken stock, and then served generously buttered with no other treatment than salt and a generous grind of black pepper.

In the second, it is boiled in chicken stock until it is quite soft, put through a potato ricer and beaten together with one-third its weight of riced potatoes and a generous amount of butter.

CORN, GREEN

The chief direction for cooking fresh corn on the cob well is a negative one: avoid, avoid like plague, those neat and attractive ears from which all the shucks and silk have been stripped and which are shown neatly encased in cellophane in the supermarket. The one requirement which overweighs all others is that corn be fresh, fresh, fresh. If you do not know anyone in the countryside who raises corn where you can buy ears plucked from the stalk not more than one-half hour before you get them, at least buy only the ears encased in their own protective shucks, which must look crisp and fresh, with the grains still delicate. The trouble of cleaning such corn and even encountering an occasional worm is a small price to pay for the difference in flavor. The next most important requirement is to buy young corn, the grains of which are still milky. The only other injunction is: Don't overcook!

CUCUMBERS

Although we in America most commonly eat the cucumber raw as a salad vegetable, it also makes a delicate and good cooked vegetable.

Stewed Cucumbers

For six persons, select three or four large, firm cucumbers. Like zucchini, they may be peeled or not as you prefer. And, like zucchini, they are somewhat more delicate in texture and flavor if you *do* peel them. Slice in pieces about one inch long; cook, barely covered, either in water or chicken stock, lightly salted. Serve with melted butter and a grind of fresh black pepper. This is my favorite way to eat cooked cucumbers; but if you like, you can fancy them up a bit by further baking them in a béchamel or mornay sauce, thereby having cucumbers au gratin or cucumbers mornay.

EGGPLANT (Aubergines)

I do not know why, but the small, slender aubergines encountered in France and Italy are more delicate than the larger, fatter eggplant of the United States. However, both are good.

Here again, I think that in general, I like the most simply prepared eggplant best, although some of the elaborate preparations are very good indeed.

Peel the eggplant and cut in slices about one-quarter inch thick. Dip in a whole egg beaten with a little milk and shake in a paper bag with three tablespoons of flour seasoned with one teaspoon salt and a little freshly ground black pepper. Sauté in hot oil until the outsides are a nice, dark brown, drain on paper towels and serve immediately. Even a few moments delay results in softening of the crisp outer crust which lends so much attractiveness to the dish.

Eggplant may also be cut in pieces the size of a man's finger, dredged and deep fried like French fried potatoes.

Eggplant Parmigana

Slice the eggplant one-half inch thick, sprinkle with salt and stack up the slices. Put your cutting board or some other plank on the pile and place a weight of five pounds or so on it (an electric iron, etc.). Let stand for one-half hour.

Peel the tomatoes and put them, together with the finely chopped garlic and the parsley in a skillet with the heated olive oil. Let simmer for one-half hour.

Heat two tablespoons olive oil in another skillet, dry the slices of eggplant, dredge them with egg and either flour or bread crumbs, and fry until they are a nice brown on each side.

EGGPLANT (Aubergines)

	eggplant, sliced 1/4 inch thick
1	egg
	milk
3	tablesp. flour
1	teasp. salt
	freshly ground black pepper

EGGPLANT PARMIGANA

1	large eggplant
1 1/2	lbs. tomatoes
	olive oil
	salt
	pepper
1	tablesp. chopped parsley
1/2	cup freshly grated Parmesan cheese
1/2	lb. sliced Mozzarella cheese
2	cloves garlic

290

Arrange some of the slices in the bottom of a baking dish greased with olive oil, cover with a layer of the tomato sauce, sprinkle with Parmesan cheese and repeat until all the eggplant is used, finishing with a layer of sauce and cheese. Cover the top of the dish with thin slices of Mozzarella cheese. Bake in a 325 degree oven until the Mozzarella cheese is melted and the sauce bubbles.

ENDIVE

The Belgian endive which appears in our markets for only a brief period each year is a truly elegant vegetable. Here are three recipes which do justice to its elegance.

Endive Braised with Lemon

Wash two pounds of endive and dry them on paper towels. Arrange in a heavy skillet and pour over them 1/4 cup of good French dry vermouth (note: I have ruined several purchases of this somewhat expensive vegetable by attempting to use American "vermouth" as a substitute), the juice of two lemons and one-third of a stick of butter. Cover the pan except for a small crack at one edge and simmer slowly until all the liquid evaporates, or for about thirty minutes. Remove the endive and concentrate the sauce until it amounts to about one-half cup. Garnish with fresh parsley and pour the sauce over the endive.

ENDIVE BRAISED WITH LEMON

2	lbs. endive
1/4	cup good French dry vermouth
	juice of two lemons
1/3	stick butter

Endive Braised with Walnuts

Arrange the washed and drained endive in a skillet in the same manner as in the previous recipe. This time, use one cup of chicken stock (or condensed canned chicken broth) and one-half cup of butter as the braising liquid. The dish is also more attractive if you add 1/4 teaspoon of sweet basil or tarragon (or 1/8 teaspoon of each) to the braising liquid. After you have removed the endive from the skillet, brown two or three tablespoons of broken pieces of walnut in the remaining butter and pour all over the vegetable.

ENDIVE BRAISED WITH WALNUTS

2	lbs. endive
1	cup chicken stock or condensed canned chicken broth
1/2	cup butter
1/4	teasp. sweet basil or tarragon (or 1/8 teasp. each—optional)
2 - 3	tablesp. broken walnut pieces

ENDIVE BAKED WITH HAM

2   lbs. endive
     salt
     freshly ground white pepper
     good grating of nutmeg
1/4 cup French vermouth
     finely chopped parsley

Endive Baked with Ham

Braise two pounds of endive as in the first recipe. Before it is quite tender, remove and wrap each stalk in a thin slice of prosciutto; arrange in a shallow buttered dish. Sprinkle with salt, freshly ground white pepper and a good grating of nutmeg. Add one-quarter cup French vermouth and the contents of the skillet. Put in a 400 degree oven for ten or twelve minutes. Sprinkle with finely chopped parsley as you serve it.

LETTUCE

This ubiquitous salad plant, like the cucumber and the endive, is just as delicious cooked as it is in a salad. It provides the wise housewife looking for changes in the family menu with one more variety of greens and one which is available the year around. All varieties of lettuce may be cooked, but the green one with the firm head called iceberg lettuce is perhaps the type most often chosen.

Strip off the outer leaves of small heads of lettuce and reserve for salads. Drain after washing and slit the heart in two. Place cut heads, face down, in a heavy bottomed skillet. Pour over them enough chicken or beef stock to come one-third of the way up the sides of the cut heads together with one-third stick of butter. Either simmer gently on top of the stove or place in a 375 degree oven until the lettuce has absorbed most of the liquid. Baste frequently. Serve sprinkled with chopped dried chervil or fresh chopped parsley. The chervil flavor is a little more attractive.

ONIONS

Most of the time, we in our household, prefer to use onions as a flavoring—an herb, if you like—in cooking other foods. But here are two ways in which onions can, themselves, serve as an excellent vegetable.

Creamed Onions

Select the small white boiling onions for this purpose. Place in scalding hot water for a minute or two (this aids in their peeling and keeps the volatile elements which may make you cry at a minimum). A sufficient quantity for six persons is one and one-half pounds. Boil the peeled onions in a minimum amount of salted water until they are barely tender. Arrange in a buttered baking dish with just enough béchamel sauce to cover. Sprinkle with bread crumbs and cook in a 350 degree oven until the top begins to brown.

By using sauce mornay and sprinkling the top with grated Gruyère cheese, you will have onions mornay.

French Fried Onions

Choose either large sweet purple Bermuda onions or the somewhat hotter, brown-skinned Spanish onions for French frying. Peel under running water and cut into slices about one-fifth inch thick. Separate the rings, moisten in milk, shake in a paper bag with two or three tablespoons of flour and one teaspoon salt, and deep fry. Drain on paper towels and serve immediately.

GREEN PEAS (Petits Pois)

When a French cook or a Frenchman dining in a restaurant says little peas, he *means* it. Both cooks and consumers would be horrified at the hard, green nearly marble size peas that all too frequently pass as "green peas" in our country. My inability, a great part of the time, to find truly small green peas fresh is the reason for breaking my own personal rule which forbids resorting to the frozen food cabinet. The truly *petits* pois in at least two of the brands of frozen peas are, in my opinion, better than the only moderately fresh, large peas available most of the time in our supermarkets.

Green Peas, French Style

Put in a saucepan, two tablespoons of butter, three cups of tiny shelled peas, six small green onions, three or four lettuce leaves, shredded, and one-half cup chicken stock. Cook covered just until the peas are tender. At this point, there should be very little liquid left in the pan. We like to serve the peas, taken up in a slotted spoon and well drained, at this point. If you wish to adhere strictly to the

CREAMED ONIONS

1 1/2	lbs. onions
	béchamel sauce
	bread crumbs

FRENCH FRIED ONIONS

	Bermuda or Spanish onions sliced
	milk
2 - 3	tablesp. flour
1	teasp. salt

GREEN PEAS, FRENCH STYLE

2	tablesp. butter
3	cups tiny shelled peas
6	small green onions
3 - 4	shredded lettuce leaves
1/2	cup chicken stock
1	tablesp. butter (optional)
1	tablesp. flour (optional)

293

manière française, cream a tablespoon of butter with one tablespoon of flour and add bit by bit to the peas. Cook gently another five minutes.

Green Peas with Water Chestnuts

Slice a can of water chestnuts thinly and add to the peas, cooked as in the foregoing recipe, when the peas are nearly done. The idea is to have the water chestnuts hot but not to cook the dish long enough to impair the crispness of this vegetable.

Green Peas and Celery

For this preparation, I always use the frozen petits pois.

Melt the butter in a heavy skillet and gently sauté the onion. When the onion is soft, add the celery, selected from tender stalks and cut in one inch pieces. Cover and sauté gently for six to eight minutes. Add the thawed peas, the pimento and the salt. Cook, covered, until all the vegetables are just tender—four or five minutes.

GREEN PEAS AND CELERY

2	pkgs. frozen small green peas
1 1/2	cups celery
1/2	small onion
3/4	stick butter
2	tablesp. pimento strips
1	teasp. salt

SALSIFY (Oyster Plant)

There are two varieties, one white and scarcely distinguishable in appearance from a parsnip, the other almost black, very slender and extremely hairy. It is without doubt the most repulsive appearing root vegetable existing and, curiously, one of the best tasting. While the taste is indeed excellent, it requires a greater stretch of the imagination than I am capable of to note its alleged resemblance to any oyster.

Peel and cut into narrow strips and cook, barely covered, in lightly salted water to which a tablespoon of vinegar or lemon juice has been added until the strips are just tender—about fifteen to twenty minutes. Drain, saving the cooking liquid for soup; serve with melted butter, or butter and lemon, or hollandaise sauce.

There are various ways to elaborate on the cooking of this root, but to my mind, none is as good as the simplest.

RATATOUILLE NICOISE

This fine and savory mixture of vegetables from the Mediterranean coast of France deserves to be more widely known. There are, as with most mixtures of vegetables, especially from the highly individualistic—not to say near anarchistic—population of France, nearly as many versions as there are restauranteurs and housewives, but the recipe given here is good, as typical as any, and simpler than most.

Peel the eggplant and cut into slices or cubes. Cut the sweet peppers in quarters and remove seeds. Slice the zucchini without peeling. Peel and slice the onions. According to the usual fashion in Nice, cook all of these vegetables separately in the oil which has been "perfumed" with a crushed clove of garlic. Place the cooked vegetables in a casserole with the tomatoes, the herbs and two more cloves of garlic. Cook gently for one-half hour, the last few minutes without the casserole's cover so that the liquid is reduced. Manage the cooking so that all of the vegetables are soft but so that they are not reduced to a purée. The liquid should be quite thin. Adjust the seasoning with salt and black pepper. Ratatouille prepared in this fashion is an excellent accompaniment to any beef or lamb daube or meat cooked in any other provençale style when it is hot; cold, it is a fine hors d'oeuvre.

RATATOUILLE NICOISE

6	medium size tomatoes
1	medium size eggplant
6 - 8	small zucchini
2	medium or 3 small Spanish onions
3	green peppers
3 - 4	cloves garlic
1/2	cup olive oil
1/2	teasp. dried sweet basil
1/2	teasp. dried thyme

SPINACH

Wash thoroughly, discarding old or shriveled leaves, and place in a large kettle. Ordinarily, if one uses low heat and covers the kettle, spinach will cook in the amount of water adhering to the leaves after washing. If there is insufficient moisture to complete the cooking, add the minimum amount that will do so.

We like to chop the spinach and cook until it is just tender and mix with the same vinaigrette that we use for salad. It can also be eaten with melted butter with or without added lemon juice. One may also drain it carefully and then replace in the kettle with a tablespoon of fresh bacon drippings and reheat, mixing well with the drippings. A grind of black pepper is also good.

WILTED SPINACH

6	slices bacon
1/3	cup wine vinegar
	spinach
	black pepper

SPINACH SOUFFLÉ

3	cups puréed spinach
3	tablesp. butter
3	tablesp. flour
1	cup boiled milk
4	egg yolks
5	egg whites
3/4	cup grated Parmesan cheese
	grating of nutmeg
	salt
	pepper

Wilted Spinach

Fry six slices of bacon in a heavy skillet until it is crisp. Remove and drain on paper towels. Add one-third cup of wine vinegar to the skillet, and then some of the washed spinach. As it wilts, add more spinach. Stir and toss until all the spinach is wilted. Drain and serve with the bacon crumbled on top. The effect is half like a vegetable and half like a salad. The taste is improved by a grind of black pepper.

Spinach Soufflé

Make a concentrated béchamel by melting the butter in a saucepan, stirring in the flour and cooking for three minutes without allowing the *roux* to brown. Add the milk and beat until all is mixed and free of lumps. Add seasonings and cook until sauce is quite thick.

Separate the eggs. Having removed the sauce from the heat, drop the yolks, one at a time, into the sauce and beat enough to mix thoroughly before proceeding to the next one.

Whip the whites, including the extra one, until they peak but are not dry. At this point, add the puréed spinach, from which all the moisture has been pressed, to the sauce. Add one-quarter of the beaten egg whites and one-third of the cheese. Mix well but without strong beating. Now, fold in the rest of the egg white, but take care not to incorporate them too thoroughly. Peaks of white should stand out a little all over the top of the mixture.

Pour into a soufflé mold—or the nearest to a straight sided baking dish that you have—which has been buttered and then either had crumbs sprinkled on the surface, or alternatively, which has been sprinkled with grated Parmesan cheese. Sprinkle the rest of the cheese over the surface and put into a 400 degree oven for a few minutes. Then turn the heat down to 375 and bake twenty to twenty-five minutes without opening the oven door.

Other puréed vegetables may be made into soufflés using the same recipe. Some persons like corn soufflés.

SQUASH

Summer squash may be had in sizes ranging from tender, very young specimen smaller than half of an orange to quite large ones measuring six or eight inches in diameter. The small ones usually are not peeled. I much prefer the more developed taste of the mature squash. The latter must be peeled. In either case, cut them in pieces, boil gently in a minimum of water, or, preferably in chicken stock, until they are tender. Drain thoroughly and serve with melted butter and a grind of black pepper. You may, if you like, purée them and beat the butter into them.

Yellow crookneck squash is cooked in exactly the same way. The flavor is slightly different and the yellow vegetable contains carotin, a precursor of Vitamin D, if that is important to you. Personally, I do not think it should be. Physician though I am, I do not eat or refrain from eating foods because they might be "healthy" or "unhealthy," but only for the reason that they are palatable or unpalatable. The dining table is not place for medical treatment!

Hubbard, Butternut and Acorn squashes all have firm outside skins and yellow, rather mealy interiors, with more or less tendency to be sweet. They are all excellent cut in serving size pieces, seasoned with salt and dressed liberally with butter, then baked. A grind of fresh black pepper just before eating adds zest. As a child, I was served these vegetables cooked with sugar and cinnamon and never liked them, but with salt, butter and freshly ground black pepper, they are excellent.

STRING BEANS

Whether you buy the green kind or the yellow wax beans, accept only small beans, fresh enough that the ends snap off readily. Limp string beans are likely to be tough and stringy and, in any case, will have lost a good deal of freshness.

However you cook them, string the beans carefully and cut in the "french" style—that is, diagonally in not too long strips. Do not overcook; after cooking, the beans should still not be limp.

String Beans French Style

Make your *bouquet garni* by tying together a bay leaf, several sprigs of parsley and several sprigs of fresh

297

STRING BEANS FRENCH STYLE

1 1/2	lbs. string beans
1/2	cup green onions
1	cup beef stock
1	*bouquet garni*
2	tablesp. butter
2	teasp. finely chopped parsley
2	teasp. finely chopped chives

thyme. Or, failing the fresh thyme, use one teaspoon of dried thyme and tie the herbs in cheesecloth for easy removal after the cooking is done.

Simmer the beans in the beef stock with the *bouquet garni* until they are tender—about fifteen minutes. Drain thoroughly and place the beans in a hot serving dish. To a little of the broth in which they were cooked, add the butter creamed with the chopped parsley and chives. Stir well and serve.

String Beans with Mushrooms

Cook the beans in broth as in the foregoing recipe. About two or three minutes before they are done, add a cupful or more of mushrooms, sliced and sautéed in butter.

String Beans Amandine

Cook the beans in broth as above. Sauté a cup of slivered almonds in butter until they are brown and sprinkle over the beans just before serving.

String Beans with Water Chestnuts

Slice a can of water chestnuts thinly and add a few minutes before the beans have finished cooking, so that the water chestnuts will be heated through but will not have lost their crispness.

TOMATOES

The beautiful red "Love Apple" that our ancestors thought poisonous finds its chief uses as a salad vegetable and, cooked, in sauces for numerous dishes in the Italian or southern French style. One also sees them, rather dismayingly, on American tables as stewed tomatoes, sometimes with lumps of white bread afloat, watery and unseasoned except for salt and perhaps stale preground pepper—the sort of thing to discourage any rational child from liking vegetables.

But properly done, tomatoes are an interesting and worthwhile cooked vegetable.

Tomatoes, Provençale Style

Cut the tomatoes in half. Shake out most of the seeds and juice. Heat the olive oil in a heavy skillet and cook the tomatoes very gently, beginning with the cut side down and turning over as that side softens. Crush the garlic and add to the olive oil. The cooking should take three or four minutes on each side. Remove the tomatoes to a hot serving dish, turn the bread crumbs into the hot olive oil and cook for a minute or two until the crumbs are browned. Spoon over the tomato halves, then pour the remaining seasoned oil over them. This dish is an excellent accompaniment to any meat or fish dish cooked in a Provençale, Basque or Italian fashion.

TOMATOES, PROVENCALE STYLE

6	ripe tomatoes
1/2	cup chopped parsley
1/4	cup fine bread crumbs
1/2	cup olive oil
1 - 2	cloves garlic
	salt
	freshly ground pepper

Cocktail Tomatoes Sauté

Wash and remove the stems from enough small, round cherry tomatoes to allow four or five for each guest. Crush a clove of garlic in a heavy skillet and add two tablespoons of olive oil. Heat over a low flame. Add the tomatoes, shaking the pan about to turn the tomatoes over and get them coated with the oil. After cooking about two minutes, sprinkle with 1/2 teaspoon of dried sweet basil and continue the cooking and shaking until a few of the tomatoes split their skins. Serve promptly. Good with scrambled eggs, cheese dishes and omelets.

COCKTAIL TOMATOES SAUTÉ

4 - 5	cherry tomatoes (per person)
2	tablesp. olive oil
1	clove garlic
1/2	teasp. dried sweet basil

TURNIPS

Here again, this pungent root is more often seen as an item in a stew or ragoût than as a separate vegetable. However, they are not at all bad: their slightly bitter taste can be an appetizing contrast to other items in a course.

Two pounds will serve six. Peel the turnips and cut either in slices or chunks. Pour over them a quantity of boiling water and let stand for ten minutes. This takes away most of the too pungent taste.

Then boil the cut up turnips until they are barely tender in the minimum quantity of chicken stock to cover them. Drain and serve with melted butter and a grind of black pepper.

Another way is to purée the turnips and beat in a little of the chicken broth in which they cooked, together with a nut of sweet butter. Then season with salt and a grind of pepper.

ZUCCHINI

These delicate Italian squash may be cooked in a variety of ways. First, they are good sliced either peeled or unpeeled, cooked in a minimum quantity of salted water or, preferably, chicken stock, puréed and served with butter. I find them more delicate if they are peeled.

Zucchini au Gratin

ZUCCHINI AU GRATIN

2	lbs. fresh young zucchini
2	cups béchamel sauce
1	tablesp. butter
1/2	cup bread crumbs

Parboil the whole zucchini for about three minutes. Then arrange in a buttered baking dish and cover with béchamel sauce. Sprinkle with bread crumbs and, if you like, a little Cheddar or Parmesan cheese. Bake in a 400 degree oven until the top is brown. This will take five or six minutes.

Zucchini Mornay

Proceed exactly as in the foregoing recipe except use a mornay sauce and sprinkle the top with a mixture of bread crumbs and grated Gruyère cheese.

Zucchini, Italian Style

ZUCCHINI, ITALIAN STYLE

1 1/2	lbs. zucchini
1	lb. fresh tomatoes or 1 lb. can Italian tomatoes
1	large onion
2	cloves garlic
2	tablesp. olive oil
1/2	teasp. dried sweet basil
	salt
	pepper

Heat the olive oil in a heavy skillet with the crushed garlic and chopped onion and cook gently until the onion is soft and golden. Add the zucchini sliced, and the tomatoes cut into quarters and peeled. Cover and cook until the vegetables are tender. If the dish seems too soupy, cook a few moments with the lid off. Add basil and season with salt and freshly ground pepper.

POTATOES

Whatever the final mode of preparation, if preliminary treatment of potatoes involves boiling them, be sure to do so with their skins on. Besides saving a considerable amount of potato, you will conserve the salts and vitamins more effectively in this manner.

New Potatoes

Select small, young Red Rose potatoes, scrub them well and boil until barely tender to the tines of a fork. Let them cool sufficiently to handle, peel off the skin, dig out any eyes and small irregularities and reheat in a saucepan with lots of butter and finely chopped parsley. A favorite at our house with most roasts and some steaks.

Use Small Potatoes

If new potatoes are not available, select small older Red Rose potatoes, cook in the same manner and after peeling, cut into serving size pieces. Nearly as good as the young ones.

Potatoes Anna

Choose medium size Idaho or Maine white potatoes. Peel and cut in thin slices (the thickness of a fifty cent piece). Soak in ice water and dry well. Arrange the slices overlapping in circles on the bottom of as straight sided a baking dish as you have. Sprinkle with salt and dot generously with butter. Arrange another layer with the overlapping circles running in the opposite direction. Again season and butter. Continue until you have used all the potatoes. You should choose such a size dish that you have five or six layers. Cover and bake in a hot oven at 425 degrees for forty to fifty minutes until the potatoes are soft. Turn out on a plate so that the brown bottom and sides are undisturbed.

Baked Potatoes

Choose medium to medium-large regularly shaped white Idaho or Maine potatoes. Scrub them well and cook in a medium hot oven, 375 to 400 degrees, until they are done. At this range of temperature, the potatoes will take from fifty to seventy-five minutes to cook. They are done when they are soft to the tines of a fork. Cut a cross on top and, protecting the fingers with a clean napkin, push the potatoes open. Dress with butter—as much as you like—and if you like, chopped chives, and even crumbled

301

crisp bacon. Avoid the bad West Coast habit of serving them with sour cream. This thoroughly reprehensible custom was begun, I suspect, by restauranteurs anxious not to spend money for butter and has been accepted by gullible clients—the same people who gladly pay the packers of ham prices for injected water on the theory that the ham is being "tenderized."

Château Potatoes

Choose the Red Rose potatoes for this dish. Peel and cut the potatoes into pieces the size and shape of olives. Cook, covered, in clarified butter, and shake the pan to prevent sticking, until the potatoes are golden brown. Sprinkle with chopped parsley and serve.

Potatoes Duchess

Potatoes prepared this way do not taste very good. One encounters this preparation as a garnish for meat dishes in pretentious but not necessarily excellent restaurants. For housewives who may want to similarly garnish a meat dish to impress their husband's boss and his wife, here is how to do it.

For each two cups of riced (or otherwise mashed) potatoes, beat in two tablespoons of butter and three egg yolks. Form a decorative (if you think it *is* decorative) border around a roast with this mixture in a pastry bag or by arranging with a tablespoon on an ovenproof platter and brown lightly. Or, fancy individual servings may be worked —either by hand with a spoon, or more conveniently with a pastry bag—and browned under the broiler. In any shape, the preparation looks ornamental but is somewhat dry and flat to the taste.

Potatoes Franconia

Peel medium size potatoes, either Early Rose or white baking potatoes and boil in salted water for ten minutes. Drain and arrange around cooking roast beef or pork about one hour before the roast is to be done. Turn frequently and baste occasionally with pan drippings so that the potatoes will be evenly browned.

POTATOES DUCHESS

2	cups riced potatoes
2	tablesp. butter
3	egg yolks

French Fried Potatoes

Peel and cut medium size or small potatoes into square shapes about as long and as thick as a man's finger. Soak in ice water for one-half hour or more. Dry well and deep fry in a basket in good-quality fat at 370 degrees until light to golden brown. Drain on paper towels, salt lightly and serve immediately. French fried potatoes must not be covered or they will become soggy. The potatoes must be of good quality and the oil ought to be either good lard, Crisco, or a thoroughly fresh liquid cooking oil. French *pommes frites* are crisp on the outside, mealy inside, are never greasy, and have no odor of strong or inferior cooking oil, all faults much too common in American restaurants. By observing the precautions outlined, yours can be as good as the best French housewife's.

Becomes Soggy When Covered

Hash Brown Potatoes

Various recipes call for starting with boiled potatoes or raw ones. I much prefer the latter. Hash your potatoes with the coarsest side of your grater or chop them fairly finely with a knife. Salt lightly and pour into a heavy skillet with fresh bacon drippings by preference, although a neutral cooking oil will do. Lower the heat and let the potatoes brown. If you start with boiled potatoes, as soon as the bottom has browned well, fold over omelet fashion and let brown a little more. If you begin with raw potatoes, stir a little and cover. When bottom is well browned and the unbrowned potatoes in the center of the skillet are soft, fold over as before. Do not hesitate to add more fat; the potatoes will not absorb more than they need.

Gratin of Potatoes

If you like, you may also call this dish, scalloped potatoes.

Peel white potatoes and cut them in as thin slices as possible. Soak in ice water for one-half hour and dry. In a buttered baking dish, put a shallow layer of light cream, then a layer of the potato slices. Salt them and sprinkle with freshly grated Gruyère cheese. Repeat these layers, finishing with a layer of cream without cheese. Place the baking dish in a pan of hot water covering one-half of the

303

depth of the dish and put into a hot oven. After three-quarters of an hour, add fresh cream to replace that which has evaporated in the cooking. The cooking is finished when the potatoes are tender to a knife point. Before serving, sprinkle the top generously with Gruyère cheese and turn the heat up until the top browns.

This is the accompaniment of choice for a leg of lamb en croûte and is fine with any other leg of lamb or with lamb chops.

A completely differently tasting dish can be made by proceeding exactly as in this recipe but substituting a sharp Cheddar for the Gruyère cheese.

Another Gratin of Potatoes called **Savoyard**

This version uses butter and a good strong beef stock in place of cream.

Peel and slice as thinly as possible, two and one-half pounds of white potatoes and soak slices in cold water one-half hour or longer. Rub the inside of the baking dish generously with butter and, after drying the potato slices well, arrange a layer in the bottom of the dish, overlapping them and using one-half of the potatoes. Sprinkle over this layer 1/2 cup freshly grated Gruyère cheese and a tablespoon of chopped parsley and dot generously with butter. Add a second layer of potatoes, reversing the direction of overlapping. Now, add enough beef stock to come to the top of the potatoes. Garnish the top layer with equal amounts of chopped parsley, grated cheese and butter. Bake about one hour in an oven at 425 degrees. If your proportions are right, the potatoes will be tender and the broth will have been virtually all absorbed.

Still Another Gratin is **Dauphinoise Potatoes Gratin**

Prepare potatoes, slice and soak them in cold water as above. Before you butter your baking dish, rub it with a clove of crushed garlic. Dry the potato slices and put them in a mixing bowl with one and one-half pints of scalded milk, four ounces of grated Gruyère cheese, one well beaten egg and salt to taste. Mix the preparation thoroughly and turn into the garlic rubbed buttered baking dish, sprinkling with a little more cheese, and dot with butter. Bake in a 350 degree oven for about one hour and twenty minutes.

DAUPHINOISE POTATOES GRATIN

	potatoes
1 1/2	pints scalded milk
4	oz. grated Gruyére cheese
1	egg
	salt

Again, a nice variation can be achieved by using a good sharp Cheddar in place of the Gruyère.

Potatoes Lyonnaise

Cook With Spanish Onions

Boil medium size potatoes (I rather prefer the texture of Early Rose, although the variety is not really critical) until they are barely done. Peel and slice in rounds about one-eighth inch thick. For two pounds of potatoes, peel and thinly slice one-half pound of Spanish onions. In separate pans, sauté each of the two vegetables gently in bacon drippings or neutral fat. When the onions are soft and golden, combine them with the potatoes and continue cooking a few minutes in order to blend the flavors.

Mashed Potatoes
(Pommes de Terre Purées)

Cook medium to large white Idaho or Maine potatoes in salted water, and when they are cool enough to handle, peel, and take out the eyes.

Put through a ricer, or purée with a potato masher. Beat into the puréed potatoes a generous amount of sweet butter and enough cream to make the beaten potatoes light and fluffy. Season with salt and, if you like, a little freshly ground white pepper. If you cannot serve at once, keep hot in a double boiler.

Souffléed Potatoes

Choose medium size white potatoes and cut into a rectangular shape, save the trimmings for hash brown potatoes, mashed potatoes or stews. Cut the smooth rectangles into slices lengthwise about one-eighth inch thick and as regular as possible. Soak the slices about one-half hour or longer in ice water and, because they are going into hot fat, dry them very thoroughly. Heat the oil in a saucepan to 350 degrees with a thermometer. Cook the slices, a few at a time, until they begin rising to the surface and are lightly brown. Remove them to absorbent paper with a slotted spoon until all the slices are cooked. Now, increase the heat of your fat to 425 degrees. Plunge the partly-cooked slices into the hotter fat. You will observe that almost immediately they puff and rise to the top. Turn them over and move about in the fat for a moment or two and again drain. Salt and serve at once. At the second heating, you should try one or two slices only and if they do not immediately puff, heat the fat a little more. If the slices tend to burn, the fat is a little too hot.

RICE

Long-Grained Chinese Rice is Best

The best and most satisfactory rice is the long-grain variety. And the best of the long-grain varieties is, if you can find it, that imported from Asia, the so-called Chinese long-grained rice. It is available in Chinese stores everywhere along the Pacific Coast and in larger cities in the East and Midwest. We even prefer the long-grained rice for making Italian risotto and various Spanish rice dishes, although I recognize that the rice native to Italy is a short, fat grain.

There are two general methods for cooking rice satisfactorily; it can be boiled and then the floury coating rinsed off and the rice dried until it is fluffy in a steamer or in the oven. This is how it should be done if you wish to serve plain boiled, unbuttered or herbed rice. Or you may sauté rice with oil until the outer, floury coating is cooked, as evidenced by its turning white. Then water or other stock, depending on the dish you are making, is added to the rice and it is cooked until the liquid is absorbed. This is the way rice is cooked for a pilaf, for Italian risottos and for the innumerable versions of "Spanish rice" including paella and arroz con pollo.

Plain Boiled Rice

Pick over, but do not wash, 1 1/2 cups of good long-grained rice. Put three quarts of water, lightly salted, to boiling vigorously and sprinkle the rice in the boiling water. Reduce heat so that the water boils quietly until the grains are tender and have no hard, starchy center. Drain thoroughly in a strainer and wash in hot water—the hot water tap is fine—until you are sure there is no loose, floury material adhering to the grains. Cover the colander with a cloth and set over a pan of hot water or in a pan in a moderate oven until it is dry. Or put it in a covered casserole and let it rest in a moderate oven until it is dry. It will take ten to twelve minutes to cook your rice and another ten minutes or so to dry it.

It is this rice that we serve with many fish and practically all shellfish dishes, garnished with chopped parsley and buttered at the table and seasoned with fresh pepper at the taste of the diner. This is also the indispensable accompaniment for all curries.

Rice prepared in this fashion may be mixed with sautéed mushrooms, onions and shallots, and is the form for making rice puddings (if you like rice pudding).

Pilaf (Pilau)

Sauté a medium size onion, sliced, in butter until it is soft and golden. Add 1 1/2 cups unwashed rice and sauté until the grains turn milky and opaque but not until they are brown, stirring constantly with a wooden spoon. Pour in three cups of whatever liquid your ultimate dish calls for—for a plain pilaf, chicken or beef stock will be fine. Season, cover and reduce heat so that the liquid boils very gently. Cook until the liquid absorbs and the rice is tender. At this point, the grains should be soft but not mushy and the grains should be separate and fluffy with little or no liquid in the bottom of the dish.

The plain pilaf is excellent with shish kebabs or lamb chops or a leg of lamb.

Here are some further interesting ways to prepare rice, using the preliminary sautéeing with a fat.

Milanese Risotto

In three-quarters of the butter, heat the onion, finely chopped, until it is tender and golden. Add the unwashed rice; here you might like to use the short, fat Italian rice if you can find it. Stir with wooden spoon until the grains are milky and beginning to become golden. Add the stock which you have heated to boiling and in which the saffron has been dissolved. Warning: it is easy to get too much saffron, with a resulting unpleasant, medicinal taste. Reduce heat, stir once or twice and cover. Let simmer about thirty minutes or until the liquid is just absorbed. Add a little more if necessary or turn the heat up a little at the end to dry the dish out a little. Just before taking off the fire, stir in the remaining butter and the cheese. A more characteristically Italian flavor will be

MILANESE RISOTTO

1	stick butter
1 1/2	cups long-grain or Italian short-grain rice
3	cups chicken or beef stock
1	medium onion
1/8	teasp. imported saffron
1/2	cup freshly grated Parmesan cheese
	salt
	freshly ground pepper

307

attained if you use olive oil instead of butter. It is also permissible to put a little crushed dried sweet basil in the stock, if you wish.

Rice Basque Style

Sauté the rice with two tablespoons of the butter until the grains are opaque and golden, stirring it with a wooden spoon. Then gradually add the hot chicken stock, a cup at a time, simmering, covered and without stirring until the liquid is nearly absorbed before the next addition. When the rice is nearly done, sauté the sliced onion and the seeded, sliced peppers until they are soft and golden in the remainder of the butter. Mix the vegetables with the rice and adjust the seasoning with salt and freshly ground pepper.

Spanish Rice

Spanish rice is a style of cooking, not a specific recipe. Here is a legitimate version; there are dozens of others.

Most of the alleged Spanish rices we eat in America are Mexican versions; these usually contain chili. Chili has no part in the cooking of Spain. So consult your own taste and that of your family.

Sauté the sliced onion and the chopped peppers in the fat until they are soft and golden. Add the rice and stir with a wooden spoon until the grains are coated, opaque and yellow. Add the stock and the tomatoes and whatever seasoning you wish. Simmer thirty to forty minutes until the rice is tender. Do not stir. Add a little more stock if needed.

Pilaf with Herbs

Cook onions in butter or drippings until opaque and beginning to yellow. Add two cups of stock together with salt and dill weed; add rice, cover, and let simmer. Watch the pan and as the liquid becomes absorbed, add gradually the third cup of stock. When the rice is soft and the liquid all but absorbed, season with a little freshly ground black pepper.

Note: This same pilaf is excellent with tarragon, and with a mixture of tarragon and thyme, is especially good with roasted meats. For lamb, make it with marjoram.

RICE BASQUE STYLE

1 1/2 cups raw rice
3 1/2 cups hot chicken stock
5 tablesp. butter
3 onions
2 sweet green peppers
1 sweet red pepper
  salt
  freshly ground pepper

SPANISH RICE

1 1/2 cups raw rice
3 cups beef or chicken stock
2 medium onions
3 tablesp. olive oil or
  bacon drippings
3/4 lb. tomatoes
2 green peppers
  salt
  pepper
  chili powder (optional)

PILAF WITH HERBS

1 1/2 cups raw rice
1/2 cup chopped onion
3 tablesp. butter or
  bacon drippings
3 cups chicken or beef broth
1 teasp. dill weed
  salt
  freshly ground pepper

DESSERTS

Dessert is, for many people, the most popular course of any meal. There is a legion of good desserts and some very bad ones. My family likes fruits, melons and various prepared desserts. We rarely have cake and never make it. Therefore, I have concentrated on recipes, classic or unusual, with which we most often terminate our meals and have omitted recipes for cakes and cookies.

Because they are refreshing and to keep our calories at a sensible level, we end many of our dinners with a fruit basket containing two or three kinds of fruit, perfectly ripe and free of blemishes. We finish other dinners with a peeled and sliced fruit or berries, usually not further sweetened, but sometimes with cream. Chilled melons bring other dinners to a satisfactory conclusion. During the winter months, we frequently have thinly sliced oranges sprinkled with a little sugar and sometimes a spoonful of Grand Marnier or curaçoa; fresh pineapple either plain or with kirsch; fresh bananas plain or sliced with sugar and cream. Still other meals terminate with dried raisins, figs and dates together with walnuts. A glass of ruby port with dried fruits and nuts adds a festive touch and recalls a romantic era of life in England.

But on the occasions when, for family or for friends, you wish a sweeter, or more elaborate dessert, here are some favorites.

Ambrosia

While I think this old Southern recipe is somewhat overnamed, it is attractive and festive, light enough to follow a heavy dinner.

Select a ripe coconut, break it and grate the meat with a relatively coarse grater.

Select four ripe oranges and peel them, being careful to remove all of the white membrane on the surface and at the center together with the seeds. Slice crosswise in slices one-quarter inch thick, discarding all of the segment membranes.

309

Slice six ripe bananas, depending on their size, one-quarter inch thick. There should be somewhat more banana than orange. Mix these fruits well in a glass bowl with the grated fresh coconut and finely granulated sugar to taste. Let marinate in the refrigerator for several hours before serving.

An ounce or two of Cointreau or curaçoa does this otherwise somewhat innocent preparation no harm.

Apples Baked in Red Wine

APPLES BAKED IN RED WINE

6	tart apples
	butter
1	cup red wine
1 1/2	cups brown sugar
	cinnamon bark
	lemon rind
	nutmeg

Peel and core six firm, tart apples and cut off their tops and bottoms. Slice the rest of the apples in pieces about one-half inch thick, cutting each ring in two. Sauté gently in butter for five minutes. Then arrange the partly cooked slices neatly in a baking dish and pour one cup of a good red Bordeaux or California Cabernet Sauvignon over them. (We usually have this dessert when there is some excellent red wine left from the previous evening's dinner.) Sprinkle with 1 1/2 cups of brown sugar and put a piece of cinnamon bark in the wine. Grate lemon rind and nutmeg directly over the apples and bake at 325 degrees until the apples are soft. Serve hot.

Apple Fritters

Make a fritter batter. Core and peel firm tart apples (green Pippins are best for this purpose). Cut of stem and blossom ends; slice into neat rounds one-quarter inch thick. Sprinkle the slices with brown sugar and pour a little dark Jamaica rum over the sugar slices. Let stand for two hours or longer, turning so that all surfaces of the slices are exposed to the rum and sugar mixture.

Dip the slices in the fritter batter and drop into deep fat heated to 360 degrees by the thermometer, or hot enough to brown a one inch cube of bread in a few seconds. Turn and brown on both sides. Drain on paper towels, sprinkle with confectioner's sugar and serve at once.

Apple Sauce

A good tart apple sauce, either made at home from Pippin apples, or a good canned variety, slightly chilled and garnished with a generous dusting of freshly grated nutmeg is a fine winter dessert, especially when the main course has been heavy.

Apricots Chantilly

Make a purée by stewing fresh ripe apricots, or by further cooking canned ones, or cook dried apricots very throughly and put through a sieve with enough sugar to sweeten them to your taste. Chill and fold the purée into an equal amount of whipped cream. Dress individual servings of the chilled mixture with slivered blanched almonds or finely crushed peanut brittle.

Bananas Flambés au Rhum

Select firm bananas only slightly, if at all, flecked with brown. Peel, cut in half lengthwise, and sauté in butter either in a chafing dish at the table or in a skillet. While the bananas are cooking, sprinkle them with brown sugar. When they are soft—in four or five minutes—add a tablespoon of your favorite rum to the chafing dish or skillet. Then pour warm rum (one ounce or more) over the bananas. Ignite and baste the fruit with the blazing liquor. Serve as soon as the flames extinguish themselves. We find a dark rum of the Jamaica type gives the best flavor with this dish.

Bananas Flambés au Cognac

A different dessert entirely, not better, but fully as good, can be obtained by substituting confectioner's sugar for the brown sugar and a good grade of cognac for the rum in the preceding recipe.

Bananas with Whipped Cream and Sherry

To serve six persons, whip one pint of heavy cream. When the cream is nearly stiff, add one-half cup of sifted (it must be free of lumps) brown sugar and two ounces of a good sherry, preferably a sweet variety. Slice one ripe banana for each person and chill the fruit, mixed with the sweetened and sherried whipped cream for two hours before serving.

BANANAS WITH WHIPPED CREAM AND SHERRY

1	pt. heavy cream
1/2	cup sifted brown sugar
2	oz. sherry (preferably sweet)
1	banana (per person)

311

Banana Orange Gelatin

BANANA ORANGE GELATIN

2	bananas, not too ripe
1	env. unflavored gelatin
1/4	cup cold water
1	cup boiling water
1/2	cup orange juice
1/4	cup sugar
1	tablesp. lemon juice
1/8	teasp. salt

Sprinkle the gelatin on the cold water. When it softens, pour on the boiling water and stir until the gelatin dissolves. Add the citrus juices and salt. Pour into a chilled mold, or into chilled individual molds, enough of the mixture to form a layer one-half inch deep and refrigerate. When the gelatin becomes firm enough to support them, arrange a layer of banana slices and pour on another layer of gelatin. Refrigerate a little each time. Finish with a layer of gelatin.

You will find this an especially refreshing dessert after a main course containing a good deal of fat.

Cherry Clafouti

CHERRY CLAFOUTI

1	can pitted Bing cherries
1	pt. milk
6	eggs
1/3	cup flour
6	tablesp. sugar
4	tablesp. kirsch
1/4	teasp. salt

Place milk, sugar, eggs, kirsch and salt in the blender. Blend for thirty seconds at top speed and add the flour. If you do not have a blender, sift the flour, salt and sugar into a bowl, beat in the six eggs and, little by little, the milk and kirsch. When you are finished by either method, you should have a batter the consistency of a crêpe or thin pancake batter.

Drain the cherries, mix them into the batter and put in a baking dish; place the dish into a 375 degree oven until the surface is browned and puffed. Test the doneness by inserting a straw which should come out clean. Dust the clafouti with finely granulated sugar as you take it out of the oven.

Cherries Jubilee

CHERRIES JUBILEE

1	can pitted, dark, sweet cherries
	sugar
	cornstarch
	vanilla ice cream
3	tablesp. kirsch

Most of the French recipes call for starting with "fine ripe cherries." The practical way for Americans to start is with a can of pitted, dark, sweet cherries.

Drain and reserve the juice. Sweeten the cherries to taste with a tablespoon or so of sugar. Add a tablespoon of cornstarch to one cup of the reserved juice, and if you wish, some sugar. Cook the juice until it is thickened and concentrated a little. Prepare six servings of vanilla ice cream.

To a chafing dish at the dining table, add the cherries to the thickend juice and heat. When the cherries and sauce are heated, warm three tablespoons of kirsch, ignite and pour, flaming, over the cherries. The flaming cherries are then ladled over the individual servings of ice cream.

Incidentally, the cherries and their juice, with the flaming kirsch added, makes a fine dessert for two or three persons without the ice cream.

Cherries with Sour Cream à la Gertrude

Drain the juice from a can of dark sweet cherries the day before you plan to serve the dessert. Reserve the cherries. Add a tablespoon of cornstarch to the juice and cook until it thickens and does not taste of raw starch. Add one cup of good brandy, preferably cognac. Pour the brandy-juice mixture over the cherries and marinate in the refrigerator overnight.

Next afternoon, beat together one eight-ounce package of cream cheese, one carton of sour cream plus a teaspoon of vanilla extract, finely granulated sugar to taste, and a tablespoon of cognac. Pile into serving dishes and chill in the refrigerator for one or two hours. Just before serving, spoon the cherries and their sauce over the mixture. Sometimes, we further dress the serving with a few slivered almonds. It is good both ways.

Fruit Compote

Here is another dessert especially useful for the winter months when fresh fruits are not too abundant.

Stew the dried apricots with the brown sugar for at least two hours. Rub them through a fine colander or purée in a blender. Put in a buttered baking dish with one can of Bing cherries and their juice; one can of peaches, drained; slice into the dish one lemon and one orange. Add the juice of an additional lemon and orange and grate a generous amount of both peels over the top of the fruits. Bake in a 350 degree oven until the fruits begin to lose their form and the top is becoming caramelized. The compote may be served either warm or cold. I prefer it cold, garnished with sour cream into which a tablespoon or two of kirsch or Grand Marnier has been beaten.

Oranges au Grand Marnier

Select good, full ripened fruit and peel it carefully so as to remove all of the white layer under the rind. Save

CHERRIES WITH SOUR CREAM À LA GERTRUDE

1	can dark sweet cherries
1	tablesp. cornstarch
1	cup good brandy
1	8-oz. pkg. cream cheese
1	carton sour cream
1	teasp. vanilla extract
	sugar
1	tablesp. cognac
	slivered almonds (optional)

FRUIT COMPOTE

1/2	lb. dried apricots
1	cup brown sugar
1	can Bing cherries
1	can peaches
1	lemon
1	orange
	juice of one lemon
	juice of one orange
	lemon peel from both fruits
	sour cream with 1-2 tablesp. kirsch or Grand Marnier (optional)

the juice which escapes. Slice the oranges thinly and arrange in a bowl with granulated sugar between layers of oranges. Add the juice which escaped from the fruit during the slicing and peeling together with one tablespoon of Grand Marnier for each two oranges. Chill one hour or more before serving.

Baked Pears

You may use fresh pears to make this dessert, but I do not think you gain anything by doing so. The winter pears, Comice and Anjou, are better eaten fresh. We reserve this dish for seasons when no fresh pears are available and use the canned Bartlett pears for the purpose. It makes a reasonably attractive dessert out of this quite uninspiring fruit.

Drain the liquid from the canned pears and place the fruit, cut side up, in a buttered baking dish. Cover with dark Karo syrup, stick two cloves in each pear half and put a piece of cinnamon bark in the hollow of each half. Add two or three thin slices of lemon, peel and all, to the dish and dust the top with a generous coating of freshly grated nutmeg. Bake in the oven at 325 to 350 degrees, basting occasionally with the syrup. Chill before serving.

Pineapple

French cookbooks are loaded with recipes for fancy ways to serve pineapple, many of which call for digging out the contents of the pineapple and replacing at least part of it with other fruits. Such activities have always seemed to me redundant; if you want a fruit salad and wish it to contain pineapple, make your salad. If it amuses you to stuff the fruit salad back into a hollowed out pineapple, by all means do so. But, to me, a pineapple has such an individual flavor that I dislike diluting it with the flavor of other fruits. Thus, we peel and core our pineapple, dice the ripe fruit, sweeten it, if need be, with a little sugar and serve it plain or with a tablespoon of kirsch added to each serving.

Marinated Prunes

Another somewhat simple minded but good dessert for everyday meals during the seasons when fresh fruit is scarce.

BAKED PEARS

canned pears
Karo syrup
cloves
cinnamon bark
2 - 3   lemon slices
freshly grated nutmeg

314

Place one pound of large, moist "dried" prunes in a quart jar. Add a few slices of lemon, including the rind. Fill the jar with a boiling liquid. The liquid may be orange juice, an inexpensive sweet California "sauterne" or a modestly priced port or sherry. You may also use a dry red wine, sweetening it with two or three tablespoons of sugar. If you do this, add two tablespoons of brandy or rum after the liquid has cooled. Now close the lid of the jar and let stand in the refrigerator at least three days—longer will be better.

Sooner or later, for festive occasions, you will want more glamorous desserts. Here are four classical ways to serve strawberries.

Strawberries Brillat-Savarin

Prepare a sauce by boiling the granulated sugar with water and the peel of a small orange carefully cut into thin strips so that none but the orange part is used. Cook until the orange peel is transparent. Add as many crushed fresh mint leaves as will flavor the syrup to your taste and let it cool.

Wash and stem the strawberries, slicing any larger ones in half. Just before serving, squeeze two cups of orange juice and mix with the syrup. Strain out the crushed mint leaves and orange peel and pour over the berries. Decorate the bowl with fresh mint leaves. Substituting one-half cup of Grand Marnier for an equal amount of orange juice will give the dish more dash.

STRAWBERRIES BRILLAT-SAVARIN

1	cup granulated sugar
1	cup water
	peel of a small orange
	fresh mint leaves
2	boxes strawberries
2	cups orange juice
1/2	cup Grand Marnier (optional)

Strawberries Cardinal

Wash and hull the berries as usual. Make a sauce by puréeing the frozen raspberries and straining out the seeds. Add the sugar, strained fresh lemon juice, and Grand Marnier, curaçao, or kirsch. Just before serving, pour the sauce over the berries in a chilled bowl. As an added flourish, you may sprinkle each serving with a few slivered blanched almonds.

STRAWBERRIES CARDINAL

2	boxes strawberries
1	pkg. frozen raspberries
2	tablesp. sugar
2	teasp. fresh lemon juice
2	tablesp. Grand Marnier, curaçao, or kirsch
	slivered almonds (optional)

Strawberries Romanoff

Wash and hull the strawberries. Mix the berries with the orange juice and curaçoa.

STRAWBERRIES ROMANOFF

- 3 boxes strawberries
- 1/2 cup orange juice
- 1/2 cup curaçoa
- 1/2 pt. heavy cream
- 1 pt. vanilla ice cream

STRAWBERRIES WITH SHERRY AND CREAM

- 3 boxes strawberries
- 4 egg yolks
- 1 cup finely granulated sugar
- 4 oz. good cream sherry
- 1/2 pt. heavy cream

VANILLA CUSTARD

- 3 eggs
- 3 cups scalded milk
- 1/2 cup sugar
- 1 inch vanilla bean
- 1/4 teasp. salt

Soften one pint of good caterer's vanilla ice cream. Whip the heavy cream and fold into the softened ice cream, beating to make the mixture as fluffy as possible. Fold in the strawberries and serve immediately.

Strawberries with Sherry and Cream

Wash and hull the strawberries. Heat in the upper part of a double boiler without allowing the mixture to boil, the egg yolks, granulated sugar and good cream sherry. Beat constantly until the mixture is thick enough to coat a spoon. Cool somewhat.

Beat the heavy cream, and shortly before serving time, fold into the custard-sherry mixture. Finally, add the berry-sherry mixture and serve at once.

Vanilla Custard

Place the section of vanilla bean in the milk and scald in a saucepan. (Milk is scalded when the first bubbles appear about the edges of the pan.)

Beat the eggs well and beat in the sugar and salt. Let the milk cool and add it slowly to the egg-sugar mixture, beating it gently. Strain through a fine strainer or through several layers of cheesecloth. Divide among six individual custard cups.

Set the custard cups in a shallow pan and fill the pan one-half way up the sides of the custard cups with hot water. Bake, starting the oven at 325 degrees. Watch carefully to prevent the water in your *bain marie* from boiling. The custard is supposed to *poach,* and if the water in the pan is allowed to boil, the milk mixture will begin to do so. This will result in bubbles in your custards, a separation of liquid after the custards are cold, and a hard texture. If the water starts to simmer, lower heat immediately.

It usually requires forty-five minutes for the custards to cook properly. They will be done when a pointed knife inserted into the edge comes away clean. When this occurs, remove the custard cups from the hot water as rapidly as possible so that the cooking will stop.

Caramel Custard

All over France, one encounters *Crème Caramel Renversée,* which turns out to be a plain vanilla custard cooked in a custard cup that has been coated with caramelized sugar. During the cooking the caramel becomes liquid. When it is served, the créme is turned out on a plate (reversed) and the caramel sauce serves as its dressing.

At our house, we like a better modification in which the custard itself is made with caramelized sugar and which is served without a sauce.

Scald the milk. Caramelize the sugar by heating it in a thick bottomed pan over gentle heat until it turns a little darker than golden brown. If you get the sugar too brown, it will be bitter. Pour the caramelized sugar into the hot milk and stir until most or all of it has dissolved.

Beat the three whole eggs and gradually pour into them the milk and sugar mixture. Strain through two layers of cheesecloth or through a fine wire strainer and add the salt and mapleine flavoring extract. Divide between six custard cups and bake as in the previous recipe. I cannot emphasize too much, the importance of not allowing the water in the water bath to boil.

Coconut Custard

Use the recipe for vanilla custard and add to it before distributing among the individual cups one-half cup of grated fresh coconut. Note: Coconut custards are not worth making unless you have fresh coconut. The dried shredded products simply are not good enough.

Pots de Crème Vanille

Separate the yolks of six eggs, reserving the whites for another use. Beat the egg yolks until they are thick and lemon colored and then beat in the sugar. Add vanilla extract and salt. Scald (heat until bubbles form at the edge of the pan) two cups (one pint) of heavy cream. Let it cool somewhat, then beat, little by little, into the egg-sugar mixture. Strain through a fine strainer or through cheesecloth into six little pot-de-crème pots. Place the covers on the pots, put them in a shallow pan and add hot water to within one inch of the tops of the pots. Bake in a 325 degree oven for twenty-five to thirty minutes, or until the mixture just begins to set around the edges, using the same precautions as in other custard recipes to see that the water never boils. Remove immediately and place on a wire rack

CARAMEL CUSTARD

1 1/2	cups sugar
2	cups milk
1	cup light cream
3	eggs
1/2	teasp. mapleine flavoring
1/4	teasp. salt

POTS DE CRÈME VANILLE

6	egg yolks
1/2	cups finely granulated sugar
1	pt. whipping cream
1 1/2	teasp. vanilla extract
1	pinch salt

317

to cool for one-half hour and then chill in the refrigerator at least four hours.

Pots de Crème de Chocolat

Melt two ounces of semisweet chocolate in the top of a double boiler and beat into the crème mixture after it has cooled somewhat. Reduce vanilla extract to one-half teaspoon. Cook in the same manner as above.

Crème Brulée

This delicate and light custard may be prepared in either of two ways. The way which gives the more delicate crème, when it is successful, is to cook the crème in the top of a double boiler over hot, but not boiling water. However, the slightest miscalculation will result in an unappetizing mess of sweetened scrambled eggs rather than a delicate dessert; therefore, the less adventurous may want to cook the crème like any other, by baking in a *bain marie* in the oven. However, there is nothing really difficult about the preferred method; it merely requires care. No housewife aspiring to this dish should be willing to give it less.

Heat cream in a saucepan, stopping as soon as the first bubbles form at the edge of the pan. It is important to watch this and remove from the heat before the cream is really scalded.

In the top of a double boiler over hot, but not boiling, water, beat the egg yolks until they are lemon colored. Then, beat in the sugar. Use an electric or hand beater. Cool the cream somewhat, and add it to the egg-sugar mixture, stirring constantly, little by little. Continue beating over the hot water until the crème is thick enough to coat a metal spoon. If you have the water temperature right, this will require about fifteen minutes. Add the vanilla while continuing to beat. Remove from over the hot water and strain into a shallow baking dish or into six ovenproof crème cups. Refrigerate overnight.

Next day, sift light brown—not the sticky dark brown—sugar over the top of the dish, or the tops of the cups thickly enough to cover the custard. If the sugar is damp, dry it in the oven before using it. Turn on broiler and pack the dish or dishes containing the crème in a pan

CRÈME BRULÉE

1 1/2 pts. (3 cups) heavy cream
6 tablesp. finely granulated sugar
6 egg yolks
2 teasp. vanilla extract
1/2 cups sifted light brown sugar

surrounded by cracked ice. Set under the broiler as close to the heat as is possible. Watch carefully, turning the cups or the dish as needed to get an even melting of the sugar. As soon as the sugar melts and browns slightly, remove and chill the crème at least three hours or longer.

You may want to tap the sugar glaze so that it cracks before serving and add Grand Marnier. However, the dish is excellent without this addition.

Bavarian Cream

Whip the cream so that it peaks firmly. Soften the gelatin in the cold water.

Beat the egg yolks with the sugar and salt until they are thick and lemony in color in the top of a double boiler. Add the gelatin and stir until it is dissolved. Scald the milk and let it cool a little. Gradually, add the milk to the egg-sugar mixture, beating in the double boiler, until the mixture is of the consistency of a soft custard. At this stage, remove from the heat, cool and fold in the whipped cream and the vanilla extract. Turn into a single mold or into custard cups that have been rinsed in water and chilled. Let chill in the refrigerator for several hours. Serve either in the custard cups or unmold, as you please.

BAVARIAN CREAM

1	cup milk
2	egg yolks
1/2	cup sugar
1/4	cup cold water
1/2	env. unsweetened gelatin
1/2	teasp. vanilla extract
1/4	teasp. salt
1	cup heavy cream

Butterscotch Bavarian Cream

Make custard in the same manner as in the preceding recipe but omit the white sugar. Instead, melt two tablespoons of butter in a skillet and add 3/4 cup of brown sugar. Cook until the butter and sugar are melted together and browned a little. Beat this mixture into the custard and begin the beating as in the previous recipe. Add 1/4 cup of broken pecan meats to the whipped cream before folding it into the custard. After turning the completed mixture into the desired mold or molds, decorate the tops with half pecans and chill as before.

Chocolate Mousse

In the top of a double boiler, break up the chocolate in three tablespoons of water. When the chocolate is melted, add sugar and stir until it is completely dissolved. Add butter and beat into the sweetened chocolate. Remove

CHOCOLATE MOUSSE

6	sq. semisweet chocolate
6	tablesp. finely granulated sugar
3	whole eggs, plus one extra egg white
1	tablesp. heavy cream
1/3	stick butter
1	tablesp. water

MOCHA-CHOCOLATE MOUSSE

1 1/2	cups extra strong coffee
7	sq. semisweet chocolate
2	cups sugar
10	eggs
6	tablesp. cognac
1/2	env. unsweetened gelatin pinch of salt

from the heat and add the cream, beating it well into the mixture.

Break the eggs, one at a time, put the whites together with one extra white. Add the yolks, one at a time, to the mixture beating each in well before adding the next. Continue beating with a wooden spoon or wire whisk until the mixture is as light as possible. Do not put over the heat again.

Add a pinch of salt to the egg whites and beat them until they peak well without becoming dry. Pour the chocolate mix into the beaten egg whites and fold the two together thoroughly. Chill in the refrigerator at least one day before serving.

Mocha-Chocolate Mousse

Separate the eggs. To make the coffee, brew 1 1/2 cups of coffee twice as strong as you usually make it and use the coffee thus obtained to drip through your Chemex or other coffee maker through another batch of ground coffee. By running the water through two changes of ground coffee, one gets very strong coffee at the same time avoiding the bitterness and tannin that would result from making the coffee with a double measure of ground coffee. A dark French roast is preferable for this entremet. (We use the same coffee that we use for our Sunday morning *café au lait,* which is French Market brand.)

Soften the gelatin in one-half cup of this coffee essence. Put the other cup in the top of a double boiler with the chocolate and melt over hot water. When the chocolate is melted, stir in the sugar and keep stirring until the sugar is completely dissolved. Remove from the heat, add the cognac and beat into the mixture the egg yolks, one at a time. At this time, add the coffee in which the gelatin has been dissolved.

Beat the egg whites stiff with a pinch of salt. Fold the cooled chocolate-gelatin mixture into the beaten eggs thoroughly. Let sit in the refrigerator overnight before serving.

Sabayon or Zabaglione

The first is the French; the second, the Italian, name of this delicious crème traditionally made with egg yolks, sugar and Marsala wine. Here is a variation with a hint of rum flavor to add to the charms of the dish.

Beat the sugar into the egg yolks. Place in the top of a double boiler over hot—not boiling—water and continue beating vigorously as you add the Marsala and then the rum, little by little. The mixture will become thick and fluffy. Remove from the heat and continue beating, as the yolks will keep on cooking.

The crème may be served hot, freshly made, or may be chilled. In general, we like it better hot. You may, if you think it adds a touch of elegance, top the crème, which should be served in a glass or silver stemmed cup, with a dab of whipped cream.

Sabayon au Champagne

Make exactly as in the classic recipe but substitute a five or six ounce cup of champagne for the other liquor. The flavor is quite different and if you make and serve it quickly, the crème will still be a little foamy and bubbly from the champagne.

Dessert Soufflés

In the minds of many, an excellent soufflé Grand Marnier or chocolate soufflé is the ultimate in elegant finishes for a good meal. In fact, at our house, we plan such a dessert only with meals worthy of our best wines and where there is a reasonable prospect the food, wine and guests will all come together for one of the memorable occasions which a successful dinner party can be. However, once you learn how to make a good soufflé, they are little enough trouble to be worth doing for a family meal also; again, providing the preceding courses and the wine are worthy of such a termination.

Dessert soufflés can be—and most frequently are—made with the same béchamel sauce base as entrée soufflés. However, here is a slight modification in making the basic sauce, taught us by our Bretonne housekeeper, which increases their delicacy without increasing the likelihood of the soufflé falling.

SABAYON or ZABAGLIONE

12	egg yolks
3/4	cup finely granulated sugar
3	tablesp. Jamaica rum
2 1/2	oz. dry Marsala wine

321

Soufflé au Grand Marnier

Grate about one tablespoon of the yellow part only of a fragrant ripe orange peel. Sliver off several more small pieces of the peel and grind into the sugar with a pestle or old fashion cocktail muddler. After grinding as much of the oil as possible into the sugar, discard the pieces of peel.

Make a smooth paste with the flour and a little of the milk. Gradually add the rest of the milk, beating vigorously all the while. Cook over brisk heat, with constant stirring, until the mixture has boiled for thirty seconds. Remove from heat and cool for a few minutes, beating occasionally.

Break the eggs, letting the whites fall into a bowl suitable for beating. Let the yolks drop into the milk-flour mixture one by one, beating each yolk into the mixture thoroughly before proceeding to the next one. Now, beat in the softened butter.

Beat the egg whites (do not forget the two additional whites) until they begin to peak. Now sprinkle into the whites the orange flavored sugar and continue beating until the eggs peak stiffly but are not dry.

At this point, add the grated orange rind, the Grand Marnier, and the vanilla extract to the milk-egg-flour mixture and then fold in the beaten whites, taking care that the whites are thoroughly distributed but not completely incorporated into the mass of batter. There should be small free floating peaks of beaten whites.

Turn into a two quart soufflé mold or baking dish which you have prepared by buttering generously and then dusting the inside with granulated sugar.

Put the soufflé dish in a pan of boiling water and immediately into the oven preheated to 400 degrees. Turn the heat down to 375 at once. Do not open oven door for thirty minutes. At that time, insert a needle or a thin bladed knife into the side of the soufflé. It is done if the blade or needle comes out clean. At this stage, shake either powdered or very finely granulated sugar on the top of the soufflé and let remain in the oven a minute or two.

You should plan your meal so that the last course before dessert is completed and the table entirely cleared. The safest way to achieve this is to make your guests wait a few minutes. If the guests are worthy, they will be happy to do so because they will know that a good soufflé is a short lived thing and that its moment of perfection is brief.

SOUFFLÉ AU GRAND MARNIER

4 1/2	tablesp. flour
1	cup plus 2 tablesp. milk
1/2	cup sugar
3	tablesp. softened butter
2	teasp. vanilla extract
1	medium orange
4	tablesp. Grand Marnier
6	eggs
2	extra egg whites

You may substitute curaçao or Cointreau for the liqueur in this recipe. To my way of thinking, one uses little enough of the liqueur in making this queen of desserts, that the saving is comparatively small but the quality of the other liqueurs makes the quality of the finished soufflé less good.

Soufflé with Honey

Use the same recipe as above but use one-half cup of honey beaten with the same amount of clarified butter instead of the liqueur; the honey-butter to be added, together with a tablespoon of kirsch or cherry brandy, to the milk-flour mixture as it is beaten. It is also pleasant to add a teaspoon of ground pistachio nuts.

Sit the soufflé mold in a pan of hot water in a 400 degree oven and immediately turn the heat down to 375 degrees, as in the previous recipe.

Coffee Soufflé

Use the basic recipe but in place of the liqueur, dissolve a tablespoon of instant espresso coffee in one-half cup of the hot milk. The dark roasted Italian coffee gives a better flavor than our lighter roasted bean does, but you may want to add extra sugar. Taste the batter and add more sugar if you wish.

Place the soufflé dish in a pan of hot water and lower the temperature of the preheated oven to 375 degrees.

Strawberry Soufflé

Slice fresh or frozen strawberries and let stand two hours or longer covered by the liqueur.

Use the flour and milk to make a thick cooked paste as in the first recipe and beat in the egg yolks, one at a time, as before. Beat in the liqueur in which the berries were marinated. Just before folding in the beaten egg whites, mix the strawberries with the batter, after sweetening them to taste. Cook as usual in a buttered and sugared soufflé mold or baking dish, in a pan of hot water at 375 degrees. Cooking will require thirty to forty-five minutes. Although we like this soufflé plain, you may want to serve it with sweetened whipped cream.

STRAWBERRY SOUFFLÉ

2	cups sliced strawberries, fresh or frozen
1/2	cup Grand Marnier or curaçao
	sugar to taste
3	tablesp. softened butter
3	tablesp. flour
1	cup milk
4	eggs
1	extra egg white

323

Chocolate Soufflé

CHOCOLATE SOUFFLÉ

2	tablesp. softened butter
2	oz. unsweetened or semisweet chocolate
3	eggs plus 1 extra white
2	tablesp. cornstarch
3/4	cup milk
1/2	cup sugar
1/2	teasp. vanilla extract

This one inevitably comes out somewhat heavier than the soufflés heretofore described, but the following way of doing it will give you as light and fluffy a one as it is possible for soufflé au chocolat.

The heaviness of the chocolate soufflé is made less by making the béchamel-like sauce with cornstarch instead of flour.

Melt butter, add starch and stir until smooth. Add the cold milk and cook until the sauce is thick and smooth and no longer tastes starchy—let cool.

Melt the chocolate in the top of a double boiler over hot—not boiling—water and add sugar. Stir the melted sweetened chocolate into the milk-starch mixture. Beat the yolks thoroughly into the batter one at a time, after the mixture has cooled.

Add a pinch of salt to the egg whites and beat until the whites form soft peaks. Sprinkle the sugar over them and finish beating until they peak stiffly. Now, fold the whites gently into the chocolate batter. Sift powdered sugar into an unbuttered soufflé mold or baking dish and turn the soufflé into it. Sit in a pan of hot water and bake in the oven set at 325 degrees. This usually requires about forty-five minutes. When the top is browned and the soufflé has risen nicely, test with a needle or the blade of a sharp knife.

Serve at once, with whipped cream or plain. This is the only soufflé that seems to me to gain by any garnishment. But the lightness, the flavor and the color contrast of the dark mass with the whipped cream are all pleasing.

Apple Pie

APPLE PIE

	enough pie pastry for two crusts (pâte brisée)
3	cups tart apple slices
1	tablesp. butter
1/2 to 3/4	cups brown sugar
	pinch of salt
1/2	teasp. cinnamon
	good grating of nutmeg

Select tart, juicy apples. Peel, core and neatly slice enough to make three good cups. If the apples seem sweet, add the juice of one-half or a whole lemon. Arrange bottom crust in a nine inch pie pan and place the apples in the crust, heaping a little in the center. Sprinkle over them the brown sugar and the spices. It is always worth the extra trouble to grate nutmeg freshly, rather than using the preground kind. Dot liberally with butter and if the apples appear juicy, sprinkle a tablespoon of flour over them; otherwise omit the flour. Cover with top crust, pinching the crusts together to seal after moistening the edges of the bottom crust. Prick the crust in ornamental designs with a heavy tined fork or make several knife slashes in it. Bake at 350 degrees until the top crust is nicely browned and the apples are tender. This will require fifty to sixty minutes.

Open-faced Apple Tart

In either a round or square dish somewhat deeper than an ordinary pie plate, fit a bottom crust of regular pâte brisée. Take particular care to peel and slice your apples so that you will have smoothly cut slices of uniform size, about one-half inch thick at the outside edge. Arrange the fruit in an orderly design of overlapping slices in at least two layers. Season each layer with cinnamon, a generous grind of nutmeg, and at least a tablespoon of butter dotted over the surface, and sprinkle heavily with brown sugar. Sprinkle the fruit with two tablespoons of kirsch. To the top layer, add brown sugar and butter so that the surface is practically covered. Bake in a 350 degree oven until the apples are soft and the sugar is beginning to caramelize.

Inspect the tart after one-half hour of baking. If an excessive amount of juice appears to be forming, sprinkle one or more tablespoons of flour over the fruit. If the top layer of apples or the crust appear to be getting brown before the fruit is soft, cover with a layer of buttered foil.

The idea is to finish with the crust crisply browned, the fruit fragrant and savorous and the top showing a partly candied mixture of juice and caramelized sugar over the apple slices.

We ate this dessert at Laserre, one of the four three-star restaurants of Paris, and found it worthy of that distinguished eating place's reputation and at the same time, not hard to duplicate in our own kitchen.

Alsatian Apple Tart

Line a nine or ten inch pie plate with your pâte brisée. Choose four nice tart, cooking apples; peel and slice, taking care to get smooth, uniform slices about one-half inch thick at the outer edge. Arrange on the layer of pastry in a regular, overlapping design. Put in an oven preheated to 375 degrees and bake fifteen minutes. While the apples

OPEN-FACED APPLE TART

	pâte brisée
	sliced apples, 1/2 inch thick at outside edges
	cinnamon
	nutmeg
	butter
	brown sugar
2	tablesp. kirsch

ALSATIAN APPLE TART

4   tart cooking apples
     pâte brisée

CUSTARD FOR TART

1/2 cup sugar
1/2 cup light cream
1   egg
1   tablesp. kirsch

and pastry are baking, mix a custard, using 1/2 cup sugar, 1/2 cup light cream, one egg and a tablespoon of kirsch, well beaten together. At the end of fifteen minutes, pour the custard over the half cooked apples and return to the oven for a further fifteen minutes, by which time the custard will be set.

Other Fruit Tarts

In France, the process described in the last recipe is frequently reversed, especially in making small individual tarts. The custard is baked into the shell which has already been in the oven for fifteen minutes. Cooked fruit is then placed on top of the custard and the surface is glazed with a little jelly of the appropriate color, the tarts then being returned to the oven for two or three minutes to dry out the glaze.

One of the favorite *tartes* encountered in French *patisseries* is made in this fashion using a red sour cherry much like (I believe identical with) our pie cherry. A tablespoon of currant jelly is diluted with an equal amount of hot water and is brushed over the surface. The result is a shiny pinkish red glaze over the surface of both fruit and custard.

Apricot tarts are made by placing peeled canned half apricots on the top of the custard and then glazing with a mixture of apricot jam and water.

Cherry Pie

Sour pie cherries make the best pie. In most parts of this country, this means using canned red pie cherries, which is just as well, because they are already ripe and cooked.

Line a nine inch pie plate with the standard short crust. Drain the cherries and, after pricking the pastry well, pour in three cups of the drained cherries. Spread over the cherries one cup of sugar, a pinch or two of salt, and one tablespoon of flour. Add 1/4 cup of the juice drained from the cherries. Put on a top crust, moisten the edges of the bottom crust and seal the two crusts well, crimping up the margin of the two. Prick the top pastry with a design with a large tined fork and put in a 350 degree oven until the top crust is nicely browned. Halfway through the cooking, dust the top with finely granulated sugar.

CHERRY PIE

     pie crust
1   cup sugar
1 - 2 pinches of salt
1   tablesp. flour
1/4 cup cherry juice
     finely granulated sugar

Raisin Pie

Soak the raisins in the water for several hours so that they may plump. Separate them well so that the liquid surrounds individual raisins.

Mix all of the other ingredients except the brandy, add the water and raisins and cook over low heat, stirring frequently, for about fifteen minutes or until the mixture thickens. Add brandy and mix.

Fit a bottom crust to a nine or ten inch pie plate, prick it in many places and add the filling. Cover either with a full top crust or a lattice crust. In either case, dust with finely granulated sugar when the top crust begins to brown.

RAISIN PIE

1	cup seeded raisins
1 1/2	cups water
1 1/2	cups sugar
1/4	cup flour
1	egg
3	tablesp. lemon juice
3	tablesp. grated lemon rind
2	pinches salt
1/2	cup brandy

Pecan Pie

In a mixing bowl, beat thoroughly together the sugar, flour and corn syrup. Beat the five eggs well and then add them to the bowl, beating thoroughly. Then, in order, beat in the salt, flavoring extract, and butter.

Turn into a pie plate fitted with an unbaked crust which you have not forgotten to prick in several places with a fork. Smooth over the top and cover with neatly placed pecan halves. Bake in a 350 degree oven for about thirty-five minutes.

Some cooks cover this pie with whipped cream before serving; but to me, the pie is sufficiently rich not to require this addition; furthermore, the taste of the whipped cream is not really compatible with the rich, sweet, but nutty taste of the pie itself.

PECAN PIE

2 1/2	tablesp. brown sugar
4	tablesp. flour
2	cups corn syrup, light or dark
3	tablesp. melted sweet butter
5	eggs
1/2	teasp. salt
1 1/2	teasp. vanilla extract
1/2	cup pecan halves

Cream Pie Filling

A cream pie filling is *not* a custard. Properly made, it bears a kinship to the French *crème pâtissière* which may be used to fill cream puffs or èclairs or as a filling for napoleons, as well as for pie fillings.

Separate the eggs, reserving the whites for another purpose. Gradually beat the sugar and the yolks until the mixture is thick and lemon colored. Sift the flour and beat into the egg mixture.

Heat the milk until it boils gently. Remove from the heat, let cool a little and then beat the hot milk into

CREAM PIE FILLING

5	egg yolks
1	cup sugar
1/2	cup flour
2 1/2	cups milk
2	tablesp. butter
1	tablesp. vanilla extract (or rum, kirsch, almond extract depending on use)

the egg mixture, at first adding it drop by drop. This addition should be made in a heavy bottomed saucepan which, as soon as the milk is thoroughly beaten into the egg-sugar mixture, is set over the heat. Beat constantly with a wire whip, being careful not to allow the contents at the bottom of the pan to scorch. When the mixture begins to bubble, reduce the heat and beat constantly while it simmers for three or four minutes, until the flour is cooked. Now, beat in the butter and whichever flavoring your recipe calls for.

Saint Honoré Cream

Make the crème pâtissière exactly as directed above. To the five egg whites, add three more. Add a pinch of salt and beat until the egg whites peak softly. At this point, sprinkle in two tablespoons powdered or confectioner's finely granulated sugar and continue beating until the whites peak stiffly. Stir part of the egg whites into the hot crème and then fold in the rest gently. With suitable flavoring, this is useful for tarts, cream puffs, éclairs and other forms of French pastry.

Coconut Cream Pie

Fit a nine inch pie plate with a bottom crust, prick it and bake until it is a golden brown. If you have trouble with the pastry puffing up in spite of being pricked, fill the pie pan with dried beans while it is baking.

Make the cream filling described above and add 1/2 cup of fresh coconut, finely chopped rather than grated. Put the filled pie in the refrigerator to settle, then cover with vanilla flavored, sweetened whipped cream to which another one-half cup of chopped fresh coconut has been added. Note: In my opinion, this pie, like coconut custard, is not worth doing unless you have fresh coconut.

Banana Cream Pie

Fill a baked nine inch pie shell about half full with slices of fully ripe banana and pour the crème, flavored with vanilla, over the bananas. Top with sweetened whipped cream.

Cheese Pie

Most cheese cake that I have encountered has left me cold. It is too floury and not interesting enough in either texture or in flavor. But here is a cheese pie which is moist, light, and full of flavor.

Melt the butter. Crush the graham crackers with a rolling pin and mix well with the melted butter. Line the bottom and sides of a nine inch pie plate evenly with this mixture and bake fifteen minutes at 350 degrees.

Blend in the electric mixer or beat vigorously with a wooden spoon, the cream cheese, eggs, 1/2 cup of sugar and one teaspoon vanilla extract. Pour into the baked shell and bake fifteen minutes at 300 degrees. Let cool five minutes.

Beat together one cup of sour cream, two tablespoons of sugar and one teaspoon of vanilla extract. Spread over the top of the cream cheese mixture and put back into a 300 degree oven for five minutes. Cool, then chill in the refrigerator before serving.

Cream Puffs

Make a recipe of cream puff pastry (*pâte à choux:* see basic chapter on breads and pastries). Arrange on a baking sheet, either with a tablespoon or a pastry bag, in mounds two to two and one-half inches in diameter and one inch high. Be sure to leave two inches of space around each puff. Bake in a 425 degree oven for twenty to twenty-five minutes, until the puffs are doubled in size and are lightly brown. Reduce heat to 375 and continue baking until puffs are well browned, firm and crusty. Immediately, slit each puff a little more than half way up the side and return to oven with the door opened and the heat extinguished. After the puffs have cooled, examine one. If it still contains damp dough inside, slice the puffs in two and remove all the damp dough. Return to oven at 200 degrees with oven door open to dry out.

Fill the puffs with sweetened whipped cream, slightly flavored with Grand Marnier or with orange water, or vanilla. Or use the crème St. Honoré which may be flavored with rum, cognac, kirsch, Grand Marnier, almond extract, or vanilla. Try different flavors; you will find the variety interesting. You will also find that, using either pure, home-

CHEESE PIE

8	double graham crackers
4	oz. (1 stick) sweet butter
3	pkgs. cream cheese
2	eggs
1/2	cup sugar
2	teasp. vanilla extract
1	cup sour cream
2	tablesp. sugar

made whipped cream, or the St. Honoré mixture, you can make better cream puffs than most of the ones you can buy commercially.

Chocolate Éclairs

Either with a pastry bag or a tablespoon, arrange pastry in shapes about one inch in diameter and four or five inches in length. Again, be sure to allow at least two inches around each shape for expansion. Bake exactly like cream puffs; watch the shapes as they bake; being smaller than puffs, they may be done a little sooner. Treat to avoid soggy interiors as with the puffs. Fill with the crème St. Honoré, with whatever flavor you like. Cover the top with your favorite chocolate icing, or use of those given below.

Pets-de-nonne

Make a recipe of cream puff paste (pâte à choux). Heat cooking oil to 375 degrees and drop the pâte into the hot oil in spoonsful approximately the size of a walnut. When the balls of pâte begin to swell, increase the heat to 400 degrees and leave the fritters in the hot fat until they are a dark golden brown. Drain on paper towels and sprinkle with confectioner's sugar.

Good with Vanilla Custard Cream

These souffléed fritters are also good with a vanilla custard cream or a caramel sauce.

One of our standard American cookbooks, initially written by a Boston housewife, has a recipe for a slightly modified version of pets-de-nonne under the more lady-like name of "Queen Fritters." Queen fritters, according to this respected authoress are exactly the same as pets-de-nonne except that when you have finished frying them, you slit them and fill the insides with preserves, marmalade, or a chocolate cream filling, then dust with sugar.

Napoleons (Mille-feuilles)

Make a recipe of puff paste (pâte feuilletée). Roll it one-eighth inch thick, cut into strips about three inches wide and four or five inches long. Prick in many places with a fork and bake on a cookie sheet in a 450 degree oven until the pieces of paste are puffed and lightly browned. Reduce heat to 375 degrees and bake another one-half hour or until the sheets are dry and crisp.

When they are cool, spread the sheets with one of the following fillings—or with assorted kinds of fillings—and stack them up in layers of three or four. Decorate the top layer or dust with powdered sugar.

Fillings

Most of these are adaptable as icings for cakes also.

1. *Whipped Cream with Assorted Flavors.* These should include vanilla, almond (incorporate in the cream thinly-slivered almonds either blanched or toasted), rum, cognac, orange water, and various liqueurs such as Grand Marnier, curaçao, etc.

2. *Crème Pâtissière, also with assorted flavors.*

3. *Caramel Cream Filling.* Melt in a small saucepan, the butter and add the brown sugar. Stir over low heat until the sugar melts. Add the light cream and beat until the mixture is thick. Add confectioner's finely granulated sugar to your own taste and a teaspoon of vanilla extract. Beat until the mixture is soft and smooth.

CARAMEL CREAM FILLING

1/2	cup butter
1/2	cup brown sugar
1/4	cup light cream
1 - 2	cups confectioner's finely granulated sugar
1	teasp. vanilla extract

4. *Chocolate Cream Filling.* In a bowl, cream the butter and 3/4 cup finely granulated sugar, beating until the mixture is smooth and fluffy. In another bowl, beat the egg whites and a pinch of salt until the whites peak stiffly, then add 3/4 cup finely granulated sugar and resume beating until the sugar is well incorporated. Melt three squares of unsweetened chocolate in the top of a double boiler. Blend the two mixtures together and add the melted chocolate, beating it in rapidly.

CHOCOLATE CREAM FILLING

1/2	stick butter
1 1/2	cup finely granulated sugar
2	egg whites
	salt
3	sq. unsweetened chocolate

5. Make a strong coffee infusion by pouring already normally strong coffee through a fresh charge of ground coffee. Let cool. Cream together 1/2 stick of butter and one cup of powdered sugar. After mixing thoroughly, beat in 2 1/2 tablespoons of the coffee essence and a heaping teaspoon of grated bitter chocolate. Add a few drops of vanilla extract. Beat until the mixture is light and creamy.

6. *Chocolate Crème Pâtissière.* In the recipe for cream pie filling, melt two squares of unsweetened chocolate in

331

the milk while you are heating it. Then, complete the recipe as directed.

FRANGIPANGI CREAM

6	stale macaroons
2	tablesp. chopped almonds
1/3	cup flour
3/4	cup powdered sugar
	salt
2	egg yolk plus 1 whole egg
2	cups milk
1	teasp. vanilla extract

RUM CREAM

2	oz. butter
1/4	cup heavy cream
1	cup (or more) confectioner's finely granulated sugar
1	tablesp. (or more) Jamaica rum

MAPLE CREAM

1	cup granulated sugar
1	cup maple syrup
2	oz. butter
1/2	cup heavy cream
	Mapleine flavoring extract

7. *Frangipangi Cream.* Allow macaroons to become stale, or dry them thoroughly in an oven at 200 degrees. Crush them finely with a rolling pin. Also, crush two tablespoons of chopped blanched almonds. Blend the flour, powdered sugar, a pinch of salt and one egg yolk. When these items are thoroughly mixed, beat into the mixture one more whole egg plus another yolk. Scald the milk and beat it into the first mixture little by little. Cook in the top of a double boiler without allowing the mixture to boil, beating all the while. Remove from the heat after two minutes, add one teaspoon of vanilla extract and the crushed almonds and macaroons, beating them in well.

8. *Rum Cream.* Melt in a small, heavy bottomed pan the butter; add the heavy cream and then beat into the mixture one cup or more of confectioner's finely granulated sugar until a workable filling is obtained. Flavor with a tablespoon or more of Jamaica rum. Vary the flavor by using other liqueurs such as Grand Marnier, curaçoa, or cognac.

9. *Maple Cream.* Mix in a saucepan, the granulated sugar, the maple syrup, butter and heavy cream. Cook over low heat ten to twelve minutes, beating all the time. A not-too-bad substitute can be made by doubling the amount of plain sugar, omitting the maple syrup and flavoring to taste (usually about one teaspoon) with Mapleine flavoring extract.

In any event, enough recipes for fillings have been given to supply you with good ideas of how to go about making your mille-feuilles. Obviously, any cake icing that you like can be used for this purpose, although it is better to have creamy rather than hard fillings on all but the top layer. The latter may well have a layer of hard icing, which can be further decorated with dribbles of icings of a different color or with little rosettes or other fancy shapes made with a pastry bag of the crème St. Honoré or whipped cream.

Dessert Crêpes

Of these, crêpes Suzette, in any one of an almost infinite number of versions, are probably the most familiar, having been chosen by many a man to impress the lady with whom he was dining. Besides, who knows at this date, exactly what crêpes Suzettes are? Herewith is an adaptation of the recipe favored by Escoffier.

Make the dessert crêpes recipe as described in the basic chapter on breads and pastries, but flavor the batter with curaçoa and an equal amount of tangerine juice. Cook the crêpes and keep warm, but do not stack them.

Rub six lumps of sugar over the rind of a lemon and of an orange. Moisten the sugar with one-half cup of orange juice. Cream the butter with the sugar. Melt the creamed butter in a chafing dish and pour the orange juice-sugar mixture into the pan. When the sauce has reduced somewhat, lift the crêpes into it and fold in quarters, ladling the sauce over them. Now, mix the Cointreau, or curaçao with the rum and pour over the pancakes. Finish by pouring over them 1/3 cup good cognac or Grand Marnier. Let this mixture heat to boiling, then tip the pan so that the sauce catches fire. Continue to ladle the flaming sauce over the crêpes and serve rapidly as soon as the flames die out. Allow three or four small crêpes per person.

DESSERT CRÊPES

3 - 4	crêpes (per person)
6	lumps of sugar
1	lemon
1	orange
1/2	cup orange juice
1	stick butter
2	tablesp. sugar
1/4	cup Cointreau or curaçao
2	tablesp. rum
1/3	cup cognac or Grand Marnier.

Another Version

Rub four lumps of sugar on an orange rind and crush with three tablespoons of sweet butter. Melt in the chafing dish, add juice of one large orange, a few drops of lemon juice and one-half cup of curaçao with another two tablespoons of butter. Douse the crêpes in this mixture, ladling it over them well and put a teaspoon of ground filberts or almonds in the center of each crêpe before folding. Finally, douse with one-half cup of brandy and ignite.

Still Another Version

Rub four lumps of sugar over the peel of two oranges until all sides of each lump have absorbed oil. Peel the oranges, being careful to discard the white part of the skin. Chop finely (some recipes direct you to grate the

333

orange peel). Next, cream together 1/4 cup sugar and two sticks of butter and, beating all the while, add the cubed sugar, orange peel and 2/3 cup orange juice. Heat this sauce to bubbling in the chafing dish and add three teaspoons of one of the orange liqueurs. Dip the crêpes into the sauce and fold into quarters. Sprinkle the folded crêpes with more sugar and add, already mixed, 1/3 cup of whichever orange liqueur you had used plus 1/3 cup cognac. Heat and ignite, ladling the sauce over the folded crêpes.

Crêpes with Marmalade

CRÊPES WITH MARMALADE

1	cup good English marmalade
2	tablesp. butter
1/3	cup Grand Marnier plus 2 tablesp.
1/2	cup good brandy

Mix a cup of good English orange marmalade with two tablespoons of Grand Marnier and spread a spoonful of this mixture on each warm crêpe. Roll and place in the chafing dish in which you have previously heated two tablespoons of butter and 1/3 cup of Grand Marnier. When all of the crêpes have been arranged in the dish, turn up the heat and add one-half cup of good brandy. When the sauce boils, ignite it and shake the pan so that all the crêpes are doused in the flaming liqueurs. Serve immediately as the flame dies down.

Crêpes with Cherries

CRÊPES WITH CHERRIES

	crêpes
1	small can pitted Bing cherries
1/4	cup cherry juice
2	tablesp. sugar
2	oz. butter
	kirsch
1/2	cup cognac

Cook the crêpes and keep warm. Heat in a saucepan, a small can of drained, pitted Bing cherries which have stood for two hours or longer in a bowl covered with one-quarter cup of their juice, a tablespoon of sugar and enough kirsch to cover. Melt two ounces of butter in the chafing dish, dissolve a tablespoon of sugar, and add two tablespoons of kirsch. Spoon a few (five or six) of the heated cherries together with a little of the liquid in which they have been standing into the center of each crêpe. Roll and arrange in the chafing dish, heat to boiling and add one-half cup of equal parts of cognac and kirsch. As soon as this is hot, ignite. Ladle the flaming liquid over the crêpes and serve as the flames die.

Frozen Desserts

You will not find in this chapter, any recipes for making ice cream. There is almost no place in the United States where you cannot buy excellent caterer's ice cream, as good or better than most of the homemade kind and a lot more convenient. The following recipes for sherbets and frozen mousses are not available commercially, and, unlike ice cream, are suitable for freezing in the ice cube trays or frozen food section of the modern refrigerator.

Espresso Sherbert

To serve six, make 1 1/2 pints of espresso coffee, using your favorite brand. Or—somewhat less good—make the espresso using powdered instant espresso coffee and following the package directions. Sprinkle one package of gelatin on the surface and after it softens, heat until the gelatin dissolves.

Beat egg whites with a pinch of salt until they hold a peak, but are not entirely dry. Stir into the coffee sugar to your taste. Then fold in the beaten egg whites. Turn into ice cube trays or into a shallow bowl in your deep freeze. When the mass becomes firm to about one inch from the edges of the trays, turn into a previously chilled bowl and beat with an electric mixer at high speed until no large crystals remain. Return to the freezer trays and let freeze until nearly solid. Serve quickly, in parfait glasses, either plain or topped with whipped cream.

Burgundy Sherbet

Obviously, you may use other red wines. If you do, change the name of your sherbert appropriately.

Sprinkle three envelopes of gelatin on the surface of 1/2 cup of water. When it softens, add two more cups of water and heat until it dissolves, together with the sugar, a pinch of salt and a piece of cinnamon bark one inch long. Strain into a mixing bowl and when it cools, add the Burgundy (or other red wine) and Calvados or New Jersey apple brandy and a little lemon or lime juice. Then add the stiffly beaten egg whites and freeze as directed for the espresso sherbet. You will get a smoother and more finely grained product if you remove the sherbet and beat it when it is frozen about one inch from the edge of the tray.

Strawberry Mousse

Slice still finer, one package of frozen sliced strawberries.

ESPRESSO SHERBET

1 1/2	pt. espresso coffee
1	pkg. gelatin
6	egg whites
1	pinch of salt

BURGUNDY SHERBET

3	env. gelatin
2 1/2	cups water
1 1/2	cups sugar
1	pinch of salt
1	pc. cinnamon bark
2	cups Burgundy or other red wine
1/2	cup Calvados or New Jersey apple brandy lemon or lime juice
6	egg whites

STRAWBERRY MOUSSE

1   pkg. frozen sliced
       strawberries
6   egg yolks
1/2 cup finely granulated sugar
1   pt. heavy cream

Take six egg yolks, reserving the whites for another use, and beat until thickened and lemon colored in the top of a double boiler over hot, but not boiling, water with 1/2 cup finely granulated sugar.

Whip one pint of heavy cream stiffly, add the egg yolks and sugar when all are cool, mix in the sliced strawberries and part of their juice. Freeze in the refrigerator trays or in a shallow pan in the deep freeze, stirring once or twice during the freezing, which will require about three hours.

Other Fruit Mousses

Fully ripe fresh or canned apricots, Babcock or other sweet white peaches, and other berries, particularly the modern varieties of blackberries and blueberries, are all good made into a mousse with a recipe similar to that given for strawberries. Cook and purée the fruit. Rub berries through a sieve fine enough to strain out all or most of their seeds.

Port Wine Mousse

PORT WINE MOUSSE

6   egg yolks
1/2 cup sugar
1   pt. heavy cream
6   oz. good-quality ruby port

Beat six egg yolks and approximately 1/2 cup sugar together in the top of a double boiler without allowing the water to boil.

Whip stiffly, one pint of heavy cream and stir the egg-sugar mixture into the cream. Then add six ounces of a good-quality ruby port. (To have the right flavor, it is necessary to use real port, but it need be only a standard ruby port, not a vintage wine.) Freeze, stirring at least twice during the process, in refrigerator trays or in a shallow pan in the deep freeze.

Maple Nut Mousse

Stirred by boyhood memories of maple nut ice cream, which seems to have disappeared from local markets, I devised the following recipe.

First beat together six egg yolks, four ounces of honey and eight ounces of real maple syrup, then heat in the top of a double boiler while continuing to beat and without letting the mixture boil. Fold into the mixture after it has cooled, one pint of heavy cream, stiffly whipped, and four ounces of broken English walnut meats. Turn into the refrigerator trays and stir at least twice during the freezing.

Honey and Orange Flower Mousse

Beat together and then heat without boiling in the top of a double boiler, six egg yolks and 1/2 cup (four ounces) of orange blossom honey. When the mixture cools, add one tablespoon of orange flower water and fold in one pint of stiffly whipped cream. Turn into refrigerator trays and freeze, stirring once or twice during freezing. A further interesting flavor note can be obtained by adding, at the same time as the orange flower water, one ounce of cognac.

Mousse au Grand Marnier

Beat together six egg yolks and four ounces of orange blossom honey and heat without boiling in the top of a double boiler. When the mixture cools, add two ounces or more, according to your taste, of Grand Marnier liqueur and then fold into the mixture one pint of stiffly whipped heavy cream. Freeze as usual, stirring once or twice during the process.

Biscuit Tortoni

Dry enough coconut macaroons in the air or at 200 degrees in the oven so that when they are crushed and sifted, there will be one cup. Next, whip the heavy cream as stiffly as possible; then beat into the whipped cream, the powdered sugar, egg whites which have been beaten with a pinch of salt until they peak firmly, and four ounces of sweet or medium-sweet sherry. Add these items alternately, a little at a time. Finally, beat in the macaroons. Pack into custard molds and freeze without stirring. Sprinkle the tops with more crushed macaroons.

MAPLE NUT MOUSSE

6	egg yolks
4	oz. honey
8	oz. maple syrup
1	pt. heavy cream
4	oz. broken English walnuts

HONEY AND ORANGE FLOWER MOUSSE

6	egg yolks
1/2	cup orange blossom honey
1	tablesp. orange flower water
1	pt. cream

MOUSSE AU GRAND MARNIER

6	egg yolks
4	oz. orange blossom honey
2	oz. (or more) Grand Marnier
1	pt. heavy cream

BISCUIT TORTONI

1	cup crushed macaroons
1	pt. heavy cream
1/2	cup powdered sugar
2	egg whites
1	pinch of salt
4	oz. sweet or medium-sweet sherry

SOME FRENCH GASTRONOMIC TERMS

French, or, in many cases, garbled and mangled fragments of that language, has become standard on menus throughout the world. The first reason, reasonably enough, is that French cooking leads all others. Furthermore, French cooks—usually men—have been and are inventive, and a man has the right to call his dish anything he likes. Finally, any hotel or restaurant owner who hopes to do a brisk trade at higher than ordinary prices feels that French words on his bills of fare give his establishment a certain *cachet* which helps to justify the prices. This is true even when no one in the restaurant, from the chef to the scullery lad, has ever been any closer to Paris than Piedmont or the Spanish Pyrenées; two places, incidentally, from whence most of the owners and cooks of San Francisco's "French" restaurants hail.

First of all, we can say something about a long list of proper names very quickly. French chefs, especially of bygone days, often named dishes in honor of their employers, the employer's wife, or one of his mistresses, the chef's own wife, daughter, mother, or mistress. Other creations were named in honor of a long list of famous actresses, lady violinists and pianists, female opera singers, renowned madames, and sometimes, the little girl in the next street. Such names do not result in informing the prospective diner of the composition of a dish. In the majority of cases, even their historical significance, slight as it may have been, has long since been forgotten.

But when a dish has a part of its name the word *Parmentier*, it means the dish is composed in whole or in part of potatoes. The designation commemorates a well-known French economist of the seventeenth century who was chiefly instrumental in inducing the reluctant French to accept the potato.

Place names usually refer to a style or manner of preparation, as in "Potatoes *à la Lyonnaise*" which describes potatoes sliced and sautéed with onion. *Chantilly* appended to a name means that the dish contains whipped cream. *Crécy* indicates the presence of carrots. *Saint Germain* means split peas are a part of the dish.

FRENCH	ENGLISH
Potages	**Soups**
Bouillons	Broth, or stock
Consommé	Clear soup
— à la bouquetière	— with vegetables
— au celeri	— with celery
— au cheveux d'ange	— with vermicelli
— à la dame blanche	— with chicken dumplings
— fausse tortue	— mock turtle
— froid	— cold clear soup
— écossais	— scotch broth
— à la jardinière	— with vegetables
— à la julienne	— with narrow strips of vegetables
— à la madrilène	— Madrid style (with tomato)
— à la moëlle	— with marrow
— aux paillettes d'or	— with cheese straws
— au Parmesan	— with Parmesan cheese
— aux truffes	— with truffles
— petite marmite	— French beef broth
— tortue claire	— real turtle consommé
Potages Liés	**Thick Soups**
Bisque de crabes	Cream of crabs
— d'écrevisses	— of crayfish
— de homard	— of lobster
— Borcht à la russe	— Russian borscht
Bouillabaisse	Mediterranean fish soup
Cream Argenteuil	Cream of asparagus soup
— de céleri	— of celery soup
— à la Condé	— of cauliflower soup
— de marrons	— chestnut cream soup
— d'orge	— cream of barley soup
— à la reine	— cream of chicken soup
— à la portugaise	— cream of tomato and rice soup
Minestrone (Italian word)	Italian vegetable soup
Pot chaudière	Clam chowder (Breton, not New England, although there are similarities)
Potage à l'ail	Garlic soup
— à l'americaine	— American vegetable soup
— bonne femme	— soup, housewife's style
— à la bretonne	— Breton bean soup
— au chasseur	— game soup
— à la chevreuse	— creamed chicken soup with rice

FRENCH	ENGLISH
— *à la Crécy*	— cream of carrot soup
— *au cresson*	— purée of Potato with watercress
— *aux épinards*	— cream of spinach soup
— *de laitues*	— cream of lettuce soup
— *à l'oseille*	— sorrel soup
— *Parmentier*	— French potato soup, not vichyssoise
— *aux poireaux*	— leek soup
— *Saint Germain*	— split pea soup
Velouté Marie Stuart	Cream of chicken soup with chervil
— *aux morilles*	— cream soup with morels, a special kind of mushroom

HORS-D'OEUVRES

Allumettes	Puff pastry straws
— *aux anchois*	— with anchovies
Artichauts à la grècque	Artichokes grecian style
Barquets	Puff-paste boats
— *de crevettes*	— with shrimps
— *diverses*	— assorted pastry boats
— *de homard*	— with lobster
Boeuf fumé	Smoked beef
Beignets	Fritters
— *d'anchois*	— with anchovies
— *à la bénédictine*	— benedictine style
Betterave	Beets
Bouchées	Small patties (bites)
— *à la bohémienne*	— bohemian style
— *à la bouquetière*	— with vegetables
— *aux huitres*	— with oysters
— *à la périgourdine*	— with truffles
— *Saint Hubert*	— with game
Brochettes	Skewers for broiling meats, etc.
Canapés	Buttered toast cut in fancy shapes
— *d'anchois*	— with anchovies
— *à l'anglaise*	— welsh rarebit
— *de caviar*	— with caviar
— *au gibier*	— with game
— *de homard*	— with lobster
Cantaloupe frappé	Iced melon
Caviar	Caviar
Choux au fromage	Cheese puffs

FRENCH	ENGLISH
Concombres	Cucumbers
Concombres farci	Stuffed cucumbers
Cornichons	Small sour pickles
Croquettes	Meat or fish balls, sometimes in a conical or cylindrical shape
Croustades	Crusty patties
— aux pommes d'or	— with Golden apples
— de ris de veau	— with veal sweetbreads
Duchesses diverses	Assorted puffs
Farci	Stuffed
Frivolitiés	Appetizers
Hareng	Herring
— à la Bismarck	— Bismarck herring
— fumé	— kippers
— mariné	— pickled herring
— à la russe	— herring with caviar
Homard	Lobster, clawed
Huitres	Oysters
Jambon cru	Raw ham
— de Bayonne	— Bayonne raw ham
— de Parme	— prosciutto
— de Westphalie	— Westphalian ham
Jambon cuit	Cooked ham (boiled)
— de Paris	— "tenderized" ham
— de Prague	— Polish ham
— de York	— Yorkshire ham
Langouste	Salt water crayfish; similar to Pacific Coast lobster
Moules	Mussels
Oeufs farcis	Stuffed eggs; the French have more kinds than your grandmother, making deviled eggs, ever dreamed of
— de pluvier	— plover's eggs
— à la russe	— hard cooked eggs cut in two and served with mayonnaise and capers
Olives farcis	Stuffed olives
Pâté de foie gras	Fat goose liver pâté usually truffled; sometimes mixed with pork liver to lessen cost
— de gibier	— game pâté

FRENCH	ENGLISH
— *de veau*	— veal pâté
Petits soufflés	Little soufflés
— *de crustacés*	— with shrimp, crayfish, lobster, etc.
— *de gibier*	— of game
— *aux huitres*	— with oysters
— *au Parmesan*	— with Parmesan cheese
Quiche Lorraine	Custard with bacon, sometimes with cheese or onions
Radis	Radishes
Rissoles aux anchois	Turnovers with anchovies
— *à la Joinville*	— with crayfish
— *aux morilles*	— with morels, a mushroom
— *aux truffes*	— with truffles
Salades diverses	Various salads
Salade Niçoise	Salad with potatoes, onions, tuna, anchovies, etc.
Sardines à l'huile	Sardines in oil; the French kind are caught in the Bay of Biscay and are stronger than the Norwegian kind
Saucisse	Small sausages
Saucisson	Larger, dry, served sliced; salami
Saumon fumé	Smoked salmon; the best is Norwegian or Scottish
Tartellettes Châtillon	Tartlets with mushrooms
— *au fromage*	— with cheese
Terrine de foie gras	Small earthen dish with foie gras
— *de canard*	— with a pâté of duck
— *de campagne*	— with pâté country style
Tomates natures	Fresh tomatoes
Truites en gelée	Trout in aspic
Viande de Grisons	Spiced dried meat from a Swiss province
Zamponi	Stuffed pig's foot
Zéphirs de homard	Light lobster soufflé
Plats d'oeufs	**Egg Dishes**
Ouefs Argenteuil	Eggs with asparagus tips
— *brouillés*	— scrambled
— *brouillés aux fines herbes*	— scrambled with fine herbs
— *en cocottes*	— cooked in earthenware pots

343

FRENCH	ENGLISH
– *à la coque*	– boiled eggs
– *mollets*	– shelled soft boiled eggs
– *sur le plat*	– fried
– *au beurre noir*	– fried with black butter and dressed with capers; typical bourgeois dish
– *au lard fumé*	– fried with bacon
– *Lyonnaise*	– fried with onion purée
– *à la opéra*	– fried with chicken livers and asparagus tips
– *Parmentier*	– with potatoes
– *à la périgourdine*	– with truffled sauce
– *pochés*	– poached
Omelettes	Omelets
– *à la bourguinonne*	– stuffed with snails
– *aux champignons*	– with mushrooms
– *chasseur*	– hunter's style
– *à l'Espagnole*	– Spanish style
– *à la fermière*	– farmer's style
– *aux fines herbes*	– with herbs
– *aux foies de volaille*	– with chicken livers
– *à la Florentine*	– with spinach
– *à la forestière*	– with morels
– *au fromage*	– with cheese
– *à la grand'mère*	– grandmother's style
– *au jambon*	– with ham
– *au lard*	– with bacon
– *Lorraine*	– with bacon, Lorraine style
– *lyonnaise*	– with fried onions
– *nature*	– plain
– *à la Provençale*	– with tomatoes and parsley
– *Rossini*	– with goose liver and truffles
– *aux truffes*	– with truffles
Poissons	**Fish**
Alose	Shad
Anchois	Anchovy
Anguille	Eel
Bar	Bass
Brochet	Pike
Cabillaud	Cod
Colin	Hake

FRENCH	ENGLISH
Dorade	Sea Bream
Espadon	Swordfish
Flet	Flounder
Flétan	Halibut
Hareng	Herring
Lamproie	Lamprey eel
Limande	"Lemon sole" – vastly inferior to true sole
Loup de mer	Mediterranean name for bass
Maquereau	Mackerel
Morue fraîche	Cod
Morue verte	Salt cod
Raie	Skate
Saumon	Salmon
Sole	The true sole of the Channel
Thon	Tuna or tunny
Truite	Trout
— arc-en-ciel	— rainbow trout
— de rivière	— river trout
— saumonée	— salmon trout

As you might expect, there are innumerable ways of preparing fish. Hundreds of recipes have proper names carrying no indication of their composition. Here are some of the more frequently encountered terms. The list is not intended to be complete.

Poisson au beurre	Fish, usually specified, with butter
— à l'arlésienne	— with marrow and onions
— à la bonne femme	— housewife's style
— à la Bordelaise	— with red wine, onion, and usually, garlic
— braisé	— cooked in covered pan with both liquid and fat
— au Chambertin	— with Chambertin; usually a fantasy with Beaujolais
— au court bouillon	— poached in fish stock and usually wine
— au fenouil	— with fennel; usually in the Midi
— au four	— baked (in the oven)
— froid	— cold
— à la Lyonnaise	— with onions
— à la Mornay	— with mornay sauce

FRENCH	ENGLISH
Coquilles St. Jacques	Not a method of preparation; it means scallops
— en papillote	— scallops cooked in paper
Coquilles de saumon	Scalloped salmon
Cotelettes de saumon	Salmon steaks
Matelote d'anguille	Eel stew, sailor's style
Mayonnaise de saumon	Cold salmon with mayonnaise
Moules	Mussels
— marinière	— sailor's style
Scampi	Adriatic crayfish

BEEF

In reality, French butchers cut the carcass so differently that equivalents are in most cases only approximate.

Boeuf	**Beef**
Aloyau	Sirloin
Cervelle	Brains
Châteaubriand	Steak from the middle of the filet at least three inches thick; frequently sautéed
Côte de boeuf	Rib of beef; rib steak
Plat, plat de côte	Plate
Cou	Neck
Culotte	Rump roast
Entrecôte	Sirloin
Filet	Filet; tenderloin
Foie de boeuf	Beef liver
Jarret	Shank, shin bone (for soup)
Langue	Tongue
Noix, fausse tranche	Thick flank
Pointe de culotte	Aitchbone roast
Queue de boeuf	Oxtail
Romstek	Rump steak
Rosbif, contrefilet	Roast loin of beef
Rognons de boeuf	Beef kidney

Ways of Cooking Steaks and Roasts

Bien cuit	Well done; no self-respecting Frenchman would be caught dead with meat cooked so

FRENCH	ENGLISH
À Point	Medium, "to the point"
Saignant	Rare; the literal meaning is bloody and this is what the Frenchman means when he orders his steak or roast this way
À La Tartare, *Steak Tartare*	Raw, but doctored with many condiments; popular with the university set
Boeuf bouilli	Boiled beef
Carbonnade de boeuf	Belgian, braised beef in beer
Entrecôte à la béarnaise	Sirloin with béarnaise sauce
— à la bordelaise	— with bordelaise sauce and
— aux champignons	— with mushrooms
— à la forestière	— with morels
— à l'hôtelière	— with herb butter and duxelles (mushrooms)
— à la Lyonnaise	— with onions
— marchand de vin	— with a red wine, butter and herb sauce; try it
— à la Marseillaise	— also with onions
— Tyrolienne	— with tomatoes and onions
— au vert pré	— with watercress
Estouffade	Steamed beef stew
Filet de boeuf	Filet of beef
— à la bouquetière	— with vegetables
— à la châtelaine	— with artichokes and chestnuts
— à la dauphinoise	— with potato rissoles
— à la financière	— with quenelles of force meat, mushrooms, cock's combs, kidneys and olives
— à la gastronome	— marinated in Madeira and served with truffles, chestnuts and other things
— à la Hongroise	— with glazed onions and soubise sauce
— Montmorency	— with artichokes and asparagus tips
— à la Parisienne	— with potatoes and artichokes
— à la Périgourdine	— with truffles and truffled sauce
— Petit-duc	— with puff-paste, artichoke bottoms and truffles

FRENCH	ENGLISH
— à la Provençale	— with tomatoes and stuffed mushrooms
— à la renaissance	— with spring vegetables and a clear gravy
— Richelieu	— with tomatoes, mushrooms, lettuce and new potatoes
— Saint Germain	— with carrots, potatoes and peas
— Talleyrand	— cooked with Madeira and truffles and served with poached macaroni and truffles
Hachis	Hash or hashed
— à l'américaine	— American style; occasionally encountered
— à la fermière	— farmer's style; French farmer, that is
— à la grand'mère	— grandmother's style
Langue de boeuf à l'Alsacienne	Beef tongue with sauerkraut
— à la Bigarade	— with orange brown sauce
— à la bourgeoise	— with carrots and onions
— à l'écarlate	— pickled ox tongue
Queue de boeuf à l'Auvergnate	Oxtail with white wine and chestnuts
— à la Cavour	— with brown sauce and a purée of chestnuts
Rognons de boeuf aux champignons	Beef kidneys with mushrooms
— bordelais	— with bordelaise sauce and marrow
— Dijonnais	— with mushrooms, mustard and cream
— flambé	— browned in butter with mushrooms and flamed with brandy
— Parisien	— with white wine, mushrooms and garlic
Romstek grillé	Grilled rump steak; contrary to most travel and cookbooks, most French menus spell steak s-t-e-a-k, although we have encountered s-t-e-a-k; never s-t-e-k
Tournedos	Steaks cut from the smaller end of the filet; usually cooked in butter

FRENCH	ENGLISH
— *sauce béarnaise*	— with béarnaise sauce
— *cendrillon*	— served on artichoke bottoms with soubise sauce
— *favorite*	— with foie gras and truffles
— *Henri IV*	— on fried bread canapés and artichoke bottoms with béarnaise sauce
— *à la moelle*	— with poached marrow and a bordelaise sauce
— *aux morilles*	— with chopped morels
— *Rossini*	— on fried bread canapés, with fried foie gras and a truffle
— *vert-pré*	— with half-melted maître d'hôtel butter and surrounded with alternating heaps of watercress and shoestring potatoes
Veal	Veal
— *blanquette de*	— stew with velouté sauce
— *côtelette de*	— cutlet
— *foie de*	— liver
— *Medaillon or Noisette*	— small cut from tenderloin
— *Ris de*	— sweetbreads
— *Rognons de*	— kidneys (preferred to beef)
— *Selle de*	— saddle, for roast
Mouton	It ought to mean mutton but it really means lamb; I never found mutton in France—in restaurant or *boucherie*
Mouton Pré-salé	Lamb, supposedly from the salt meadows of Britanny and Normandy, but I do not believe these provinces have that many salt meadows; I suspect that it really means grade A lamb
Agneau	Lamb
— *Côtelette de*	— chop
— *Carré de*	— rack
— *à la bonne femme*	— with onions and potatoes
— *à la boulangère*	— with onions and fried potatoes
— *à la soubise*	— with an onion sauce
— *Cassoulet de mouton*	— stew with navy beans
— *à la Bretonne*	— with navy beans

349

FRENCH	ENGLISH
Côtelette de mouton (d'agneau)	Lamb chop
— grillé	— grilled
— Maréchale	— fried, served with truffles and asparagus
— navarraise	— with ham, truffles and mushrooms in béchamel sauce
— à la Perigueux	— stuffed, with truffle sauce
Gigot d'agneau	Leg of lamb
— à l'Anglaise	— boiled with vegetables
— à la Bretonne	— roasted with navy beans
— à l'estragon	— roasted with tarragon
— à la soubise	— with onion sauce
Porc	Pork
— Carré de	— loin
Lard	Bacon or salt pork
Andouillettes	Pork sausages
— à la bourguignonne	— Burgundy style
Cochon de lait	Suckling pig
Côtellette de porc	Pork chop
— à la charcutière	— pork butcher's style
— à la grand'mère	— grandmother's style
Crepinettes de porc	Bulk sausage in flat cakes

The list of ways to cook pork is long and largely duplicates those for beef and lamb; you will not encounter pork on the dinner menus of three-star restaurants.

FOWL AND FEATHERED GAME

Unlike the laws in the United States, French law permits the sale of game of all sorts. Owners of farms and woodland regard game as a cash crop, although the regulations as to seasons and limits are as strict, and as strictly enforced, as in our country. Consequently, one finds game on restaurant menus and also for sale in shops.

FRENCH	ENGLISH
Volaille	Poultry
Canard	Duck
Caneton	Duckling
Chapon	Capon
Coq	Cock, rooster
Dinde, dindon	Turkey
Dindonneau	Young turkey

FRENCH	ENGLISH
Oie	Goose
Pigeon	Pigeon
Pigeonneau	Squab
Pintade	Guinea fowl
Pintadeau	Young Guinea fowl
Poularde	Fattened pullet (young hen)
Poule	Hen
Poulet	In French, the word is masculine and simply means "young chicken" with no distinction as to sex
Poulet de grain	Young chicken; fryer or broiler
Gibier à Plumes	Feathered game
Bécasse	Woodcock; highly esteemed
Bécassine	Snipe
Caille	Quail
Canard sauvage	Wild duck
Faisan	Pheasant; as in U.S., chiefly reared and freed for shooting
Grouse	Grouse
Perdreau	Young partridge
Pedrix	Old partridge; tough!
Sarcelle	Teal

Ways of Cooking Poultry and Game Birds

Aspic de bécasse	Woodcock in aspic
— de foie gras	— goose liver in aspic
Ballotines de canard	Stuffed duck's drumsticks
Bécasse à la fine champagne	Woodcock in champagne sauce
— à la riche	— in a rich sauce; coals to Newcastle
— aux truffes	— with truffles; don't miss it if you see it on a menu
Blanquette de Chapon	Capon in a velouté sauce
— de Dinde	— turkey in velouté sauce
— de volaille	— chicken in velouté sauce
Caille à la broche	Quail on the spit
— en casserole	— stewed
— aux cerises	— with cherries
— grillée	— grilled; in France as in the U.S., the best way

351

FRENCH	ENGLISH
— *lardée*	— with bacon; relieves dryness
— *aux truffes*	— with truffles; a shameless display of luxury but delightful
Canard à la bordelaise	Duck with bordelaise sauce
— *aux morilles*	— with flavorful wild mushrooms
— *aux olives*	— with olives; dish of the Midi
— *à la vigneronne*	— with glazed chestnuts
— *à la bigarade*	— with orange; featured by every restaurant catering to Americans; not as bad in France as in the U.S., because the oranges are bitter ones
— *à la choucroute*	— with sauerkraut; good if you like duck with sauerkraut
— *aux cerises*	— with cherries
— *à la Lyonnaise*	— with onions and chestnuts
— *à la rouennaise*	— the style of Rouen; with red wine, shallots, brandy and the liver of the duck
Chapon braisé	Capon, stewed with butter
— *roti*	— roasted
— *à la périgourdine*	— roasted with truffles also offered as *chapon truffé*
— *Alexandre Dumas*	— with cognac, chicken livers, basted with heavy cream
Dindonneau farci aux marrons	Young turkey stuffed with chestnuts
faisan à la vigneronne	Pheasant braised with chestnuts
— *à la broche*	— not advisable; pheasant on a spit tends to dryness
— *Alsacienne*	— pheasant buried in overcooked cabbage. Good if you like pheasant in overcooked cabbage
— *à la crème*	— with cream sauce
— *à la Périgord*	— with truffles
Foie de volaille	Chicken livers; as in U.S., used in many ways
Fricassée de volaille	Chicken fricassee
— *de pigeon*	— the only possible way to eat a pigeon
Galantine de volaille	Cold chicken in aspic

FRENCH	ENGLISH
Mousse froide de bécasse	Cold creamed woodcock in mold
— *de caneton*	— same, with duck
— *de faisan*	— with pheasant
— *de foie gras*	— with goose liver
— *de volaille*	— with chicken
Oie à l'Alsacienne	Goose stuffed with sausage and cooked with sauerkraut
— *à la bordelaise*	— with bordelaise sauce
Pigeonneau à la financière	Squab with sauce financière previously noted; good at a restaurant, too much trouble at home
— *à la minute*	— sautéed
— *à la nivernaise*	— with carrots and onion
— *aux olives*	— with olives
Poularde bouilli	Fat hen, boiled
— *aux céleris*	— with celery
— *aux champignons*	— with mushrooms
Poularde à l'estragon	Hen roasted with tarragon
— *à l'Espagnole*	— Spanish style
— *à l'indienne*	— flavored delicately with curry; *not* chicken curry
— *à la paysanne*	— peasant style
— *Marengo*	— with tomatoes and herbs
— *à la Périgeux*	— with a truffle sauce
— *à la Portugaise*	— with tomatoes and rice
— *soufflée*	— chicken soufflé
Quenelles de faisan	Pheasant dumplings
— *de volaille*	— chicken dumplings
— *à l'estragon*	— same, with tarragon
Salamis de bécasse	Slices of woodcock
— *de caneton*	— of duckling
— *de faisan*	— of pheasant

Salmis ordinarily implies a dish made from slices of leftover meat with a different sauce. Obviously useful, sometimes good, but be a little skeptical.

Suprême de bécasse	Breast of woodcock. Note: French chefs refer to breasts of all fowl as suprêmes; the word means the breast and *not* a way of cooking it

FRENCH	ENGLISH
— de caneton	— of duckling
—de faisan	— of pheasant
— de pigeonneau	— of squab
— de volaille	— of chicken
— aux champignons	— of chicken with mushrooms
— à l'indienne	— with *delicate* curry flavor
— en papillote	— cooked in a paper bag with spiced wine sauce
— à la Parisienne	— with a delicately herbed cream sauce
Timbales de bécasse	Patties of woodcock
— de cailles	— of quails
— de caneton	— of duckling
— de poulet	— of chicken
Vol-au-Vent de Pigeonneau	Squab pie made of puff pastry; you will frequently encounter *vol-au-vents,* which are meat or game pies of puff-pastry

Gibier de Poil	Furred Game
Cerf	Stag; specifically male European red deer
Chamois	You are not likely to see it
Chevreuil	Venison
Lapin, lapereau	Rabbit, young rabbit
Lièvre	Hare
Marcassin	Young wild boar
Sanglier	Wild boar
Chaud-froid de chevreuil	Venison in aspic
— Chevreuil rôti	— roasted
Civet de cerf	Jugged stag
— de chevreuil	— venison
— de lièvre	—hare
Cotellete de chevreuil	Venison chop
— sauce poivrade	— with pepper sauce
Cuissot de chevreuil	Leg of venison
— piqué	— larded
Cuissot de marcassin	Leg of young wild boar
Jambon de marcassin	Ham made of young wild boar leg
Rable de lièvre	Saddle of hare
Selle de chevreuil	Saddle of venison; choice

354

FRENCH	ENGLISH
Légumes	**Vegetables**
Ail	Garlic
Artichauts	Artichokes
Asperges	Asparagus
— pointes d'	— asparagus tips
Aubergines	Eggplants; the European kind is smaller than ours
Betteraves	Beets
Brocolis	Broccoli
Carottes	Carrots
Celeri	Celery
Celeri-rave	Celery root
Champignons de Paris	Common white domestic mushroom
Chanterelles	Wild mushroom with unique taste
Chicorée	Salad green sometimes called endive in the U.S.
Chou	Cabbage
Chou frisé	Savoy cabbage
Chou rouge	Red cabbage
Choucroute	Sauerkraut
Choux de Bruxelles	Brussels sprouts
Chou-fleur	Cauliflower
Ciboulette	Chives
Concombres	Cucumbers; longer and thinner than ours
Courgettes	Zucchini squash
Echalote	Shallot
Epinards	Spinach
Fenouil	Fennel
Haricots blancs	White (navy) beans
Haricots verts	Green beans
Laitue pommée	Head lettuce
Laitue romaine	Romaine
Lentilles	Lentils
Marrons	Chestnuts
Morilles	Morels; species of wild mushrooms
Navets	Turnips
Oignons	Onions
Oseille	Sorrel
Persil	Parsley
Petits pois	Green peas; the French like them really small

FRENCH	ENGLISH
Poireaux	Leeks
Pommes de terre	Although Parmentier had a difficult time introducing them, potatoes are now France's chief source of starch after wheat
— *allumettes*	— matchstick potatoes
— *à l'Anglaise*	— boiled potatoes; not 100 percent English because the French usually get them to the table still warm
— *à la Berrichonne*	— potatoes cut in shape and size of olives and steamed
— *chips*	— potato chips; the British call them crisps
— *dauphine*	— potato fritters
— *frites*	— "French fried potatoes"; not all those so named in the U.S. resemble the French kind, which are prepared fresh for each patron
— *à la Lyonnaise*	— potatoes sliced thin and fried with onions
— *maître d'hôtel*	— creamed with parsley
— *menagère*	— housewife's style
— *mousseline*	— mashed with cream
—*purée de*	— mashed potatoes
— *nouvelles*	— new potatoes
— *Quenelles de*	— potato dumplings
Soufflé	Potato soufflé
Radis	Radishes
Raifort	Horseradish
Salsifis	Oyster plant, salsify
Tomates	Tomatoes
Topinambours	Jerusalem artichokes
Truffes	Truffles; a kind of black mushroom which grows under oaks chiefly in Périgord; they are found both by specially trained dogs and pigs on a leash

FRENCH	ENGLISH
Entremets et Fruits	**Sweets, Desserts and Fruits**
Beignets	Fritters
Crèmes	Creams, custards
Crêpes	Not exactly pancakes; thinner and more delicate
Croquettes douces	Sweet rissoles
Entremets	Sweets
— chauds	— hot
— froids	— cold
— glacés	— frozen
— à la pâte à chou	— cream puff desserts
Fondants et glaçages	Icings and glazings
Gateaux	Cakes
Glacés	Ice creams, ices
Omelettes sucrées	Sweet omelets
Patisseries	"French pastries"
Sirops	Syrups
Soufflés sucrés	Dessert soufflés
Tartes aux fruits	Not American pies; they often have custard as well as fruit and are open-faced
Tourtes	Rich cakes
Abricots	Apricots
— à la Condé	— with rice pudding
— gratinés	— glazed
— meringués	— apricot meringue
Amandes	Almonds
Ananas	Pineapple
— Chantilly	— with whipped cream
— au kirsch	— with kirsch; a favorite in France
Babas au rhum	Little rich cakes soaked in a syrup heavily laced with rum; very good good and very full of calories
Bananes	Bananas; the French ones come from Africa and can be overripe at the center and still have the skin unflecked with brown
— flambées	— flamed with rum or brandy
— soufflées	— banana soufflé is delicate
Bavaroise	Bavarian cream

FRENCH	ENGLISH
au chocolat	Chocolate flavored
— *aux fraises*	— with strawberries
— *aux noisettes*	— with hazelnuts; unusual and delicate
— *à la réligieuse*	— nun's style; made with plain instead of whipped cream
— *rubanné*	— with alternate layers of differently colored creams
Beignets d'abricots	Fritters with apricots
— *aux fraises*	— with strawberries
— *à la crême*	— with cream
— *de pomme*	— apple fritters
— *à la vanille*	— vanilla fritters soufflé
Biscuit à la cuillère	Ladyfingers
Blanc-manger	Blanc mange
Bombes	Popular iced or whipped cream mousse preparations formerly in round molds, now more often shell-shaped. One Escoffier book lists 66 varieties—not an exhaustive list. Herewith a few samples
— *Aida*	— bombe coated with strawberry ice and filled with kirsch ice
— *Andalouse*	— with apricot coating and vanilla filling
Bourdaloue	— of vanilla and anisette ices decorated with candied violets
Cardinale	— coated with red currant and raspberry ice and filled with pralined vanilla ice cream
Clarence	— coated with banana ice and filled with violet ice
Diable Rose	— coated with strawberry ice and filled with kirsch ice and cherries
— *Grande Duchesse*	— coated with pear ice and filled with ice flavored with Chartreuse
— *Hollandaise*	— coated with vanilla and filled with curaçoa ice
— *Mascotte*	— coated with peach ice and filled with kirsch ice

358

FRENCH	ENGLISH
— *Nesselrode*	— coated with vanilla ice cream and filled with whipped cream a and purée of chestnuts
— *Pompadour*	— coated with asparagus ice and filled with pomegranate ice
— *Vénitienne*	— coated half with vanilla and half with strawberry ice and filled with a preparation of maraschino and kirsch
Broiches	Characteristically shaped buns of an egg dough
Cacahuètes	Peanuts
Café glace	Coffee ice; good when it is made of espresso coffee
Cassis	Black currants
Cerises	Cherries
Cerises jubilées	Cherries jubilee
Charlotte	Charlotte pudding
— *à la Chantilly*	— with whipped cream
— *de pommes*	— apple Charlotte
Choux	Puffs
Choux à la crême	Cream puffs
Citron	Lemon
Compote de fruits	Stewed fruits
Corbeille de fruits	Basket of fruits
Coupes	Bowls filled with combinations of ices or ice creams with whipped cream and candied fruits
Dame Blanche	— one such bowl; a massive construction of almond ice, poached peaches, *Bar-le-duc* jelly and lemon ice, which is scarcely worth the trouble
Crêpes Sucrées	The most notorious is perhaps crêpes Suzette found chiefly in restaurants patronized by Americans
Dattes	Dates
Figues	Figs
Fraises	Strawberries

359

FRENCH	ENGLISH
Fraises de bois	"Woods strawberries" small and highly perfumed; every *maître d'hôtel* in France will swear they grow wild, but you can buy the plants in Connecticut and raise the berries, with all their beautiful perfume, in California
Fraises Cardinal	See the recipe in this book
Fraises Romanoff	See the recipe in this book
Framboises	Raspberries
Fruits assortis	Mixed fruits
— refraîchis	Fruit salad
Gateau au chocolat à la Sacher	Sacher torte
Gaufrettes	Waffles, also wafers
Gelées	Jellies; the French have all that we have plus some of their own, such as violet jelly
Glace, Crêmes glacés	Ices, ice creams; the flavors are numerous, the quality is frequently like U.S. iced milk
Groseilles	Red currants; chiefly as jelly
Macarons	Macaroons
Macedoines de fruits	Iced fruit salads
Marrons glacés	Glazed chestnuts
Meringue	Meringue
— Chantilly	— with whipped cream
Mille-feuille	Layers of puff-paste with fillings; "French pastry"
Mirabelle	Small yellow plum
Mousse glacé	Frozen mousses
Myrtilles	Blueberries
Noisettes, avelines	Hazelnuts
Noix	Walnuts
Omelettes sucrées	Sweet omelets
— au chocolat	— with chocolate
— aux confitures	— with jams
— au rhum	— with rum
Pain d'Epice	Gingerbread
Pamplemousse	Grapefruit

FRENCH	ENGLISH
Parfaits	Layered ice creams
Pêches	Peaches
— *Cardinal*	— poached and covered with raspberry and kirsch sauce
— *Petit-duc*	— with vanilla ice cream and red currant jelly
— *Melba*	— poached in vanilla syrup, served with with vanilla ice cream and puréed raspberries. There are dozens more; if you like cooked peaches you might experiment
Petits-beurres	Small sweet crackers
Poires	Pears; many recipes
Pommes	Apples
— *au beurre*	— baked with butter
— *en cage, en chemise*	— like apple dumplings but with a better pastry
— *au four*	— baked apples
Prunes	Plums
Pruneaux	Prunes
Raisins	Fresh grapes, *not* raisins
Reines-Claude	Pleasant greenish-yellow plum
Sabayon	Italian dessert, *zabiglione,* made by heating egg yolk, sugar and Marsala wine
Sauce aux abricots	Apricot sauce
Sauce au caramel	Caramel sauce
Sauce au chocolat	Chocolate sauce
Sauce au vin	Wine sauce; go down the list of wines and fruits; you will find sauces made from all of them
Sorbet	Sherbet
Soufflé aux abricots	Apricot soufflé
— *aux avelines*	— soufflé flavored with hazelnuts; unusual and good
— *au chocolat*	— chocolate soufflé
— *aux fraises*	— strawberry soufflé
— *au Grand Marnier*	— Grand Marnier soufflé; soufflés are also made with other liqueurs

FRENCH	ENGLISH
Timbale de fruits	Molded fruit patties
Timbale à la Parisienne	Brioche hollowed out, coated on outside with apricot jam and filled with pieces of pears, peaches, apricots in a vanilla syrup, plumped raisins, pineapple, angelica, half-almonds, all mixed with a kirsch and apricot purée

INDEX

A

364

365

𝒞

373

M

377

379

383

385

Y

#

This book was designed and typeset by Westype Graphic Services, Beverly Hills, California, on their IBM Composer in 11 point Press Roman. The line art in the book was drawn by Laurie Jordan. All but one of the color plates were supplied by Kimberly-Clark Corporation; the other by the Wine Institute. The display type used is Oakwood. The text paper is 60# Simpson Publishers Offset, supplied by the Zellerbach Paper Company. The cover material is Kivar 6 supplied by the Plastic Coating Corporation. The book was printed and bound by Stecher-Traung-Schmidt, San Francisco, California.